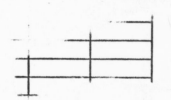

The Golden Antilles

THE
GOLDEN
ANTILLES

Timothy Severin

A L F R E D · A · K N O P F

N E W Y O R K / 1 9 7 0

CONTENTS

Contents

    SURGEON   233

14 LIFE WITH THE CUNA   251

15 THE COMPANY PROMOTER   263

16 A SMILE ON THE FACE OF THE SUN   288

17 THE COLLAPSE OF DARIEN   312

18 THE TURN OF THE LEGEND   328

    Author's Bibliographical Note   335

    Index   FOLLOWS PAGE 336

ILLUSTRATIONS

FOLLOWING PAGE 144

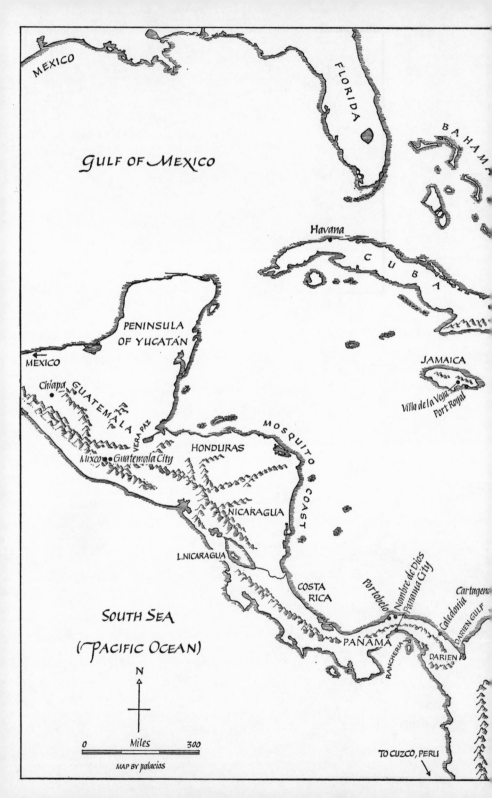

MEXICO

GULF OF MEXICO

FLORIDA

BAHAMA

Havana

CUBA

PENINSULA
OF YUCATÁN

MEXICO

JAMAICA

Chiapa GUATEMALA

Villa de la Vega
Port Royal

HONDURAS

Mixco Guatemala City

VERA PAZ

MOSQUITO COAST

NICARAGUA

L. NICARAGUA

Nombre de Dios
Panama City

Cartagena

COSTA
RICA

Portobelo

Caledonia

DARIEN GULF

SOUTH SEA

PAÑAMA

(PACIFIC OCEAN)

RANCHERIA

DARIEN

N

0   Miles   300

MAP BY palacios

TO CUZCO, PERU

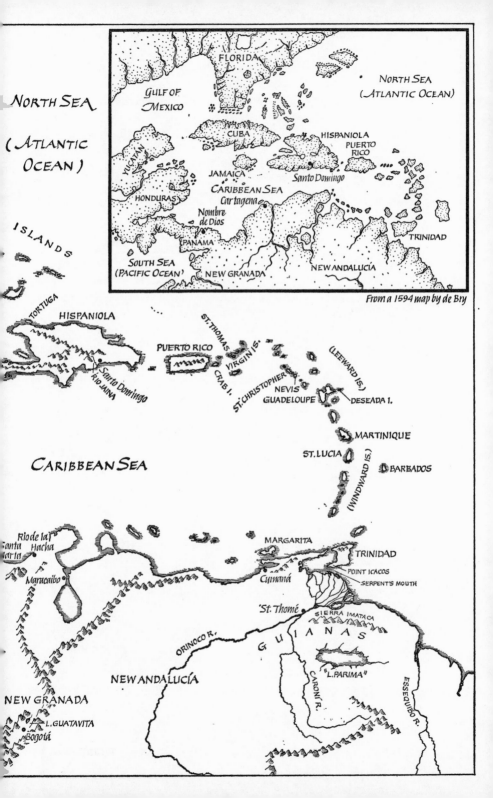

NORTH SEA

(ATLANTIC
OCEAN)

ISLANDS

FLORIDA

GULF OF
MEXICO

NORTH SEA
(ATLANTIC OCEAN)

CUBA

HISPANIOLA

PUERTO
RICO

YUCATAN

JAMAICA

CARIBBEAN SEA

Santo Domingo

HONDURAS

Cartagena

Nombre
de Dios

PANAMA

TRINIDAD

SOUTH SEA
(PACIFIC OCEAN)

NEW GRANADA

NEW ANDALUCIA

From a 1594 map by de Bry

TORTUGA

HISPANIOLA

ST. THOMAS

Santo Domingo

PUERTO RICO

VIRGIN IS.

CRAB I.

RÍO JAINA

ST. CHRISTOPHER

NEVIS
GUADELOUPE

(LEEWARD IS.)

DESEADA I.

MARTINIQUE

ST. LUCIA

BARBADOS

CARIBBEAN SEA

(WINDWARD IS.)

RÍO de la)
Hacha
Santa
Marta

Maracaibo

MARGARITA

TRINIDAD

POINT ICACOS

Cumaná

SERPENT'S MOUTH

St. Thomé

SIERRA IMATACA

ORINOCO R.

G U I A N A S

NEW ANDALUCIA

"L. PARIMA"

CARONÍ R.

ESSEQUIBO R.

NEW GRANADA

L. GUATAVITA

Bogotá

The Golden Antilles

Introduction

S OME TWELVE YEARS BEFORE CHRISTOPHER COLUMBUS and his inquisitive flotilla of three small ships first appeared off the coasts of the New World, an Indian tribe living in the highlands of Bogotá celebrated what was to be the final performance of a peculiarly spectacular religious ceremony. On the appointed day each year the tribal chief was stripped naked by his attendants and smeared from head to foot with a sticky layer of balsam gum. Then powdered gold was puffed through tubes of cane over the gum until the chief appeared like a living statue of gold. Glittering in this magnificence, he presented himself before his people and led them in solemn procession to the shores of Lake Guatavita. There he stepped into a canoe and was paddled by his nobles out across the water while his people lined the bank, made music, and chanted praises to their gods. When the canoe reached the center of the lake, it drifted to a halt. Then, in a splendid climax, the chief plunged overboard so that the lake would wash away his golden coat in a symbolic cleansing of the sins of the entire tribe. The ritual complete, the Indians celebrated with a de-bauched evening of singing, dancing, and heavy drinking.

About the year 1480 the splendid ceremony at Lake Guatavita was snuffed out when a hostile tribe invaded the area and defeated the practitioners of this strange rite. But their reports of "El Dorado," or the "Gilded Man," as he came to be called, survived and flourished, because it was a spectacle far too brilliant to be forgotten. It became deeply entwined within the folk myths of the Indians, who had never seen the fabulous ceremony at the lake for themselves, but whose imaginations easily added gaudy accretions of fantasy, exaggeration, and awe to the original truth. In their wondering tales the Gilded Man was turned into a fabulous king who ruled over a lost tribe of great sophistication and huge wealth. He held his court in a golden city whose palaces were sheathed with plates of gold, his soldiers wore golden armor, and the nobility were decorated like their lord in crusts of powdered gold whenever the court held its week-long banquets. In a rather homely touch, it was also said that the golden coats were scratchily uncomfortable in bed and therefore the *noblesse dorée* washed clean before retiring at night and were gilded anew every morning.

Extravagant though the fable of El Dorado may have been, it was to receive serious attention, if not wholehearted acceptance, for nearly three centuries after the last ceremony at Lake Guatavita. Even as the colonists of British North America were deliberating whether to declare independence from England, French cartographers were still marking El Dorado's golden lake on their maps of South America. As late as 1772 a Venezuelan artillery lieutenant was given solemn instructions to take a squad of men, march off into the jungles of the interior, and report back when he had captured the city of the Gilded Man.

But the legend of El Dorado was something more than a crackpot aberration or a wistful curio dreamed up by a handful of gullible optimists and avaricious adventurers. El Dorado and his glittering city was merely the brightest thread within a far broader tapestry of make-believe that depicted those lands fringing the Caribbean Sea as a demi-paradise on earth. Here, so the legend ran, Nature had showered her gifts more lavishly than on any other region of the world, and the results were stupendous: around the Caribbean were rich mines, ancient civilizations of great wisdom, vast plantations under balmy skies, and an unopened Pandora's box of trade and commerce. In tropical

America, it was said, the humblest adventurer might make his fortune in the flash of a sword blade or the blow of a miner's pick. For this reason the Spaniards had named the place after Antilia, a lost civilization of dazzling achievement where seven bishops had ruled over seven cities in peace, serenity, and prosperity. The lands of the Caribbean were indeed a new and golden Antilia, the greatest prize of the New World.

Of course the Spaniards had first claim to this alleged cornucopia, but this did not prevent the English, Scots, French, Germans, Danes, and Swedes from being equally fascinated by the legend. And the more these nations envied the Spanish mastery of the fabled Antilles, the more they magnified the value of the prize they had been denied. Inevitably, too, they strove to swoop in and grasp a share of the vast Antillean wealth, and by use of diplomacy, open war, piracy, or legal sleight of hand they tried to oust the Spaniard from his Antillean empire. Several of these attempts were successful enough to win the assailants a few toeholds in the area they coveted: the odd little trio of Guianas, wartlike on the shoulder of Brazil, and the English, French, Dutch, and Danish islands sprinkled around the rim of the Caribbean. But these crumbs were miserable consolation for all the armies, fleets, and effort the invaders expended in pursuit of the mirage of the Golden Antilles.

No country fell more under the spell of the myth than England, and as befitted one of Spain's major colonial rivals, she made several strokes against the circle of Spanish possessions that bounded the Caribbean. Three of these English onslaughts, the first during the declining years of Elizabeth I, the second under her successor, James I, and the last under Protector Cromwell, can be seen together as acts of national self-delusion. They were occasions when the myth of the Golden Antilles shone so powerfully in England that ambitious men from a small and relatively puny country were sufficiently dazzled to sail to the American tropics, confident that they would make fools of the Spaniards, line their pockets with bullion, and return home as heirs to the richest empire of their day. The fourth attempt on the Antilles came from farther north, from Scotland. And here again the myth was the mainspring, for the Scots, a nation not normally known for chasing after will-o'-the-wisps, were induced to sink huge amounts of hard cash into a venture by which they hoped to tap the inestimable trade of the Golden Antilles. In pursuit of this mercantile dream the Scots were deluded into putting forth a prodigious national effort to finance and equip a powerful expedition that was then shipped out to the fever-stricken coast of the Central American isthmus. There they met with utter calamity, and the financial penalties of that disaster were so burdensome that, if England had not come to the rescue, the Scottish economy would have been crippled.

Thus four times the myth of the Golden Antilles was tried and found wanting. Three abject failures and one, almost accidental, success were the price of disillusionment. They provide the subject of the chapters that follow.

1.

The Quest for
El Dorado

T HE EMPTY HEART OF THE GOLDEN ANTILLES IS the gently circulating expanse of the Caribbean Sea, stretching almost two thousand miles from west to east, and nearly a thousand miles from north to south at its widest point. Warm water, carried along by the north equatorial current, filters into one end of the sea through the arc of West Indian islands facing across to Africa. Swirling gently westward and north, this warm current then crosses the breadth of the sea and escapes into the Gulf of Mexico, where it doubles back to re-emerge in the Atlantic Ocean as the infant Gulf Stream. The unceasing movement of this circulation makes the Caribbean a huge basin constantly scoured by the water within it. The rim of this basin forms the legendary circlet of the Antilles.

Half the ring is mainland, that curve of the South and Central American coastline that sweeps up from the mouth of the Orinoco River to the Peninsula of Yucatán and embraces what are now the coasts of Venezuela, Colombia, Panama, Costa Rica, Nicaragua, Honduras, Guatemala, and southern Mexico. Opposite is the matching half of the basin's rim, the chain of islands whose names read like a roll call of tropical luxury, from Cuba (the largest), through Jamaica, Hispaniola (Haiti and the Dominican Republic), Puerto Rico, and the Virgin Islands, to the Leeward and then the Windward Islands, and finally back to Trinidad, scarcely twenty miles off the starting point at the delta of the Orinoco. The circle is complete and the Caribbean almost landlocked, a huge salt lake whose shores and islands share a common geographical identity of blue sea, gentle breezes, and soft scenery, far different from the wilder, more extreme, mountainous interior of the mainland.

Cautiously investigating the perimeter of this sea, the first European visitors may be excused for eulogizing what they found. They were accustomed to the harshness of life in Europe at the turn of the fifteenth century, where famine and pestilence were commonplace. Here on the fringes of the Caribbean they came ashore in lands that seemed, by comparison, almost indecently well endowed by Nature. The virgin soil was deep and rich, the climate proverbially benign, and the vegetation spectacular as well as lush. Columbus, expecting to find the idyllic islands of the Orient where men lived to advanced age in the ease of life, was so carried away with what he found that he called the islands the "Indies," and it was not until 1502 that the name was amended to its slightly more accurate "West" Indies.

Yet it was not such a bad name at that. After all, the West Indies offered almost everything that the travelers had hoped to find in the East Indies. The coasts of the Caribbean provided sheltered, almost tideless, anchorages and careenages, streams of clear water, beaches of powdery white sand, and enticing vistas of tree-clad hills or open savannah. Sometimes in the distance there was a glimpse of splendid gray-blue mountains. "There is a river," Columbus wrote to King Ferdinand from Cuba, "which discharges itself into the harbour that I have named Porto Santo, of sufficient depth to be navigable. I had the curiosity to sound it, and found it eight fathoms. Yet the water is so limpid, that I can easily discern the sand at the bottom. The banks of this river are embellished with lofty palm-trees, whose shade gives a delicious freshness to the air; and the birds and the flowers are uncommon and beautiful. I was so delighted with the scene, that I had almost come to the resolution of staying here the remainder of my days; for believe me, Sire, these countries far surpass all the rest of the world in beauty and conveniency; and I have frequently observed to my people, that, with all my endeavours to convey to your Majesty an adequate idea of the charming objects which continually present themselves to our view, the description will fall greatly short of reality."

Unfortunately for Columbus's hopes of trade, there were no spices in the islands, but the natives were friendly enough and their golden amulets hinted at an even greater reward. Another obvious attraction was the absence of disease, for compared to the fevers and epidemics that regularly decimated the crews of vessels trading to the East Indies, the Spanish sailors found little sickness in the West Indies. Then, too, the fauna and flora of the Antilles combined to produce a fairyland effect. The islands were the natural habitat of such oddities as the armadillo, iguana, hawksbill turtle, and opossum, all of which might have stepped from the pages of a medieval bestiary. There were endlessly colorful varieties of hummingbirds and parrots, flamingos, and that curious creature, the diablotin, or oilbird, which lives in the caves of Trinidad and flies only at night. According to Bryan Edward, a resident of Jamaica in the late eighteenth century, the plumage of the "colibry" or hummingbird, was so brilliant that "no combination of words, nor tints of the pencil can convey an adequate idea. The consummate green of the emerald, the rich purple of the amethyst, and the vivid flame of the ruby, all happily blended and enveloped beneath a transparent veil of waving gold."

In the seas there were barracuda, shark, and ray, while on land the less exotic creatures included monkeys, wild pig, and the rabbitlike agouti, desperately twitching his nose like a man perpetually anticipating a sneeze. Less amusing, naturally enough, was the insect life, which ranged from the merely minor nuisances of chiggers and sandflies to the more virulent types of tarantula and scorpion. Perhaps the greatest curse of the natural world of the Antilles was the boring worm, teredo and bankia, which riddled the hulls of the Spanish ships.

But what really impressed the explorers from Europe was the astonishing fertility of the Antilles. Cocoa, tobacco, vanilla, arrowroot, cassava, coconut, sweet potatoes, avocado, the cotton plant, and that "princess of fruits"—the pineapple—were all indigenous. To this list the European settlers, who soon followed on the heels of the explorers to populate the new-found lands, added oranges, lemons, figs, sugar cane, and bananas, all of them lucrative plantation crops. Only the vine, wheat, and olive failed to thrive, to the understandable regret of the Spaniards. But maize was an excellent substitute for wheat, and there was ample compensation in the extraordinary behavior of the other imported crops. They grew prodigiously, and an early account noted with amazement that the plants and animals taken to the Caribbean grew "muche better, bygger, and of greater increase" than at home. Citrus fruits swelled to nearly twice their usual size and were much sweeter; horses, mangey from the transatlantic crossing, grew sleek and glossy within a month of landing. Swine escaped from the pioneer farming settlements and bred so rapidly that the strays began to ravage the plantations and hunting parties had to slaughter the pigs in order to control the problem. Cattle were an even more notable success. Conditions were so favorable for stock raising that it was not even necessary to look after the herds. A farmer simply turned a few animals loose at some convenient location, preferably a small island where they could not wander too far, and the creatures obligingly multiplied and increased in weight and size without further attention. Their owner needed only to return to the place from time to time in order to shoot as many as he needed, flay the carcasses, and carry off the hides and tallow for market. The meat was left to rot because it was not worth salting and preserving when other foodstuffs were so plentiful. Amid all this plenty it was small wonder that the Spanish settlements in the Antilles multiplied as fast as men and their families could be ferried out from the homeland. The first major colonizing fleet arrived in 1502—thirty ships carrying 2,500 settlers—and by the 1520's the wave of settlement had washed across the Caribbean from Hispaniola to the shores of Darien.

The idyll of the Antilles did, however, have flaws. Hurricanes, aptly named after the wind god of the Mayans, were the chief menace. Periodically they would sweep across the islands, uprooting and smashing everything in the path of raging winds that could reach speeds in excess of 140 miles an hour. In a single day a bad hurricane might destroy years of husbandry, though a catastrophe of this scale was an isolated incident, attributable in the settlers' opinion to an act of God. The real nuisance of the hurricanes was the regular disruption they caused to shipping. Every year, during the hurricane season in late summer and autumn, the sea-borne traffic of the Caribbean became semidormant. A few small boats might work round the coasts on short journeys, ready to dash for shelter; but the Spanish captains of the larger vessels rarely put to sea unless they had to, and the pulse of the Caribbean beat languidly as the flow of shipping across the empty heart dwindled to a trickle.

The earlier occupants of the Antilles, both insect and human, also posed something of a problem to the settlers from Europe. The first plantations established by the Spaniards disturbed the natural ecology of the region, and in retribution the luckless planters were afflicted with plagues of insects like those of ancient Egypt. Between 1518 and 1520, for example, an army of ants attacked the orange groves of Hispaniola and Puerto Rico, nibbling their way through the roots of the trees that then turned black and died. On another occasion a great carpet of marching ants was measured at eleven inches deep. Equally unexpected, though easier to deal with, were the incursions of the Carib Indians, after whom the central sea was named. They were a warlike tribe preying on weaker neighbors, and their custom of eating human flesh was to introduce the word *cannibal* into European languages. When Columbus reached the New World, the Caribs were migrating northward from their homelands in the interior of South America, and their fleets of war canoes were already raiding as far north as Puerto Rico. But the guns and steel armor of the white men made the Indians pause, and, fortunately for the Spanish settlers, the Caribs were never powerful enough to do more than capture the smaller, weakly defended islands or launch pinprick attacks against the better-protected settlements. By way of retaliation a Royal Edict of 1504 decreed that all Caribs could be exterminated or sold into slavery, on the moral grounds that their cannibalism rendered them undeserving of Christian sympathy. This pious attitude led to much brutality, and it was not uncommon for captured Caribs to be tortured mercilessly, their flesh being ripped with iron pincers or, as in another recorded instance, both ears nailed to a plank while the victim struggled to break free. During those brutal days a young Carib girl could be sent into perpetual slavery for the price of no more than a single ordinary knife.

But the Caribs were themselves newcomers to the Caribbean islands. The true natives of the Antilles were the Arawaks, an unsophisticated race whose gentle way of life admirably suited the European concept of a demi-Paradise on earth, and whose harmless existence was smashed by the invaders. The first explorers were enchanted by the Arawaks. They reported that these copper-skinned, beautifully proportioned aborigines were true denizens of the fortunate Indies. Like children in the Garden of Eden they lived a carefree life, gathering wild fruit, catching fish or raising a few poultry and the occasional crop. Utterly at ease in that mild climate, the Arawaks neither wore clothes nor built permanent houses. Sometimes they had crude huts made of fronds, but more often they went near-naked and slept at night in cunningly made nets called *hamacas*, which they strung in the open air between two trees. The white men were welcomed with childlike delight by these harmless creatures, and accepted the Arawaks' pleasing little gifts of fruit, feathered ornaments, and small quantities of gold in the form of pellets or dust.

But unfortunately for the Arawaks, the Spaniards looked upon the natives as being as much a part of the natural resources of the Antilles as the stands of timber or the shoals of fish in the sea. And so, by sporadic mismanagement, some downright cruelty, and a great deal of misunderstanding, the Spaniards utterly wasted that resource. Eager for cheap labor, they cajoled, hurried, and frightened the Arawaks out of the Stone Age in less than two decades. Quite naturally the Arawaks bitterly resented the process. Thousands of them quietly decided that they would be better off dead than living the new way of life. They committed suicide in droves, some refusing to eat the food the white men gave them, others deliberately drinking the poisonous juices of the cassava root. Many more seemed only too happy to succumb to smallpox or measles, both introduced from Europe. These wretches slipped away from the mines and plantations to rejoin their families, the infection spread, and the wastage was enormous. According to one quite conservative estimate, sixty thousand Arawaks lived on Jamaica when the Spaniards reached the island. By 1655 there was not a single Arawak left.

Indeed, the first twenty-five years of Spanish rule in the Antilles had proved to be something of a disappointment. Of course the early Spanish administrators wrote home long dispatches showing how diligent and successful they had been in their new appointments; the military captains reported victory upon glorious victory; and the missionary priests added up the souls of the saved heathen like so many entries in a celestial account book. But there were discordant notes in this paean of self-congratulation, particularly the recurrent incidents of bickering among the colonial leaders and the never-ending demands for more men, more ships, and more supplies to be sent from Spain. Year after year the royal advisers found it increasingly pertinent to ask why, amid all the alleged plenty of the legendary Antilles, did the colonists quarrel so bitterly, and why did they require so much external assistance. To those who had the wit to see it, the myth of the Golden Antilles was becoming markedly frayed at the edges.

The Casa de Contratación, the panel of accountants set up in Seville to oversee and audit the finances of the Spanish Americas, bluntly skewered the stark reality of the early years of the myth in their annual account ledgers. Between 1504 and 1516, according to their neat calculations, the Crown of Spain received as its "royal fifth" of all the proceeds of the colonies a yearly income of some thirteen to twenty-seven million maravedís.* Only in 1512 and 1513 did the royal fifth exceed these limits, because in those years the conquest and spoils of Cuba almost doubled the annual profits. Yet not even the Casa de Contratación could make any precise record of how much money went the other way— from Spain to the Caribbean to pay for the fleets, troops, and

---

* *At that time a Spanish maravedí was worth slightly more than eleven English pence and so the Spanish monarchs were doing well, though not fabulously, from their stewardship of the Antilles.*

supplies that were opening up the new colonial territory. It could not have been an inexpensive venture, and the idea of the humble peasant becoming a millionaire in the Antilles was in reality wide of the mark. A sugar estate on Hispaniola, for instance, required an initial investment of ten thousand ducats, followed up by at least four times that amount to pay for the necessary milling machinery, the purchase and instruction of slaves, the salaries of sugar refiners (usually free men brought under contract from Andalucía), and other expenses. Yet once the capital was there, the returns were good. The same mill would enrich its owner to the tune of at least six thousand ducats a year from then on.

Few colonists, however, could afford this scale of outlay, and most of the early settlers in the Antilles found that the terrestrial paradise in the West was a matter of carefully tended paprika and tobacco crops, regular shipments of hides and tallow, and the nagging problem of finding the ready cash to pay their taxes. Life was a small plantation and an occasional visit to the nearest colonial town, each like the next, faithfully duplicating the standard pattern of plaza surrounded by church, town hall, prison, and barracks. Very slowly the first flush of the legend was being smothered under a lifetime of hard work and monotony.

Then, in 1519 and 1533, two insubordinate and opportunist military adventurers reversed the decline: Hernán Cortés seized Montezuma's treasure in Mexico, and Francisco Pizarro looted Peru. These two extraordinary achievements took place outside the limits of the Antilles, but their effect on the Caribbean area was immense. The golden fabric of the myth had at last found its substance. Bags of gold dust, crates of precious inlay work, and stacks of silver bars really did lie waiting for the lucky venturer; and the West was indeed golden. Once more the Casa de Contratación had the stark details: the year Pizarro sacked the Inca capital at Cuzco, the royal fifth soared to 119 million maravedís. Twenty years later, when the silver mines of Mexico and Peru had been brought into production, the Crown's revenue climbed to 847 million maravedís. It was as much money in a single year as the rulers of Spain had received during the first thirty years following the discovery of America, and every ducat came back home via the original gateway of the Caribbean. Inevitably, some of the luster rubbed off on the Antilles. There, at Havana, the two streams of riches converged. One fleet arrived from Panama with the dividends of Peru and the Pacific, the other fleet came from Vera Cruz in Mexico. At Havana they kept rendezvous, revictualed, and, when the winter storms were over, they sailed for Spain in convoy, bearing a cargo that was the envy of every European monarch. History had reinforced geography in refurbishing the legend of the Golden Antilles.

Paradoxically, the immediate result of the conquistador feats in Mexico and Peru was the near-collapse of the Spanish colonies on the rim of the Caribbean. The success of the conquistador armies on the South American mainland tempted many of the Antillean settlers to join a convulsive stampede to share the rewards of the conquest. The islands were stripped of men and materials to maintain the conquistador armies. In Cuba, for example, De Soto ransacked the island so thoroughly before his abortive invasion of North America that the price of a good horse, vital to military success, rose too high for the ordinary colonist to afford one.

Some sort of balance was restored only when a fresh influx of colonists arrived in the Antilles from the mother country to take the place of the hotheads who had rushed off to the new frontiers. This second wave of colonists included a good number of men from the middle class, men interested in the solid, less glamorous wealth of the Antilles. They reorganized the farms and plantations along more economic lines, and closed the handful of unprofitable mines which had destroyed so many of the natives. Then, like the solid citizens they were, they watched the high-born and hopeful chase a dream that the Peruvian conquest had started. The hunt for El Dorado was on.

WHEN FRANCISCO PIZARRO AND HIS EXPEDITIONARY FORCE boldly invaded the empire of the Incas of Peru and smashed it to fragments, a band of native dissidents refused to accept defeat. Led by a prince of royal blood called Tupac Amaru, they crossed the mountains in the east and vanished into the jungle-clad slopes where the Amazon draws its headwaters from the Andes. Through their spies the Spaniards heard about this retreat, and with characteristic greed assumed that the refugees had taken with them as much of the Inca treasure as they could haul away. This, in itself, was ample reason for the conquistadors to follow the runaways, but the pursuit was made even more attractive by the rumor that the ruling Incas had originally come to Peru from a mysterious kingdom to the east. There in the Amazon basin, it was said, flourished the ancestral home of the Incas, the great empire of Pay-titi the "Tiger Father," which boasted a civilization even more magnificent than the Inca realm in Peru. Historically the tale may have had its roots in an Inca legend that their first priest-king had come to the Andean highlands from the east, but what mattered to the Spaniards was that the Peruvian natives seemed genuinely convinced of the existence of Pay-titi. Moreover their information tallied neatly with the fact that Tupac Amaru had fled in the same direction.

If this information was not enticing enough to send the Spanish probing eastward for gold, a third legendary element also came to the Spaniards' attention to reinforce the theory of a fugitive empire in the interior. By strange coincidence a few months after the fall of the Inca empire, an Indian messenger from a then-unknown tribe appeared in Peru from the northeast. He came in search of Atahualpa, the last Inca ruler. Not knowing that the Inca was overthrown, the messenger walked straight into the hands of the Spaniards, and, when they interrogated him about his mission, he revealed that he had been sent by the Zipa of Bogotá. Asked to describe his homeland, the messenger embellished his narrative with an extraordinary description of still another kingdom, far away to the east of Bogotá, where a priest-king, covered in gold, dived into a lake surrounded by high mountains. The legend of El Dorado had finally come to the ears of Europeans.

The precise number of Spanish expeditions that went to find the Gilded Man has never been successfully computed. Contemporary chronicles list at least twenty attempts, and there were probably other, less publicized, ventures. In the early years when the Spaniards' spirit of optimism ran high, expedition after expedition went out in quick succession to locate and sack the golden palaces. But later, when hundreds of lives and several fortunes had been squandered, the pace slowed down, a tinge of desperation became apparent, and El Dorado was pursued with a sense of grim determination rather than cheerful expectancy. Tantalizingly, the golden kingdom always seemed to lie just over the next mountain or a single day's march away. The natives generously pointed out the route so that they would be rid of the white men, and even as the glistening mirage slipped out of range, every expedition brought back fresh rumors to add to its charisma. The reports of Pay-titi and Tupac Amaru (who was eventually captured and executed), the tale of the ceremony at the lake, the evidence of emerald chips brought from the mines of Bogotá and macaw feathers from the Amazon basin were woven together into the greatest illusion of them all. Even such unexpected allies as the geographers and savants of the day assured the public that gold was by its natural properties more likely to be found near the equator than in higher latitudes, and that a final super kingdom could exist. In this fashion the realm of El Dorado became a distillation of greed and hope, and a target to attract adventurers and desperadoes of every shade.

Between 1536 and 1541 five major sorties went out from the Andean mountains, while another search party, led by a German officer operating under Spanish license, tried marching inland from Venezuela. Every venture failed, and one group under Gonzalo Pizarro, Francisco's half-brother, blundered into such appalling difficulties that the starving soldiers turned cannibal as they clawed their way back to Peru through the jungle. This expedition had sent off a flying column of the fittest men to bring help, and it was typical that the lieutenant in command was so consumed by the lust for El Dorado that he callously abandoned the main force to its fate and tried his own luck. He and his men built a brigantine on the upper Amazon and sailed down the length of the river to its mouth. They found no Gilded Man but did discover river tribes whose fighting women gave the great river its name.

By now the viceroy of Peru had taken the unusually shrewd point of view that these zealous El Dorado hunts were an ideal distraction for the worst ruffians in his charge, and he therefore encouraged the quest. As a result, the next expedition to leave

Peru was the goriest and most notorious calamity of all. A young and noble commander led a band of cutthroats into the region of the Amazon headwaters and there, on New Year's Day, 1561, his troops mutinied bloodily. They hacked the nobleman to death and then turned on his mistress, Dona Inés de Atienza, who, legend has it, was a lovely mestiza widow who had sold all her possessions to follow her lover. But she had incurred the wrath of the rebels by bringing along an excess of baggage, and was murdered. When the massacre was done, the leader of the insurgents, Lope de Aguirre, took command of the expedition and to everyone's horror turned out to be mentally unbalanced. Neurotically suspicious of his associates, he inaugurated a reign of terror. One by one his cronies were accused of plotting against their leader, and were garrotted or stabbed. No one dared to protest, for the expedition was hopelessly immersed in the jungles and a second internal upheaval would have finished it off entirely. Under Aguirre's malign direction there was a nightmare march as the column groped across the entire width of the continent toward the Spanish settlement on the island of Margarita, a few miles off the Venezuelan coast. On reaching Margarita, Aguirre seems to have gone completely insane. His men launched a treacherous attack on the unsuspecting town, sacked it, looting and murdering their own countrymen, and vanished back into the interior. Aguirre himself in the depths of his dementia wrote out a message of defiance to the King of Spain, declaring that Philip II was deposed and that one of his own men was "Lord and Prince of Peru."

Aguirre's atrocities stirred the Spanish authorities from their usual lethargy and they were obliged to treat Aguirre like the mad dog he had become. Every colonial governor was ordered to hunt him down, and a punitive force finally trapped the crazed expedition and annihilated them in a bloody battle. In a final welter of destruction Aguirre first killed his own children and then committed suicide so that no member of his family should face disgrace. The Spanish authorities completed their task by pulling down the Aguirre home and ordering that the site be strewn with salt to obliterate his memory.

As if Aguirre's blood bath were not enough, within a few years two other conquistador bands, both hunting for El Dorado, met head-on in the jungles of the upper Amazon and fought a pitched battle to decide who should continue the search. The contest was so fierce that both forces were virtually wiped out, and the few miserable survivors fell easy prey to the forest Indians, who picked them off without mercy.

Elsewhere on the continent it was much the same story: heat exhaustion, disease, starvation, and hostile Indians decimated one expedition after another. The only appreciable result was that the supposed location of El Dorado and his kingdom withdrew farther and farther into the remaining, unexplored portion of the interior. Finally, there was nowhere left for it to be found except in the dim fastnesses of "Guiana," the name by which the Spaniards knew the great, unmapped basin of the Orinoco and its tributaries. Here, like a hunted hare doubling back on its tracks, the legend came to rest on the fringe of the Golden Antilles. And here, too, it became the personal ambition of a little-known but remarkable conquistador, Don Antonio de Berrio, governor of New Granada, whose fate was to be so closely associated with the search for the Gilded Man that one of his appointments was the worthless governorship of a purely mythical Spanish colony —the province of El Dorado itself.

Governor Berrio came to the search for El Dorado by accident. A professional soldier who had already served a full and very active life in the armies of Emperor Charles V, he was obviously an outstanding officer, for he had reached the rank of captain in one of the four companies that composed the Old Guard of the Kingdom of Granada. Then his wife's uncle died, leaving him his estate. This somewhat distant relative was no less a personage than Gonzalo Ximénez de Quesada, adelantado of New Granada in the Americas and a man rumored to have made a vast fortune for himself during his conquest of the Chibcha Indians in Colombia. Now, unexpectedly, Quesada had left his New World estates to Berrio, to whom the legacy seemed an ideal opportunity to retire and enjoy the yearly income of fourteen thousand ducats which the American property was said to be worth. So, loading his family and belongings aboard the annual American convoy, Berrio sailed in 1580 to the Antilles, expecting to retire in well-earned ease.

He was to be disappointed. Quesada's will included a stipulation that the heir to his estate should justify his inheritance by using part of the income to finance the search for El Dorado. And so the hapless Berrio, instead of settling down on some opulent plantation with a great house, manicured gardens, and obedient servants, found himself back in the saddle, leading third-rate colonial troops on long treks into the interior where the rains and the sun beat down with equal ferocity, and the Indians had an unpleasant habit of using poisoned darts and arrows. The insect-infested campsites bore little resemblance to a retirement idyll, but Berrio persevered. For fifteen years the aging warrior doggedly hunted for El Dorado, and succeeded more nearly than any of his predecessors. His first quest took him into the interior for seventeen months; a second trip lasted three years; and from his third venture, only forty-five of the original 112 men returned. Disease, accidents, and the Indians claimed the rest.

Yet Berrio's tenacity established one important fact: somewhere on the right bank of the Orinoco River was a huge lake where, or so the Orinoco Indians claimed, a great and powerful tribe lived in splendor. Naturally Berrio tried to find this lake and he traveled down the length of the Orinoco, attempting to lead exploring parties up its right-bank tributaries. But on every occasion his progress was blocked by a range of mountains which ran parallel with the Orinoco. He surmised that these might be the mountains which were supposed to surround the lake of the El Dorado legend, and he was heartened to hear from the natives that the powerful tribe on the lake had arrived only some twenty years earlier, and had established their supremacy with payments of gold and irresistible military organization. The various strands of the El Dorado legend were tantalizingly obvious—the fugitives from Peru, carrying the salvaged treasure of the Incas; the lake; the presence of an advanced native civilization. At last Berrio felt sure that he was on the threshold of the great discovery that had eluded the Spanish search parties for so long. He was to die before he could learn the truth: his so-called "lake" was nothing more than a temporary lagoon formed by the flooding of the rivers in the rainy season, and the mysterious tribe of invaders were not refugee Incas but Caribs migrating northward.

Simultaneously, and as though to confirm the final identification of the kingdom of the Gilded Man, a strange and almost prophetlike figure emerged from the interior, claiming actually to have visited this legendary ruler of the golden city. Juan Martínez de Albujar, sole survivor of a lost expedition to El Dorado that had vanished ten years earlier, stumbled out of the interior one day and dramatically appeared in the church of Margarita to ask for confession. He was dressed in the clothes of an Indian chief and he spoke broken Spanish, as though the words were strange to him. For years, he claimed, he had been living among the tribes of the interior and they had taken him to visit the city of the Gilded Man. Blindfolded, he had been led through the jungle for many days, and when the bandages were removed from his eyes he had found himself standing at the outskirts of a city so vast that it had taken him and his guides from dawn to dusk to walk from the main gate to the palace of the ruler. The streets of this city were lined with tall, stone-built houses, and in the great palace he had seen with his own eyes the fabulous carousals of the Gilded Man and his courtiers glistening in their golden skins. For seven months he had witnessed the grandeur of El Dorado, and the Gilded Man himself had welcomed him and questioned him about the ways of the white men. Then Martínez had been released. His eyes were bandaged once more, and he was escorted back through the jungles. As a farewell gift the Gilded Man had given him a quantity of gold and jewels, which, Martínez said, had been stolen from him by forest Indians as he made his way back to the Spanish settlements. All he had left was a single calabash full of gold beads. To prove his story, he produced this precious evidence and offered to swear on the Bible that he was telling the truth.

Of course Martínez was a monumental liar, and quite likely his long stay in the jungles had unhinged his mind. Nevertheless, his dramatic arrival in the sleepy little town, his outlandish costume, and his wonderful yarns made a great stir. He was positively identified by men who had known him before he had left the settlement to hunt for El Dorado, and he had a plausible answer to every skeptical question. Eventually it was decided that he should be shipped off to Spain to tell his story there. But Martínez never reached his mother country. At Puerto Rico on the homeward voyage he caught a fever and died, still clinging to the story even on his deathbed that he had indeed visited the fabulous realm of El Dorado.

Berrio was away on the third of his El Dorado quests when Juan Martínez appeared so fantastically from the interior, and in consequence the conquistador never met the castaway. Yet every detail in Martínez's story, which Berrio heard on his return to the coast, seemed to corroborate what the conquistador had already learned about the upper reaches of the Orinoco. Clearly the time was ripe for a final, grand assault along the Orinoco and on to the mysterious kingdom by the lake.

Berrio did not rush his preparations for his fourth trip. He had been a long time in the field and he knew that it was not enough to mount a powerful and well-equipped force; he needed also to protect himself from jealous rivals who would swarm in as soon as Martinez's story was common knowledge. So first he sent one of his lieutenants, Domingo de Vera Ybarguen, up the Orinoco to make contact with the river Indians and gain their friendship. Ybarguen's role was to secure the river route while Berrio himself occupied the island of Trinidad, which was the key to the mouth of the river. Ybarguen did his job well. By May 1593 he had returned down the Orinoco with new versions of the Indians' tales about the mysterious lake, a quantity of native garments, and some jewelry collected from the natives of the river. In addition he reported the satisfactory news that he had left a tiny outpost of Spanish soldiers on the river itself. Berrio, who immediately saw the propaganda value of his lieutenant's achievements, instructed Ybarguen to go on to Spain to recruit men for the venture and gain royal support for Berrio's expedition. It was a wise maneuver. In Madrid Ybarguen put on such a splendid show, wearing the looted trinkets and boasting of Berrio's achievements, that the lieutenant successfully obtained royal confirmation of Berrio's title, optimistically granted five years earlier, to the governorship of El Dorado. In the meantime, Berrio's eldest son had traveled from Venezuela to New Granada to beg reinforcements for his father's cause.

With the prize so near and his arrangements going so well, Berrio's plans were abruptly shattered on April 4, 1595. That day four strange vessels appeared off Trinidad where Berrio had his camp and dropped anchor. Their crews were observed to be preparing and victualing a flotilla of launches. To the watching Spanish it was all too obvious that the unidentified newcomers intended to enter the Orinoco and forestall Berrio's expedition. The veteran conquistador, now seventy years old, immediately dispatched a squad of heavily armed soldiers to the beach to demand the identity of the brash interlopers. To his sharp dismay he learned that the ships were English and that their commander's name was "Guatteral."

His name mispronounced in the Spanish fashion, Sir Walter Ralegh had arrived to search for El Dorado.

2.

Enter Sir Walter
Ralegh, Knight

WHEN RALEGH WENT TO SEEK THE GILDED MAN, he was on
the high plateau of his career. So there is something
supremely appropriate in the fact that the most resplendent and
romantic courtier of Elizabeth's court should have gone in search
of El Dorado, the dazzling priest-king of myth. Already Ralegh
had won a reputation for himself as a soldier and administrator in
Ireland; he had received his knighthood, enjoyed lucrative patronage from Queen Elizabeth, served as captain of her Guard (a post
somewhat similar to Berrio's earlier rank, though much closer to
the monarch), and had converted a profitable wine monopoly
into a small private fortune. Still in his early forties, Ralegh held
the titles and offices of Lieutenant of Cornwall, Deputy Lieutenant of Devon, and Lord Warden of the Stannaries, the tin-
mining districts of the West Country. With prosperous estates
in Dorset, friends and family at court, and an enviable reputation
as a poet and author, he had come a long way from his early days
as a hopeful gentleman-adventurer.

Yet in 1595, the year he went to seek his star in the Golden
Antilles, Ralegh chafed under one all-pervading disappointment:
three years earlier his clandestine marriage to Elizabeth Throck-
morton, the Queen's blonde and blue-eyed maid of honor had

plunged him into disgrace. The marriage had been supremely injudicious and quite counter to Ralegh's usually deft behavior. The marriage had forfeited the Queen's favor and reduced him to virtual exile from her court. To a man of Ralegh's tastes and ambitions, such exile was intolerable. Banished from the hub of fashion and applause, he was an orchid deprived of light and warmth; and, from a more down-to-earth point of view, his absence from the Royal Presence could easily mean his ruin. What the Queen had given, the Queen could take away. Ralegh knew as well as any man in the kingdom that while the shortest road to riches in Tudor England was by way of royal largesse, the converse was also true—no one flourished in the shadow of royal displeasure. Shut out from his natural surroundings and obliged to sit idly in the provinces, Ralegh fretted. Emotionally incapable of hiding his light under a bushel, he missed those lost days when he could have been scintillating with elegance, taste, and wit in the galaxy of courtiers that centered on Gloriana. It was while casting around for a stratagem to extricate himself from this dreary limbo that he hit upon the discovery of El Dorado as the ideal escape. In the Golden Antilles a single fortunate stroke would regain him the royal favor, supply the additional wealth he craved, and thrust him back to the center of England's stage.

In some ways England's own condition at the end of the sixteenth century bore a strange resemblance to Ralegh's plight. The country boasted power and prestige far beyond her humble situation at the middle of the century. The Spanish Armada had been defeated seven years before; the nagging problem of the Irish rebellion was soothed for the present; at home a strong central government ruled firmly, if ruthlessly, while an enterprising merchant class was busy laying the foundations of a great commercial empire. Yet, like Ralegh, England was isolated. On the fringe of Europe, the country was part of the continent without playing any important role in European politics. Nor had she yet found her place as a colonial power. Her economy was fragile, her trade embryonic, and there was an acute shortage of hard currency. Above all, there was the constant threat of a renewed Spanish attack. The Great Armada had been repulsed, but there was no reason to suppose that Philip of Spain might not try a second time. Every summer the country was rocked by a fresh invasion scare.

Through English eyes, and certainly in Ralegh's opinion, one root of the problem could be traced directly to the Golden Antilles. There was something almost indecent about the way in which the wealth of Philip's American colonies was pouring into Spain's coffers. Year after year Spain's infernal luck was bloating her with riches, and it seemed to the English that the golden flow might swell Philip into an invincible juggernaut. Knowing nothing of the financial morass into which Philip's military adventuring had actually led him, Elizabeth's advisors tried to stall the Spanish with a mixture of bluff and deception. On the one hand, they carefully dangled before Madrid the temptation of a marriage between Elizabeth and a Spanish prince; but just as adroitly they hinted at a wedding between Gloriana and a French prince. On land England smilingly signed peace treaties with Spain, while at sea English sailors harried Spanish shipping. It was a delicate international balancing act designed to gain time and preserve England's independence, but no one believed that it offered long-term security. The crux of the matter was that as long as Spain loomed over European politics, England was in danger. And, according to Ralegh's way of thinking, a possible solution to the problem was an overseas empire to provide England with the same bulging opulence that Philip deployed to pay his troops, outfit his navies, and bribe his vast network of spies, which extended even into the Privy Council of England. Thus the Golden Antilles held promise for England, as well as for Ralegh himself. If El Dorado could be found, England might tap that "Magazin of all rich mettells," as Ralegh neatly put it. America would do for Elizabeth what it had done for Philip, raising that Spaniard "from a poore king of Castille to the greatest monarche of this part of the worlde and liklie every day to increase, if other Princes forsloe the good occasions offered." The trick was to seize the kingdom of the Gilded Man before the Spaniards did.

In his West Country exile, Ralegh had ample time to develop this argument. And, like Berrio, he went about the matter thoroughly. It was characteristic of Walter Ralegh that once his interest was fired by a project, his enthusiasm and energy were formidable. Intent on ferreting out everything that was known about the Gilded Man, he located the captains of vessels that had traded in Caribbean waters and questioned them about conditions in the Antilles. He cross-examined travelers who claimed to have visited Spain's colonies in the Americas, and he consulted eminent geographers about their theories concerning the Golden Antilles. Then he ransacked the libraries for information, and read every book about South America that he could lay his hands on, until it was his boast that he knew of twenty-three Spanish "gentlemen, knights, and noble men" who had tried and failed to enter the supposed realm of El Dorado. Their failure, he pointed out with more patriotism than truth, indicated that Divine Providence had reserved El Dorado's kingdom specially for the English nation and that they should now grasp the opportunity.

In fact, most of Ralegh's ideas on Spanish American history came from two books, *Historia de la Conquista de Nueva-España*, published in Seville in 1552–3, and *Crónica de las Indias*, both written by Francisco López de Gomara, a Spanish author who made great play with the idea of fabulous empires in the Americas, where native princes lived in munificence. Ralegh, whose Spanish was excellent, read Gomara in the original and was tinged with the Spaniard's romantic viewpoint, which he then proceeded to reinforce with some equally optimistic geographical notions taken from a French scholar, André Thevet. According to Thevet's treatise, *Les Singulartez de la France Antartique*, the logical place to look for the lost empire of the Gilded Man would be in the vast, unmapped expanse of South America that lay between the courses of the Orinoco and the Amazon. If so, Ralegh calculated, an English expedition stood a good chance of slipping past the Spanish patrols guarding the more northerly approaches to the Antilles and entering the Orinoco unnoticed. With this idea in mind, Ralegh contacted and interviewed John Hampton, a Plymouth sea captain, who had recently traded "with divers others" to Trinidad and the Orinoco regions and returned safely. From Hampton he gained invaluable information about the navigation of those little-known waters "under the line equinoctial."

So, piece by piece (though not always with great clarity or particular accuracy) Ralegh scraped together the information he needed. This preliminary research was vital, because the expense of mounting an expedition to the New World was enormous, and Ralegh had to be well informed and circumspect, persuading a friend here, cajoling a courtier there, until he had the financial backing necessary for the venture. The truth of the matter was that Ralegh, the convinced expansionist, was aiming at no less than a complete English empire in South America, and already he had a name for it—"Guiana," the word which Martínez had used in connection with the realm of the Gilded Man. Yet (and this is the strangest riddle of all), Ralegh's extensive researches may simultaneously have convinced him that there was no such place as the kingdom of the Gilded Man.

To explain this paradox and so get closer to Ralegh's true understanding of the legend of the Golden Antilles, Ralegh's character must be placed in the balance. He was by all accounts the sort of person who in any day or age would be considered an incurable romantic. His letters were filled with curlicues of imagination, and he took an almost sensuous delight in expounding the most fanciful and glossy view of any subject which caught his attention. Poesy and knight-errantry, the perfect breeding grounds for such notions as the myth of El Dorado, flavored his everyday existence and he could be as quixotic as any fairy-tale hero. Yet none of this romanticism was entirely casual. In the last analysis, Ralegh was a Renaissance courtier par excellence. He survived and was successful only because he knew how to manipulate his talents to suit the occasion, and his visions of romance were matched by a corresponding down-to-earth pragmatism. Perhaps nowhere was this more clearly brought out than in his advocacy of the Guiana scheme. At one moment he would laud his own visionary genius, and with the next breath mercilessly ridicule his fellow gallants for their own high-flown dreams. Sir John Harington, the Queen's godson and one of his rivals, put the matter shrewdly when he gibed:

But while he [Ralegh] scorns our mirth in plain simplicity
Himself doth sail to Afric and to Ind,
And seeks with hellish pains, yet doth not find,
That bliss in which he frames his wise felicity.

In short, Harington accused Ralegh of using a double standard, and most of Ralegh's acquaintances would probably have agreed with the accusation.

But the question whether or not Ralegh actually believed in the existence of El Dorado was still further complicated by Ralegh's extraordinary ability to warp the truth to serve his own purposes. He was a magician with words and a most extraordinarily competent liar. As an adept with the half-truth, the fading exaggeration, and the innuendo, he could open his thesis on Guiana with one set of facts, and close it with quite another version, just as he was soon to praise his men on the Orinoco expedition to their faces and then shift the blame for failure onto them the moment he reached home. His performance was a masterpiece of egotism and duplicity, and by Renaissance standards one of Ralegh's finest achievements was the mendacity with which he cloaked his venture to Guiana.

But the motive, at least, for these Machiavellian tactics is easily identified. Pent up behind all Ralegh's arguments in favor of the expedition to Guiana was his harsh enmity toward Spain. It was a simple enough formula. Ralegh, the Spanish-speaking Hispanophobe, was positive that anything beneficial for England was also bad for Spain, and vice versa. Thus the great attraction of his Guiana scheme was that it would strengthen England and harm Spain at the same time. It was Ralegh's argument, expressed time and time again, that if England did not forestall the Spanish in Guiana, Philip II would surely add the realm of El Dorado to his possessions. Ralegh pleaded that the positions should be reversed, and to drive home his thesis, he brazenly cast Elizabeth in the role of an American empress, drawing huge revenues from Guiana and sending out surplus population in return. Then as soon as her fiefdom was established and England had amassed the necessary wealth for the campaign, Gloriana's armies would break out of

Guiana and thrust against Philip's colonies. Guiana would be the springboard for an offensive against Philip's land empire in America. English armies would march up the feeder streams of the Orinoco and fight their way into Venezuela and Peru. In his vaunting belligerence Ralegh wanted no less than to sever Spain from the very tap root of her power and inject poison into the arteries of her financial structure.

So the genius of Ralegh's use of the El Dorado myth becomes apparent. With remarkable astuteness he had drawn a vital distinction between the idea of El Dorado and the much wider concept of the Golden Antilles. His real belief was that the natural assets and strategic location of the Guiana country would support a flourishing English colony, just as once he had hoped that the settlers at Roanoke would find subsistence in the natural bounty of Virginia. His Guiana scheme was, therefore, a serious attempt at colonization and not a wild goose chase in the manner of the conquistadors. Yet he was also aware that his colonial ambitions could be achieved only if he invoked the idea of El Dorado. The lure of the Gilded Man and his gorgeous city was the essential bait to attract men and money, and Ralegh did not hesitate to use it. In the Earl of Northumberland's phrase, he was a man who sought "to sway all men's fancies—all men's courses," and the Guiana scheme was a brilliant illustration of his style. For the first time in the long-drawn-out quest for El Dorado, it did not matter that the Gilded Man might turn out to be a fiction. The primary aim was to lure the English to the Caribbean in force. Once they were there, Ralegh was confident that the more substantial benefits of the Golden Antilles would encourage them to stay. To this end he continued to work patiently and, if need be, unscrupulously.

So matters stood in 1594, when fate took a hand. An English privateer cruising in Caribbean waters under the command of Captain George Popham intercepted a Spanish ship with dispatches for Madrid. The ship was boarded and looted, and all her documents seized. Among them was a bundle of letters giving a complete description of the most recent developments in the hunt for El Dorado. The famous pedantry of the Spanish colonial functionaries had rebounded against them. The author of the captured dispatches carefully provided a complete résumé of all the evidence in support of the El Dorado theory, listed the achievements of earlier expeditions, and then brought the matter up-to-date with a report of Berrio's most recent expedition on the Orinoco and the strange affair of Martínez the castaway. With one scoop, the English had caught up with all the knowledge that the Spaniards had so painfully put together about El Dorado.

The same year Joseph Whiddon, a sea captain whom Ralegh had sent to reconnoiter the coasts of Trinidad, returned to England to say that Berrio was in possession of the island and had built a small stockade there. He also reported that Berrio had been savagely resentful of the intruders. His men had ambushed and massacred eight of the English sailors who had gone ashore to hunt for fresh meat. First disarming their prisoners and lashing their hands behind their backs, the Spaniards had then tied the sailors to a long rope like a string of slaves, and calmly proceeded to slit their throats in cold blood. The atrocity was to have dire consequences for the handful of Spaniards on Trinidad, because instead of frightening Ralegh off, the incident led him to think that Berrio believed very seriously in an El Dorado on the Orinoco and that it was time for the English to intervene before it was too late.

Ralegh's squadron which set out for the Antilles on Thursday, February 6, 1595, was small, heavily armed, and showed signs of having been hastily thrown together. Despite months of lobbying, Ralegh had still not received the Queen's financial backing for his venture, and it was as much as his friends could do to obtain for him an official commission for the trip. With neither the financial resources nor the necessary time to assemble a larger force, he had to be satisfied with only four vessels—his flagship, a light sailing galley called a galleass, a small bark, and *The Lion's Whelp*, a vessel on loan from Lord Admiral Howard. In addition to their regular crews, the ships carried a supernumerary force of about one hundred and fifty gentlemen volunteers (some of whom had actually purchased shares in the venture), a number of ordinary soldiers, and a smattering of officers. Obviously Ralegh had postponed his grandiose scheme for starting a major campaign against the Spanish colonies, and his 1595 expedition was, in effect, no more than a reconnaissance in strength for the greater effort yet to come. At the last moment the English government somewhat grudgingly gave him an official commission, instructing him to "offend and enfeeble the King of Spain." But it was more in keeping with his own grand design that he should be going to inspect in person just what the legendary Antilles had to offer.

The voyage out to Trinidad was very nearly a fiasco. Off the coast of Portugal the little squadron was scattered by bad weather, and Ralegh, aboard the flagship, found himself escorted only by Captain Cross, commanding the small bark. For a week they delayed at Tenerife in the Canary Islands, hoping that the two stragglers would come up and also waiting for Captain Amyas Preston, an English privateersman, who had been toying with the idea of joining the expedition on its way to the Antilles. But after eight days when no other sails had appeared over the horizon, Ralegh decided to press on. The flagship and the bark set their course across the Atlantic and, after a superior feat of navigation, arrived at precisely their destination, Icacos Point at the extreme southwest corner of Trinidad. Their landfall was March 22 and, as far as they knew, no Spanish ships had seen them slipping into the Caribbean.

Berrio was blissfully unaware of Ralegh's menacing presence. The Spanish leader had set up his headquarters at the village of St. Joseph, a short distance inland from the present-day Port of Spain and some 90 miles from Ralegh's position. The Spaniard was still awaiting his reinforcement from New Granada and the mother country. The only English activity in the area that he knew about had been the appearance almost two months earlier of Sir Robert Dudley, another trader-cum-privateersman whose ship lurked around the island for six weeks. But eventually Dudley had sailed away without molesting the colonists, and Berrio had no way of knowing that the English captain had in fact been waiting for a rendezvous with Ralegh, and had abandoned the vigil only after deciding that St. Joseph was too miserable a place to be worth an assault. Now, though Dudley was en route for England. Ralegh was a few hours' sail away, impatiently awaiting the arrival of *The Lion's Whelp* and the galleass, so that he could press ahead with his campaign for Guiana.

This delay was not wasted. Ralegh had read, heard, talked, and dreamed so much about the Golden Antilles that he was thrilled to be there in person at last. The moment his flagship dropped anchor off Trinidad, he had his personal barge lowered into the water, and with picked rowers at the oars he embarked on a miniature voyage of discovery.

Contrary to popular opinion, Ralegh was a poor sailor who loathed sea voyages for the very good reason that he suffered acutely from seasickness. Calm passages, on the other hand, bored him so much that he used to take a small library in his cabin so that he might shut out the tedium and discomfort of the trip. Indeed, it was to be one of his more famous quips that he preferred a year in the Tower of London to a month at sea. Now, however, the dreaded transatlantic voyage was safely over and he was in high spirits. Splashing along in a little boat beneath a blue sky "under the line equinoctial" was a delicious conceit. The excursion tickled his sense of adventure without being too dangerous, and flattered his sense of scientific inquiry without being too irksome.

Gazing eagerly at the beach and occasionally dashing ashore in hopes of meeting the "naturals," Ralegh industriously took notes on such topics as the configuration of the coast, the quality of the soil, the plants and animals, and the most convenient watering places. This potpourri of information was all part of his grand design, for he was planning to produce a geographical survey of the Antilles in support of his colonial thesis when he got back to England and he even had ambitions to make a new map of all the areas he visited. To his chagrin, the "naturals" steadfastly refused to put in an appearance, and he had to content himself with inspecting the clusters of tree oysters that clung to the roots of the trees in the mangrove swamps like bunches of misshapen grapes, shooting out little jets of water as the ripples from his boat disturbed them. The oysters were considered to be genuine "curiosities," because contemporary naturalists maintained that they were nothing less than the fruit of the mangrove tree and grew, rather like plums or oranges, from the tree itself. It was held to be a singular instance of a vegetable giving birth to an animal and an excellent example of the renowned fecundity of the Antilles. Ralegh's scientific curiosity had a more practical bent, and he promptly prized off some of this "fruit" in order to taste it, pronouncing the oysters (generally considered inedible) to be "very salt and wel tasted." His visit to Trinidad's famous pitch lake was, if anything, even more of a triumph, as he proudly carried off samples of the tarry pitch so that he could experiment with it as a caulking material for his ships. Again his practical approach was uppermost, for he declared it "most excellent good, and melteth not with the sunne as the pitch of Norway, and therefore for ships trading to the south partes very profitable."

But these dilettante investigations were strictly incidental to the main purpose of his visit to Trinidad. Ralegh knew that sooner or later he would have to come face to face with the Spanish garrison holding the island, and perhaps with Berrio, the one man who knew more about Guiana and El Dorado than anyone else alive.

The anticipated encounter finally took place when Ralegh's two ships had worked their way round to the Spanish landing place at "Puerto de los Hispanioles" on the west coast of the island. There on the beach the Englishmen saw the squad of soldiers sent by Berrio to spy out the strangers' strength and intentions, and when an English officer went forward with a flag of truce, four of Berrio's men rowed out to visit the ships. Once on board they were plied with copious draughts of wine and bland assurances that the English squadron was really on its way to Virginia with supplies and had only stopped in Trinidad to take on water and wood. For their part the Spaniards gamely tried to stay sober (a task made more difficult by the fact that there had been no wine available to them on Trinidad for several months) and tried to pump the visitors for information. Neither side had much success, though the Spaniards did at least find out enough about the English to warn Berrio that Walter Ralegh was in command of the interlopers.

Later in the afternoon an Indian chief, or *cacique*, risking Berrio's threat to hang, draw, and quarter any Indian who made contact with the foreigners, paddled his canoe out to the English ships. Ralegh already had with him two Arawak Indians whom Whiddon had brought back to England the previous year and trained as interpreters, and now through these men Ralegh learned that Berrio's position was extremely weak. Apparently the old conquistador had been caught offguard, for he had less than eighty men with which to hold the island. This welcome piece of intelligence decided Ralegh that there was no longer any need to keep up his pretense of neutrality. Accordingly, he opened hostilities with typical ruthlessness. He sent a boatload of food and drink to the Spaniards guarding the landing place, and when these men had settled down to their supper, they were surrounded and massacred by an English landing party. At the same moment the four Spaniards who had so foolishly ventured aboard the ships were cut down without regret. This killing, Ralegh later wrote, was to avenge the deaths of Whiddon's men the previous year. Whiddon himself must have found peculiar satisfaction in the deed, for he had returned to Trinidad with Ralegh and was the officer who had carried the flag of truce to the Spaniards on the beach.

Now that Ralegh had revealed his warlike intentions, he acted quickly to press home his advantage. He stripped his ships of men for an attack against St. Joseph, and two companies of forty and sixty men, commanded by himself and one Captain Calfield, were rowed ashore. Tramping briskly through the sultry tropical night, the English halberdiers and musketmen covered the nine miles to St. Joseph in short order and at daylight next morning they swept into the town with scarcely a shot fired. Fourteen Spanish men, several women, and the local Franciscan friar managed to scuttle to the safety of the woods, but most of the garrison was killed, and Berrio, as well as his chief lieutenant, was taken prisoner. In St. Joseph five Trinidadian *caciques* were found manacled to a single chain and half dead from starvation. After releasing the captives, the English soldiers went through the settlement, ransacking the shabby little houses, and smashing strongboxes and chests in search of papers or valuables. When they were disappointed, they set the place to the torch and burned St. Joseph to the ground. This destruction ended the first phase of Ralegh's Guiana campaign. Without loss he had crushed the Spaniards on Trinidad and captured his chief rival in the hunt for El Dorado. It had been a cheap and easy victory, and the real difficulties still lay ahead; but at least Ralegh had put the Spaniards in check. Trinidad, the vantage point commanding the mouths of the Orinoco delta and the last known place before entering the unmapped wilderness of the Orinoco basin, was now firmly under English control.

Doubtless Ralegh had hoped to profit from Berrio's knowledge of the Orinoco navigation once he had the Spaniard within his grasp, but to his annoyance he soon discovered that he had badly underestimated his seventy-year-old prisoner. Berrio was taken to the English flagship, where at first Ralegh treated him lavishly enough, hoping that he could wheedle the old man into describing his journeys in search of the kingdom of the Gilded Man. Berrio, however, was no maundering dotard and proved far too cunning to be drawn out. Rather, he turned the tables on the younger man, and made a fool of him by lapsing into feigned senility or rambling off into long and tedious lamentations over the difficulties of the Orinoco. It was useless, he chided Ralegh, to think of going up so fearsome a river. Sandbars blocked its mouth; there were wild animals and even wilder Indians farther upstream, and excruciating discomforts all the way. If the Englishmen were so thick-headed as to attempt to row up against the current, they would exhaust themselves and consume all their provisions before they had gone very far. Even if they did succeed in penetrating to the interior, they would only find abandoned Indian villages whose inhabitants had fled before the terrifying white men.

Berrio's weary jeremiads were not so far from the truth, but Ralegh had his heart set on his plans for the luxurious Antilles, and finally came to the conclusion that he was being duped by a deliberately uncooperative prisoner. So his honeyed words turned to menaces, and he warned Berrio that he would hand the old man over to the Trinidad Indians, who were itching to use the Spaniard for target practice. Ralegh knew that it was an empty threat: Berrio was useful to the Englishmen only if he were kept alive and, besides, both men were bound by those courtly rules of war which encouraged persons of high birth to cheat one another over the dinner table rather than permit the common folk to spill such noble blood.

By now the English squadron was back at full strength. The galleass and *The Lion's Whelp* had turned up safely on the day that Ralegh and his men attacked St. Joseph, and the reunited squadron then moved back southward to Point Icacos. There Ralegh set his men to felling trees and clearing the ground for a stockade on the headland which faced across to the delta of the Orinoco, for he wanted his squadron to have a secure base against any counterattack from the nearby Spanish colony at Margarita. Three pieces of artillery were transferred from the ships to the new strong point, and while the palisades were being strengthened, *The Lion's Whelp* and Captain Cross's bark made a quick trip across to the mainland of South America some twenty miles away to inspect the Orinoco delta and select a suitable channel to enter the river. To their dismay the English pilots discovered that Berrio's warning about the existence of sandbars was entirely correct: there was dangerous shoal water at every entrance to the delta, and the Caribbean tide was much too feeble to carry the ocean-going ships over the shallows and into the river itself. Crestfallen, the scouts returned with the dismal news that there was no more than five feet of water at the bar and that none of the larger English vessels could possibly enter the Orinoco.

This was serious news, for Ralegh had not brought with him enough boats and launches to carry all his men, and he did not dare attempt the river with a reduced force in case he should be attacked by hostile Indians. In this predicament, Ralegh and his officers showed considerable ingenuity. The light galleass was leaking so badly that she had already been pronounced unfit for the homeward voyage, and the sea officers had decided to abandon her at Trinidad. Now, however, a shrewd feat of improvisation transformed the galleass into a makeshift river craft. Her masts were rooted out; her entire superstructure chopped off and dumped overboard; extra oar holes were cut in the stripped hull, and additional benches installed for rowers. When the refit was complete, the remodeled vessel was no longer a sailing ship but a pure rowing galley drawing a fraction less than the critical five feet of water. Furthermore, she was large enough to carry sixty men, more than half the total expeditionary force. The remainder of the expedition was divided among the cockboat from the flagship, a wherry from *The Lion's Whelp*, another wherry under the command of Captain Calfield, and of course Ralegh in his favorite barge. Each of these smaller boats held ten men, so that the expedition now had a total strike force of one hundred optimistic Englishmen, plus sundry Indians to serve as their guides and interpreters. With them as a hostage went Don Antonio de Berrio, reluctantly returning for the fourth time to the quest for the Gilded Man.

3.

Along the Orinoco

THE RIVER FLOTILLA MADE A WOEFULLY SHAKY START. The first leg of the journey was the crossing of the Serpent's Mouth, the aptly named straits which divide Trinidad from the mainland. It was a dangerous place for small boats, being notorious for the overfalls and short seas which were kicked up whenever the wind blew counter to the current in the narrows. A queasy Ralegh was not the man to dawdle in such fickle waters and he ordered a quick dash across the open straits. His little armada, creeping out from under the shelter of Point Icacos, ran blindly for the opposite shore. It was an ill-conceived maneuver, for it made accurate navigation impossible and the scurrying flotilla merely turned into the first mouth of the Orinoco it found, and then began groping up against the current. As a result neither Berrio nor the Indian guides had the least idea which distributary of the Orinoco they had entered, and the English adventurers promptly lost their way, wandering in aimless circles through the great maze of interconnecting waterways.

The delta of the Orinoco was indeed immense, a huge maze some 150 miles wide composed of streams and rivers, among them seventeen major channels, which braided, divided, rejoined, and looped in such bewildering confusion that the current sometimes ran backward away from the sea. Ralegh and his sailors had never seen anything like it. There was no life, human or animal, to be seen in this wasteland. Nothing moved except the muddy swirling flow of the river, bounded by a thick, unfriendly horizon of dense green where the forest came down to the water's edge. "We might have wandred a whole yeere in that laborinth of rivers," marveled Ralegh, "ere we had found any way, either out or in, especiallie after we passed the ebbing and flowing, which was in fower days; for I know all the earth doth not yield the like confluence of streames and branches, the one crossing the other so many times, and all so faire and large, and so like one to another, as no man can tell which to take: and if we went by the Sun or compasse hoping thereby to go directly one way or other, yet that waie we were also carried in a circle amongst multitudes of Ilands and every Iland so bordered with high trees, as no man could see any further than the bredth of the river, or length of the breach."

Ralegh and his bewildered oarsmen were in a sorry state, and only their good luck saved them from real disaster. On May 22 (the fitting-out of the boats and the construction of the Icacos fort had delayed them nearly seven weeks) they were fortunate enough to surprise a party of three Indians ferrying themselves across the river in a canoe. Immediately Ralegh dashed off in pursuit, for his eight-oared barge was easily the fastest boat in the flotilla, and, after a hectic chase, he succeeded in overhauling the Indians before they could reach the bank. Then, instead of seizing their quarry as the three terrified Indians had fully expected, the English bargemen rested their oars and gestured that they meant no harm and only wanted help. The effect of this unlooked-for friendliness was almost magical: the woods along the bank disgorged an entire tribe of "naturals" who, like shy wild animals, had been surreptitiously watching the passage of the English expedition. Now these Indians timidly came forward from the shelter of the trees, some of them holding up offerings of fruit and gifts to show that they were peaceful, and others beckoning the English to pull into the bank. Ralegh, of course, was thrilled, not merely because the expedition could now ask its directions, but also because his long-sought-after "naturals" had finally materialized. So, while his men cheerfully bartered for fresh food and stared curiously at the near-naked savages, he busily jotted down his first impressions of these denizens of the Golden Antilles.

"Those people," he wrote, "which dwell in these broken Ilands and drowned lands are generally called Tivitivas, . . . a verie goodlie people and verie valiant, and have the most manlie speech and most deliberate that ever I heard of what nation soever. In the summer they have houses on the ground as in other places; in the winter they dwell upon the trees, where they build very artificial townes and villages, . . . for between May and September the river of Orenoke riseth thirtie foote upright, and then are those Ilands overflowen twentie foote high above the levell of the ground, saving some few raised grounds in the middle of them; and for this cause they are enforced to live in this manner.

"They never eat of anie thing that is set or sowen, and as at home they use neither planting nor other manurance, so when they com abroad they refuse to feed of ought, but of that which nature without labor bringeth forth. They use the tops of Palmitos* for bread, and kil Deere, fish and porks for the rest of their sustenance; they have also manie sorts of fruits that grow in the woods, and great varietie of birds and foule."

It was a portrait of the wretched Tivitiva which few of the English sailors on the expedition would have recognized. By any more objective judgment the Orinoco River Indians were a poverty-stricken lot who scraped out a meager existence in a water-logged land that was scarcely fit for human habitation. Yet Ralegh was not being naïve; he knew that he was writing for an assortment of Privy Councillors, merchants, and courtiers in England who would probably never visit the Orinoco and to whom the idea of a happy aboriginal was an integral part of the myth of the Golden Antilles. So, in order to persuade them that Guiana was good colonial material, he deliberately warped the truth. The Tivitivas, he wrote, were "for the most part Carpenters of *Canoas* . . . [selling] them into *Guiana* for gold, and

---

* *Probably the edible crown of the cabbage palm.*

Trinedado for *Tobacco*, in the excessive taking whereof they exceed all nations, and notwithstanding the moistnes of the aire in which they live, the hardness of their diet, and the great labors they suffer to hunt, fish, and foule for their living, in all my life either in the Indies or in Europe did I never behold a more goodlie or better favoured people, or a more manlie."

The Tivitivas almost immediately demonstrated just how "valiant" and "manlie" they really were, by nearly murdering Ralegh's two Arawak guides. The guides were brothers who came from a tribe nearer the coast, and one of them had apparently been in contact with the Spaniards before joining up with Ralegh, for he had somehow picked up the name Ferdinando. During the parley with the Tivitiva, these two men had slipped away from the main expedition and peacefully ventured into the nearby Indian village looking for palm toddy, the favorite native brew. But they were promptly set upon by the villagers, seized, and accused of guiding the Englishmen upriver in order to attack and despoil the Tivitivas. As the English were at that very moment trading hatchets, knives, and other desirables for the Indians's surplus food stores, this was hardly a fair accusation. But the angry villagers were in no mood to argue the point, and Ferdinando and his brother prudently decided that their only chance was to run for the safety of the English boats. Wrenching themselves free from their captors, they bolted out of the village with a mob of Tivitivas in close pursuit. Unfortunately for Ferdinando he was no runner, and although his brother managed to sprint clear, the panting guide was obliged to swerve aside from the path and plunge breathlessly into the forest, hoping to hide in the undergrowth. But the maneuver only won him a few moments' rest. The Tivitivas were soon on his trail with the help of a pack of hunting dogs that chivvied their luckless victim through the bushes to the accompaniment of much excited hallooing and yapping. This uproar could easily be heard at the riverside, and just as the English were wondering what had caused the commotion, Ferdinando's brother arrived at full tilt, sprang aboard, and blurted out that Ferdinando was taken and would surely be killed.

As Ralegh had no intention of losing the services of his chief pilot, however useless Ferdinando had been up to that point, he immediately ordered his men to seize the nearest Tivitiva as a hostage. Their prey, an old tribesman, was snatched up before he could run away from the landing place with the rest of his tribe, and found himself suddenly hoisted into Ralegh's barge, which then stood out into the river. But it turned out that the old man was a poor choice as a hostage. The Tivitivas were much too absorbed in their raucous hunt for Ferdinando to concern themselves with redeeming the captive, and the old man found himself willy-nilly a member of the English expedition. In the meantime Ferdinando's luck had finally turned. After blundering through the thickets the guide somehow found himself at the riverbank, and managed to clamber up into the comforting foliage of an overhanging tree, where he clung, too exhausted to move. When Ralegh's barge swept past, the truant guide splashed limply from his perch and was hauled aboard, quivering with fright. Ralegh now found himself with three guides instead of the original two, and as the old Tivitiva soon showed that he knew a good deal more about the river than anyone else, the English commander abducted him for the time being.

The English now learned to their mortification that rowing against the Orinoco's current was not the easiest way of reaching El Dorado. During their first five days on the river they had made satisfactory progress by riding the floodtide when it was in their favor, and then hanging on their anchors during the ebb. Indeed, they were swept along at such a smart pace that when the galley ran on to an underwater snag, she went aground so vigorously that Ralegh worried lest "even there our discovery had ended, and that we must have left 60 of our men to have inhabited like rookes upon trees with those nations." But Ralegh ordered the removal of the galley's ballast, and after waiting for high tide, the men succeeded in getting her off by dint of much "tugging and hawling." Two days later, however, tidal water was left behind and the oarsmen found that they had to bear the full brunt of the Orinoco's current, which at that season was flowing strongly because of summer rains falling in the interior. It was excruciatingly hard work, and the men strained at the oarhandles, knowing that the boats were swept back one foot for every two feet they gained. The crawling pace was enough to take the heart out of the sailors, and it did not help their morale to know that their commander was puzzled by this great empty delta which had played no part in his original plans. Ralegh's sparkling promises of El Dorado were poor compensation for blistered palms, aching backs, and daily reduction of the food ration. Every bend of the river and every new panorama looked monotonously like the last. The temperature crept upward as the expedition penetrated deeper into the humid interior; the men's clothing began to rot on their sweating bodies, and inevitably they started to flag and to grumble—against Ralegh, against the overcrowding of the boats and the slimy drinking water scooped from the silt-laden river, against the whole ill-begotten idea of looking for the Gilded Man. Ralegh did what he could to appease the malcontents. He ordered the men to work shifts at the oars— each shift was no longer than one hour—and he insisted that the gentlemen-volunteers and the officers should also take their turn at the oar benches. But it was not enough, and he was forced into the time-honored ruse of promising his men that the realm of the Gilded Man lay only two or three days upriver.

Before long, however, Ralegh had to admit that no further progress could be made unless the expedition found some way to replenish its food supplies. The fruit and meat obtained from the Tivitivas had all been eaten, and there was less than three days' rations remaining. Since leaving the Tivitiva village the flotilla had not encountered a single Indian, and the only wild animals that were occasionally seen on the bank were too nimble to be shot with the expedition's clumsy weapons. There was not even enough food to allow the expedition to turn back and head for the fleet at Icacos.

Under the circumstances Ralegh decided that it would be better if the galley dropped anchor in the main distributary which the expedition had been following, while a small search party went out to find a native village which the old Tivitiva guide believed lay a short distance up a minor tributary. Accordingly Ralegh and eight musketeers in his barge, Captain Calfield in a wherry with four musketeers, and Captain Gifford, formerly commanding *The Lion's Whelp*, in the second wherry with another four musketeers, turned into the tributary, intending to visit the Indian village, load supplies, and return before nightfall.

Ralegh's description of this side trip takes less than two paragraphs in the book which he eventually wrote about his first Guiana expedition. Yet these two paragraphs crystallize both his genius as a travel writer and the skill with which he could invoke the concept of the Golden Antilles. His subtle touch transmuted what was really a minor jaunt into a fine episode of adventure and romance: confidently the little band sets out at noon, taking no food with them because their guide has assured them that the Indian village lies only a few hours ahead. But by nightfall the oarsmen are still in the unmapped wilderness, and they have gone too far to turn back. They can only press forward, rowing into such pitch darkness that when the stream narrows to a trickle they must haul out their cutlasses and hack through the over-hanging creepers, groping their way through the obstructions. They grow faint from hunger; the guide is suspected of treachery and the boats's crews debate whether they should hang him; but they are too "hart broken and tired" to do anything about it. Finally, at one o'clock in the morning they glimpse a light ahead and hear the barking of dogs. Summoning up the last of their strength, they wearily reach their destination.

This, in essence, was Ralegh's description of the outward trip. It was a neat story of exploration and adventure that delicately underscored the gallantry of the expedition under his command. But by the same token it was a tale that risked leaving its readers with the impression that the Orinoco's tributaries were inhospitable, danger-infected backwaters quite unsuited to future colonization. Therefore Ralegh brazenly reversed the whole trend of his narrative in describing the return journey. When the little boats head back downstream, the explorers find that the terrors of the previous night were largely imaginary. The black and trendriled wilderness becomes "the most beautiful countrie that ever mine eies beheld; . . . heere we beheld plaines of twenty miles in length, the grasse short and greene, and in divers parts growes trees by themselves, as if they had been by all the art and labour in the world so made of purpose: and stil as we rowed, the Deere came down feeding by the waters side, as if they had beene used to a keepers call." Trying to redress the balance of his tale, Ralegh was in danger of letting his pen run away with him; this new and bosky pleasance was more reminiscent of the Thames at Hampton than the wild "Orenoke" in far Guiana.

After returning to the galley and before the expedition resumed its progress, there occurred a minor tragedy that was to affect Ralegh very deeply. Among the sailors aboard the galley was a young Negro of whom Ralegh had taken some note and considered a "very proper yoong fellow." This young man rashly decided to go for a swim in the river, and had scarcely leaped into the water when he was attacked by a crocodile. In full view of his horrified companions, he was dragged under and drowned before anyone could go to his assistance. It was a sobering reminder that the expedition knew nothing of the real hazards of the country. Ralegh himself was so shocked by the accident that fifteen years later he was to refer to it again.

The flotilla had not gone much farther before Captain Gifford, who had gone on ahead with the galley to find a campsite, suddenly met four canoes running downriver toward him. His lumbering vessel moved to intercept the strangers, and with a fortunate burst of speed he managed to force two of the larger canoes ashore, where their occupants immediately leapt out and ran off into the woods. The English were very pleased to discover that the abandoned canoes were loaded to the gunwales with loaves of cassava bread, and they were congratulating themselves on this windfall when Ralegh came up in his barge and guessed, correctly as it turned out, that the canoes had been headed for the Spanish colony at Margarita. He was poking about the undergrowth on the bank hoping to turn up some further clues to the identity of the mysterious runaways when he uncovered a wicker basket hurriedly concealed among the bushes. Dragging his prize into the open, he found that he had stumbled across a refiner's portable assay kit, complete with its neat array of saltpeter, phials of quicksilver, and all the other paraphernalia used in the testing of rocks for their mineral content. There was also a small quantity of powdered rock which the owner of the basket had evidently been assaying shortly before he hid the basket.

This was a momentous discovery, and it changed the whole complexion of Ralegh's attitude to Guiana. He himself had dabbled in alchemy and metallurgy (and was to do so again when he was incarcerated in the Tower of London) so he had no difficulty in recognizing the importance of his find. Only the Spaniards could have spies so far up the river looking for gold with such sophisticated equipment, and it was essential to catch and interrogate the fugitives in the canoes. Immediately Ralegh sent every available man in pursuit, promising a reward of five hundred pounds to whoever caught the Spanish refiner. But it was too late; the Spaniards had escaped in the smaller canoes. The English search parties could only find their frightened canoemen, who were cowering in the forest, terrified of being caught by the Englishmen who, they had been told, were cannibals and would eat any prisoners that fell into their hands. From the frightened Indians Ralegh learned that the Spanish party had been made up of three white men, an officer, a man-at-arms, and a metallurgist-refiner, and that they had been upcountry to search for gold deposits. According to the canoemen, the Spanish survey party had actually located several possible mining sites and were bringing back a quantity of likely looking ore for more exhaustive tests when they had fallen foul of the English expedition.

This report of gold mines gave a new twist to Ralegh's hopes for Guiana. Until now he had been concentrating on the agricultural potential of the region, and perhaps finding the mysterious kingdom which Berrio had been searching for. Ralegh must have noticed the few gold ornaments worn by the native *caciques,* but he probably thought little about them beyond the idea that perhaps these trinkets might be imported into Europe and sold as quaint Indian curios. The natural assumption was that the gold itself was obtained by trading with the kingdom of the Gilded Man or from the farther tribes, some distance away. Now, however, it appeared that the Spaniards were expecting to find gold mines near the river itself, and they actually had prospectors in the field. If their theories had any foundation, then a Guiana colony would be a much more lucrative affair than a gigantic tropical farm. Its mines might rival Mexico or even Peru itself. Best of all, Ralegh and his expedition were poised to snatch the opportunity from the Spaniards, open up the mines, and present a gold-rich Guiana to Queen Elizabeth.

This was, of course, wishful thinking of the wildest kind. No one in the English party had the least idea whether the Spaniards's ore (which had conveniently vanished along with the two smaller canoes) was of any real value; and if so, whether the Spaniards's canoemen could take them to the place where it had been dug up. Indeed, the irony of the situation was that Ralegh, the one person who had been hard-headed enough to resist the myth of El Dorado, was now falling prey to much the same temptations as his less critical followers. His newly kindled hopes, it was true, had more practical foundation than the will-o'-the-wisp reports of the Gilded Man, but Ralegh had nothing like conclusive proof of the existence of major gold deposits in Guiana.

As if to encourage Ralegh even more, the expedition at last began to mend its pace, and the tempo of the adventure suddenly quickened. On the same day that the Spanish canoes were taken, Ferdinando and the aged Tivitiva were sent back downstream with letters for the fleet at Trinidad. Ralegh could spare both men, since the English flotilla had long since passed beyond those parts of the Orinoco which were familiar to them. It was a compliment to Ralegh's treatment of the two Indians that when Ferdinando and the abducted Tivitiva were turned loose and left to their own devices, they obeyed their instructions conscientiously and took the English commander's dispatches safely to Point Icacos where the sea-going ships were impatiently waiting for news. As his new pilot Ralegh hired "Martyn," the head canoeman from the Spanish party, and although the Indian had only the vaguest idea where the Spaniards had found their ore samples, he took the English expedition off at a brisk pace. Understandably, the oarsmen no longer needed to be coaxed forward. The rumor of the gold mines was sufficient spur, and they were so eager to push ahead that when the galley went aground yet again, her crew ran out a cable to an anchor which they buried in the bank and whisked her off by brute force and in quick time.

On the fifteenth day after leaving Trinidad there came an-

other taste of impending success. Far away to their left the
oarsmen began to make out the distant outline of a mountain
range. It was, in fact, the jagged crest of the desolate Sierra de
Imataca, the same great five thousand-foot mountain barrier that
had blocked Berrio's progress years before. But to the excited
imaginations of the Englishmen the distant peaks were the long-
awaited "mountains of Guiana" which they had come so far to
find. Beyond the mountains, they thought, would lie the capital
city of El Dorado on the shores of the ceremonial lake. The
rowers applied themselves even harder, and as if to crown their
persistence a favorable breeze sprang up and blew the flotilla
forward so that by evening Ralegh recorded in his diary that "a
slent of northerly winde . . . brought us in sight of the great
river of Orenoque." The expedition had at last emerged from the
trials of the delta and was entering upon the broad highway of
the main river, which, they saw to their amazement, flowed
majestically before them in a huge flood spreading four miles in
width between the banks.

The next few days on the main river proved to be a happy
time for the men. Once the expedition entered the large channel,
they began to meet considerable numbers of Indians fishing from
their dugout canoes. The natives' first reaction was invariably one
of terror, and they would paddle frantically for the bank as
though their lives depended on it. But curiosity quickly overcame fear, and the Indians would usually reappear, furtively
showing themselves on the edge of the forest and holding up the
usual peace offerings of food. From them the Englishmen bought
flat cassava cakes, bushels of wild fruit, and baskets filled with the
eggs of the freshwater turtles that swarmed in great profusion on
the Orinoco's sandbars. To vary their diet the sailors took to
fishing with seine nets from the islands in the river. And they
greatly enjoyed the local palm toddy, which the Indians brought
down to the bank in huge earthen pots holding ten or twelve
gallons apiece. The toddy was heady stuff, and the Englishmen
quickly acquired a taste for it, the pungent drink making them
tipsy in the sultry tropical heat. According to Ralegh the Orinoco Indians were themselves "the greatest garousers and drunkards of the world." One of the sights on the entire trip which

impressed him most was the Bacchanalian tableau at one village where he found a pair of lordly *caciques* lolling graciously in their hammocks and quaffing endless toasts to one another. The toasts were called three cups of toddy at a time, and it was the duty of their womenfolk to ladle out the liquor until their masters were blind drunk. Not surprisingly, the English expedition found that the most valuable trade items they had brought with them were the few bottles of Spanish wine which they had put aboard for their own consumption.

The friendliness of the Orinoco Indians was entirely sincere, and it was with genuine hospitality that they insisted Ralegh and his men should visit their villages. The Englishmen gladly accepted the invitation, for they were delighted to have a chance to get away from the monotony of the boats. Ralegh, however, was worried that his sailors might cause trouble. He warned each member of the landing party on pain of immediate punishment that he must pay for all food or other goods which he received from the Indians. To enforce this rule, Ralegh always made a point of inquiring at the end of every visit to a village whether his men had taken anything without permission. If the villagers had a complaint, it was investigated on the spot and the culprit was either forced to pay for the loss or summarily punished in the presence of the watching tribesmen.

It was more difficult to restrain the English sailors from molesting the Indian women, for the latter were a real temptation. They had graceful, well-proportioned bodies, handsome features and glossy skins, and they wore their long black hair in elaborate and very elegant coiffures. This seductiveness was further enhanced by their disconcerting habit of walking stark-naked among their visitors, smiling and serving them food, apparently unconscious of the devastating effect they had on their ogling audience. Yet despite the provocation Ralegh was able to boast when he got back to England that never once did any of his men lay hands on an Indian woman, even though "we saw many hundreds, and had many in our power, and of those very yoong and excellently favoured."

But, sadly, Ralegh's benevolent Indian policy, achieved at the cost of such iron discipline, was largely a waste of effort. He had hoped to win the friendship of the Indians and then cement a formal alliance with them against the Spanish. He was successful to the extent that the Indians never attacked or hindered his expedition, but he never really received the wholehearted cooperation he wanted. In truth his "naturals" were a happy-go-lucky, simple people with a primitive social organization. They had almost no concept of concerted action, and their *caciques* were really little more than a succession of village headmen and petty chiefs who had no notion of what Ralegh was talking about when he requested formal alliances and treaties. Only a very few senior *caciques*, particularly those who had suffered at the hands of the Spanish explorers, were prepared to listen patiently to Ralegh's schemes, hoping that perhaps the English could protect their villages in the future.

The most important of these senior *caciques* was an imposing old gentleman by the name of Topiawari. He boasted that he was a hundred and ten years old, and considerably impressed Ralegh by walking a brisk fourteen miles from his village in order to greet the Englishmen at the riverbank and then marching all the way home again the same evening. With him he brought a motley entourage of men, women, and children, hauling along a variegated assortment of gifts for the white men, ranging from pineapples and slabs of venison to a noisy aviary of parrots, macaws, and parakeets of all sizes and colors. For Ralegh himself, as a special mark of favor, Topiawari had "a beast called by the Spaniards *Armadilla*, which they call Cassacam, which seemeth to be all barred over with small plates somewhat like to a *Renocero*." Ralegh noted sagely that the tail of this ungainly creature, if powdered and placed in the ear, was reputed to cure deafness, and put the armadillo aside (he later ate the luckless creature to see how it tasted) while he tried to explain to the old *cacique* why the English had come to Guiana and what they were seeking.

His speech was the same one that he had been declaiming to astonished aborigines all along the river, "dilating at large her Maiesties greatnes, her iustice, her charitie to all oppressed nations, with as many of the rest of her beauties and vertues, as either I could express, or they conceive." Admittedly this description of his speech was written when Ralegh was back in England and attempting to gain the Queen's favor once again, but there is no reason to suppose that he did not follow the diplomatic custom of his day in describing the magnificence of his own sovereign when suggesting an alliance with Topiawari and his clan. Topiawari, of course, was largely bemused by this grandiloquent rigamarole. When Ralegh tried asking him about matters "touching Guiana, and the state thereof, what sort of common wealth it was, how governed, of what strength and pollicy, how farre it extended, and what nations were friends or enimies adjoining," the old *cacique* could only produce a garbled tribal history which told of his own tribe's migration from the interior and the peoples who had replaced them. But it was enough: from the man's answers Ralegh was able to find references to the hoary tale of the fugitive Incas, who came "from so far off as the *Sun* slept," the mountains of Guiana, and the city of gold. Yet, as always, the Indian *cacique* did not know where to find the route which led across the mountains to the kingdom of the fabulous invaders. He could only advise Ralegh to proceed upstream until he reached the mouth of the Caroní, a large right-bank tributary of the Orinoco. The Caroní, suggested Topiawari, was the key to El Dorado, for the river rose in the mountains of Guiana and by following it the Englishmen might reach El Dorado. It was precisely the kind of vague half-promise which had misled Spanish conquistadors for nearly seventy years.

At this point in his great adventure, Ralegh did the totally unexpected. Just when it would have been logical for him to rush off in hot pursuit of the new rumor, he suddenly lost interest in the search for Guiana and virtually abandoned the project. It was an extraordinary reversal, attended by a strange attack of lethargy which utterly drowned that sense of urgency that had been driving him forward. Instead of pushing smartly up to the mouth of the Caroní and then advancing along it toward the mountains and the fabled kingdom, Ralegh slowly frittered away his advantage with a succession of inconsequential side trips, which culminated in a flying visit to the Caroní that can scarcely be called anything more serious than a casual tourist's inspection.

Here, at the mouth of the Caroní and the alleged road to El Dorado, Ralegh's curiosity vanished. The Caroní was the Ultima Thule of his exploration. He neither continued along the main river nor turned up its tributary to try to reach the mountains. His vacillation squandered the achievements of his expedition, yet he did not care. His only excuses, which he was later to plead to disappointed backers in England, were that the rising floodwater in the Orinoco made it impossible for the expedition to continue, and that he was worried about the fate of his squadron waiting at Point Icacos. But neither explanation carried any weight. He could just as easily have spent a few more days, or even weeks, before the floods became too dangerous, or he could have transferred the expedition from the boats and struck overland toward the mountains. And as for the fleet at Icacos, there was no reason for him suddenly to be so concerned about its safety.

Indeed, the only plausible excuse for Ralegh's sudden abandonment of the Guiana trip was a personal one: he seems to have dropped the idea in a fit of whimsy. It was typical of the man. Mercurial of temperament, Ralegh was accustomed to titillating his intellect by constantly bombarding it with a diversity of interests and schemes. Now, however, this singleminded, uncomfortable journey into the wilds of South America had gone on too long. It was no longer a diversion but a bore, and despite its importance to his own career and status in England, Ralegh had grown tired of it. Already the flaws in his colonial paradise were disturbingly apparent: the climate was enervating, the natives primitive, the prospects for white settlement dim, and his own efforts at leadership were a severe strain without being particularly illustrious. By the time Ralegh met Topiawari, he had seen enough of the countryside to know that the wealth of Guiana was not to be won without prolonged exertion, and he himself had neither the inclination nor the resources to mount a sustained effort. So, rationalizing his disappointment and eager to escape the tedium, he abruptly made up his mind to return to Trinidad before conditions became any more difficult. In a sense, therefore, Ralegh had reached the same disillusionment with the idea of the Golden Antilles that had blunted the efforts of the early Spanish settlers in the lands of alleged plenty. But like them too, he would soon forget the disappointment of his own experiences and resurrect the myth when the memory of failure had softened. Ironically, he was to be his own seducer in leading himself back to the Orinoco.

4

The Bewtiful Empyre

RALEGH'S LAST ACT BEFORE TURNING DOWNSTREAM was his brief excursion to see the famous cataracts of the Caroní. The tributary river, as it approached its union with the Orinoco, plunged abruptly down a steplike series of waterfalls. Tumbling over and over in a roaring cloud of spray, it provided a magnificent spectacle. There were, wrote Ralegh, "ten or twelve overfalls . . . , everyone as high over the other as a Church tower, which fell with that fury, that the rebound of the waters made to seeme as if it had beene all covered over with a great shower of rayne: and in some places we tooke it at the first for a smoke that had risen over some great towne." But, he confessed, only the pleadings of his companions had made him take the trouble of walking over from the main river to view the falls.

By contrast, his sailors and several of the gentlemen-adventurers were not at all disposed to give up their hopes of the golden realm so readily. Outcrops of mineral-bearing rock around the falls of the Caroní encouraged these optimists to suppose that they had finally reached the area where the Spaniards had quarried their specimens of gold ore. With their bare hands and the blades of their daggers, the Englishmen greedily prized out any rock or pebble which looked as if it might contain traces of gold, and triumphantly carried their spoils back to the boats. Ralegh, of course, blasted their hopes. He was prepared to believe that veins of genuine gold-bearing rock might perhaps lie several feet underground, but his river force had not brought along the "pioneers, bars, sledges, nor wedges of Iron" needed to dig down to the *madre del oro* or "mother of gold" as he called it. He warned his men that they were wasting their time in gleaning the trash on the surface. But his sailors paid no attention, and sourly he noted that "such as had no judgement or experience kept all that glistered, and would not be perswaded that it was rich because of the lustre."

Then Ralegh ordered the retreat from the Caroní and, falling back to Topiawari's village, he held a last interview with that wily old chieftain. Topiawari cannily took the opportunity of asking the English commander, a little pointedly, if he could not show his good faith in the proposed Anglo-Indian alliance by leaving behind a garrison of fifty English men-at-arms to defend the tribes against the Spanish. To Ralegh's acute embarrassment a number of the more rash gentlemen-volunteers immediately offered to stay behind on this assignment, and he was obliged to quash their enthusiasm. Brusquely he insisted that he could spare neither the men nor the gunpowder and weapons which would be needed for the scheme. As a rather poor substitute, he suggested that Topiawari's son might like to come back to England with him and train as an interpreter for future liaison between the English and the tribes.*

In the event, Ralegh did allow two Englishmen from the expedition to stay behind in Guiana. They were Francis Sparrey and Hugh Goodwin; and they must have possessed courage and confidence far beyond the ordinary, for they volunteered to be left behind—marooned would be a more accurate description— almost three hundred miles up the Orinoco until Ralegh returned to South America at some future, and as yet unspecified, date to pick them up again. Both volunteers knew that the risks were appalling. They would be completely at the mercy of the Indians; the Spaniards were certain to come hunting for them; and

---

* *The son did in fact go with the English expedition. But his fate is not known.*

if they were captured, they could expect torture, imprisonment, and possible execution as spies. Also they would be obliged to live off Indian food, to abandon all vestiges of European life and clothing, to expose themselves to all manner of tropical diseases, and yet have no firm assurance that Ralegh would ever be able to return and rescue them. Their willingness to face this formidable array of dangers was one of the more remarkable examples of the much-vaunted Elizabethan spirit of adventure.

Hugh Goodwin was no more than a boy. His assignment was to live among the Indians in order to learn their language and their way of life, and he was, in effect, a hostage for Topiawari's son. Francis Sparrey, on the other hand, was given a much more ambitious role: he was to learn if there was any truth whatever in the tale that the Gilded Man lived in a city on the other side of the distant mountains. It was an extraordinary assignment for one man, but Sparrey was considered to be particularly suited for the hare-brained task. He had joined the Guiana expedition as a servant-cum-clerk, and it was precisely because he could read and write that he was selected for his mission. It was proposed that, with the Indians to guide him, he would walk through the jungles until he reached the mountains that had defeated Berrio, and somehow find a way through them to the city of the Gilded Man, if it existed. Entering the city Sparrey would quietly spy out the place, draw sketches of its defenses and location, and prepare a complete intelligence dossier for Ralegh. He would then extricate himself and make his way back to the Orinoco. If by that time Ralegh had not returned to the river, Sparrey was to head for the coast. Being careful to avoid the Spaniards, he was to attract the attention of the first English trading ship that came his way, and arrange his passage back to England and to Ralegh.

The plan was heartbreakingly impractical. Even if Sparrey had succeeded in finding a way to the city of El Dorado, he would have been identified immediately as an interloper and a spy. He did not speak any of the Indian dialects and he would have had the greatest difficulty in communicating with his guides. Even in the unlikely event that he did return from the mountains of Guiana with the answer to their mysterious secret, it would have been virtually impossible for him to contact an

English ship before the Spaniards were alerted and captured him. Indeed, under the circumstances, Sparrey was exceptionally lucky ever to see England again, and it was not surprising that his return was not at all in the manner he had hoped. Soon after Ralegh left Orinoco, the Spanish colonists at Margarita did hear rumors of the two Englishmen living with the tribes, and they promptly sent a special expedition to capture the intruders. Poor Sparrey, wandering vaguely through the jungles in search of the mythical El Dorado, was ambushed by a posse of Spaniards disguised as Indians and taken off to Margarita. There he was thoroughly interrogated and then shipped off to a dungeon in Spain. After about six years in prison he eventually managed to smuggle out word of his plight, and the English authorities saw fit to negotiate his release. But naturally Sparrey had nothing of importance to tell them about El Dorado's mysterious city, and in the end it was left to the Reverend Samuel Purchas, editing a collection of travelers' tales, to publish a short account of Sparrey's luckless experiences in search of the Gilded Man.

Young Hugh Goodwin fared slightly better. The boy made an excellent start with the Indians, and rapidly became so popular with them that when the Spaniards came looking for him, his hosts concocted a story that he had been killed and eaten by a jaguar. Apparently the Spaniards accepted this tale, for they abandoned the search and Goodwin was left to live unmolested among his protectors. In course of time the young Englishman immersed himself so thoroughly in the native way of life that when Ralegh eventually found him again, twenty-two years later, Goodwin, like Juan Martínez before him, had virtually forgotten his mother tongue and was a curiosity rather than of any practical use.

Now that the English expedition was on its way home, Ralegh's oarsmen had the Orinoco's current in their favor. This was just as well, for the water level in the river had begun to rise alarmingly, going up several feet each day and running with a powerful and treacherous current. To make matters more difficult the flood was also bringing down huge rafts of driftwood, some of them containing whole treetrunks like great battering rams. In the eddies and crosscurrents of the spate, the rowers needed all their skill to prevent the boats from being swept out of control. There was a very real danger that the hulls would be dashed to pieces against the rocky banks or collide with the bobbing, gyrating masses of flotsam. Then too, the boats were increasingly difficult to manage, for they were overloaded and unstable, and to make the task more awkward, the heavy summer rains had begun to fall. Two or three times a day torrential downpours would cascade from the sky with all the fury of a tropical storm, and enormous raindrops, as if sprayed from a gigantic hose, blotted out the horizon. In a few seconds the men would be soaked to the skin, their supplies drenched, and the bilgewater slopping around their shins. When the downpour ended, the situation scarcely improved, for the air remained moist and heavy, the men's clothes flapped soggily against their bodies, and the rainwater mingled with their sweat to drip clammily on the thwarts. "The fury of the Orenoque beganne daily to threaten us with daungers in our return," wrote Ralegh, "for no halfe day passed, but the river began to rage and overflow very fearfully, and the raines came downe in terribel showers, and gustes in great abundance: and withall, our men beganne to cry out for want of shift, for no man had place to bestowe any other apparell then that which he ware on his backe, and that was thoroughly washt on his body for the most part ten times in one day."

The shore landings also grew more irksome. The expedition had no choice but to stop from time to time in order to obtain supplies of food from the natives, and these halts cut down the speed of travel. They did give Ralegh an opportunity to visit the other senior *caciques* and tell them of his plan to oust the Spaniards, but he had to keep such side trips very brief, because the rising floodwater made it dangerous to leave the flotilla for more than a few hours at a time. Indeed the Orinoco's rise was phenomenal. During the rainy season the river rose as much as ninety feet over low-water mark, and this extraordinary increase was achieved by daily increments that were so sudden as to be grotesque. Ralegh's men quickly learned that an insignificant creek which they had splashed across ankle-deep in the morning on the way to some village could have swollen that same evening into a raging torrent forcing the men to struggle back with their muskets held high above their heads and the water close to shoulder level. It was an unnerving experience, and no one relished these conditions less than Ralegh himself. He hated discomfort, particularly when he considered it to be futile. He grew less and less inclined to go ashore, preferring to stay with the flotilla, and increasingly he delegated command of the land excursions to his lieutenants. It was a lackadaisical attitude, though his disinterest was not entirely without excuse. After one long and unusually tiring march to an Indian village whose *cacique* was supposed to be waiting for a conference, Ralegh arrived to find the entire conclave of Indian dignitaries "all drunke as beggers, and the pottes walking from one to another without rest." Furious, he withdrew to his boats, and his enthusiasm for the Guiana venture dimmed still further.

Ralegh's aversion to the idea of long route marches—disarmingly he described himself as "a very ill footeman"—was to have a very important consequence. An Indian chief by the name of Putijma sent a messenger to intercept the expedition while it was returning downstream, and offered to show the Englishmen a mountain near his village which he claimed "had stones of the cullor of Golde." The offer was too tempting to be dismissed without further investigation, and Ralegh with most of the gentlemen-volunteers and a number of the sailors went ashore to follow their guide as he led them away from the river. As usual the journey turned out to be thoroughly unpleasant. The weather was very hot, the men sweated profusely, and the party was obliged to wade across several creeks. By noon they were exhausted and had arrived at a small backwater inhabited, interestingly enough, by a number of manatee or "sea cows." Here Ralegh ordered a halt so that his men could rest and dry out their sodden clothes over a fire. He himself had reached the limits of his endurance, and when he learned from the guide that it was another half-day's march and several more river crossings to the "mountain of gold," Ralegh decided that he could go no farther. Turning back with the main party, he ordered Captain Keymis, his chief lieutenant, to press ahead with a flying squad of six musketeers to investigate Putijma's alleged gold mine. When he had done this, Keymis was to cut back diagonally toward the Orinoco, and, traveling by forced marches, he was to reach the main river in time for Ralegh to pick him up as the boats passed downstream.

It was a sensible plan, and Keymis (of whom more will be heard later) carried out his part conscientiously enough, except for one crucial omission. He himself did not personally test the validity of Putijma's gold mine, but only went to the Indian's village, from where he was able to see the so-called golden mountain. Then, worried that his detachment would be stranded if he did not reach the riverbank in time, Keymis accepted Putijma's assurance that the rocks on the mountain seemed to be made of gold and promptly hurried off for his rendezvous with his commander. When he rejoined the flotilla, Keymis told Ralegh that in his opinion there was a potential gold mine near Putijma's village, and he stupidly omitted to point out that this opinion was based on hearsay and not on first-hand evidence. By coincidence, Ralegh had already noted several promising out-crops of mineral-bearing rocks in the area and he was therefore inclined to believe Keymis's report. It was an unwarranted conclusion that was to have catastrophic results.

For the moment, however, it was much too late to follow up Keymis's encouraging tale of the gold on the mountain. The galley with half the expedition on board had already gone on ahead toward the sea, and Ralegh was unwilling to split his command at a time when they might well encounter a Spanish force in ambush at the mouths of the delta. He therefore decided that Putijma's alleged gold mine, together with the possible underground deposits near the mouth of the Caroní, would have to wait until he returned to Guiana with a larger and better-equipped force. His immediate problem was the successful with-drawal of his men. So the entire expedition—less one Negro taken by the crocodile, Francis Sparrey, and Hugh Goodwin—headed with all possible speed for Trinidad and Point Icacos. There, to their profound relief, they found the precious ocean-going ships unharmed and their crews bored by more than a month of complete inactivity. Apart from an occasional scouting canoe, the Spanish colonists had left the English support fleet alone.

Re-embarking without incident, Raleigh immediately took his squadron along the Venezuelan coast, where he intended to make a show of strength before the Spanish colonists and, he hoped, to recoup some of the expenses of the Guiana venture by looting their coastal trading vessels. But his luck continued poor. The Spanish ships wisely kept to the safety of their harbors, and the three feeble attacks which Ralegh launched against their ports at Cumaná, Santa Marta, and Rio de la Hacha, were singularly undistinguished for a man who had boasted of the vulnerability of the Spanish cities in the Antilles. The only honorable result of this halfhearted campaign was that Governor Berrio finally received his freedom. Apparently Ralegh had grown fond of the old man, for he was to refer to him later as a "gent. well descended . . . very valiant and liberall, . . . of great assuredness, and of great heart." Yet this esteem for the aging conquistador did not prevent the English commander from attempting to put his prisoner up for ransom to the Spanish colonists. When they would have nothing of it, Ralegh was eventually obliged to set Berrio ashore scot-free.* Then the English squadron swung away to the north, out of those Caribbean waters where there was constant danger of meeting a Spanish battle fleet, and set course toward the coast of North America, perhaps with the idea of going in search of the "lost colony." But the winds proved contrary, and the scheme was soon abandoned in favor of taking the shortest way back to England, where the ships arrived in August 1595.

Ralegh's Guiana expedition had been away for seven months. During that time he had led a small English squadron into the Spanish Antilles and penetrated unscathed for three hundred

---

* The old man stubbornly made his way back to the Orinoco, built a small settlement on the river, and brought over colonists from Spain. But the experiment was a fiasco. Most of the settlers died of disease, malnutrition, or were killed by the Indians. When Berrio died two years later, his governorship of the province of "El Dorado" was a sorry affair and much of his fortune had been lost.

miles up the Orinoco, farther than any English had gone before. He had also set the Spanish colonial administration at defiance. But that was the limit of his real achievement. His attempt to find the kingdom of the Gilded Man and to open up a rich new colony for Gloriana had brought back nothing more substantial than a handful of Indian trinkets, a few hogsheads of tobacco looted from St. Joseph, a quantity of dubious-looking gold ore, and several more rumors to add to the legend of the Gilded Man and his whereabouts. The expedition had fallen abysmally short of the stunning success which Ralegh had hoped would restore his fortunes and his reputation with the Queen.

If Ralegh expected a hero's welcome upon his return to England or hoped that his expedition might strike a spark of favor from the public imagination, he was quickly disillusioned. In England the popular response to his return was lukewarm, short lived, and not a little deflating. His supporters, particularly those like Sir Robert Cecil, the Queen's chief minister, who had invested money in the project, were frankly disgruntled that the voyage had failed to show a profit on their money. Having listened to Ralegh's promises of El Dorado, his financiers had anticipated a quick return on their investments and they were understandably piqued when the expedition's promoter came back empty handed. Their discontent, however, was trifling by comparison to the hostility of Ralegh's enemies. When it was known that his much-publicized expedition had reappeared with nothing better than vague promises and another sackful of tales, Ralegh's detractors and rivals launched a chorus of criticism. Gleefully they mocked his friends for the money they had wasted on the madcap venture, and sought to hang the expedition like an albatross about its promoter's neck. The entire Guiana project, they claimed, had been a gigantic hoax. Ralegh had never left England at all. Instead of sailing to South America he had been skulking comfortably in the inlets and hidden places off Devon and Cornwall. Another equally preposterous cavil suggested that Ralegh had planned on defecting with his squadron to the Spaniards, but they had refused to have anything to do with him. More credible, and therefore more damaging, was the tale that the so-called Guiana ore that he had brought back for analysis by the assaymasters was not from the Orinoco at all, but had been picked up on the west coast of Africa where his ships had secretly called on their way out to the Caribbean. To compound Ralegh's discomfiture, the rumor also got about that whatever its provenance, this gold ore was utterly worthless, for it had been assayed in London and found to contain no trace of gold whatsoever. This last canard probably referred to the specimens of "fool's gold" which members of the expedition had brought back privately, against Ralegh's advice, from the Caroní falls. But the damage was done. Ralegh's enemies deliciously glossed over such distinctions and attacked their target with any calumny that was at hand.

Goaded by these tormentors, Ralegh was quick to defend himself and did not hesitate to use the most effective weapon at his command—his pen. His brilliant counterstroke to the campaign against him was the publication of his personal account of the Guiana trip designed to show that the venture had been well planned, well led, and promised well for the future. Commonly known as *The Discovery*, his book is one of the most elegant travel classics ever written and a major contribution to the literature of the legendary Antilles.

In the manner of the time the book's full title left no doubt about the extent of the subject matter. It was called THE DIS-COVERIE OF THE LARGE, RICH, AND BEWTIFUL EMPYRE OF GUIANA, WITH *a relation of the great and* GOLDEN CITIE *of* MANOA (*which the Spanyards call El Dorado*) *And of the Provinces of Emeria, Arromaia, Amapaia, and other Countries, with their rivers, adioyning. . . . Performed in the year 1595 by Sir W. Ralegh Knight, Captain of her Maiesties Guard, Lo. Warden of the Stanneries, and her Highneffe Lieutenant Generall of the Countie of Cornwall*. It opened with a fulsome dedication to Lord Admiral Charles Howard (provider of *The Lion's Whelp*) and to Sir Robert Cecil, both men whose influence at court was calculated to give pause to the critics.

With these daunting advance piquets tactically displayed on his title page, Ralegh proceeded straight into his rebuttal of the malicious tales against him. He challenged the rumormongers to prove their allegations; and he contemptuously dismissed their products as the vicious fabrications of men who sought to do him harm at all costs. Was it likely, he asked sarcastically, that he, Walter Ralegh, a man long accustomed to the soft and easy life, would undergo "long voyages, to lie hard, to fare worse, to be subiected to perils, to diseases, to ill savours, to be parched and withered, and withall to sustaine the care and labour of such an enterprize" merely to perpetrate a bad practical joke? His expedition had indeed visited Guiana, as his expert knowledge of the area would testify. And as for the rumor that his gold ore was worthless, he reminded his readers that his followers had picked up specimens of worthless marcasite, thinking them to be true *madre del oro*. He had warned his men against this folly at the time. Clearly he could not be held responsible for such people. On the other hand, if his readers wished to learn the true value of the specimens that he had brought back officially from Guiana, they could consult either Master Westwood, refiner living in Wood Street, or Master Dimmock, an assaymaster of Goldsmith's Hall, or no less a personage than Master Palmer, Comptroller of the Royal Mint. These metallurgists were men of unimpeachable character and wide experience, and they had all tested the ore samples and pronounced them to contain gold in excellent commercial quantities.

But happily, Ralegh's *Discovery* was much more than a fusillade against his detractors. It glittered with as many facets as its author. It was a treatise of empire, a plea for personal recognition, a geographical handbook, and a work of pure literary entertainment. Regrettably, it was also marred by excessive vanity, considerable exaggeration, and several downright lies. In fine, *The Discovery* provided not only an excellent and highly readable account of the Guiana expedition, but it also gave an intriguing glimpse into Ralegh's character.

His skill as an author was beyond question. Although forced to rush the book to press (and probably to pay for its printing himself), *The Discovery* was beautifully written. Interweaving the thread of the narrative with digressions into such topics as empire-building, Spanish colonial history, and indigenous cultures, Ralegh mustered his somewhat meager raw material into a full-length, well-rounded book. Literary talent infused every page. The reader was carried forward along curlicues, flourishes, and sudden spurts of style and content; and although at first impression this movement seemed merely to follow the haphazard ramblings of Ralegh's own mind, closer inspection showed a carefully designed structure. From the opening Dedication to the final sentence of his conclusion, Ralegh was in unswerving pursuit of those same goals that had induced him to sail for the Golden Antilles. *The Discovery* was designed to win its author public recognition, restore him to the Queen's favor, and initiate his country's colonial future. Again and again Ralegh hammered away at these themes and, fortunately for his cause, he was a far better writer than he was an explorer.

His digression on the native use of the poison curare, for instance, showed how ably he could use his material. The very topic, as Ralegh knew, was precisely the right sort of *bizarrerie* to enliven his narrative and catch the attention of his readers. And so, unblushingly, he interrupted the smooth flow of his account of the expedition's progress upriver in order to add the spicy tidbit. He described the effects of the poison with special panache: "the partie shot [with a poisoned arrow] indureth the most insufferable torment of in the world, and abideth a most uglie and lamentable death, sometimes dying starke mad, sometimes their bowels breaking out of their bellies, and are presently discoloured, as blacke as pitch, and so unsavory, as no man can endure to cure, or to attend them." According to Ralegh, the Spaniards had failed to discover how to counteract this virulent poison, even though they had tortured the native medicine men to reveal their secret.* The tenacious Berrio himself, try as he might, had been unable to worm out the secret, for the Indians guarded their medical lore closely and passed it only from father to son. "And yet," boasted Ralegh, "they taught me the best way of healing as wel thereof, as of all other poisons. . . . This is the generall rule for all men that shall hereafter travell to the Indies where poisoned arrows are used, that they must abstaine from drinke, for if they take any licor into their body, as they shall be marvellously provoked therunto by drought, I say, if

* *Apparently garlic juice was an effective antidote against the lesser sorts of venom.*

they drink before the wound be dressed, or soone vpon it, there is no way with them but present death." Ralegh must be given credit for providing what was, by sixteenth-century standards, a remarkably good prognosis of curare poisoning and the best available treatment.

Yet Ralegh's bragging was so repetitious in the pages of *The Discovery* that the sin cannot be easily overlooked. By some slant of temper he managed to impart a tone of condescension to almost every page of his text. Clearly he despised anyone his inferior, and in this context his idea of an inferior included nearly everyone he had encountered during the expedition. Thus Berrio was well bred but dimwitted; the English lieutenants were willing but fumbling; and the rank and file were uncouth poltroons who would have turned back if they did not have their leader's example to encourage them on. Nowhere was this air of superiority more obvious than when Ralegh allowed himself to lapse into false modesty. In his Dedication he announced that his writing had "neither studied phrase, forme, nor fashion," yet even by Renaissance standards this disclaimer was absurd, for every paragraph of *The Discovery* was obviously the work of a painstaking craftsman of literary elegance. Even more hollow was the claim that he and his "poore troope" successfully penetrated farther up the Orinoco than that old master Berrio, who had lavished more than eight hundred thousand ducats on his quest for the Gilded Man. In point of fact, Ralegh's self-styled "poore troope" had been better equipped and more numerous than any task force which Berrio had ever been able to put into the field. Furthermore, the Englishmen had been following in the older explorer's footsteps at every turn.

In truth, Ralegh would have been far wiser to have avoided all comparison with the Spanish explorers. By conquistador standards the Guiana expedition had been no more than a cosy jaunt, and Ralegh had flinched and then retreated at a stage in his El Dorado hunt when most conquistadors would have pushed ahead. The Englishmen never suffered unduly for lack of food; they were never in any real danger from the natives or the elements; and, most damning of all, they had never even ventured into unexplored territory. *The Discovery* was no "discovery" at all—

every inch of the Orinoco and every tribe which Ralegh visited were already known to the Spaniards. The Spanish colonists at Margarita regarded the Orinoco as a well-traveled artery which took their explorers into the interior and brought out canoeloads of food for the townsfolk. Ralegh and a hundred heavily armed Englishmen had actually met a tiny party of three Spaniards returning downstream with an escort of a few native canoemen. The Englishman's claim to have discovered "Guiana" was utter nonsense. And where Ralegh boasted to have traveled at least four hundred miles up the Orinoco, his farthest point was really only 125 miles from the sea in a direct line, and less than three hundred miles along the most tortuous river route he could have devised.

Strangely enough, in view of his inclination to stretch distances as they suited him, Ralegh was in fact a quite competent geographer. Despite the handicaps of discomfort and the strain of leadership, the author of *The Discovery* had done an excellent job of putting together his promised geographical synopsis of the area he had visited. Unavoidably, he made mistakes. For example, he seriously exaggerated the size of the Orinoco and described it as being larger than the Amazon, a river which he had not seen for himself and which was several times the size. But on the whole his book was an honest attempt at a summary of such features as the topography, drainage, climate, and inhabitants of the Trinidad-Orinoco area. Certainly *The Discovery* was far superior in this respect to any of the earlier descriptions of the region which Ralegh might have consulted before he left England. As for his map of Guiana, the adverse conditions had not deterred Ralegh from his self-appointed task of compiling a dossier of notes and drawings on the subject. When his "Guiana map" duly appeared—at about the same time as the first edition of *The Discovery*—it was a notable contribution to geographical knowledge. Drawn with the south toward the top of the sheet, the map showed most of what later became known as "Caribeana," the large segment of South America lying between the mouth of the Amazon and the isthmus of Panama. Special emphasis was given to Trinidad, the course of the Orinoco, its huge delta, the Spanish settlements on the coast, and the Indian villages of the interior. The map's only serious inaccuracy was the obvious one: there, behind the clearly marked line of the "mountains of Guiana," lurked the tantalizing outline of a huge lake, its bristling fringe of feeder streams giving it the appearance of an enormous centipede which has somehow strayed onto the page. Here, for several generations, was to be the fictitious "lake of Guiana," home of El Dorado, and because the remainder of Ralegh's map was so accurate and so workmanlike, subsequent mapmakers accepted the existence of this lake along with the other features he marked. In consequence, Ralegh's imaginary lake was to show up in reputable atlases for another 150 years, sometimes drawn to a scale that made it larger in area than the Caspian Sea.

But Ralegh's geography was not accepted so credulously by everyone who read it. There were some critics who pored over *The Discovery* with the particular intention of selecting its faults; and in Ralegh's extraordinary story of the outlandish "Ewaipanoma" they found a stick with which to belabor the hapless author.

The Ewaipanoma, Ralegh wrote, were a freakish tribe of club-wielding giants who lived in the remote fastnesses of Guiana. He himself had never actually seen any of them, but the Orinoco Indians had solemnly assured him that such a tribe really existed, and they even claimed that they had captured an Ewaipanoma in battle. According to the Indians, these giants were true monstrosities, for they had no heads. And since they were headless, their eyes, nose, and mouths were, perforce, located in the middle of their chests, while a thatch of long hair grew backward from their shoulders.

This preposterous yarn, as Ralegh should have known, was one of the hoariest of all travelers' tales. Its antecedents went back more than a thousand years, and during the Middle Ages the same headless giants had appeared in the *Travels* of that glib arch-liar, Sir John Mandeville. By the sixteenth century, in fact, the fable of the "men with their eyes beneath their shoulders" was beginning to be recognized as humbug. So it was all the more extraordinary that Ralegh should have chosen to dust off the venerable myth and parade it forth once again as though it were true, even saying that since many of Mandeville's tall stories had turned out to be based on fact, there was no reason to suppose that a tribe of headless men did not exist in the depths of the Guiana jungle. More cynically, perhaps, Ralegh had resurrected the monstrous Ewaipanoma because he knew that the taller his story, the more it would delight his more credulous readers and draw attention to his book. In fact the tale became one of *The Discovery*'s most popular, and in some cases most ridiculed, passages, with later editions showing fanciful pictures of the hideous Ewaipanoma with great war clubs in their hands and surly scowls on their chests. In the long run, however, the story of the headless men probably did more harm than good, for it reduced the overall credibility of *The Discovery*. Ralegh's readers might have paid serious attention to his claim that in certain South American rivers the water was deadly poisonous unless drunk at high noon, or that in Guiana he had seen a mountain of solid crystal, or that the banks of the Orinoco were studded with rocks of blue adamantine. But the headless men were sufficiently notorious to make other stories in the book less believable.

The same lack of credibility applied, in a lesser degree, to his claim that there was a nation of Amazon women living on the borders of Guiana. Once again he was repeating a hoary legend of considerable antiquity; though in this case, Ralegh protected himself by stating that he had only heard about the Amazons from the natives, and had not seen them himself. Quite possibly the Indians had given Ralegh a grossly muddled account of some matriarchal tribe living in the interior; but he, of course, could not resist the temptation to dress up the legend in his own fashion. Every April, according to *The Discovery*, in order to procreate their own kind the Amazons held a great orgy, to which the menfolk of the neighboring tribes were invited. From the most virile of their guests the Amazon queens selected their lovers, while the humbler tribeswomen would cast lots for the less promising-looking males. Then for a whole month, everyone would "feast, daunce, and drinke of their wines in abundance, and the Moone being done, they [the men] all depart to their owne Provinces." The results of these festivities were of the greatest importance to the Amazons, for "if they conceive, and be delivered of a sonne, they returned him to the father, if of a daughter they nourish it, and reteine it, and as many as have daughters send unto the begetters a Present, all being desirous to increase their owne sex and kinde." On a more cautionary note, Ralegh warned that should any man stray into the realm of the Amazons uninvited, he would be used at stud for a time, "but in the end for certain . . . put . . . to death: for they [the Amazons] are said to be very cruell and bloodthirsty." To illustrate the point, *The Discovery*'s publishers gladly served up pictures of Amazon women shooting arrows into trespassers whom they had caught and hung upside down from the branches of trees.

Ralegh's somewhat racy story of this love-making was unusually outspoken, for he intended that Queen Elizabeth should read *The Discovery* and be impressed by the author, and it was no secret that the Queen could be erratically waspish about anything to do with sex. Usually Ralegh, like most of Gloriana's courtiers, was careful to adopt a more prudish approach about sexual matters. Elsewhere *The Discovery* was replete with sycophantic references to the "virgin queen," her chastity, her dazzling charms, and similar virtues. In fact, in one unconsciously humorous passage Ralegh claimed that the Orinoco Indians so fawned on Her Majesty's image that he was obliged to hand out shiny new twenty-shilling pieces because they were stamped with the Queen's portrait. This largesse, he said, meant that he left more gold in Guiana than he ever took out of the place.

Despite all its faults, exaggerations, and purple passages, Ralegh's *Discovery* earned a well-deserved popular success. The first edition, hastily set and with many printer's errors, was followed in the same year by a second edition. Three years later an abridged version was translated into Latin and appeared on the Continent, where its scholarly language was amply balanced by several lurid illustrations. Among the leading editors of travel literature of the time, Hakluyt and De Bry both included *The Discovery* in their collections. In Germany the book acquired such vogue that no less than three editions were published in 1602, while an early Dutch translation was eventually reprinted five times.

Amid all this success, however, Ralegh knew that his *Discovery* had failed in its true purpose: it did not persuade the financiers and Privy Councillors of England to assemble the great colonizing fleet which he had begged for. Worse yet, there was not the slightest flicker of interest from the Queen herself. Just where it mattered most, *The Discovery* had slipped across the narrow line dividing a hard-headed report on Guiana's colonial potential from a woolly-minded eulogy of the Golden Antilles. *The Discovery* was, by the very nature of its author, more suited to the romance of the Orinoco than its colonization. William Shakespeare probably borrowed from its pages Othello's reference to

> *The Anthropophagi, and men whose heads*
> *Do grow beneath their shoulders*

and his monstrous Caliban may have been an amused acrostic of Ralegh's "canibal" Indians. But in the politicians' eyes Guiana remained a demi-fairyland too good to be true, where according to *The Discovery*, the countryside was "all faire greene grasse, the ground of hard sand easy to march on, eyther for horse or foote, the deere crossing in every path, the birds towardes the evening singing on every tree with a thousand several tunes, cranes and herons of white, crimson, and carnation perching on the rivers side, the ayre fresh with a gentle easterlie wind, and every stone that we stooped to take up, promised eyther gold or silver by his complexion." Ralegh's pen had been too successful in providing the stuff of legend and wistful illusion. He was the tale-telling wanderer who had visited the earthly paradise and now come back to say that its treasures and pleasures really existed. His yarns of the Golden Antilles certainly enchanted the arm-chair travelers who read of his *Discovery* by their firesides and did not know the extent of the fraud, but the policy-makers of England merely smiled at the grosser conceits and counted the appalling cost of the colonial scheme that Ralegh was trying to sell them. In view of their skepticism, it was all the more extraordinary that Ralegh, who knew the somber truth about the place, should then have risked his life to return to the discomforts and disappointments of the Orinoco.

5.

Raleana Revisited

RALEGH'S SECOND AND FINAL EXPEDITION TO the Golden Antilles was so overshadowed with gloomy foreboding that it had an eerie, almost macabre, quality about it. The leading actor of the drama moved as though drugged, and held in the style of true tragedy to a predetermined course which appeared to bear little relation to the events taking place around him. Conscious from the inception of his second trip that he was facing tremendous odds and that he would need phenomenal luck to achieve success, Ralegh proved singularly ineffectual. When it became clear to him that everything about the venture was ill-starred, he neither attempted to adapt his plans nor tried to improve his chances of winning through. Instead he blundered forward, and when at last he returned home and his friends melted away, there was almost a feeling of relief that the whole debacle had ended and that he could be left alone to plead his excuses for the failure of a venture which never had more than a marginal chance of success.

Sixteen eventful years separated Ralegh's first Caribbean trip from the second, and in that time much had changed. Ralegh himself was much older, mentally as well as physically. Sixty-four years old, he described himself as an "ould and Sorrowe-

worn Man, whom death would shortlye deliver." He walked
with a limp, the result of a splinter burst which had injured his
leg during the naval attack on Cádiz in 1596, and he was increasingly prone to attacks of fever, abscesses of the body, and severe
headaches. Nothing had yet blunted his spirited imagination, but
the restlessness of his early days was reduced. He no longer
darted from one scheme to the next with quite the same lightning
vivacity, and was content to spend more time on fewer projects.
This new patience, however, had been painfully learned. In his
heart of hearts Ralegh still yearned to be poet, alchemist, politician, historian, and adventurer, all in one, but his wings were
closely clipped—for thirteen years preceding his second Guiana
voyage, he had been a prisoner in the Tower of London.

As always, Ralegh's fate had been intimately bound up with
the politics of the land. In 1603, on the death of Queen Elizabeth,
James I had ascended the English throne, and the change of
sovereigns had shaken Ralegh's life to its very foundations. His
carefully garnered monopolies, privileges, and estates began to be
whittled away by his new master. Fresh cronies and rearranged
power groups emerged from the old patterns of royal cliques and
favorites—and Ralegh was not among the lucky ones who were
intimately close to the throne. In the previous reign, Elizabeth
had been a dangerous enigma, who ruled her court with a shrewd
balance of one faction against its rival and seasoned everything
with a dash of feminine capriciousness. Now, superficially, James
was very similar. He too played off rival factions and behaved
with a willfulness that was wholly unpredictable. But the new
regime had a more sinister bent than the old. Because of his
character—a mixture of ambition and deceit, cleverness and
caution—James was emotionally unable to exercise the tight
control that his predecessor had managed so ably. He was inclined to slide temporarily under the influence of men of stronger
character, and then to turn on his advisers. In consequence his
policies veered sharply from one extreme to the other, and these
wild swings of royal opinion were often fatal to those who
dabbled in affairs of state. Ambitious men, no longer held in
check, had greater power to damage one another, and a man like
Ralegh was constantly vulnerable.

Within four months of Elizabeth's death, Ralegh had been arrested on a charge of high treason and accused of conspiracy in a plot against James. The plot was real enough and Ralegh personally knew a number of the conspirators, but he himself almost certainly had nothing to do with their plans. Yet his innocence was irrelevant; his real fault was that his enemies ruled the King's councils and wanted him out of the way. So, convicted by a browbeaten jury, sentenced to death and then reprieved at the last moment, he was left to cool his ambitions in the Tower. Ironically, the man most responsible for his downfall was Robert Cecil, to whom he had dedicated *The Discovery*.

Despite this catastrophic downturn in his fortunes, Ralegh did not entirely abandon his dream of an English colony in the Golden Antilles. While Elizabeth still lived, he had stubbornly continued to advertise Guiana's potential and to ask for a colonizing fleet to follow up the promises of *The Discovery*. But England's shipping had been desperately needed for the struggle against Spain, and Ralegh himself could not be spared for another wild goose chase in South America. So, seeking an alternative, Ralegh had tried to interest the Swedes in loaning him a fleet for the Guiana venture, and when this scheme came to nothing, he patiently continued to send a trading vessel to the Orinoco delta every second year at his own expense with orders to maintain contact with the "naturals."

One other approach was also tried. In 1596 while Ralegh himself was busy fighting the Spanish, he despatched Laurence Keymis, the captain who with six musketeers had seen Putijma's alleged golden mountain, on a carefully planned reconnaissance trip. Keymis had two objectives: he was to examine the coastline south of the Orinoco delta to see if there was another river which might lead inland behind the mountains of Guiana to the lake of El Dorado; and he was to pay a return visit to the Caroní falls where he was to collect a second and larger batch of gold ore for analysis. The first part of the mission was accomplished without much difficulty. Captain Keymis explored the coast and learned from the Indians that the Essequibo River was a likely route to El Dorado, since its source was said to lie within a day's portage of the lake of the Gilded Man. The return visit to the Caroní, on the other hand, was not a success. Three miles below the falls of the Caroní, Keymis found that the Spaniards had established a small garrison to prevent intruders from proceeding upriver. Furthermore, it appeared that the Spanish soldiers had established themselves permanently, for they had gone to the trouble of clearing the ground and building themselves a small hamlet of some twenty huts, complete with palisade, at a strategic location from which their artillery could control the passage of the river. Since Keymis had neither the troops nor the instructions to risk an attack, he withdrew quietly, believing that the Spaniards had fortified their position because they had opened the mines on the Caroní and were working the gold ore. In point of fact, the Spaniards were doing nothing of the sort. Like cocks on a dunghill they were still hopefully scratching around near the mouth of the Caroní, expecting to uncover the gold which they suspected had lured Ralegh to Guiana. Thus it was that the two sides, Spanish and English, thrust each other forward, each convinced that the other had possession of the splendid mineral wealth of Guiana or knew where potential mines were located. The myth of the Golden Antilles, seductive enough already, was considerably enhanced by this new element of direct rivalry. And Keymis, retreating down the Orinoco without firing a shot, returned to England more certain than ever that there were gold mines in "Raleana" as he called the Orinoco basin in honor of his imprisoned patron.

Keymis's visit to South America was not the only English venture in this area. The following year an English pinnace, probably also sent by Ralegh, poked around near the mouth of the Essequibo River and came back with a confirmation of Keymis's report that the river offered an alternative route to El Dorado's supposed city. About the same time, too, the publication of *The Discovery* had its repercussions. Ralegh's book might have failed to conjure up a colonizing fleet for its author, but his glowing account of the "bewtiful empyre" in Guiana prompted other adventurers to try their hand at finding the Gilded Man or planting a colony in South America. The French and the Dutch both sent scouting ships to the area, and no less than three English attempts were made to follow up Ralegh's lead. The last of these attempts, in 1610, was led by Sir Thomas Roe, later ambassador to the Great Mogul, the Sublime Porte, and Gustavus Adolphus. Ralegh himself invested six hundred pounds in Roe's venture, and so it was doubly disappointing when Roe came back to report that although he had spent more than a year exploring the region lying between the lower Amazon, the Essequibo, and the Orinoco, he had been unable to locate the famous inland lake. Roe did not go so far as to say that the realm of the Gilded Man was an utter fabrication, but his experience considerably dampened English enthusiasm for ever finding El Dorado. From this time forward it was noticeable that Ralegh spoke less and less of El Dorado and the fugitive "Inga," and concentrated instead on the alleged gold mines which he and Keymis believed to exist near the Orinoco.

The persistence of Ralegh's self-delusion about the wealth of Guiana was one of the most remarkable traits of a very remarkable man. His Orinoco trip had already shown quite clearly that he lacked the stamina to see such an exhausting and long-drawn-out project through to its grinding conclusion. Yet this frailty was compensated by an intellectual stubbornness of surprising strength. Once Ralegh had seized hold of an idea, he refused to let it rest. His implacable hatred of the Spanish was one example of this tenacity, and his unquenchable vision of Guiana was another. Thus, while incarcerated in the Tower, he gnawed away ceaselessly at the problem: In 1607 he volunteered to fit a ship with "six paires of great bellowes" in her hold, and send her to the Caroní as a floating smelter to bring back a shipload of refined ore; but his offer was declined by the English government. Two years later he invested in Roe's venture, and lost his money. In 1611 he was again petitioning, this time in a letter to James's wife, Anne, that he be allowed to return to Guiana in search of gold. Once more he was refused. Finally in 1616, when most of his enemies were dead and he had outlived his original opposition, he was still asking the same permission of the Crown. At last his pleas were answered. On March 19 the Lieutenant of the Tower received an official warrant instructing him to allow Ralegh to come and go as he wished, escorted only by a single keeper, in order that the celebrated prisoner might prepare for a second voyage to Guiana. On this condition Ralegh had regained his freedom.

Ralegh emerged from the Tower into a political landscape which would have daunted a lesser man. The King, presiding uneasily over every detail of his country's policy, was apparently incapable of making up his mind whether to be friend or foe of Spain; two powerful cliques at court were engaged in bitter rivalry to decide the issue for him. To confuse the situation still further, the Madrid government had sent to England a brilliant new emissary, the future Count Gondomar, who had begun to wield considerable personal influence over King James. Ralegh, the aging adventurer now released from captivity, was the newest pawn to be introduced into the internecine struggle. To the anti-Spanish group he was a weapon to be used against Spain; while in the opinion of the shrewder members of the pro-Spanish party, he was a sacrificial lamb whose carefully engineered ruin could be made to humor the councillors in Madrid.

Ralegh of course knew his danger, just as he knew that while he had been in the Tower, every English expedition to South America had ended in utter failure. There had been several attempts to plant a colony on the coastal bulge of Brazil, but no venture had lasted more than four years before disease, crop failure, and accidents had killed or discouraged the settlers. The few survivors usually packed up their belongings and sailed away, only too thankful to be going back to the mother country and to be rid of their tropical fields where the weeds and the encroaching jungle quickly swallowed up any traces of their sad little efforts to found a new colony for England's greater prosperity. But the real threat to Ralegh's long-delayed ambitions for the Antilles was not the inhospitality of his beloved Guiana, nor the small band of Spanish men-at-arms sweating out their monotonous vigil on the banks of the Orinoco. The real menace lay at home, where his king was desperately short of money, frustrated by a contentious parliament, and outmaneuvered by Ambassador Gondomar. Within his devious mind King James twisted and havered between greed and caution. At first he had been tempted to release Ralegh from the Tower and send him off to Guiana because the man might find gold enough to solve the problems of the exchequer. But at the same time James was nervous that this course of action would exacerbate Anglo-Spanish relations. Certainly the Spaniards would be outraged at the idea that Ralegh, a known Hispanophobe who was considered little better than a pirate, was being sent by his monarch to the Caribbean where on the previous occasion he had sacked St. Joseph and seized hold of one of his Imperial Majesty's governors.

The Spanish ambassador played on these fears with considerable cunning. When his informers told him that a new Guiana scheme was under serious consideration by the King and his ministers, Gondomar called on James and staged a blazing scene. Pointing out that Ralegh had an appalling record as a troublemaker, he demanded guarantees that his new expedition would neither molest Spanish citizens in the Antilles nor harm Spanish property there. Without such guarantees Madrid would regard any second Guiana trip as an act of hostility toward Spain. As usual James reacted with an ill-managed blend of caution and foolhardiness. He refused to call off the proposed expedition, but at the same time he promised that if Ralegh damaged the Spaniards in any way, he would be condemned to death on his return. Furthermore, the King undertook to keep the Spanish government fully informed of Ralegh's preparations and movements, so that they could assure themselves of his intentions. As a gruesome earnest of good faith, James even offered to turn a guilty Ralegh over to Spanish authorities so that they could execute him publicly in the main plaza of Madrid.

Gondomar had completely outmaneuvered the English king. The Spaniard knew that when Ralegh arrived on the Orinoco a second time, his advance would be blocked by the garrison commanding the approach to the Caroní. If at that point Ralegh turned back, he would be discredited as a coward and a fool, and Spain would win a notable psychological victory. If, on the other hand, Ralegh pressed forward to attack the Orinoco garrison, his own king had already put him under sentence of death. Gondomar's counterploy was, therefore, a trap for Ralegh. To all practical purposes the newly released prisoner was committed on a perilous trip to a land where he and others had already tried and failed. This time, however, the price of failure would be his life.

Ralegh was politician enough to realize these dangers, and his seemingly lunatic decision to accept James's conditions and return to Guiana was heavily influenced by the events leading up to his release. Clearly the most important factor in his decision was the knowledge that the new Guiana expedition gave him an opportunity to regain his freedom. After thirteen years in the Tower, almost any chance to leave the place was worth the gamble. Yet Ralegh's willingness to risk a second Guiana venture needed some additional motive, for his prison years had utterly failed to break his spirit and he was still pleading his innocence of the original charge on which he had been convicted. Indeed, Ralegh had continued to make his life in the Tower more comfortable than might be expected. Visitors could, and did, frequently come to see him in his suite of rooms, and he kept himself busy on a multitude of projects. A team of writers, including Ben Jonson, was helping him to compile his ambitious *History of the World*, and he had set up his own laboratory where he tinkered endlessly with alchemy, metallurgy, and his favorite pharmaceutical concoction, that renowned "elixir" which the Queen herself used as a cure-all. Most unlikely of all, this convicted traitor, a person "civilly dead" according to his monarch, had been acting as personal tutor to Prince Henry, heir apparent to the throne of England.

In fact it may have been Prince Henry's sudden death—he caught typhoid from swimming in the polluted Thames—that thrust Ralegh back to Guiana. The prince's death was a staggering blow, for Ralegh had lavished affection and education on the youth, hoping that he would prove to be the ideal prince and, of course, that through the prince he himself would regain his freedom. But with Henry's death, such hopes were brutally snuffed out. Years of effort were wasted, and Ralegh seemed further away from release than he had ever been. To make the blow harder to bear, he knew that he would not have a second chance, for there was the insidious knowledge that he himself was weakening. He was an old man by the standards of his day, and he must have felt acutely that he was hardening into an anachronism. He was almost the last famous Elizabethan still alive who had fought against the Armada, and he was that strange and lonely figure—the gallant courtier accidentally preserved in captivity like a sugared plum while everything around him had withered away. Under such circumstances, Ralegh must have known that the second Guiana trip was his last chance to use those talents and few years remaining to him. Pride, too, must have played its part, for he despised James's less illustrious cronies, and his own arrogance led him to believe that he could succeed where all others had failed. Ralegh possessed in excess that quirk of flamboyance which dared a man to snatch at the prize denied to all others; and that same confidence, which had already allowed him to challenge the conquistadors in their search for El Dorado, now encouraged him to risk both James's strictures and Gondomar's overt hostility in a last attempt to seize victory where it was least expected.

But to Ralegh, victory had to be nothing less than a shipload of bullion brought back to fill James's coffers, and such a climactic achievement depended upon the discovery and exploitation of rich gold deposits near the Orinoco. So, to have agreed to James's conditions for the trip, Ralegh must also have believed that he could find gold mines in Guiana. The myth of the Golden Antilles must have found favor a second time with one of the very few men who knew the uncomfortable realities of the Orinoco. Keymis's tale of the "golden mountaine" and Ralegh's own observations of the geology of the area may have provided a few scraps of hopeful evidence, but in the final analysis Ralegh must have convinced himself. Locked up in the Tower, he must have brooded on the attractions of that land he had described so glowingly in *The Discovery*, until finally the glistening lure paraded so convincingly in his book dazzled even its creator. The disappointments of Sir Thomas Roe's trip and the collapse of the abortive English plantations in the Antilles may have damaged the myth, but Keymis's reports and his own memories of the "bewtiful empyre" made good the difference. In its new guise, the mirage of the Golden Antilles was Putijma's mountain and the mines at the Caroní, not El Dorado and his golden city. The myth's enchantment was unimpaired. It held out to Ralegh those same promises of rescue which had previously deluded him in 1595, and by a strange mirror effect of fate, his career was repeating itself. Once before, Guiana had seemed the way to escape from exile and regain royal favor; now, two decades later, the same delusion about the Antilles was his only immediate hope of freedom and the King's pardon. Therefore Ralegh, for the second time, threw himself wholeheartedly into the task of preparing an expedition to the Orinoco.

On this occasion, however, he made up his mind that his expedition would be a full-scale affair. Larger and better equipped than his previous venture, it was to be strong enough to push ahead where the last expedition had been forced to turn back. Although such a massive venture was an extremely expensive proposition, Ralegh did not flinch. Right from the beginning he staked his entire resources to the project, knowing that if he failed on this occasion, there would be little point in clinging to the last shreds of his personal fortune. It cost the enormous sum of thirty thousand pounds to assemble, equip, and supply his expedition, and Ralegh had no hope of providing all the money himself. So he organized the new venture as a joint-stock project, and many of the gentlemen-volunteers who elected to try their luck with him invested fifty pounds apiece on the understanding that they would receive a proportionate share of the profits. Larger sums were put up by Ralegh's wealthier friends, and several of his wife's distant relatives contributed money. Typically, King James offered very little, although he stood to gain one fifth of all "Golde and Silver Bullion or Oare of Gold or Silver and Pearl or Precious Stone" brought back. The most the Crown could manage was the paltry sum of 170 pounds, paid out as an incentive toward building new ships for the voyage. Inevitably, the real burden fell on Ralegh himself. He could not expect others to invest heavily unless he himself was fully committed and, besides, every penny was desperately needed. To this end Ralegh cast his entire financial position into the balance, until eventually he managed to raise about half the capital from his own private resources. He sold virtually everything that he or his wife possessed, even including her private estate in Surrey, which brought in some 2,500 pounds; he wrote to his debtors, calling in his outstanding loans; and in the final pinch, he even disposed of his family plate for ready cash.

For his money Ralegh put together such an impressive-looking fleet that there were worried inquiries from one or two European countries who wanted assurance that Ralegh was really on his way to South America and did not plan to go adventuring in European waters. The French envoy in London was sufficiently concerned to make a trip to Deptford in order to inspect Ralegh's flagship and interview the commander himself. This flagship was, in fact, the pride of the fleet and her armament of thirty-six cannon made her its most formidable component. Aptly named *Destiny*, she had been built by Phineas Pett, the royal shipbuilder, and she was such a splendid vessel that it became quite the fashion for courtiers to make an excursion downriver to see the *Destiny* during fitting-out. With her in the Thames lay five smaller vessels: *Star*, 25 guns; *Encounter*, 17 guns; *Thunder*, 20 guns; *Flying Joane*, 14 guns; and *Husband*, 6 guns. An additional three or four ships were expected to join from the Channel ports where they were being prepared for the transatlantic passage. Even the runt of the fleet, the little three-gun *Page*, was a workmanlike boat. She carried three robinets—small brass cannon weighing about two hundred pounds—and was fully capable of doing considerable damage to any piraguas and other light craft which she might be expected to encounter in the shallow waters of the Orinoco delta. But James's officers were also keeping an eye on Ralegh's growing fleet, and their lists of his ships, the strength of their crews, and their armament were being passed on to the king's advisers. They, in turn, added a map of Ralegh's intended Guiana destination and, acting on James's instruction, forwarded the information to Gondomar. As a result, the Spanish authorities were forewarned of every detail of Ralegh's dispositions.

On paper Ralegh's heavily gunned ships were probably more than a match for any Caribbean fleet which the Spaniards might be able to put together at short notice. Yet the English ships were of little use without well-trained sailors and gunners to man them, and in this department Ralegh's expedition was desperately poorly served. Ultimately, the success of his scheme depended upon the quality of the adventurers who enrolled under his command, and by all accounts the thousand and more men who sailed to Guiana were unfit material. A few, noticeably some of the officers (among whom was Ralegh's own son, Wat), were steadfast and reliable men, but the majority of the troops were dross. They were an undisciplined, shiftless rabble—wastrels and incompetents who had stumbled into the Guiana venture because they believed that it would provide them with a quick and easy fortune. Ralegh quite rightly despised them; yet he had no choice but to take them with him, hoping that by the time the fleet reached the Antilles some sort of discipline would have been drilled into them. They were, he wrote, "the very skume of the world, Drunkards, blasphemers, and such like, as their fathers, brothers, and frends thought it an exceeding [good] gaine to be discharged of, with the hazard of some thirtie, fortie, or fiftie pounds, knoweing they could not live one whole year soe good cheape at home." Many of these lackluster rowdies had picked up their fighting experience in no sterner battlefields than tavern brawls, and the worst elements were soon making such a nuisance of themselves—there were scuffles between expedition men and townsfolk at both Gravesend and Plymouth—that Ralegh thankfully turned a number of them loose and left for the Orinoco without them.

In truth, everything about the expedition went wrong from the start. The original plan had been to leave in February, but poor coordination between the ships' captains meant that their vessels loaded with widely differing degrees of speed and success. Thus by the spring of 1617 one half of the fleet was manned, victualed, and ready to sail; while the remainder were still only partly loaded, and a number of their captains had not even managed to recruit their full complement of men. One vessel, the *Star* under Captain Pennington, was so poorly victualed that she went no farther than the Isle of Wight before her food supplies ran out. Pennington had to scuttle back to London and borrow money from Bess Ralegh to buy additional stocks of bread for the trip. Unavoidably, these delays made havoc of the expedition's timetable, and although Ralegh moved his fleet round to

Plymouth to try to instill a sense of urgency, the same problems continued.

Ralegh would have been blind not to have seen that his expedition was disintegrating before it had even set out on its mission. And so, in a futile attempt to impose some sort of discipline on the chaos, he issued his "Orders for the Fleet." Delivered in Ralegh's usual sparkling prose, these "orders" were in fact much too priggish to have any hope of success among the riff-raff they were meant to control. The men of the expedition, Ralegh directed, were not to employ foul language at any time, nor to smoke below decks but only "aloft the upper Decke." All crewmen were to sing a psalm twice a day for the good of their souls and the success of the expedition. Some idea of the poor quality of the ships' crews can be gained from the fact that Ralegh felt he needed to warn them that he would make a deckswabber of anyone who gambled away his weapons or his clothes. There were also instructions on the operation of the cannon; the best method of dousing shipboard fires; the correct stowage of personal belongings; and even a self-evident caveat against carrying loose gunpowder while also holding lighted linstock. Significantly, too, the Orders made it clear that the fleet was already short of essential material. Gunpowder, for example, was in such short supply that the gunners were ordered to hold their fire until they were at point-blank range and were certain to hit their marks. Food was to be kept under lock and key, and any man caught stealing it would "receive the punishment of a thiefe and the murtherer of his fellowes." Owing to a shortage of trained sailors with the fleet, it was decreed that the landsmen would have to learn the various parts of the ships so that they could help the sailors. Conversely, the sailors were to train as landsmen for the time they reached the Orinoco.

Ralegh's Orders also laid down the rules which would govern his men when they reached Guiana. Once again he gave strict instructions that nothing was to be taken by force from the natives, and he warned that anyone who raped an Indian woman would be executed. Cowardice, by contrast, met a less drastic punishment: the craven would be stripped of his weapons, made

to forfeit his share in the expedition's profits, and would spend
the rest of the trip as a "Labourer and carrier of victuals for the
rest." In its other clauses, the Orders relating to Guiana were
remarkably sensible. The Englishmen were forbidden to eat any
unidentified fruit unless they had first observed that the same
fruit was food for the birds and animals of the area; they were
not to sleep on the ground; and they were not to eat any freshly
killed meat without first steeping it in salt for at least two hours.
If they failed to take this precaution, Ralegh warned, acute
diarrhea would be the result. Finally, echoing an earlier tragedy,
he notified his men that no one was to go swimming in the rivers
of Guiana "except where you see Indians swim, because most of
the rivers are full of Allegators."*

Although the Orders were issued to the fleet on the third day
of May 1617, another five weeks dragged by before the expedition actually put to sea. Even then it set sail only because Ralegh
could wait no longer. His last desperately mortgaged trickle of
money had finally dried up, and his men were consuming their
provisions at such an alarming pace that he feared that his ships
would be eaten bare of supplies while still in sight of the English
coast. So, on June 12, half set for the venture, the Guiana fleet
weighed anchor and left Plymouth Sound, only to sail straight
into the teeth of a storm which drove them back to Plymouth. A
second departure was attempted, and this time the fleet had
worked round to Falmouth before heavy weather once again
forced it into shelter. Some good came of the delay, for Ralegh
cut down the number of hungry mouths by the simple expedient
of announcing to his men that the expedition would be away
from home for a minimum of twelve months. This was longer
than the faint-hearts had bargained for, and many of them discreetly jumped ship. The fleet then made a third attempt to clear
the Channel, and had even less luck than before. A gale hit the
undermanned vessels off the Scilly Isles, one pinnace capsized and
went to the bottom with all hands, and the other vessels ran

---

* More probably Orinoco crocodiles, which commonly exceed ten feet in
length. Ralegh was referring to the local Spanish name el lagarto (a
"lizard") from which the English "alligator" is derived. To this day crocodiles in the Antilles are popularly known as "alligators."

helter-skelter for refuge at Cork. There the fleet stayed for almost a month, bottled up in the Irish harbor by unseasonable gales and rough seas, and draining the supply of foodstuffs even more.

In this lame fashion the better part of the summer sailing season glided away, and every lost week gave the Spaniards added opportunity to strengthen their defenses on the Orinoco. But Ralegh could not put back to England. If he returned home, even temporarily, he knew his expedition would never sail again. His men would desert, and his creditors would demand their payments. And so, when the weather finally improved in mid-August, his fleet bravely left Cork and pressed on full sail in a belated attempt to win the golden prize of Guiana before their supplies were exhausted or the Spaniards closed the Orinoco to them.

This unbroken succession of early misfortunes had already sapped the expedition's morale. Below decks there was an unpleasant rash of fights between the sailors and the landsmen. The officers of Ralegh's loosely knit command also began to complain about their conditions of service, the chief malcontents being a small group of the shipmasters who were scarcely better than off-duty pirates. They had grown frustrated during the months of delay in harbor and now hankered after their former trade. Ralegh's Guiana scheme seemed to them to be a poor waste of such a powerful English fleet, and they advocated taking the easy pickings which could be found in the waters off the European coast.

Their insubordination suppurated beneath the surface until the fleet overtook four small French vessels near Cape St. Vincent. Ranging in advance of the *Destiny* with Ralegh on board, several of her consorts hungrily snapped up these pathetic little prizes. When Ralegh came up to investigate, there was a bitter argument between the English commander and his rebellious captains. The latter claimed that the French ships were corsairs and therefore legitimate prey; but Ralegh, finding insufficient evidence of French piracy and rather too much proof of English rapacity, brushed aside all protests and insisted that the captured vessels be released. His decision infuriated those captains who had secretly anticipated a comfortable profit from the Guiana venture by indulging in a little piracy on the side. One of them, Captain Bailey, soon afterward took the opportunity to desert the fleet. Sailing back to England (and playing the pirate en route), he had his revenge by reporting to James's council that Ralegh had duped them and had no intention of going to Guiana. He was, said Bailey, planning to seize the Spanish Plate Fleet and start a full-scale war with Spain. Unfortunately for Bailey, his lies came home to roost when contradictory reports began to filter back from the Canary Islands, Ralegh's next port of call, and Bailey's own misdemeanors were discovered. The Privy Council made a formal inquiry into the whole affair, and for once Ralegh was exonerated. Bailey was found guilty of spreading false rumors, and was thrown into prison until he offered a groveling apology.

Ralegh, meanwhile, had far too much at stake to risk a clash with Spain. At Lancerota in the Canary Islands, for example, where belligerent Spanish settlers ambushed and killed two members of his shore party, he restrained his men from retaliation and meekly moved on to the island of Gomera. There he had an easier time because the governor's wife was half-English and acted as a mediator between the two sides. In consequence the English were allowed to take on water peacefully and to buy supplementary stocks of fresh fruit. As a nice touch of appreciation Ralegh gallantly sent the lady a gift of a half-dozen pairs of gloves. Not to be outdone, she promptly responded with baskets of oranges, lemons, figs, and pomegranates. Whereupon the urbane English commander countered with a present of rose water, ambergris, and a picture of Mary Magdalene. This was repaid with a consignment of chickens, fruit, and bread from the shore, and even a letter from the governor himself, testifying to the probity of Ralegh's behavior and the good conduct of his men while the fleet was in harbor. Only the fleet's belated departure finally put an end to this surfeit of gallantry and mutual applause.

It was now late September, and thus far the fleet had been moving at a snail's pace toward its destination. But the worst was yet to come. Soon after their departure from England several of the sailors had been afflicted with a mysterious illness, probably scurvy, and three days out of Gomera this sickness suddenly flared into a raging epidemic. On a single day, fifty men aboard the *Destiny* went down with the strange disease and were rendered unfit for duty. The surgeons were baffled, and could do nothing to prevent the illness from spreading. Soon the conditions aboard the other ships were equally pitiful. Ralegh, trying desperately to control the epidemic, set course for the Cape Verde Islands where he intended to land the very sick and take on fresh meat and vegetables. But the English fleet had scarcely anchored in the poorly protected roadstead at Brava Island, when a hurricane roared down on the ships. Another pinnace went to the bottom; anchor cables snapped; and the leaky, pestilence-ridden vessels were driven helplessly out to sea. Eight days later, when the fleet had collected itself together again, the weather switched to the other extreme. The wind dropped away, a dreary stillness descended, and Ralegh's fleet with its sick and dying men lay sweltering and becalmed.

Again Ralegh's luck had been atrocious. In latitudes where normally the trade winds would have wafted his fleet across to the New World in a matter of days, his hapless vessels rocked quietly under a fierce tropical sun. Below deck the makeshift sickbays were like ovens, and the invalids never had a chance. Day after day the stretcher bearers dumped corpses over the rail. On the flagship forty-two men, more than a quarter of the *Destiny*'s crew, died before the fleet reached South America. Among the dead were the expedition's chief refiner-metallurgist, who had been brought to assay the supposed Guiana ore; the chief surgeon of the expedition; the senior officer appointed to command the land forces, his second-in-command; and the provost marshal. Also dead, and a very personal loss to Ralegh, was John Talbot, his devoted manservant who had stayed by his master for eleven years in the Tower. "He was," wrote Ralegh sadly, "my honest friend, an excellent general scholar, and as faithfull and true a man as lived. I lost him to my inestimable grief." Ralegh himself was in no condition to alleviate the general distress. He had tripped and taken a heavy fall. Carried down to his cabin, he was soon showing symptoms of malaria, and for twenty-eight days lay shivering in bed, semidelirious and unable to take solid food. He survived, he later said, only by sucking the juice from the fruit which he had been given at Gomera and which he had fortuitously preserved in a box of sand.

Only in mid-November did the long-drawn-out agony finally come to an end. On the fourteenth day of the month, the sickly fleet limped into the protected estuary of the Cayenne River, still several days' sail from the Orinoco delta. Too weak and too dispirited to face the Spaniards on Trinidad, Ralegh's men crept quietly ashore on this out-of-the-way corner of South America in order to gather edible wild plants and beg food from the natives. For three weeks they stayed there, slowly shaking off the effects of their ill-fated Atlantic crossing. As Captain Keymis bitterly noted in his log, the voyage from the Cape Verde Islands to South America, which he had previously accomplished in twelve days, had taken the second Guiana fleet forty days.

6-

Apology for the Impossible

STILL UNABLE TO WALK, RALEGH WAS CARRIED ASHORE in a chair
at Cayenne, so that he could supervise the convalescence of
his men and the cleansing of the ships. The comparative relaxa-
tion of life on the beach and an exotic diet of pineapple and armadillo (apparently he had acquired a taste for both on his previous
trip) gradually restored him to health. But many of the other invalids were so chronically sick that a ship had to be detached from
the fleet to take them home to England. With this vessel Ralegh
sent a letter to his wife, telling her of his difficulties. "Dear Heart,"
he began, "I can write to you but with a weak hand, for I have
suffered the most violent calenture for fifteen days, that ever man
did, and lived: but God that gave me a strong heart in all my
activities, hath also now strengthened it in the hellfire of heat."
He then went on to describe the ravages of the epidemic and to
give her the names of the more important officers who had died,
so that their relatives might be informed. Almost the only cheerful news he could provide was that his son, also named Walter
but more usually referred to as Wat, was alive and well.

The loss or incapacity of so many high-ranking officers meant
that Ralegh now had to find men to fill their places. Undoubtedly
the most important post was the command of the river force

which Ralegh proposed to send up the Orinoco and which he could not lead himself as he was still too weak. The task called for the greatest skill and tact, because the river force would have to locate the gold-producing area, keep on good terms with the Indians, and avoid a brush with any hostile Spaniards. A leader was needed who knew the country and was able to keep his men under tight control, and yet could also evaluate the tactical situation clearly and sensibly. Only one man, besides Ralegh himself, seemed to fulfill all these requirements, and that was Captain Keymis. Keymis had been up the Orinoco twice already; he knew where Putijma's alleged golden mountain was to be found; and he was a familiar figure with the Indian *caciques*. Keymis was so obviously the person to lead the river force that Ralegh appointed him without hesitation. Apparently he had no thought that Keymis might let him down.

It is difficult to know what to make of Captain Laurence Keymis. He was a man who should have stood head and shoulders above his contemporaries, and yet he remains something of a mystery, a self-effacing figure who never completely emerged from the shadows. According to contemporary Spanish accounts he was tall and slim, and had a cast in one eye. By education and appointment he was not a seafaring adventurer at all, but a university man (from Oxford) whose Latin verse and well-couched letters showed a cultivated turn of mind. Apparently he found the academic life dull, for at an early stage he had thrown in his lot with Ralegh and served him faithfully for many years on various errands. In 1595 he had captained the decrepit galleass which reached Trinidad in such a shoddy condition that it was converted for the river trip; and in the following year he had commanded the reconnaissance vessel that Ralegh sent to look for an approach to Guiana from the south. In 1603 he had been imprisoned briefly alongside Ralegh in the Tower on the same charge as his captain, and after his release he had steadfastly continued to work and lobby on Ralegh's behalf. To all appearances, therefore, Keymis was the ideal second-in-command, intelligent, loyal, and capable of carrying out the responsibilities delegated to him. But he had one dangerous weakness: he was as much a dreamer as Ralegh himself, and he too had been mesmerized by the myth of the Golden Antilles. This was disaster, and Ralegh could not know that his optimistic lieutenant had already misled him twice: once over Putijma's golden mountain, and once with his report from the 1596 trip that the Spaniards were guarding fabulous wealth on the Caroní. In short, Keymis's castle-building had only served to accentuate his captain's weakness. And though Keymis himself had never shown the slightest intention of deceiving Ralegh, he would soon learn the extent of his earlier mistakes and realize that he had betrayed the man he most admired.

Sadly, this tragic denouement might never have happened but for Wat Ralegh, the youth who pricked the bubble of Keymis's dreams. Wat Ralegh was the apple of his father's eye. The parent had spared no pains to make his son the epitome of Elizabethan gentility—fencing lessons, an Oxford education, moral instruction, and a stay in Paris had all been lavished on the boy. And, as so often happens, the product of this parental zeal, now in his early twenties, was a spoiled, impudent, and reckless young man, whose palpable faults were lightly camouflaged beneath their customary accompaniment—a certain rather attractive quickness of mind and a facile wit. This latter trait was well illustrated by the tale that as a student in Paris Wat Ralegh had tempted his tutor and guardian, Ben Jonson, into taking too much wine one evening. When Jonson duly slid into an alcohol-sodden stupor, Wat had hired a gang of men to wheel the playwright in a cart through the streets of Paris so that the citizens could mock the negligent tutor. Pranks of this stripe were harmless enough in undergraduate days, but the willful and precocious young man was a volatile companion on an expedition which was about to enter hostile territory, especially when the same young man was the son of the overall commander. Wat Ralegh, who had already been promoted to captain of the *Destiny,* was now appointed to command a company of pikemen in Keymis's river force. His recklessness was to bring calamity.

On December 4 the English fleet left the Cayenne River and limped round to the Triangle Islands near the Orinoco delta. There Ralegh divided his force. Keymis with 250 soldiers and 150 sailors embarked on the five ships which drew the least water. He also took with him a number of special launches that had been brought out to Guiana in pieces and were now assembled for the river journey. With this flotilla he was ordered to proceed as fast as possible up the Orinoco, taking care to avoid the Spaniards, until he reached the gold-bearing area and opened a gold mine. Meanwhile Ralegh would take the rest of the fleet and cruise off the southern tip of Trinidad where he would cover Keymis's rear. It was no secret that Gondomar had alerted the Spanish authorities, and the Englishmen expected a punitive Spanish fleet to show up at any moment. With his earlier experience of the insubordination of his sea captains, Ralegh felt that only his personal supervision would stop them from deserting as soon as the river flotilla had started out along the Orinoco. "You shall find me at Puncto Gallo [Point Icacos on the southern tip of Trinidad] dead or alive," he assured Keymis, "and if you find not my ships there, yet you shall find their ashes for I will fire with the galleons if it come to extremity, but run away I will never."

In complete contrast to these fighting words, he cautiously ordered Keymis to be very circumspect in his dealings with the Spanish garrison near the Caroní cataracts. If possible, he was not to make contact with them at all, and was to take the river force upstream only as far as Putijma's golden mountain, several miles short of the estimated position of the Spanish garrison. At that point, Keymis was to land his men, throw out a covering wing of skirmishers between his main force and the Spaniards, and open up the golden mountain at leisure. Only if the Spanish launched an attack on the English was there to be an open clash, for the English would then be obliged to defend themselves. Under these circumstances King James's strictures about not harming the Spanish colonists were scarcely applicable. If Keymis was unable to find enough gold to warrant opening a mine, he was to retreat quietly, bringing with him a basket or two of any likely looking ore as proof of Ralegh's early contention that gold did exist in Guiana.

Superficially, Ralegh's plan of campaign avoided any risk of violating the conditions laid down for him by his king. Unfortunately, however, the success of the entire operation hinged upon Keymis's bold report of Putijma's golden mountain on the first expedition; and Keymis himself, who had never actually visited the supposed mine, was a good deal less optimistic about its existence than Ralegh. Twenty years earlier Keymis had allowed his enthusiasm to run away with him and he had never had the courage to alter his story. Now that it was time for him to make good his recommendations and bring back the ore from Putijma's golden mountain, it was only natural that he should privately revert to the original idea of the gold deposits near the falls of the Caroní. This second mine was alleged to be only a few miles farther upstream than the golden mountain, and for Keymis, seeking to please his commander, the Caroní mine offered much the better hope of success. But it lay on the other side of the Spanish garrison, and although there was the chance that the English flotilla could slip past the Spaniards unobserved, or might even overawe the Spanish into allowing them to go through unmolested, Keymis was running a considerable risk if he decided to go for the Caroní mine. And this was precisely what he chose to do, without telling Ralegh.

Keymis's force took three weeks to reach the spot where the Spaniards had established their Orinoco garrison at the village of St. Thomé. It was a miserable place, scarcely more than a cluster of shabby houses behind a palisade on the left bank of the Orinoco about three miles downstream from the mouth of the Caroní. The village—it was really only a plaza surrounded by scrawny buildings—boasted a tiny church, a government storehouse, a water cistern, several poorly constructed houses, and a slightly more impressive residence for the newly arrived royal administrator, Diego Palomeque de Acuna.

Palomeque was intensely unpopular. A recent appointment, he had been sent to St. Thomé with specific orders to suppress the illicit trade in tobacco that was being carried on with considerable profit between the citizens of St. Thomé and the captains of small Dutch and English smuggling vessels that occasionally ventured up the Orinoco. Unfortunately, Palomeque had obeyed his instructions to the letter, and the colonists at St. Thomé, who had taken up this illegal sideline in the days of his predecessor, Don Fernando de Berrio, were outraged. Don Fernando, son of Ralegh's old antagonist Antonio de Berrio, had inherited his father's estates and offices, and his lax and light-handed administration had eventually led to his being recalled to stand trial for deliberate evasion of the King's revenue. Under the stricter rule of the man who replaced him, St. Thomé's fortunes had slumped. When Keymis arrived, the settlement was poverty-stricken and neglected.

For eight months, too, the inhabitants of St. Thomé had known that an English fleet under Sir Walter Ralegh was once again preparing to sail for the Orinoco. Ambassador Gondomar's intelligence reports had given them advance notice of the size and strength of the intended expedition, but because the machinery of Spain's colonial government creaked into action with so many delays, frustrations, and deliberate procrastinations, the smallest decision took months to put into effect between the huge triangle of London, Spain, and the Orinoco. In the mother country the Council of the Indies had gravely considered Gondomar's warnings, had written back to London asking for more information and an assurance that Ralegh was not headed for Virginia, had mulled over the ambassador's reply, had forwarded their recommendations to the King for his signature, had interviewed other informants who claimed to know about "Guatteral" and his plans, and had asked the military authorities to provide ships and men to defend Guiana. The council was advised in no uncertain terms that the Spanish navy was heavily committed elsewhere, and feebly ended up by telling the colonial governors what they knew already: namely, to beware of Ralegh and to help one another if the English attacked. Thus, while the dossier on Ralegh's Guiana trip grew thicker, the inhabitants of St. Thomé had not yet received one ounce of practical help when on January 1, 1618, an Indian canoe came frantically paddling upriver to tell them that an English flotilla was a day's journey from the settlement. At that moment Palomeque had thirty-six effective soldiers, plus an unknown number of surly civilian noncombatants, with which to face Keymis's four hundred.

Keymis was also having his difficulties. Two of his five ships had been hung up on sandbars and were lagging behind the main body of the river force, and his men were dispirited and tired. Nevertheless, the English commander had more than enough men to crush St. Thomé. Significantly, he made no attempt to look for Putijma's golden mountain but moved directly to a landing place some three miles downstream from St. Thomé. There, at about four o'clock on the afternoon of January 2 he began to land his men. As soon as the disembarkation was complete, the three English ships continued upriver and took their stations in midstream opposite the palisades of St. Thomé. In that anchorage they came under fire from a Spanish mortar at about nine o'clock in the evening, but no damage was done and the English ships did not deign to reply.

At this stage Keymis's plan seemed to be straightforward. He had chosen to disregard Ralegh's instructions, and rather than avoiding all contact with the Spaniards he had deliberately moved up against them so that his vastly superior force could hold their garrison at its mercy. His three ships brazenly anchored in mid-channel commanded St. Thomé with their guns and could batter the town to pieces within a few hours. From this overwhelmingly strong position, Keymis should have been able to keep the Spaniards at bay while his miners either opened up the golden mountain or an advance party visited the Caroní falls to investigate the rumors of a Spanish gold mine there. Logically, Palomeque and his thirty-six soldiers were helpless and would not dare to attack.

But Palomeque refused to be cowed. Although he was poorly supported by the townsfolk, he bravely determined not to give up St. Thomé without a fight, and had evacuated the women and children to the island of Seiba a few miles up the Orinoco. So when the English landed from their ships, he sent forward a handful of men under his second-in-command, Captain Geronimo de Grados, to spy out the enemy positions. The events that followed happened very quickly.

It was almost midnight by the time Grados moved out with ten musketeers, and in the darkness the Spanish scouts blundered into the English pickets. There were some scattered shots, a few brave yells of "Perros ingleses" ("English dogs"), and a momentary panic among the English soldiers, who thought that they had been surrounded by a much larger enemy force. Losing their few shreds of discipline, the English huddled together in fright, facing every direction and not knowing what to do. At this crucial juncture Wat Ralegh seized what he thought was his moment for glory. Pounding up at the head of his pike company, he rushed past the English sentries and charged off in pursuit of Grados and his men. The English rank and file were caught up in the excitement of the rush and streamed after him right to the gates of St. Thomé, which stood open to receive Grados. The whooping, out-of-breath straggle of undisciplined Englishmen poured through the gate and into the plaza. There they ran head-on into a desperate defensive stand by Palomeque and his officers. There was a brisk hand-to-hand struggle as the Spaniards put up futile resistance, but they were soon overwhelmed as more and more of the English arrived. Palomeque was killed when his head was almost split in half by a blow from an English halberd, and the rest of the Spaniards very sensibly retreated into the safety of that night. But Wat Ralegh, who had been the direct cause of this unlooked-for fight, lay dead. Running recklessly into the town at the head of his men, he had been shot down and his skull smashed by the butt of a Spanish musket.

Keymis had won a calamitous victory. For the loss of five officers (the Spaniards had suffered the same number of casualties) the Englishmen had seized a settlement for which they had slight use. Their only loot was a little tobacco, the abandoned Spanish weapons, the church's sorry collection of plate, two small gold ingots worth about 2,600 reales, and Palomeque's municipal treasure chest filled with the records of town council meetings, copies of official correspondence, and notices of uncollected debts. Worst of all, every condition laid down by King James for the conduct of Ralegh's expedition had been flouted. Keymis's disobedience and Wat Ralegh's impetuosity had cost Spanish lives and wantonly destroyed Spanish property. It was said that in London when Gondomar heard about the storming of St. Thomé he hurried off to see King James and burst into the royal audience chamber, shouting, "Pirates! Pirates! Pirates!"

Faced by this unforeseen and disastrous turn of events, Keymis went to pieces. Wat Ralegh and the other English dead were buried in the church at St. Thomé after a funeral parade in which the five shrouded palls were solemnly carried around the plaza behind trailed banners, but it was not until January 7, five days after the fatal battle of St. Thomé, that he could bring himself to write to Ralegh, telling him the gloomy news.

If, at this stage, Keymis had gone ahead with his search for a gold mine and had returned downstream with a cargo of bullion, Ralegh might possibly have forgiven him the attack on St. Thomé, though not the death of his son. Certainly King James would have hesitated to punish the leader of an expedition which brought back sufficient riches to discharge the royal debt. But as it was, Keymis now behaved like a man in shock. The appalling blunder at St. Thomé had jolted him into facing the truth that neither the Caroní mines nor Putijma's golden mountain really existed. He did take a small group of his most loyal men to check on Putijma's mine, but it was a surreptitious, doubting gesture. The party left and returned under cover of darkness, and when the assayer found that the rock samples they brought back contained no gold, Keymis hushed up the whole affair.

Unwilling to face Ralegh and too confused to give his men a firm lead, Keymis took the easy way out. Shirking the responsibility of his command, he abandoned his men at St. Thomé, and led three boatloads of soldiers on a wild goose chase up the Orinoco. In his torment he may have been looking for the promised gold deposits of the Caroní, but it is more likely that he simply could not control his junior officers any longer. Certainly he did not pursue his quest with any great determination. Opposite Seiba Island his party was fired on by Grados and his refugees, who succeeded in killing two and wounding six of the English. The attack was enough to dissuade Keymis from continuing. Later he was to plead that the Spaniards were so firmly entrenched around their Caroní mine that his men would have been cut to pieces.

Keymis's pointless and time-wasting trip lasted just under three weeks, and in this time the English troops left behind at St. Thomé disintegrated into an unmanageable rabble. For the first few days they made some attempt to find out where the citizens of St. Thomé had obtained the two gold ingots which they discovered in the town, and the Spaniards' Indian servants were picked up and questioned, but they knew nothing. Probably the ingots had been made from metal washed out in small streams locally. Some of the English rank and file, however, still clung to their visions of fabulous underground mines, and small squads went out into the countryside, hoping to stumble across exposed seams of auriferous rock. But they were searching at random, without direction or system; and often they did not even bother to take with them the crowbars, blasting powder, and other mining equipment they would need. Grados's Spaniards of course took advantage of their ignorance and harassed the disorganized Englishmen mercilessly. There were night attacks; exploring parties were ambushed; wood-cutting gangs were shot at by hidden snipers; and stragglers were picked off by the Spaniards, who knew the terrain far better than the newcomers. Before long the victors of St. Thomé gave up. They stayed behind their palisade, cowed and hungry, while their officers bickered among themselves and the food shortage became worse. Several groups of men mutinied. They stole the light boats and set out for the delta, though few of them ever reached the fleet; they were either drowned or killed by the Indians. By the time Keymis arrived back in St. Thomé, he found that in a last act of wanton stupidity the troops had set fire to the town. Hungry and without shelter, the English began their retreat, and it was a measure of their disgust that when Keymis offered to make another attempt at finding Putijma's mine, his own officers refused point blank to tramp off in search of this last mirage.

Meanwhile Ralegh, deeply hurt and furious after reading the report that Keymis had sent him, was waiting for his lieutenant. No Spanish fleet had been seen near the delta, and the English ships had spent two fruitless months tacking idly back and forth with an occasional detour to Trinidad so that Ralegh could add to his collection of "curiosities." Keymis's letter describing the capture of St. Thomé and the death of Wat Ralegh had been a cruel betrayal, and when Keymis finally put in an appearance with his shamefaced followers, Ralegh poured out his pent-up anger and bitterness. Aboard the *Destiny* he upbraided Keymis for negligence and cowardice, and scathingly demolished his lieutenant's excuses. Keymis was contrite, pleading that he had not expected to come upon St. Thomé so soon and that the Spaniards must have moved their garrison post at least twenty miles down-stream since he last visited the river. But he was only trying to cover up the fact that he had disobeyed his orders, and his excuses did not stop Ralegh from acidly pointing out to him that a greatly superior English force had failed to dislodge a small, unsupported Spanish garrison. The river expedition, he said, was a disgrace to England and a dishonor to Keymis.

Ralegh was a master of sarcastic invective, and he quickly reduced Keymis to the depths of despondency. The faithful lieutenant had acted in what he had believed were Ralegh's best interests, and so the virulence of Ralegh's wrath only increased his gloom over the entire St. Thomé debacle. Unable to withstand the odium, Keymis reached his breaking point when Ralegh refused to support a letter of apology which Keymis had drafted to one of the expedition's supporters in England. It was a churlish rebuff. "You have undone me with your obstinacy," he told Keymis, "and I will not favour or colour in any sort your former folly." Crestfallen, Keymis asked Ralegh if that was his final word on the subject. When Ralegh told him that it was, he replied, "I know then, Sir, what course to take," and left Ralegh's cabin. A few moments later there was the sound of a shot, and Ralegh sent a messenger to discover what had happened. The messenger found Keymis in his cabin, holding in his hand a small pistol, which, he explained, he had fired because it had been loaded for a long time and needed cleaning. This answer satisfied Ralegh, but about half an hour later a cabin boy entered Keymis's cabin and found Keymis lying dead. The disgraced lieutenant had killed himself by thrusting a dagger into his heart. An examination showed that the earlier gunshot had been a less successful suicide attempt, for the lightweight pistol ball had been deflected after striking and breaking a rib. At the last moment, it seemed, Keymis had found the resolution which he so badly needed at St. Thomé.

Ralegh took Keymis's death calmly, if not callously. Flailing against other troubles, he had little time to brood over the suicide of his most staunch supporter. Wat's death had been a far greater blow, and now his attention was completely taken up with his own future and the problems of the English fleet. His sea captains were openly blaming him for their misfortunes. The men were refusing to obey their officers, and there was a widespread and dangerous undertow of resentment. Ralegh's authority had vanished with the collapse of his high-sounding tales of Guiana gold, and with neither a common cause nor any confidence in their leader, the expedition fell apart like the staves of a barrel whose hoops have burst. When Ralegh suggested that he personally would lead a second river force up the Orinoco to look for gold, his suggestion was rejected out of hand. The officers and shareholders still dreaded the arrival of a Spanish fleet and were eager to leave the exposed delta area as quickly as possible. So, against Ralegh's wishes, the English ships moved north to the anonymous safety of the Leeward Islands, where the quarrels, indecision, and mutual recrimination continued.

Ralegh was too worn out and downhearted to try to cajole his disgruntled captains back into line. "My brains are broken," he wearily confessed in the letter telling his wife of the death of their son, "and 'tis a torment for me to write, and especially of misery." Wat's useless death had sickened him of the whole Guiana venture, and he no longer cared what the other captains decided to do with the ships and crews they had contributed toward the project. One by one his consort vessels abandoned the *Destiny*, either sailing directly for England or turning pirate in order to use their heavy guns against lightly armed merchantmen. By the end of March Ralegh was alone.

Eventually the *Destiny* too went home. Her commander had no choice. If he failed to return to England, his wife and family would be disgraced and his friends persecuted. His second venture to the Golden Antilles had been a greater failure than the first, and he was honor-bound to bear the consequences. On June 21 the *Destiny* dropped anchor in Plymouth, and in a gesture of finality the ship's sails were sent ashore.

Ralegh had come back to a nation whose political realities gave him not the slightest chance of survival. King James was in the middle of very delicate negotiations concerning the marriage of Prince Charles to a Spanish princess, and he did not want Ralegh's continued existence to disrupt the proceedings. A pro-Spanish faction was in power at court; and Ambassador Gondo-

mar was still exercising his customary dexterity. Indeed, Ralegh's
Guiana venture had been prejudged even before its leader set
foot again on English soil. Thirteen days before the *Destiny*
sailed into Plymouth Sound, a royal proclamation had been
issued, inviting all persons who could give evidence about the
"hostile invasion of St. Thomé," to make their information
available to the Privy Council, which was conducting an investigation into an act of belligerence for which the King had "an
utter mislike and detestation." The *Destiny* herself was already
forfeit. The High Admiral had issued orders for the ship to be
seized, and as Ralegh made his way toward London to stand trial,
the King's agents descended like scavenging vultures to auction
off the ship and her contents.

Threatened with this deluge of troubles, Ralegh reacted in the
same way as he had done twenty-two years earlier: he turned to
his pen. His defense and counterblast for the first Guiana trip had
been *The Discovery*. For the second Guiana catastrophe it was
his *Apologie*.

The genesis of *The Apologie* was worthy of the Arabian
Nights. Ralegh, who had been arrested in the West Country, was
under escort to London, when at Salisbury his path crossed the
route of King James's summer progress through the provinces. It
was an unforeseen opportunity for Ralegh to present his sovereign with his case in his own defense, but he needed several
days in which to prepare and set out his arguments. And so at
Salisbury Ralegh gained vital time by pretending serious illness. It
was a well-known political ruse, but under Ralegh's able stage-
management the trick became a virtuoso performance. He bribed
the physician accompanying his party to supply him with a
powerful emetic, and the same evening feigned dizziness, lurch-
ing and staggering in the presence of his chief captor, Sir Lewis
Stukely. Ralegh eventually ran his head spectacularly into a pillar
and fell to the ground. On the following morning a guard entered
Ralegh's bedchamber to find him stark naked on all fours and
gnawing dementedly at the rushes on the floor. Stukely was
hastily summoned and came hurrying into the room just in time
to see his cherished prisoner fall into a fit of violent convulsions
brought on by the emetic which Ralegh had surreptitiously

swallowed. Stukely was beside himself with anxiety and desperately frightened that his prisoner might die en route to London.
So he helped the doctor put Ralegh to bed and massage the
supposed invalid, an act which later led Ralegh to gibe that he
made a perfect physician out of his jailer. When it was safe to do
so, Ralegh then had his doctor accomplice smear him with a
virulent ointment which caused the skin on Ralegh's face, arms,
and chest to break out in hideous pustules, great purple lumps
with yellow heads in their centers, a revolting development that
quite appalled Stukely and caused him to suspect some exotic
Orinoco disease. Hurrying off to the Bishop of Winchester, he
beseeched the services of consultant physicians, and when these
sages in their turn had examined the prisoner, they pronounced
Ralegh too ill to be moved.

So Ralegh won four days of quarantine. Shut up in his room
for fear of the contagion spreading, he lived on slabs of bread and
mutton smuggled to him by his bribed physician, and composed
his *Apologie*.

Written under such pressure, it was impossible for *The
Apologie* to be as well organized or as elegant as *The Discovery*.
Nevertheless, it was a cogent piece of writing. One by one,
Ralegh examined and refuted the criticisms made against his management of the second Guiana expedition. He pointed out that he
could not be held responsible for the late departure of the fleet
from England, the inadequate outfitting of the ships, or the bad
weather and illnesses which they had suffered at sea. But these
were minor considerations. Ralegh knew that as supreme commander of the expedition he was ultimately responsible for
everything that had displeased King James. Essentially he stood
accused on two counts: first, he had committed a deliberate act
of war against the Spanish garrison on the Orinoco; second, his
fine stories about the gold mines of Guiana had been no more
than a confidence trick to get himself out of the Tower.

The Apologie's defense against the first charge was straightforward enough. Ralegh maintained that the Spanish at St.
Thomé had brought their fate down upon themselves because
their scouts had attacked the English in the dark, and Keymis's
men had merely retaliated against the unprovoked ambush. This

excuse was the obvious one, and Ralegh was adroit enough to support his thesis by claiming that St. Thomé had been built on English colonial territory and its citizens were therefore trespassers. The town had been founded subsequent to his first Orinoco trip, when he had claimed Guiana as an English possession, and by international law, the Spanish nation had no right to place a garrison on the river.

Ralegh's specious claim to England's ownership of Guiana was a red herring, intended to coax King James into a territorial squabble with Spain. Rather more interesting—for it revealed Ralegh's new vision of the Golden Antilles—was *The Apologie*'s reasoning that he had gone to the Orinoco in good faith, fully expecting to find a rich gold mine.

"What madness," he asked, "would have made me undertake this journey [to the Orinoco], but the assurance of the Myene?" Only a lunactic would have risked his health, already weakened by long imprisonment, and his entire fortune to a project which he knew to be a sham. Surely it would have been a "strange fancy . . . to have persuaded my sonne, whome I have lost, and to have persuaded my wife to have adventured eight thousand pounds, . . . and when that was spent, to persuade her to sell her house at Micham in hope of enricheing them by the Myenes of Guiana, if I myself had not seene them [the gold deposits] with my owne eyes." The Orinoco mines, Ralegh stubbornly maintained, really existed. Only Keymis's indecision had robbed the expedition of fabulous wealth. Those who doubted the Golden Antilles were either "sillie fools" or "puppies."

So, to the last, Ralegh clung to his belief in the paramount wealth of Guiana. Twenty-five years earlier, he had seized on the golden myth as a glittering bait to lure the English to an overseas empire, and he had never looked back. Yet in the end it was the myth which defeated the man who sought to manipulate it. Once Ralegh had committed himself to the concept of the Golden Antilles, he was a victim of its charms. Though he had successfully survived the collapse of his El Dorado theory, his failure to find his promised gold mines was too great a reversal. King James was disappointed of his bullion and, ironically, had already turned to Spain for loans and financial assistance. One of the merits to the Spanish marriage alliance, as far as the English king was concerned, was that it would make it easier to borrow money from Spain. Ralegh's unswerving pursuit of Guiana gold had not only proved vain, but had made him an international embarrassment. It was time to be rid of him.

The story of the last few weeks of Ralegh's life is justly famous—his journey from Salisbury to London, his attempt to escape by ship, his betrayal at the hands of "Sir Judas" Stukely, and his reimprisonment in the Tower, where he was spied upon by his warders and mercilessly cross-examined in order to establish a modicum of legal guilt. During this harassment, the attack gradually drifted away from the specific events of the Guiana trip and concentrated on nebulous "plots against the throne" and other vague accusations of faithlessness to his sovereign. Yet the prosecution dared not allow Ralegh an open trial, for fear that the silver-tongued and nimble-witted prisoner might find a pulpit from which to arouse popular sympathy. Instead, a board of commissioners examined him in private, found him guilty of treason, and, to avoid a legal tangle, his judges resurrected the long-standing 1603 sentence of death. Ralegh, they decided, had committed sufficient new offenses to have "stirred up his Majesty's justice, to remember to revive what the law formerly cast upon you."

The death sentence was carried out at nine o'clock in the morning of Friday, October 29, 1618. Standing on the headsman's scaffold in the Old Palace Yard at Westminster, Ralegh was permitted to deliver a final speech. Using a list of notes he had prepared for the occasion, he again denied the various accusations against him, and among those matters which he considered important at this final hour was "a report that I meant not to go to Guiana at all, and that I knew not of any Myene, nor intended any such matter, but only to get my Liberty, which I had not the Wit to keep. But it was," he pledged yet again, "my full intent to go for Gold, for the Benefit of his Majesty and those that went with me, with the rest of my Country-Men."

Ralegh meant sincerely what he said. When rearrested after his bungled attempt to escape, the goods found on his person were a microcosm of his life and ambitions. The inventory included fifty pounds in gold, "one ring with a diamond which he weareth on his finger, given him by the late Queen"; a lodestone in a red purse, some assays of a silver mine; and—from Guiana—a gold and copper image, several rough maps of the area, one or two small ingots of gold (probably those taken at St. Thomé), and a piece of the fabled golden Guiana ore.

7-

The Man Who Liked Chocolate

WHEN RALEGH AND HIS THOUSAND "SCUM" of the second expedition were ineffectually challenging Spain's claim to the elusive gold mines of Guiana, England's next great propagandist of the Golden Antilles myth was still a boy in school. The young student, later to call himself the "English American," would be the first Englishman to travel widely inside the Spanish-American empire and the first northern European to write a full-length description of what he saw there. His lively account of Spain's American colonies would pick up the theme of the Golden Antilles where Ralegh's *Discovery* had left it; and like Ralegh, he would deliberately encourage the English nation to seek its place in the Caribbean sun. But at that point the comparison with Ralegh ends, for while Ralegh was a glittering genius who twisted and turned in his struggle to fulfill grand ambitions, the newcomer was a man of straw, a lesser creature with lower aims, who crept and cheated, lied and connived, wrote and preached merely to take the best advantage of every situation that arose. He was a minor player who did not strike high at any scheme, but slyly contented himself with choosing and then joining the winning side. Yet he, more than Ralegh, was to shape England's destiny in the Caribbean.

Thomas Gage, the "English American," was an apostate and a renegade, a prig and a gourmand. Yet it was precisely because he had so unsavory a character that he managed to retain a certain charm. In his own lifetime he was reviled and threatened sufficiently to punish him for all his sins, whether committed or intended, and later commentators proceeded either to condemn him with equal venom or, rather condescendingly, to pass him off as a misguided weakling. Few people, it seemed, were prepared to acknowledge the lighter side of Thomas Gage's life and adventures, and to recognize him for what he was—a natural-born buffoon. For Gage's greatest failing was his unerring ability to bungle everything he turned his hand to. It was a knack which brought him much unhappiness and unfailingly left him slightly out of step with events around him. Unceasingly he tried to order his own life with aplomb and skillful timing, but nothing ever turned out quite as it should have; and he only succeeded in precipitating himself from one catastrophe to the next. On every occasion Gage contrived to wriggle out of trouble, yet it was never anything more than a temporary escape, and he never really checked his own slapstick slide through life. Seen in this light, the English American was not a malicious villain, but a gently incompetent, thoroughly second-rate opportunist.

Thomas Gage lived during the religious turmoil of seventeenth-century England, and the root of all his troubles and travels was his birth into a sternly Roman Catholic family. His great-grandfather and founder of the family fortunes, Sir John Gage, had risen to power as an unswerving supporter of the Church of Rome. Appointed Constable of the Tower when Queen Mary was on the throne, he had been the officer responsible for the safe imprisonment of Princess Elizabeth when she was locked up by her half-sister. Sir John Gage had also played a leading part in the suppression of the anti-Spanish Wyatt rebellion, and had strongly advocated Mary's marriage to Philip of Spain. In short, everything about Sir John marked him as zealously Papist and staunchly pro-Spanish, and in due course his heirs followed his example. One grandson, Robert Gage (Thomas's uncle) went so far as to involve himself in the notorious Babington plot to assassinate Queen Elizabeth and to place the Catholic

Mary Stuart on the throne. When he and most of his fellow conspirators were discovered and duly executed, the Gage family had its first martyr. Thereafter they were regarded with even more pride by their co-religionists and with even deeper suspicion by the Protestants. When a Catholic party was in power at court, the Gages prospered; when the Protestants ruled, they were investigated and harassed. Thomas Gage's father, who had married into another prominent recusant family, was arrested twice—once on suspicion of complicity in the Babington plot, and once for harboring a Jesuit priest. In consequence, he forfeited much of his property and was forced to spend a temporary exile in the Spanish Netherlands. Thomas's mother, too, had been in trouble on her own account. Shortly before Thomas's birth, she was arraigned on the usual charge of concealing a Jesuit priest in her house, and although powerful friends interceded on her behalf and secured her release, a fellow culprit and the Jesuit priest concerned in the matter were both hanged. Inevitably, Thomas Gage's childhood was colored by these religious adventures.

Yet the Gage family not only survived these vicissitudes, but actually flourished. Somehow they managed to entrench their position as one of the country's best-established families.* Moreover, the religious persecution of the Gages only served, as so often happens, to strengthen their convictions, which soon took on a pronounced and understandable bias in favor of the missionary activities of the Society of Jesus. As a result Thomas himself was trained with a view to joining the Society, and of his six brothers and half-brothers, two actually became Jesuits and two more were secular priests. The eldest boy, Sir Henry Gage, received a Jesuit-directed education and then spent most of his adult life on the Continent as an officer in the English legion, a body of Catholic expatriates who offered their service to the Spanish Crown. As was customary for the leading English Catholic families of the time, the Gages sent their sons overseas to be educated in a manner suitable to their religious beliefs. Nearly all

---

* One descendant, General Gage, was to command the royal garrison in Boston at the outbreak of the American Revolution, a task he discharged with little danger to the revolutionaries.

the Gage boys were shipped across the Channel to the Jesuit-staffed college at St. Omer in French Flanders, where, since the English authorities naturally frowned on such practices, all foreign students of the school were registered under suitable aliases. At St. Omer, therefore, when Sir Walter Ralegh returned from Guiana, was one Thomas "Howard," in reality Gage, spending his last year in school.

The following year, when Thomas was eighteen, he graduated, and his father sent him to Spain, where it was intended that he should continue his religious studies until he was ready to be ordained a Jesuit priest. But in Spain, well removed from his father's presence, Thomas Gage showed for the first time that chronically maladroit spirit of independence which was to plague his later life. While at the College of San Gregorio in Valladolid, he came under the influence of Dominican teachers, and in his happy-go-lucky way made up his mind that he would prefer to become a Dominican rather than a Jesuit. There was no evidence that his decision was based on any matters of deep religious faith, and indeed it was just as likely that young Thomas was merely trying to save his own skin, for it was an uncomfortable fact that many of the Englishmen who became Jesuits were then clandestinely sent back to their homeland as undercover priests. Thomas Gage may have been genuinely reluctant to provide the next martyr in the Gage roll of honor. But whatever his reason for changing to the Dominican Order, Gage managed the transfer with characteristic ineptitude. Instead of placating his father, who had set his heart on Thomas's joining the Society of Jesus, he floundered deep into a vitriolic exchange of letters with his parents over the whole affair, a correspondence which ended, according to Thomas, with "a harsh and angry letter . . . from mine own father. In this he had signified to me the displeasure of most of my friends and kindred, and his own grievous indignation against me. . . . He added that he would have thought his money better spent if I had been a scullion in a college of Jesuits than if I should prove a General of the Order of Dominicans." To make his displeasure abundantly clear, Thomas's father informed his son that he was cutting him out of his will.

The pro-Jesuit Gages had good reason to be piqued, for when

the errant Thomas turned Dominican, it was tantamount to defection. In the early seventeenth century, religious enmity was
not confined to the hatred between Papist and Protestant. There
were also fierce rivalries within the Catholic Church itself, among
Jesuits, Dominicans, Franciscans, Mercedarians, and the other
preaching orders. This internecine rivalry went far beyond solemn questions of casuistry and dogma. Often there were bursts
of savage political infighting as the several orders tried to expand
their influence at one another's expense. In such circumstances
the contesting orders did not disdain to seduce each other's
trainee priests (in Thomas' case successfully), to lobby for the
exclusion of their rivals from choice areas of missionary activity,
or, at a more frivolous level, to wrangle over which seminary had
the most melodious choir. At other times the disputes took on a
chauvinist air, and in Valladolid in particular the College of San
Gregorio was notorious for the constant uproar between "Spanish" priests and "foreigners." Such bickering was hardly con-
ducive to the serious-minded religious training of young novi-
tiates, and Thomas Gage, who, it must be remembered, had been
given little or no choice in his profession, was not the only cleric
who paid scant attention to spiritual affairs and changed orders to
suit his own ambition.

So it was that in May 1625 Thomas Gage, aged twenty-two or
thereabouts and not overly concerned with religious matters,
found himself at the Dominican friary in Jerez, when a Papal
Commissary visited the cloisters in order to recruit missionaries
for service in the Philippines. One of Thomas's friends, a former
school-fellow named Antonio Meléndez, had already volunteered
for the mission, and it was only natural that the young Englishman should think of joining him. Short on religious zeal, Gage
was endowed with a well-developed wanderlust. He decided to
travel abroad, he later said, because of "the inducing argument of
the increase of knowledge natural by the insight of rich America
and flourishing Asia." He wanted to see the world, and the
wandering life of a Dominican missionary priest was an excellent
way of doing so. So he, his friend Antonio, and a young Irish
friar from the same cloisters left Jerez and traveled by donkey to
Cádiz, where they joined a larger group of Dominicans impa-

tiently awaiting the departure of the annual Indies fleet to the New World.

Officially, Thomas Gage should never have been admitted to the Dominicans' western mission. Under Spanish law all Englishmen were banned from visiting Spanish America, and to reach the Philippines, Gage and his fellow priests would first have to land at Vera Cruz on the east coast of Mexico, cross from one side of Mexico to the other, and then board the Manila galleon at Acapulco. The Spanish authorities regarded all Englishmen, whatever their political complexion, as potential spies, and the Council of the Indies dreaded the very thing which was about to happen —namely, that an outsider would visit the Caribbean colonies and then reveal to an envious world the frailty of Spain's grip on her colonial possessions. The Spanish authorities intended to prevent this exposé at all costs, and Thomas Gage was extraordinarily fortunate not to have been intercepted at Cádiz and turned back. As it was, another English priest, who lived in the port, happened to hear that Gage was waiting to take ship for the Americas and raised the alarm. The governor sent a search party to look for Thomas, but he had been forewarned. He had quietly slipped off by himself, boarded his ship, and hidden in an empty biscuit barrel. There he stayed—with the connivance of his fellow Dominicans, who had no intention of being deprived of a budding missionary—until the signal gun announced that the Indies convoy should make for the open sea.

The July departure of the Indies fleet was one of Europe's great spectacles. Writing many years later, Thomas Gage remembered the scene in vivid detail. At the second signal gun from the flagship announcing the beginning of the voyage, the vast concourse of vessels began to weigh anchor in unison and then swung majestically into line. Dressed overall, they dropped down with the tide and went sweeping past the town walls where the citizens of Cádiz stood waving goodbye while the guns of the forts along the shore thundered out their farewell salvos. That year, wrote Gage, forty-one ships set out: "Some for one port in the Indies, and some for another . . . All laden with wines, figs, raisins, olives, oil, kerseys [coarse woolens], linen, iron, and quicksilver for the mines, to fetch out the pure silver of Zacatecas from the earthen dross where it is digged." Among the more illustrious passengers were the Marquis de Serralvo, recently appointed viceroy of Mexico, the new president of Manila, and Inquisitor Don Martin de Carrillo who, Gage noted with delicious horror, had "full commission and authority to imprison, banish, hang, and execute all delinquents." Until the Canary Islands were reached, the fleet was to be escorted by no less than eight of His Majesty's fighting ships led by his Admiral of the Galleons, Don Carlos de Ybarra.

On that occasion the summer voyage of the Indies fleet unfolded with copybook perfection. It was the kind of trip which seven years earlier might have saved Ralegh from the debacle of his second Orinoco venture. From Cádiz to the Canary Islands the Spanish convoy made a fast, choppy passage and successfully evaded the predatory attentions of the Dutch and Arab corsairs which normally infested those waters. The Canaries marked the edge of the danger zone, and, as soon as they were no longer needed, the escorting warships prepared to turn for home. But before they left, there was a splendid ceremony of farewell. Amid a general shuttling back and forth of cockboats, the Admiral of the Galleons was invited to dine aboard the fleet flagship, while the lesser captains similarly entertained their opposite numbers. Final letters for Spain were hastily written and sent across to the returning warships, and with them went one or two deserters who had already lost heart. When the final sailing orders had been prepared and circulated round the fleet, the merchantmen and the royal men-of-war separated into their respective squadrons and sailed past one another with flags flying, trumpets blaring, ordnance booming, and the passengers lining the rail to shout, "*Buen viaje,*" "*Buen viaje,*" and receive the reply "*Buen pasaje,*" "*Buen pasaje.*" From thence forward, the Indies fleet was on its own.

Westward from the Canaries the voyage was, quite literally, plain sailing. "A thing worth noting," wrote Gage in his account of the trip, "in that voyage from Spain to the Indies is that after the Canary Islands are once left, there is one constant wind continuing to America still the same without any opposition or contrariety of other winds. This is so prosperous and full on the sails, that did it blow constantly and were it not interrupted with many calms, doubtless the voyage might be ended in a month or less." But of course there were calms; and like Ralegh's ships, the Spanish vessels spent day after day almost motionless on the water. The Spaniards, however, were in no hurry, and were well prepared for the doldrums. Every year for more than a century the Indies fleet had been setting forth from Spain to the New World, and the Atlantic crossing had long since fallen into a well-established routine. No one expected record mileages; the entire fleet proceeded at the pace of the slowest vessel; and anticipating long delays, the passengers had prudently buttressed themselves against discomfort with supplies of live sheep, pigs, and chickens, kept in pens on deck until they were ready for slaughter. In addition, Gage noted, they took along barrels of white biscuit, jars of wine, and "store of rice, figs, olives, capers, raisins, lemons, sweet and sour oranges, pomegranates, comfits, preserves, conserves, and all sorts of Portugal sweetmeats."

In a good year, in fact, the passage of the Indies fleet had the relaxed air of a pleasure cruise, at least for the richer passengers. When there were no storms, the sailors seldom needed to trim the yards, and on windless days the fleet patiently huddled together on the water like a small, floating town. Passengers were ferried between the gently rocking ships, so that they could make up card parties or entertain each other with dinners and musical performances. Fishing was an obvious and favorite pastime, and Gage remarked on the huge numbers of "dorado," the golden fish, which were caught. In fact many more fish were caught than could be eaten, and most of them were thrown back into the sea. For their gala occasions, the passengers observed the various saints's days, and especially those days dedicated to the patron saints of the missionary Orders. Thus on the last day of July, the mission of thirty Jesuits (also destined for the Philippines), traveling aboard the *Santa Gertrudis,* prepared a magnificent show in honor of their founder. They trimmed their ship round about with white linen, and on her sails they painted pictures of St. Ignatius and the arms of their Society. Then the *Santa Gertrudis* was sailed jauntily around the fleet while her crew lined up on deck to sing anthems. After dusk her standing rigging was hung with strings of lighted paper lanterns, and against this splendid backdrop the Jesuits put on a display of fireworks, while the envious Dominicans were forced to wait, sourly counting the number of squibs which their rivals had fabricated from the *Santa Gertrudis*'s powder store.

Naturally, the Dominicans refused to be outdone by the Jesuits, and since St. Dominic's Day fell only four days later, the twenty-eight Dominicans aboard the *San Antonio* (the different Orders were wisely assigned to separate ships in order to reduce squabbles) tried hard to eclipse their rivals. They put on a similar pageant of fireworks, decorations, and choral singing for their vessel. Then all the Jesuits and the captain of the *Santa Gertrudis* were invited to a lavish dinner aboard the *San Antonio*, so that the Dominicans could produce their trump card to best effect—a Lope de Vega play which was performed by a scratch troupe drawn from the passengers and the younger Dominicans. In Gage's unashamedly prejudiced opinion this *coup de théâtre* gave the palm to his Order, for the play "was as stately acted and set forth both in shows and good apparel, in that narrow compass of our ship, as might have been the best stage in the Court of Madrid."

Gage also took a lively interest in the operations of the Spanish sailors and shipmasters. The latter were an unusually cautious group of navigators, and indeed it was not uncommon for the Indies fleet to lower its sails at night in case the pilots had so seriously miscalculated their position that they ran the ships aground in the dark. Certainly Gage and several of the other passengers thought it a great joke when, in the middle of August, the Admiral of the Fleet confessed that he had completely lost his bearings, and despite a flawless crossing had not the least idea how far his ships were from the nearest land. A general conclave of pilots was summoned to advise him but failed to pierce the fog of ignorance. Some said "three hundred miles, another two hundred, another one hundred, another fifty, another more, another less, all erring much from the truth save only one old pilot of the smallest vessel of all. He affirmed resolutely that with that small gale wherewith we then sailed we should come to Guadeloupe the next morning." At dawn the next morning in fact, Guadeloupe came in sight, and the admiral was relieved to discover that he had reached the outer fringe of the Golden Antilles.

After the six or seven weeks of the Atlantic passage it was customary for the Indies fleet to lie over for a few days at one of the Leeward Islands in order to cleanse and refill the watercasks, obtain fresh vegetables, and allow time for those travelers who so wished to wash their laundry. Guadeloupe was the favorite island for this stopover, as a conveniently sheltered roadstead gave on to a beach where there was a spring of fresh water. Guadeloupe itself had not been permanently settled by Spanish colonists; and the Carib population of the island had become so used to the annual visits of the fleet, that they looked forward eagerly to the frenetic bartering spree when they traded fruit, plantains, turtle, and segments of sugar cane for the white man's manufactured goods and, above all, for his wine. Gage, however, was rather scornful of the Caribs. He claimed that "one reasonable cup of Spanish sack presently tumbled up their heels, and left them like swine tumbling on the deck of our ship," an impression enhanced by the "thin plates hanging at their noses, like hog rings."

HAVING SATISFIED THE IMMEDIATE DEMANDS of the islanders, whose dugout canoes swarmed thirstily around the fleet, the Spaniards began to go ashore. For most of the passengers it was their first visit to the New World, and naturally they were agog with curiosity to see what exotica the Golden Antilles had to offer. No one was more ardently inquisitive than the tyro missionaries. Impatient for the chance to convert the heathen wherever they might be found, the credulous and thoroughly inexperienced Jesuits, Dominicans, Franciscans, and Mercedarians swept ashore in a race to win souls for heaven. As the young missionaries did not speak a single word of the Caribs' language, they could scarcely have hoped to reap a rich harvest during the two or three days that the fleet was at Guadeloupe, even if the Caribs, who saw a similar rush of newly fledged apostles from the fleet year after year, had not learned how to avoid their ministrations. But as luck would have it, a band of Jesuits happened to stumble across a Spanish-speaking mulatto on the island. He was an ex-slave who, having decided that he liked the Antillean way of life, had run away from an earlier Indies fleet. He had taken himself a Carib wife, started a family, and utterly abandoned his former religion. Now, unexpectedly, he found himself deluged with eager missionaries who were concerned with his welfare and quite determined to save him. While one posse of Jesuits entrapped him and proceeded to berate the unfortunate mulatto for his lapse, a second group of priests stood guard to fend off the attentions of rival preaching orders, who might intrude upon their prey. Thomas Gage, typically unenthusiastic, sauntered up and was allowed to join in the haranguing of the mulatto, but his subsequent description of the episode showed quite clearly that his sympathies lay with the besieged ex-slave. The Jesuits, however, would not be satisfied until the man had promised to return to the fleet, bringing with him his wife and children. Working in unison and in relays, they finally obtained the mulatto's reluctant agreement and rushed off jubilantly to demand from the admiral that he should send a cockboat to collect this poor sinner and his heathen kin.

Such enthusiasm was infectious; and aboard the *San Antonio* several of the younger Dominicans were so carried away with the success of this trial attempt at proselytizing in the New World that they began a serious discussion whether or not to stay on in Guadeloupe and convert the entire population. They were still praising the docility and apparent gentleness of the Caribs when they saw sudden pandemonium on the beach. Apparently the mulatto had never had the slightest intention of returning to Christianity and his former state of slavery, and as soon as the Jesuits had left, he had assembled his Carib friends and crept down to the beach where they laid an ambush. When the priests returned to collect their supposedly reformed sinner, they were met with a hail of arrows and driven back. The attack was a complete surprise, especially for those unfortunate Spaniards who had been minding their own affairs and quietly washing their clothes on the beach. Everything was thrown into uproar. Men abandoned their laundry and dashed pell-mell for the safety of the cockboats. Some tripped and fell; others hauled themselves into the little boats until the vessels were so overloaded that they sank. A few even tried vainly to swim out to the fleet. A half-dozen were killed outright by the Caribs, several more were so panic-stricken that they drowned, and at least thirteen men were wounded, some seriously, before the hidden attackers finally withdrew in the face of a bombardment opened up by the heavy guns of the fleet. From then onward the admiral forbade any more laundering on the beach, and the last of the water casks were hurriedly filled under the guard of a full company of soldiers. Thus ended Thomas Gage's first experience of missionary work in the West Indies, and his only satisfaction was that the marked targets for the Carib bowmen had been the black-robed figures of the Jesuits.

Considerably chastened by this incident, Gage and his Dominican brethren were obliged to endure the gibes of fellow passengers who teased them unmercifully about the lack of success of their Guadeloupe mission. Thomas Gage himself was not unduly despondent, for he was interested in other things beside the salvation of the American aborigine, and already his appetite for New World edibles was beginning to make itself felt. The sailors of the *San Antonio* had purchased from the Guadeloupe natives several bunches of plantains and hung them up to ripen. The fruit met with Gage's unreserved approval. It "is not gathered ripe from the tree," he wrote, "but being gathered green, it is hung up some days, and so ripens and grows yellow and mellow, and every bit as sweet as honey." Nor was the plantain his only happy discovery, for he had a sweet tooth and was enjoying his first taste of sugar cane. Giant turtles too, "in some cases two yards broad," were speared up from the blue waters of the famous sea, and when their flesh had been hung up to dry, Gage pronounced that it tasted as good as veal.

But this last leg of the voyage to America, from Guadeloupe to Mexico, was not without its tragedy, for a number of the men who had been wounded on Guadeloupe died. The Caribs had used poisoned arrows in the attack, and, like those unfortunates Ralegh had described in his *Discovery*, the bodies of their victims began to puff up and discolor. Aboard the *Santa Gertrudis* one of the Jesuits died, and on the *San Antonio* the Dominican friar Juan de la Cueva also succumbed to the effects of the poison.

Both corpses were weighted with heavy stones and slung over the ships' sides at the end of ropes while a Mass was sung. Then, to a boom of cannon, the ropes were loosed and the bodies splashed into the Caribbean. Several days later a similar service had to be held to dispose of the mangled remains of a sailor who had been chewed in half by a large shark as the poor wretch was attempting to swim from one ship to another on a calm day.

At about seven o'clock in the morning of September 11, the Indies fleet, now reduced by the departure of those ships bound for other Caribbean destinations, at last came in sight of the Mexican coast. It was a perfect landfall, for they found themselves exactly opposite their destination, the Mexican port of San Juan de Ulloa. This feat of navigation was, however, due to luck rather than good seamanship, and the admiral was so surprised to find himself running directly toward the coast that he once again assembled his pilots to ask for their advice. As always, they recommended caution and warned him that it would be dangerous to try to enter San Juan de Ulloa so late in the day. Therefore the fleet performed the extraordinary maneuver of reducing sail even while in sight of their destination and hanging back lest they should run aground in the dusk. The penalty for their timidity was a sudden change of wind during the night and a mild storm which sent the sailors scurrying aloft to trim sail and the friars to their knees to beseech the intercession of the Virgin Mary. Luckily at dawn the wind veered back to its normal quarter again, and, as Gage sarcastically noted, to cries of *"Milagro, Milagro, Milagro,"* the fleet was carefully shepherded into harbor by the pilot boats of San Juan de Ulloa.

In Gage's day, the Viceroyalty of Mexico was already slipping into that colonial stagnation which characterized the middle age of Spain's American empire. The sense of urgency which the conquistadors had brought with them had long since died, and the new generation of Spanish Mexicans was much more inclined to the peaceful pursuits of farm, mine, and trading company. Huge fortunes could still be made, and indeed some of the colonists were men of enormous, almost legendary, wealth. The viceroy and many of the senior Crown officers were still regularly sent out from Spain to run the colony's affairs, but most of the real power had devolved into the hands of the richer Creoles, men of Spanish descent born in the colony and making their lives there. The Creoles's wealth and their permanent attachment to Mexico gave them a built-in advantage over the temporary colonial administrators, who in turn looked down upon the "colonials." As a result Mexican life was notorious for its perennial feuds between the Creoles and the expatriate Spaniards. These quarrels often spilled over into religious life. Mexico, which like the other central provinces was liberally dotted with churches, friaries, convents, and monasteries, re-echoed to the squabbles of Creole and Spanish priests, in addition to the more traditional rivalries between the various orders.

The Mexican clergy, as Gage soon discovered, led a remarkably privileged life. They were well paid, well housed, and well respected by their parishioners. Every community had its own church buildings, and often a friary as well. There the clergy lived in considerable comfort, waited on by small armies of Indian servants who were obliged to supply their labor free of charge. The priests, it must be said, repaid this attention by being more closely in touch with the great mass of the native population than any other segment of the white culture they represented. Even so, the Mexican priesthood was comparatively well cushioned against the harsh realities of life; while, for their part, the attitude of the Mexican Indians toward the priests can best be described as one of apathy. The vast majority of the native population lived a simple existence that demanded and received little more than the bare essentials of survival—a small shack to live in, a straw mat for a bed, a cotton shirt, and an uncompromisingly monotonous diet based on maize flour and beans. Here and there one found a few rich Indians, but not many; the mixed bloods, the mestizos, where the only real link across the otherwise impassable gulf which separated the native Mexicans, concentrated in the small towns and in the countryside, from their white conquerors, who lived in the cities or dwelt on their large estates.

Thomas Gage attached great importance to this gap between the Spaniards and the Indians, and in this respect his description of social conditions in Central America echoed Ralegh's propaganda about the Orinoco Indians. Both authors went out of their way to foster the impression that if England sent an army to the Spanish colonies in America, this would trigger off a general uprising. The native population, they claimed, would expel the hated Spaniards, and welcome the Englishmen as their deliverers. Ralegh's nascent guerrillas had been the natives of Guiana, Thomas Gage saw them in the huts and market places of Mexico and Guatemala. According to the English American, the gross and enfeebled Spanish colonists were dissipating themselves in lascivious vice while their maltreated Indian subjects, whose sweat paid for this pleasure, seethed silently for revenge. Spanish America was a large and succulent plum waiting to be plucked by the English nation. Mexico itself was Babylon in need of cleansing, a place where priests kept mistresses, and great men paraded strings of half-caste paramours gorgeously arrayed in the finest jewelry. Such tales, though palpable exaggerations, gave new life to the tarnished image of the Golden Antilles, and those who read Gage's subsequent account of his American travels either burned with Puritanical fervor to reform the Romish ways of Spanish America or were equally eager to lay their hands on the mouth-watering opulence which Gage so lovingly and enticingly described.

In fact it is abundantly clear from Gage's comments on the New World that secretly he envied those worldly delights which he castigated so vehemently. He betrayed himself with his own ornate descriptions of the lotus-life in Mexico, for there was a little too much enjoyment in his lip-smacking and he was a little too quick to cast an appreciative eye at pretty women. Unashamedly, too, he set about collecting his own share of the New World's treasures. Scoffing at the Creoles for their avarice, he hoarded a small fortune for himself as soon as he had his own parish. Accusing the other friars of peculation, he falsified the financial accounts of his own ministry so that he could divert the surplus into his own pocket. And to cap it all he had the brazen nerve to jeer at the failure of Spanish missionary activity, when he himself turned tail and ran away on the only two occasions on which he was faced with hostile natives.

The first of these desertions was the reason for the next crisis in Thomas Gage's checkered career. His Dominican mission

spent the winter months in Mexico City preparing to move on to
Acapulco, where it would embark for the trans-Pacific voyage to
the Philippines. But in Mexico City Gage met a friar who had
just recently returned from Manila, and learned from him that a
missionary's life in the Philippines was so hazardous that few
missionaries ever returned from the islands. Gage was not the sort
of man who dismissed such warnings lightly, and his unfailing
sense of self-preservation told him it was high time to execute
another *volte-face* in order to avoid the least glimmer of future
unpleasantness. So, with typical incisiveness, he washed his hands
of the entire (and now obviously misguided) Philippine affair,
and resolved to desert the Dominican mission at the very first
opportunity and to stay in America.

He was not alone in this plan. Four other Dominicans, among
them his friend Antonio Meléndez, had also lost their enthusiasm
for the Philippine venture, and they too wanted to stay in
America. So the five malcontents plotted together. Pooling their
resources, they secretly sold their books and other possessions to
raise money and buy horses, which they kept at a stable at a safe
distance from the friary where they were staying. But above all,
they needed to arrange their escape with the greatest care, because runaway priests, who had broken church discipline, were
normally hunted down by government officers and handed over
to the superiors of their Order for punishment. To reduce the
risk of capture, Gage and his fainthearted companions agreed that
it would be better to postpone their flight until the very last
evening before the Dominican mission set out for Acapulco.
They hoped that this would prevent the Papal Commissary from
staying on in Mexico City and personally supervising the hunt
for his missing charges, as the main body of the Dominican
mission would have to move forward to Acapulco to meet the
departure of the Manila galleon. Gage reasoned that once the
Papal Commissary was out of the way, he and the other runaways would stand a better chance of clemency when they
finally surrendered themselves to the permanent Dominican representatives in America and asked for asylum.

The plot worked more smoothly than the conspirators had
dared hope. On the night before the mission's departure for

Acapulco the runaways slipped quietly out of the friary in pairs so as not to attract attention, and hurried off to the stables in town. There they mounted their horses and with the help of a hired guide left Mexico City at ten o'clock at night. To confuse any pursuit they at first rode westward along the dark and deserted country side-roads, heading directly away from their true destination, the province of Guatemala more than six hundred miles to the south and east. Only in Guatemala, they had been told, would they find refuge, for in Guatemala the vast majority of Dominicans were friars who were themselves Spanish-born and Spanish-trained and would welcome additional recruits of the same background in the constant struggle against the Creole faction. In the other provinces, by contrast, the Dominican monasteries were already dominated by Creoles who could be expected to ship the truants summarily off to the dreaded Philippines.

Either the runaways' precautions were unusually effective, or the Mexican authorities paid little heed to the defection of five very insignificant friars, for Gage and his party got away without difficulty. Traveling as far as possible in the first night, they hid during daylight in a small Indian town. Here their guide turned back, leaving them to push ahead as fast as their horses would carry them through a second night, and at dawn the next day they reached the pleasant and fertile valley of Atlixco. They were now far enough from Mexico City to have outstripped the news of their escape, and so, in Gage's florid expression, "we began to shake off all fear, and would no more, like bats and owls, fly in the night, but we travelled by day that we might with more pleasure enjoy the prospect of the valley, and of the rest of the country."

For the moment Gage and his friends still avoided the larger country towns for fear of being recognized, but they altered their route so as to describe a wide circle around Mexico City and arrive upon the road to Guatemala. To their surprise and gratification they quickly discovered that they would have no difficulty in obtaining food or shelter, even though they had set out with only twenty ducats among them—a paltry sum, according to Gage, "which in that rich and plentiful country was not much more than twenty English shillings, and this seemed to us but as morning dew, which would soon be spent in provender only for our horses." But luckily the "dew" was not exposed to the evaporation of day-to-day travel expenses, for at one estancia after another the Dominicans found themselves greeted hospitably by the owner, feted with lavish meals, given beds for the night, and in some cases sent on their way next morning with presents of money. These landowners, said Gage, were so isolated that they seldom saw a priest and were overjoyed to hear good Spanish spoken again. They felt themselves amply rewarded by a single evening's conversation with five friars so lately arrived from the mother country and were so open-handed that, instead of spending the twenty ducats, the runaways's capital actually increased to twice that amount. A good part of this increase was due to the generosity of one unusually homesick but highly successful expatriate farmer, who, on hearing that Meléndez came from the same town in Spain as himself, insisted that the Dominican party stay three days with him and then gave the friars a large sum of cash to defray future expenses.

The best, however, was yet to come. The overwhelming liberality of the landowners had given the runaways enough confidence for them to abandon their furtive cross-country progress and take to the open highway. There they pretended to be an official Dominican mission en route to Guatemala, and to their great glee this bold maneuver made them eligible for the special privileges accorded to itinerant members of the Church. In every town or large village the Indian populace unquestioningly provided food, stabling, and shelter to the travelers free of charge. Everything the friars needed for their comfort was obtained merely for the asking. In return they had only to note down in the village account book what services had been rendered. Later the value of these services would be paid for out of the community chest. It was a paternalistic and remarkably convenient arrangement for those travelers lucky enough to be eligible for such services, and Thomas Gage was very impressed to find that when settlements were too far apart for a comfortable day's travel, the authorities had thoughtfully provided *ventas*, or inns. Here the wayfarer could find bed, board, and such welcome touches as crystal-clear water stored in great porous jars, which sweated a thin film of moisture so that their contents were cold enough to make the travelers's teeth chatter on the hottest day.

But the wayfarer in Spanish America did not always travel with such lordly ease, and before long Gage was complaining bitterly of some places where the swarms of mosquitoes were so thick that they managed to penetrate the crude mosquito nets the party carried. Once, too, the English American was obliged to spend the night by himself in the open. His horse had balked toward the end of the day and Gage, being far too tight-fisted to abandon an animal for which he had paid good money, decided to let his companions go on ahead while he waited for his horse to recover. He soon regretted his decision. Stranded on a dark and windy night in the wilds of Mexico, he succumbed to an acute attack of fright. He swore that during the night he heard the "howling, barking, and crying" of packs of demons disguised as wild dogs, the piercing shrieks of witches, and the bellowing of tormented Christians. He solemnly advised the reader of this tale that should a similar situation befall him, the only defense was to lie as still as quaking muscles would allow, in the hope that the evil spirits and ravening beasts would lose interest and wander off in another direction. Only by this stratagem, he assured his audience, had he saved his own life in Mexico and been able to rejoin his traveling companions.

Gage was less frightened, but equally uncomfortable, when he and his party ran out of food while crossing a desolate mountain pass on the way to Guatemala. Faint from hunger, the travelers unwisely attempted to eat green lemons straight from the tree. Naturally, this diet had played havoc with their digestions and to remedy their distress the Dominicans were obliged to purchase half a bag of maize flour from their guide. He, a local Indian, was promptly relegated to Gage's bad books because he took a sharp profit from the tormented friars.

Fortunately, these adventures did not prevent the English American from putting together a colorful description of lands which he was probably the first Englishman to visit. "My desire," he wrote in his subsequent *Travels*, "is to shew my reader what parts of America I travelled through, and did abide in." But that was only half the story, for Gage gave his reader something more substantial than a vade mecum of the New World, and he obviously enjoyed himself hugely in the Golden Antilles. He trumpeted his propaganda for an English attack on Spain's American empire, delved into the minor details of Mexican and Guatemalan life in both town and countryside, and made careful, if slightly bizarre, remarks about the geography of the isthmus. Thus he firmly advanced the medieval theory that earthquakes were a symptom of terrestrial flatulence and were caused by the eruption of wind imprisoned in huge subterranean caverns. And he poked fun at a certain Spanish friar, who, he said, believed that volcanoes were filled with molten gold. This deluded priest had climbed up to the peak of one volcano and, hoping to scoop up a bubbling fortune, let down into the crater a pot on the end of a long chain. But the chain melted and he lost his cauldron. Such anecdotes came easily to Gage's jaunty style of narration as, with an odd mixture of cynicism and solemnity, he set about describing to an English audience the details of everyday life in the colonies.

Nowhere was Gage's own character more delightfully portrayed than when he was writing about chocolate, at that time one of Central America's most renowned and exotic products. Gage adored chocolate, though it was a novelty to most Englishmen of his day. For this deplorable oversight he berated his countrymen sternly, lecturing them that English privateersmen wantonly dumped overboard sack after sack of chocolate beans from captured Spanish vessels simply because the English sailors were too ignorant to know what to do with the strange objects which they dubbed "sheep's dung." To remedy this lamentable ignorance Gage gave a painstaking description of how chocolate was grown and exactly how it should be prepared. He himself had tasted his first cup of chocolate soon after landing at San Juan de Ulloa, and from that moment chocolate was never far from his thoughts or his lips. It was his boast that he drank chocolate a half-dozen times a day—at meals, between meals, as a nightcap, or as a stimulant to keep him awake when studying late at night. For extra pungency he recommended flavoring it

with sugar, or cinnamon, or clove and aniseed, hazel nuts, al-
mond, vanilla, rose water, and even pepper. And to help the
traveler he listed various ways of compressing chocolate into
easily portable blocks which could then be broken up and used as
required en route. Gage himself had a portable chocolate-making
kit, comprising a small leather pannier with blocks of dried
chocolate, cups, sugar, spices, labels, and all the other appurte-
nances of a wayside brew. Indeed, it would not be too much to
say that Gage's *Travels*, literary as well as physical, were punc-
tuated from start to finish with a long succession of cups of
chocolate. And he boasted how the Creoles and Indians so enjoyed
their chocolate that in some church services it was difficult to
make oneself heard above the clattering of crockery as the Creole
women sipped cup after cup brought in by their Indian maidservants. The Bishop himself had tried to put an end to this
practice and decreed that there was to be no chocolate-drinking
during divine service. But, hinted Gage darkly, the bishop died
soon afterward, poisoned of all things by a cup of chocolate
handed to him by a page who was friendly with one of his
disgruntled Creole parishioners.

Other American foods, besides chocolate, tickled Thomas
Gage's palate. With the curiosity of a true gourmet he sampled
both hedgehog and iguana. The latter was something of a disappointment, for despite its dragonlike appearance and encrusta-
tions, Gage found it to be no more gastronomically exciting than
an ordinary English rabbit. On the other hand, he was loud in his
praises of such dishes as lake trout from Guatemala, mamey
apples from Mexico, melons, corn on the cob, American grapes
and, oddly enough, the nauseatingly sweet fruit of the sapodilla.
The latter, better known as the source of chicle gum, bore a
fruit "so juicy that at the eating, the juice like drops of honey
falls from them, and the smell is like unto a baked pear." Gage,
who had found shark meat to his liking during the trans-Atlantic
passage, unhesitatingly placed the cloying sapodilla plum on his
list of New World delicacies, as he munched his way undaunted
through nearly every dish that Guatemala or Mexico had to offer.
In the end his only gastronomic defeat was from the homemade
Indian liquor in Guatemala. This concoction, of frightful smell

and uncertain extraction, was so foul that Gage swore it was flavored in the jar with dead toads, and that its very smell made him retch. By happy circumstance Gage's ultimate verdict on all American food was that, though attractive and bulky in appearance, it lacked the solid substance of its European equivalent. In consequence, a man in the New World who gorged himself on the local food was soon hungry again and faint for lack of sustenance. Naturally enough, this rapid depletion was a splendid excuse for Thomas Gage to recommend at least one or two cups of chocolate between every insubstantial meal.

The English American was also, it seemed, a frustrated farmer at heart, for he lost no opportunity to describe the agricultural bounty of the New World. From Mexico City to Panama, he reeled off details of plantations and crops, landlords whose sideboards groaned with fabulous collections of silver, and encomendero serfs who were forced to work the land for their Spanish masters. He described cattle ranches so huge that their owners had not the least idea of their own wealth or the size of their herds, and valleys so fertile under irrigation that the farmers could raise two crops every year. On the coasts there were prosperous fishing villages, and around every town was a circle of lush market gardens. At the lowest end of the scale the Indians cultivated humble plots of chili and maize outside their huts, while on a grand acreage the great landowners ran enormous plantations which produced everything from coconuts and tree cotton to vanilla and cochineal. To the readers of his *Travels*, Gage's Antilles were not so much the fabulous lands of gold and silver, which *The Discovery* had portrayed, as a vast garden of unsurpassed fecundity where industrious natives tilled the soil for their rulers and awaited their deliverance by the first nation bold enough to challenge Spain's rule over them.

8.

The English American in Guatemala

WHEN THOMAS GAGE AND HIS FELLOW RUNAWAYS eventually arrived in the province of Guatemala, they were relieved to learn that they had found the sanctuary they had been seeking. At the town of Chiapa on the border of Guatemala the travelers called at the local Dominican friary and were redirected to a meeting with the regional Provincial, Father Peter Alvarez, who alone had the authority to decide their fate. Luckily for the fugitives, Father Alvarez was a kindly judge, himself Spanish-born and Spanish-trained, and fully prepared to forgive the misdemeanors of the truant Philippine missionaries once he had heard their story. Gage, crafty as ever in his own interests, felt that the Provincial's decision was unduly influenced by the fact that his own prior had run away from the Philippine mission under very similar circumstances some ten years earlier. In any event, Alvarez ruled that Gage and his companions could stay as priests in Guatemala provided they atoned for their disobedience to the Papal Commissary with three days spent on bread and water. It was a mere slap of a punishment even for someone of Gage's sybaritic tastes. For the benefit of the Creole friars the penitents kept to their official diet during public meals in the refectory, but Spanish-born Dominicans smuggled sweetmeats and cups of chocolate to Gage and his friends in their cells late in the evening. Then, as soon as the three days were over, the runaways emerged and were officially welcomed into the ranks of the Dominicans of Guatemala. And Gage, whose strict Jesuit education at St. Omer now stood him in good stead, found himself assigned as a teacher of Latin syntax and grammar to the youths of Chiapa studying in the cloister school.

Gage was less than impressed with Chiapa. The little place was scarcely more than an overgrown market town, dull, quiet, and singularly lacking in sophistication of any sort. The rustic simplicity of this backwater, however, did not deter its wealthy Creole inhabitants from adopting ludicrously conceited airs, and Gage, who took an instant dislike to the parents of his numskull pupils, could not abide their pretentiousness: "The gentlemen of Chiapa" he complained, "are a by-word all about that country [for] fantastic pride, joined with simplicity, ignorance, misery, and penury. These gentlemen will say they descend from some duke's home in Spain, and immediately from the first Conquerors; yet in carriage they are but clowns; in wit, abilities, parts, and discourse, as shallow-brained as a low brook, whose waters are scarce able to leap over a pebble stone. Any small reason soon tries and tires their weak brain, which is easily at a stand when sense is propounded; and slides on speedily when nonsense carrieth the stream." As an example of this Chiapan stupidity, Gage claimed to have persuaded one local dignitary that all English privateersmen abstained from eating garlic so that they should be able to smell the presence of Spanish merchant vessels at night.

Fortunately for Gage's sensibilities, he was soon rid of Chiapa's dullards, for after less than a year in their town, he received his Provincial's permission to transfer to the capital of the province, Guatemala City, where he was to enroll as a graduate student in theology at the College of St. Thomas Aquinas. There Gage spent three years, the happiest of his New World career. He was on good terms with his Dominican brethren; he actively enjoyed his studies and was quickly promoted to the rank of Reader of Master of Arts; and as a Reader he was inordinately proud that he held a position of some responsibility within the college hierarchy. Moreover, he was an able scholar who worked hard, studying late into the night, so that when he came to be examined by a panel of judges, he defended his thesis capably and was passed with credit.

Guatemala City at that time stood some ten miles from its present-day site, and was a far grander place than little Chiapa. Capital of the Captaincy General of Guatemala, it was the focus of trade and government for a considerable area of the isthmus, including Honduras, Nicaragua, Vera Paz, and Costa Rica. By sea it traded with Peru and Spain, and by land well-traveled mule tracks led to Mexico in one direction and to Panama in the other. According to Gage, its wealth was so great that five of its merchant princes were each worth more than five hundred thousand ducats, and the governor himself normally amassed a private fortune because the bribery for state monopolies reached such enormous heights. The city was also very beautiful. Spreading out from a central plaza, its wide avenues were dominated by the ornate splendor of a host of monasteries and nunneries and the massive town houses of wealthy Guatemalans. And always, bounding every horizon, rose the magnificent peaks of the surrounding mountains, several of which were volcanic cones, and two in particular were famous throughout Central America. The first was extinct, its fertile slopes renowned for "pleasant springs, gardens, fruits, flowers and every green and flourishing prospect"; but the other remained active, and would periodically threaten to erupt, rumbling and shaking as though the end of the world were at hand. At such times, wrote Gage, the inhabitants of the city would rush into their churches to pray for salvation, while the mountain flared so brightly that it was said that at night one could stand by the window and read a book by the light of the lava's glow.

Amid such spectacular surroundings lay the College of St. Thomas Aquinas. Organized and operated by its Dominican founders (the Jesuits had their own college), it was linked to the Dominican friary by a long cloister, and thus Gage's life, apart from an occasional outside sermon, was very sheltered. It was also, if he is to be believed, a luxurious existence. His friary boasted several splendid treasures which were on permanent display, including a solid silver picture of the Virgin Mary and a silver lamp so heavy that it required the combined efforts of three men to haul it up to the ceiling. And the Dominicans' cuisine—a matter of some consequence to their Reader of Master of Arts—was superlative. All this comfort was made even more delightful by a small army of Indian servants who daily attended to the needs of the friars. Gage never mentioned just how many servants were attached to the friary, but the lavish use of staff can be judged from the fact that even a country priest would employ, at minimum, three butlers, a pair of cooks, a half-dozen errand boys, several maidservants to wash the dishes and laundry and to bake tortillas, two gardeners, at least six stableboys and grooms, and sometimes a group of fishermen whose sole task was to keep the household supplied with fish. This plethora of helpers was quite separate from a similar horde of sacristans, cleaning women, bell ringers, major domos, and other factotums who looked after the church and assisted at divine service. It was only to be expected that Gage found the well-padded life of Guatemala City very much to his liking.

At the end of his three years in the college, Gage's wanderlust began to prick him again, and this time he took a fancy to the idea of joining a Dominican mission which was setting out to explore a land route from Guatemala into the Yucatán peninsula. The aim of the mission was to convert the forest Indians, and it had the full support of the colonial government, which was supplying a detachment of troops as escort. The spiritual side of the expedition was entrusted to a Dominican, one Father Francisco Moran. The latter was an old friend of Gage's and a former student at Valladolid, so the English American had no difficulty in arranging to be enrolled as a member of the exploring party. In the event, however, the mission was a complete failure, for it ran into such stiff resistance from hostile tribes that all progress was abandoned. Gage, laconically describing the expedition, confessed with his usual disarming candor that when danger threatened, "[I] began to repent me of what I was engaged in," and conveniently contracted a sharp attack of the flux. Thus at the critical moment when his companions were hard at work fighting off a night attack on the Spanish bivouac, Thomas Gage dangled in his invalid's hammock, lying quite still, while "uproar and sudden affrightment added sweat and fear to my fever." Naturally, when the expedition decided to turn back, he was possessed of a sudden and miraculous cure, left his hammock, and joined briskly in the retreat.

Later the same year Gage also paid a flying visit to the wild backlands of Honduras, but after his experiences in the Yucatán, the English American had little stomach for missionary work amid the savage heathen. He became, instead, increasingly homesick for England. Unfortunately for his plans, there was a rule that any Dominican priest who had been sent out to the New World should spend at least ten years in the Americas before being allowed to return to Europe. It was a sensible policy, which made the best use of the missionary resources available, and, as Gage still had another five years to serve, he found himself appointed parish priest of Mixco, a small community about a day's journey from Guatemala City. The parish was in the gift of the central Dominican friary, and it was a congenial post that certainly did not call for too much hard work. But Gage's mind was made up—he had set his sights on going back to England, and in consequence he saw his new appointment as nothing more nor less than a stepping stone on his homeward path.

Gage went to work with that buoyant enthusiasm which characterized his every action when his own interests were at stake. It so happened that the previous incumbent of Mixco, an octogenarian priest, had shown very little business acumen, so that during his tenure the parish had provided only a small, but adequate, income with a meager surplus for the central friary. As soon as Gage discovered this fact, he immediately took the trouble to find out how much money the old man had been sending to the Dominican friary. Then he arranged with the Provincial that if the revenue of the parish should increase, the friary would reward Gage with free clothing and wine. It was a shrewd move, because the wily appointee had already calculated that he could increase Mixco's revenue far beyond the Provincial's expectations. With his living expenses thus reduced, Gage knew how he could keep his superiors in contented ignorance, pay his own way, and cream off the surplus income to pay for his return passage to England.

With this plan in mind, he set about his parish finances with the ferocity of an ambitious entrepreneur. And for once he managed to live up to his own expectations. Indeed, there was scarcely a money-making device to which Thomas Gage did not apply his ingenuity with remarkable success. First, he made sure that all his official income—from the community chest, regular Masses, sodality payments, and so forth—was fully and punctually paid up. Then he made an extraordinary review of the religious house and calendar, ejecting from his church any statue which was no longer profitable because its donor had stopped paying the incumbent for prayers and upkeep. Into the vacated niches he then persuaded his richer parishioners to install more lucrative saints. The newcomers, he carefully noted, brought in a healthy income of seven crowns apiece, four crowns in cash for prayers and processions on the relevant saint's day, and three crowns in kind, usually presents of chickens, turkeys, or chocolate. Next, Gage turned his attention to the ecclesiastical calendar. After careful inspection he revived numerous obscure days of observance, making sure that his parishioners knew of every major or minor occasion on which they were expected to show up in church, attend divine service, and reward the priest for his diligence. Thus within a few months Gage's flock was attending every Communion, christening, and burial in the parish; the number and frequency of confessions had greatly increased; and the parish had been utterly transformed by a diligent pastor who did not miss a single opportunity to wrest a few more coins from the public.

But Gage was not yet done. Once he had put Mixco's parochial finances in order, he turned his attention to the monetary possibilities of expanding his catchment area. And, like the good businessman he was, he concluded that two fast thoroughbred mules would soon pay for themselves and more. So, to the parish of Mixco, he added the adjacent parish of Pinola, and by dint of rushing back and forth on his mules, he managed to double his income, preaching two sermons (and taking two collections) each Sunday, observing every saint's day twice over, and making sure that he gave Mass and heard confessions from two paying populations. At its wildest extreme, his avarice even extended to collecting and reselling the candles left by devotees in his church, and ghoulishly counting up the sudden increase in burial payments when a plague afflicted the province. Other acts of God, all cheerily regarded as manifestations of divine charity, included a plague of locusts, which encouraged people to pray and pay for a miracle to save their crops, and a handy series of earthquakes, shooting stars, and thunderbolts, which also gave a sharp fillip to his profits.

This all-embracing rapacity should, by rights, have turned Thomas Gage into a particularly revolting human predator, battening on the simple-minded piety of his trusting parishioners. Yet this would be an unfair judgment on the English American, for lickpenny though he was, Thomas Gage was neither callous nor malicious in his treatment of the Indians entrusted to his care. Although he pocketed their money whenever he could, it was obvious that he did his best to protect them and to look after their spiritual well-being. On behalf of the Indians, who formed most of his parish, he intervened against their Creole masters whenever there was cruelty or injustice. And during the worst ravages of the plague he courageously visited the houses of the sick, trusting only to a vinegar-soaked handkerchief held over his nose and mouth to protect him from the disease. He was equally indefatigable in his campaign against the last vestiges of the indigenous Indian animistic cults, which he sincerely believed did great harm. On one memorable Sunday, after a thunderous hell-fire sermon blasting all secret devil-worshippers, he triumphantly capped his performance by producing from under his pulpit rail a wooden idol which he had found hidden in a cave in the country-side. This "Dagon," as Gage proclaimed it, was thereupon smashed into pieces with an ax and in the presence of his congregation the fragments were hurled into pans of burning coal. So virulent an onslaught against traditional beliefs was bound to cause resentment among the superstitious villagers, and some weeks later Gage was waylaid and beaten up by a gang of foot-pads. Thenceforth he took the precaution of hiring his own bodyguard, an impressively pugnacious Negro named Michael Dalva who, Gage boasted, "alone was able to fight any half-dozen Indians."

Then, too, Gage himself saw no reason to be in the least ashamed of his financial chicanery. Rather, the English American recounted the outcome of his money-making stratagems with all the effervescent glee of a schoolboy proudly describing how he has repeatedly duped his teacher. There was nothing secretive about Gage's knavery. With scrupulous attention to tiny detail he explained the intricate workings of his embezzlements, and with innocent frankness he gloated over every coin tucked away in his secret hoard. Indeed, his facts and figures were so conscientious and so very precise that it was possible that one of his proud souvenirs brought back from the New World was a well-kept ledger, showing exactly how a nimble-witted parish priest in Spanish America could make a profit from his calling.

Of course, these telltale reminiscences also chimed with Gage's own propaganda theme, for when he came to write his memoirs of travels, he had no better way of illustrating the opulence and evils of the Catholic missionaries in the Americas than to produce examples from his own experience. The twist was that when the English American sought to impress his audience with damning tales of the pernicious priest of Mixco and Pinola, he was also telling the unpalatable truth about himself. So once again, with his buffoon's prerogative, Thomas Gage stumbled blithely into a trap of his own making, and few of his readers were to set much store by a man who in his ministry counted ducats rather than Christian souls.

After nearly seven years as a parish priest and with two transfers to other churches in the same area, Gage had finally saved almost nine thousand pieces-of-eight. It was a tidy sum and a tribute to his parsimony as well as sufficient to see him back to Europe. And as he still could not be sure that his Provincial would allow him to leave Guatemala, Thomas Gage began to lay his plans for the next departure in that succession of surreptitious leave-takings at which he was becoming so adept. Item by item he quietly sold most of his personal belongings—the books, furniture, pictures, and other household equipment he had accumulated during his time in Guatemala. Taking care that his preparations were not remarked, he converted most of his capital into pearls or other precious stones which could be conveniently carried and easily sold when the need arose. Moreover, like another Marco Polo, he ensured his escape by sewing part of his stock of jewels and coin into the padding of a traveling quilt which was the standard item of equipment for travelers in Central America. Then, not daring to trust any of his own parishioners to keep his secret, he summoned an Indian muleteer from the neighboring province and paid the man to set out in advance with a pair of mules laden with Gage's loot from the New World—two leather chests filled with clothes and books, several pictures of worked brass, the well-lined traveling quilt, a quantity of conserves to eat on the road, and, of course, the indispensable chocolate-making kit. Four days later, at midnight, Gage stole quietly out of his house, now empty of everything except a bundle of old papers. Leaving the key in the door so as to allay suspicions about his absence, he bade "adieu," as he put it, "to all my friends throughout America."

Two incidents during this departure from Guatemala showed that Gage was by no means the complete blackguard of repute. In the first place his Negro bodyguard refused to allow Gage to travel unescorted. Gage tried hard to persuade Michael Dalva that he should stay behind, but the "Blackamoor" had become so devoted to his master that he insisted on accompanying Gage until he was safely out of Guatemala. Second, Gage's sense of propriety and his gratitude to the Dominicans of Guatemala who had given him refuge induced him to compose a farewell letter of apology to the Provincial. In this letter Gage asked the Provincial not to blame him too harshly for running away again. He explained that he had made up his mind long ago to return to Europe and had written direct to Rome for permission to leave America. Furthermore, he wrote, he was confident that the Dominican mission in Guatemala would not suffer by his departure, for they would have little difficulty in filling his vacant parish with one of their many dialect-speaking missionaries. Typically, the English American could not refrain from one last touch of guile: He gave the letter to a friend of Dalva's to be delivered to the Provincial four days after he, Gage, had left Guatemala. Gage also dated his letter incorrectly so as to show that he had left several days later (thereby giving himself a head

start), and he confused his trail still further by pretending that he
was writing from a town on the road to Mexico. In point of fact
he had resolved to flee in quite the contrary direction, southeast
along the spine of the Central American isthmus to the province
of Nicaragua. There Gage hoped to buy passage aboard ship for
Europe and home. So began the penultimate phase of the English
American's wanderings in the New World. It was a voyage
which was enlivened, according to the editor of his *Travels,* by
"divers occurents and dangers that did befal in the said journey."

All went smoothly enough at first. Gage and Dalva set such a
smart pace that by the end of the first day they had covered sixty
miles and were well clear of the region where the priest was a
familiar figure. Soon afterward the two travelers overtook the
baggage mules which Gage had sent on ahead, and the ex-parish
priest was greatly relieved to discover that his precious belongings were all intact. Then, pushing on by forced marches, they
succeeded in crossing into Nicaragua before there was any hint
of a pursuit. At that point, however, Gage met with an unforeseen crisis. He had planned to go to the Caribbean coast aboard
the Nicaragua flotilla, a bevy of river craft which annually took
the province's output of cochineal, indigo, hides, and silver down
to the sea via Lake Nicaragua and the Rio San Juan. But that
year there were rumors that a squadron of Dutch and English
privateers had occupied the mouth of the river and were lying in
wait for the flotilla. This report had thrown Nicaragua into
panic; and at the last moment the governor canceled the sailing of
the flotilla until the situation was safer. Gage, who had already
contracted for his passage and gone so far as to lay in an extra
supply of chocolate for the voyage, was left stranded. Clearly he
could not linger in Nicaragua, as he was far too close to Guatemala for comfort and there was a very real risk that he would be
recognized by someone who had known him in Mixco or Guatemala City. He had already had one bad fright when a Guatemalan
mule train had arrived unexpectedly in town, and he was obliged
to duck for cover into his lodging house and stay there day and
night until the Guatemalan muleteers left for home. This scare
was enough to make him decide that he should put as much
distance as possible between himself and his old haunts. So,

sending Dalva back with a special bonus for his loyalty, Thomas Gage joined forces with three Spaniards, who had also been stranded by the cancellation of the Nicaraguan flotilla, and to-gether they set off on muleback for Costa Rica farther along the isthmus. There they hoped to find a small coasting craft bound for Portobelo, the most easterly port of call of the Indies fleet.

The journey to Costa Rica was a routine affair, very similar to Gage's earlier travels on the road from Mexico, and he had little of interest to record in his journal except for an untoward adventure with a cayman, or crocodile. The creature was sunning itself on the mule path when the four travelers rode up, and Gage and his companions, mistaking the crocodile for a fallen log, were casually riding past when ". . . on a sudden we knew the scales of the cayman and saw the monster move, and set himself against us. We made haste from him, but he, thinking to have made some of us his greedy prey, ran after us, and when we perceived that he was like to overtake us, we were much troubled." To save themselves, said Gage, the terrified travelers urged their mules into running a zig-zag course, and this maneuver soon left the lumbering crocodile far behind, for "though his straightforward flight was as swift as mules could run, . . . as the elephant, once laid down, is troubled to get up, so this monster is heavy and stiff and therefore much troubled to turn and wind about his body." It was one of Gage's few lapses into a traveler's tale.

Arriving at the Costa Rican seaboard, Gage and his com-panions made inquiries at the fishing villages until they found the captain of a small coaster who was willing to ferry them south-ward to Portobelo. It was a stroke of luck, and Gage was still congratulating himself on the apparently successful outcome of his alternative plan, when the coaster put to sea and immediately fell foul of two Dutch privateering ships. These two marauders had been hovering off the coast for just such prey, and in a trice they swooped down on the little coaster which, even to Gage's landlubber eye, was far too slow to outsail them. Sensibly, too, the Spanish captain had not the slightest intention of putting up a fight. He had only four or five muskets and a half-dozen swords on board with which to face the privateers's cannon, and his paltry cargo of bacon, hides, honey, chickens, and cornmeal was scarcely worth defense. Gage, on the other hand, was thunder-struck. With the peculiar sense of injustice of one rascal about to be fleeced by another, he saw that his hard-won spoils, scrimped together during seven years of niggardliness, would be whisked away in as many minutes of piracy. To add sting to his mortification, he also realized that he was the only passenger aboard the coaster who had so much at stake. His three Spanish companions possessed no more than a few hundred pieces-of-eight between them; while he, officially a priest with neither use nor love for money, stood in jeopardy to the amount of eight thousand in pearls, jewels, and specie.

Gage's robber, as matters turned out, was something of a celebrity, for the two Dutch privateer ships were under the command of the almost legendary figure of Diego el Mulato. Half Negro and half Spanish, El Mulato was a picturesque ruffian and virtually the prototype for the popular idea of a Caribbean buccaneer. He had been born and brought up a slave in Havana, where the Spaniards had badly mistreated him. After one particularly brutal flogging, El Mulato had turned against his former masters and, swearing to be revenged on them, he had put to sea in a tiny boat hoping to reach a Dutch privateer lying offshore. The success of this feat so impressed the Dutch seamen that he was taken on as a member of their crew, and in a very short time El Mulato had proved himself to be a man of exceptional abilities, both as a seaman and as a fighter. The Dutch authorities, appreciating such talents, eventually promoted him to command of his own ship, and it was even reported that he married a Dutch girl. At all times, however, El Mulato's driving passion remained his feud against the Spaniards, and as soon as he commanded his own vessel he pursued this vendetta with an unswerving singlemindedness that soon won him a near-fabulous reputation. In 1633, four years before he met Gage, he had capped his career with the sack of Campeche. For this feat he and the even more notorious captain, Pie de Palo, the original Peg Leg, had brought together ten privateering ships. It was a combined operation which presaged the heyday of Caribbean piracy when the "Brethren of the Coast" would unite to terrorize the Antilles.

When Thomas Gage encountered him, Diego el Mulato was

conducting his day-to-day trade of harassing Spanish colonial shipping wherever he could find it. Almost certainly he had broken away from the privateer squadron that was blockading the mouth of the Rio San Juan, and now, making the best of an abortive venture, he was cruising the Costa Rican coast, picking off any stray vessel that was so foolhardy as to venture out of port. Gage's coaster was an unexpected plum, for the English American's stock of valuables was an unusually large sum to be carried aboard such a mean ship. In addition, the coaster's humdrum cargo was a good opportunity for the raider to revictual his own vessels. So for twenty-four hours the hapless coaster was lashed alongside her captors and stripped of her lading. The privateersmen, said Gage, even took away the cattle hides in her hold, carrying them off against the day when they would need to make themselves new boots and shoes. Of course Gage's cache of valuables was among the first loot to go, and the dismayed traveler looked on helplessly while he was robbed of all his money except for the thousand pieces-of-eight hidden in his quilt and sewn into his doublet. In the event, Gage nearly lost his precious quilt as well, for the Dutch sailors had taken it away from him, when he appealed directly to Diego el Mulato and begged that a poor priest should at least be allowed to keep his bedding. Gallantly, the privateer captain ordered his men to return the priest's quilt, spare clothes, and books.

When the transfer of cargo was complete, El Mulato invited his prisoners to dine with him aboard his boat, and was vastly amused at the idea of serving the Spaniards with their own bacon and fowls. Gage, determined to salvage something from the disaster, bided his time until he had the chance to take the privateer captain on one side, and confided to him that he was an Englishman who was running away from the Spanish colonies and trying to return to his native country. Under the circumstances, Gage suggested, and since Holland and England were at peace with one another, it would be only fair if the privateersmen returned his missing seven thousand pieces-of-eight, or, at the very least, allowed him to stay aboard their vessel so that he could sail back to Europe with them. To his chagrin, his proposition fell flat. Diego el Mulato found the renegade priest's story too farfetched to be true and, as he told Gage, he did not want to have someone on board who would be a deadly informer if the Dutch ship were captured by Spanish patrol vessels.

Thus, gloomily, ended Gage's experiences at the hands of the Caribbean privateersmen, a flamboyant group whose well-publicized activities would soon add their own luster to the myth of the Golden Antilles. With the sarcastic thanks of the Dutch seamen ringing in their ears, the coaster's crew and passenger returned to their own ship; the privateersmen cast off and sailed away; and the little Spanish ship crept back to exactly the same port which Gage had left so jauntily two days earlier.

Back in Costa Rica, the English American and his three Spanish traveling companions found themselves worse off than before. Near-destitute, they had no hope of finding another ship to Portobelo, because the presence of Diego el Mulato off the coast had brought all coastal shipping to a standstill. But Gage was not yet defeated; it was one of his more attractive traits that he could rebound in the face of overwhelming adversity. With his customary resilience, he cast around for a stratagem which would not only recoup some of his lost fortune, but also return him to Europe in the process. Taking his companions into his confidence—although without telling them of the thousand pieces-of-eight he still had hidden in his baggage—he proposed that the four of them should retrace their steps across the isthmus and travel on to the Pacific shore. There they would try to pick up another coaster sailing south to Panama. From Panama City they could then travel by mule across the narrow neck of the isthmus to Portobelo on the Caribbean and make their hoped-for rendezvous with the Plate Fleet. To finance this trek, Gage pointed out, the travelers could turn their recent misadventure to good use if they agreed to act in unison and spread such a tale of hardship and woe that they became a public charity and everyone along their path gave them alms to help them on their way.

As with Gage's earlier money-making schemes, his new financial stratagem worked admirably, and neither he nor his companions suffered from lack of funds as they journeyed to the Pacific coast. Most of the credit for this success went to Gage himself, for it was on his insistence that the party spent all religious holidays staying in towns where he could help the local priest with his duties and dip for his share into the church offering.

Thus, living by his wits, the English American found his way to the Pacific coast and took passage aboard the first ship bound for Panama. But his troubles were far from over, for his latest maneuvers had landed him into even more perplexing difficulties. Scarcely out of port, his new ship ran into a severe gale which blew her far to the south of Panama. Then the wind died away and the coaster was left becalmed for a week, until a second gale came, this time from the opposite direction, and swept her north again. Just as her captain was hoping to swerve aside into Panama, the wind dropped once again, and the ship was caught in an adverse current that began to push her south once more. By this time, wrote Gage, all the provisions and water supplies on board had been consumed, and he and several others were driven to drinking their own urine and sucking on bullets to relieve their thirst. Finally the situation became so bad that the crew mutinied and threatened to kill the captain if he did not put into the nearest land. For a few minutes the captain ignored their demands, but when faced with the drawn swords of his crew, he agreed to alter course, and made for a group of small islands nearby.

Gage managed to find a place with the watering party which rowed off in the ship's cockboat to look for a spring on the nearest island. But on going ashore, he somehow became separated from his companions, who, failing to find water on the island, rowed off in the cockboat without him. The sailors were merely going off to search the next island, but Gage was convinced that he was marooned and immediately fell into a panic that he would never see home again. In a fever of anxiety he dashed wildly about his little island, hallooed uselessly to the departing cockboat, ran to the beach, and jumped up and down, frantically waving his arms to attract the attention of the men aboard the coaster. But he utterly failed to produce any reaction and, having exhausted himself completely, curled up on the ground and fell asleep. He was still asleep when the cockboat returned to pick him up and found their supercargo half-delirious

The gilding of El Dorado. Attendants puff gold dust on his body through a tube while his lords carouse in their hammocks. From Pieter van de Aa: *De Aanmerkenswaardigste Zee-en Landreizen* (1727).

BELOW   The city of El Dorado situated on imaginary Lake Parima.
At top left a party of travelers portage their boats to the lake from the
headwaters of the (real) River Essequibo, a theoretical approach
much favored by the early explorers. From Hulsius: *Travels* (1599).

OPPOSITE ABOVE   An Indian bacchanalia, showing their supposedly happy and
carefree life in the demi-paradise of the Antilles. From de Bry: *America*.

OPPOSITE BELOW   Indians of the Golden Antilles bring their produce to
market. From de Bry: *America*.

Ralegh and his soldiers invade Trinidad and burn St. Joseph to the ground. From Pieter van de Aa: *De Aanmerkenswaardigste Zee-en Landreizen* (1727).

OPPOSITE ABOVE   Spaniards languidly survey the mining and refining of gold by their slaves. From de Bry: *America*.

ABOVE   The cutting, pressing, and boiling of cane to make sugar—source of immense West Indian fortunes. From de Bry: *America*.

LEFT   A boatload of English soldiers discovers the inhabitants of an Antillean island singing, dancing, and feasting. Center, a naked swimmer coyly runs for cover. From Pieter van de Aa: *De Aanmerkenswaardigste Zee-en Landreizen* (1727).

ABOVE The Tivitiva tribe living in the tops of trees during the floods of the Orinoco, from Walter Ralegh's description. Hulsius: *Travels* (1599).

BELOW A "crocodile" devours a member of Ralegh's expedition as it advances up the Orinoco in search of El Dorado. The artist, never having seen a crocodile, has relied on the standard concept of a voracious sea serpent. From Hulsius: *Travels* (1599).

ABOVE   Sir Walter Ralegh greeted by Orinoco "naturals" bearing gifts. From
Pieter van de Aa: *De Aanmerkenswaardigste Zee-en Landreizen* (1727).

BELOW   The Indians of gold-rich Guiana molding figurines from molten
ores. From Hulsius: *Travels* (1599).

ABOVE Love feast of the Amazons; held once a year with men from neighboring tribes in order to beget children. From Hulsius: *Travels* (1599).

BELOW Punishment meted out by the Amazon women to males who trespassed on their territory. From Hulsius: *Travels* (1599).

ABOVE Men "with heads beneath their shoulders" who, it was rumored, lived in the fastness of the upper Orinoco. From Hulsius: *Travels* (1599).

BELOW The wondrous animals of Guiana. From Hulsius: *Travels* (1599).

Simi Vulpa.   *Haute.*   *Armadilio.*

Nieuwe en seer Nauwkeurige
Reise
door de Spaensche Westindien
van
THOMAS GAGE
met verschei'de Curieuse plaeten
Voorsien overgeset door
H.V.Q.

ABOVE Thomas Gage, dressed in Dominican habit, preaches in the New World to adoring natives. The frontispiece to the 1682 Utrecht edition of his *Travels*.

OPPOSITE ABOVE A shore party from the Spanish fleet is ambushed on Guadeloupe by Caribs. From Gage: *Travels* (1699 Amsterdam edition).

OPPOSITE BELOW Traveling in Central America in the seventeenth century— mountain roads and an Indian church. From Gage: *Travels* (1682 Utrecht edition).

Surprise des INDIENS, de la Guardeloupe.

Onnoselheyt der Indianen.

A plague of locusts darkens the sky as native farmers (mid-distance) blow trumpets and flail with sticks to frighten away the insects. From Gage: *Travels* (1682 Utrecht edition).

LEFT A richly dressed and portly traveler in the West Indies. The frontispiece to a French translation of Gage's *Travels*.

BELOW The great market at Porto Bello when the Plate Fleet was in. From Gage: *Travels* (1699 Amsterdam edition).

ABOVE Privateers raiding a coastal town. From de Bry: *America*.

BELOW Rioting in Mexico City. Thomas Gage claimed that the dissatisfied colonials of Central America would rise against their fainthearted and debauched Spanish administration. From Gage: *Travels* (1699 Amsterdam edition).

OPPOSITE Colonial Havana in Thomas Gage's time. The city's full name was "La Siempe Fidelissima Ciudad de San Cristobal de la Habana." From Gage: *Travels* (1699 Amsterdam edition).

Bounteous nature pouring out her riches on the Golden Antilles.
From Esquemeling: *The History of the Bucaniers* (1684).

ABOVE The pirate leader Francis Lolonais against a background of his achievements. From Esquemeling: *The History of the Bucaniers* (1684).

BELOW Seventeenth-century sensationalism: the pirate Lolonais tears the beating heart out of an uncooperative prisoner and forces his companion to eat it. From Esquemeling: *The History of the Bucaniers* (1684).

LEFT One of the most renowned pirate captains, Bartholomew Portugues, said to have escaped from a Spanish ship by swimming ashore using two empty wine jars as floats. He then returned with reinforcements, boarded the ship in a surprise attack, and cut her out from under the Spanish shore batteries. From Esquemeling: *The History of the Bucaniers* (1684).

RIGHT Sir Henry Morgan, later to sue Esquemeling's publisher for describing him as a pirate. Morgan died, according to his doctor, from a surfeit of good living. From Esquemeling: *The History of the Bucaniers* (1684).

Henry Morgan's men sack a Spanish town. From Esquemeling: *The History of the Bucaniers* (1684).

As a surgeon Wafer was fascinated by the native method of letting blood by shooting small arrows into the patient's flesh. From Wafer: *Voyage and the Description of the Isthmus of America* (1699).

ABOVE An Indian hammock and the Indian method of smoking tobacco.
A child blows smoke into the face of the smoker, who inhales the cloud. From
Wafer: *Voyage and Description of the Isthmus of America* (1699).

BELOW "Indians marching upon a Visit, or to a Feast," led by Wafer's
friend, Chief Lacenta. From Wafer: *Description of the Cuna* (1699).

The Indians marching upon a Visit, or to a Feast. P. 140.

Lacenta.   his Lady.   Attendants.

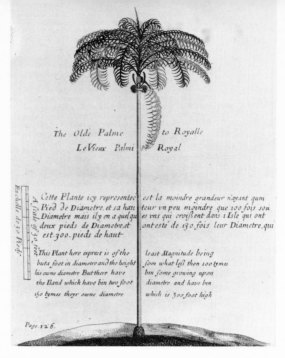

The Olde Palme   to Royalle
Le Vieux Palmi   Royal

Cette Plante icy representee est la moindre grandeur n'ayant qu'un
Pied de Diametre, et sa hau teur vn peu moindre que 100 fois son
Diametre mais il y en a quelqu es vns qui croißent dans 1 Isle qui ont
deux pieds de Diametre, et onteste de 130 fois leur Diametre, qui
est 300 pieds de haut

This Plant here exprest is of the least Magnitude being
buta foot in diametre and the height som what leß then 100 tymes
his owne diametre But ther have bin some growing upon
the Iland which have bin two foot diametre and have bin
150 tymes theyr owne diametre which is 300 foot high

Page. 126.

ABOVE The royal palm, credited in this seventeenth-century description with a height of three hundred feet. From *Recueil de Divers Voyages faits en Afrique et en l'Amérique* (1674).

BELOW LEFT The pineapple--Ralegh's "princess of fruit" and to many European travelers the epitome of succulent nature in the West Indies. From *Recueil de Divers Voyages faits en Afrique et en l'Amérique* (1674).

BELOW RIGHT The banana plant, one of the fecund marvels of the Antilles. From a seventeenth-century description of the West Indies.

Reyne ou l'Ananas
The Queene Pine

The Plantine
Le Bananas   de Fleurs

from a combination of heat-stroke and plain fright. Gage was in such a poor state that he had to be picked up and carried unceremoniously to the cockboat and ferried out to the coaster. There he was placed like a sack of potatoes in a cabin, while the captain again tried valiantly to make Panama. But Gage did not stay below decks for long. The wind and current continued to be against the little coaster, and in his frustration her captain tried to take an inshore channel and nearly split his ship into matchwood when he ran her onto the rocks. The shuddering shock of the ship striking, the cries of terror from the deck, and the shrill prayers of the helmsman performed restorative prodigies on the invalid cooped up below. The following morning Gage struggled up on deck, grimly determined to be better placed for jumping overboard if the vessel foundered with her next mishap. To his relief such drastic action was not necessary, for with her fourth attempt to enter Panama, the coaster made harbor, working her way in with the help of an anchor borrowed from another vessel, as she had managed to lose her own earlier in the voyage. With that landfall, Gage bluntly noted, "I made no stay in that frigate, which I thought would have been my last abiding place in the world."

Nor did the English American linger in Panama. The place had an unwholesome reputation as a pest-hole, and he hoped to reach Portobelo before the Plate Fleet sailed. To reach Portobelo he had the choice of either going by mule train all the way across the mountains or traveling by mule only as far as the watershed and then floating down the Rio Chagres on one of the cane rafts which descended that river to the Caribbean. Gage chose the river route and had a memorable ride as the ungainly river craft were coaxed, pushed, poled, and cursed along by crews of highly professional Negro and mulatto raftsmen. Usually the water level in the Chagres was so low that relays of mules worked the portages around the shallow sections of the river, but on this occasion heavy rains had swollen the river so high that his raft shot downriver "with the swiftness of an arrow."

At Portobelo, however, Gage began to regret that he had made such a fast passage, for he found that he had arrived there several days ahead of the Plate Fleet. Normally Gage would have put any such delay to excellent use, preaching a few sermons, helping out the local priest for a small fee, picking up a ducat here or a crown there, and generally replenishing the purse that had been so badly depleted by Diego el Mulato and his companions. But to his annoyance, Gage discovered that Portobelo in the weeks before the Fleet arrived was a catastrophically expensive place to live. During eleven months of the year the visitor could find board and lodging for next to nothing; but when the Fleet was about to come in, landlords and tavern-keepers made up for their lean months with tariffs of astronomical proportions. Travelers came there from the Philippines, from Peru and other parts of South America, from Central America and several of the Antilles islands. Most of them were seeking a passage to Europe, some waiting to greet incoming dignitaries or immigrants, and a few were there because they wanted first option on the manufactures brought in by the fleet. To compound the confusion, the fleet itself disgorged a similar horde of travelers, who were headed in the opposite direction, together with an escort of four or five thousand regular troops whose duty was to protect the immensely rich cargo being carried back to Spain. This influx of transients overwhelmed Portobelo's inns and lodging houses like a host of passenger pigeons squabbling for space in a small wood. Men took up residence in warehouses, in stables, in the street, or in barrooms. The lucky few who found rooms, even though shared with several other inmates, did so only by paying the most exorbitant prices, sometimes as much as six months' wages for the two-week rent.

The town was thronged with returning colonists flush with the profits of years in the colonies. They spent lavishly, and were convinced that they were having a roaring good time. Portobelo under these conditions was more like a gold-rush town than a seaport. From the farthest outposts of Spain's empire, the "royal fifth" of gold, silver, precious gems, and fine curios trickled in toward Portobelo—only Mexico's was excluded, because her exports went through San Juan de Ulloa. As the rivulets converged on the isthmus, they coalesced into streams of wealth, and then into a rolling flood of opulence, as merchants and planters took advantage of the protection afforded by the heavily escorted convoy to add their own contribution of commodities and produce. According to Gage's eyewitness account, one could see wedges of silver casually stacked in heaps on the wharves of Portobelo, waiting to be stowed in the holds of the fleet, while merchants sold "their commodities, not by the ell or the yard, but by the piece and weight, not paying in coined pieces of money, but in wedges [of silver] which were weighed and taken for commodities. This lasted but fifteen days, while the galleons were lading with wedges of silver and nothing else." It was a distillation of the very essence of the Golden Antilles.

Naturally Gage, with his pitifully few pieces-of-eight, was hopelessly outclassed in this outpouring of wealth. He was shriveled with envy, but, more than that, he was furious that he had to spend his meager funds simply to rent what he called a "miserable mousehole" of a room, "no bigger than would contain a bed, a table, and a stool or two, with room enough besides to open and shut the door." Fulminating at his misfortune, he retired to his room in a huff and consoled himself that he would soon be away, for the fleet never stayed long in Portobelo, which, like Panama, was notoriously unhealthy. Gloomily gnawing dried fish and tortoise flesh, he stubbornly refused to buy chickens, which had soared in price from one real to twelve reals each, while beef, which was commonly half a real for thirteen pounds, now cost two reals a pound.

But his chief concern, apart from saving money, was to search out a ship to take him safely back to Spain, and he diligently made inquiries for a berth aboard one of the large and powerful warships. The English American had had his fill of privateers, and he was not ashamed to admit that his ideal vessel was "a galleon, well manned and fortified with soldiers and guns of brass." But the cost of his fare aboard one of these floating castles was the staggering figure of three hundred crowns, and in the end Gage's unquenchable parsimony won out over his sense of self-preservation. He swallowed his caution and contracted to work his passage home as ship's chaplain aboard the merchantman *San Sebastian*. This ship proved to be a fortunate choice because, as Gage noted with obvious if uncharitable relief after a few days at sea, "the ship I was in was swift and nimble under sail, and kept under the wings either of the Admiral or of some of the best galleons, but all the other merchant ships were not so, for some came slowly on behind, and of them, two were carried away by the Hollanders in the night."

Thus, sailing back to Europe with the convoy, Gage witnessed the celebrated homeward trip of the ladened Plate Fleet, the corollary to his outward passage twelve years before. From Portobelo the fleet first went to Cartagena, where eight or ten days were spent taking on additional cargo and passengers, including by coincidence a group of captured English privateersmen who were being shipped back to Spain. There was also a rumor that the Dutch had a fleet of sixty sail waiting to pounce; but on investigation this scare turned out to be a mischievous invention of certain merchants of Cartagena who hoped to keep the fleet bottled up while they took commercial advantage of the delay. Once the truth had been discovered, the fleet moved sedately northward across the Caribbean to Cuba, where at Havana it expected to rendezvous with the squadron of galleons and merchantmen that was to come from San Juan de Ulloa with Mexico's tribute and merchandise.

The Mexican squadron had not yet arrived when the Portobelo fleet reached Havana, and for a week Thomas Gage had nothing to do but wander about the city, seeing the sights. He inspected the defenses of the harbor with its famous twelve-gun battery nicknamed the Twelve Apostles,* and he also took the opportunity to call on Diego el Mulato's mother, who still lived in the town where her son had been brought up. Then eight days later, when the Mexican squadron had still not put in an appearance, he went back aboard the *San Sebastian*, as the Admiral of the Fleet had decided that he could delay no longer and was determined to put to sea. On a Sunday morning the twenty-seven ships of the convoy cleared Havana and began to move at a leisurely pace toward the Bahama channel.

The same night, however, the fleet heard the sounds of other vessels, and caught glimpses of strange ships maneuvering about them in the darkness. Wild reports of a Dutch fleet blazed up,

---

* *Gage was shrewd enough to note that the place was vulnerable to a landward assault since most of the ordnance pointed out to sea.*

and there was much frenzied activity as the Spaniards cleared for action. Even Gage was hard worked, busily hearing confessions all night from frightened sailors who were sure they would be killed in the coming engagement. Their confessor, on the other hand, took some comfort from the fact that the *San Sebastian* had been detailed off to shelter under the broadsides of the admiral's galleon. To make doubly sure of his safety, he also prepared himself a bolt hole behind a pile of barrels in the ship's hold. But with daylight next morning the Spaniards, match in hand, found themselves peering over shotted cannon, not at the Dutch, but at their own Mexican squadron, which had spent an equally unhappy night, running out their guns, filling fire buckets, and generally preparing for a battle-royal the next morning. "Then," wrote Gage with a flourish that betrayed his vast relief, "the martial colours began to be taken down; the joyful sound of trumpets with the help of Neptune's kingdoms echoed from ship to ship, and the boats carried welcoming messages from one to another. The Spanish *'brindis'* with *'Buen viaje,'* *'Buen pasaje,'* was generally cried out, and the whole morning was spent in friendly acclamations and salutations from ship to ship."

Amid this froth of congratulation and camaraderie, the Spaniards failed to observe that two strange vessels had mingled with the combined fleet and were quietly working their way to windward. By the time their presence was finally noticed, it was too late. Even as the Spanish admiral was hoisting signals, calling upon the two ships to identify themselves, the two strangers suddenly wheeled about and, running alongside a straggling merchantman loaded with sugar and other goods valued at eighty thousand crowns, they raked her point blank with their broadsides. All but two of the merchantman's guns were knocked out of action, and within half an hour the privateersmen had boarded her, overwhelmed the crew, and coolly cut their prize out of the fleet while the Spanish warships were still trying to claw up into range. Then, said Gage, "the Spaniards changed their merry tunes into *Voto a Dios* and *Voto a Cristo;* in raging, cursing, and swearing, some reviling the captain of the ship which was taken, and saying that he was false and yielded on purpose without fighting. . . . others cursing those that took her, and calling them *hijos de puta, borrachos, infames ladrones,* bastards, drunkards, infamous thieves and pirates. Some took their swords in their hands as if they would cut them in pieces, some lay hold of their muskets as if they would shoot at them, others stamped like madmen and ran about the ship as if they would leap overboard, and make haste after them."

But the fleet could neither turn back to rescue their comrade, nor detach a warship to chase the impudent raiders. The precious convoy had to press forward at all costs, for the Spaniards knew from bitter experience that if they faltered, other privateers would arrive on the scene like sharks scenting blood and maul the fleet to shreds. The galleons lumbered on, wheeling away in panic a few nights later when their pilots almost ran the entire convoy headlong on to the rocks and shoals of the Bahamas. Only a last-minute change of course saved them, and as they sheered away from the terrifying sight and sound of water breaking over the reefs, the pilots muttered prayers for help and swore that the islands were inhabited by wreckers and sorcerers who created fogs and blackness to lure ships to their doom.

In Gage's opinion, however, it was the incompetence of the Spanish seamen, rather than any black magic, which threatened the passage of the Plate Fleet. The only bad storm of the entire voyage sent one merchantman to the bottom and badly strained the rigging and mainmasts of two of the galleons. And then, when land was sighted to cries of *"España! España!"* and many of the passengers had celebrated by slaughtering the last livestock and preparing a feast from their food hoards, the pilots confessed that they had miscalculated their position and the land was not Spain at all, but Madeira. The fleet still had another seven hundred miles to sail. Twelve days later, when Cádiz's outport, Sanlúcar de Barrameda, actually came in sight, Gage noted thankfully that the ships were to be guided into harbor by Sanlúcar's own pilots and not by the Indies navigators.

The English American stayed only long enough in Sanlúcar to purchase a suit of civilian clothes to replace the black-and-white Dominican habit, and then slipped quietly aboard a Dutch ship bound for England. At Dover the customs officials mistook him for a Spaniard born and bred, for he could remember only a few broken scraps of English and spoke his mother tongue with a thick and stumbling accent. His sister-in-law, whom he immediately went to see in London, teased him that he sounded more like an Indian or a Welshman than an Englishman. But Gage was overwhelmingly thankful to be home. It was almost twenty-three years since he had left England as a schoolboy to go to school in Flanders, and he had come back a deserter and almost penniless. But he was also proud of his wanderings and adventures. As the final sentence of his *Travels* put it: "Thus, my good reader, thou seest an American, through many dangers by sea and land, now safely arrived in England."

9-

England's «Rubidg»

IF THOMAS GAGE THOUGHT THAT HE HAD SEEN THE LAST of the
Golden Antilles, he was wrong. A compulsive opportunist,
he was possessed of a restless energy that constantly goaded him
to try one scheme after another in the hope of furthering his own
career; and so it was inevitable that once back in England his
nagging ambition should seize upon his recent experience in
America as a convenient handhold in the climb toward success.
Thomas Gage was, as he well knew, a rarity of his time—an
Englishman who had seen for himself the Spanish empire of the
New World and had returned with a firsthand knowledge of
those legendary lands coveted by half the nations of Europe.
Among Spain's enemies, such a man was a rare treasure, a source
of intelligence to be nurtured with great care, and an expert
whose opinions would receive respectful attention. So it was in
this role of the "American expert" that Gage now cast himself.
To use his own unabashed phrase, he saw no reason why he
should "hide his light under a bushel."

But Gage had to proceed cautiously, for when he returned to
the land of his birth, the anti-Spanish policies of Cromwell's
Commonwealth were some years off. Charles Stuart ruled England, and the quarrel with Parliament still festered beneath the

surface. These were the cankerous years when King and Commons maneuvered for advantage, high and low churchmen thrashed out matters of religious dogma amid accusations of heresy and self-interest, and the lesser fry darted in frightened shoals between one menace and the next. In these troubled waters, Gage very wisely kept out of sight. He spent the first fifteen or eighteen months after his return with members of his family in Surrey who seem to have forgiven him his conversion to the Dominicans (his father had died some four years earlier, omitting Thomas from his will, just as he had threatened). Then he took a trip across to Ghent to visit his eldest brother, Sir Henry, who was at that time colonel of the English legion stationed in the Low Countries. Apparently this cross-channel jaunt reawakened Thomas' wanderlust, for he set off from Ghent on a grand tour of Europe, visiting Cologne, Frankfurt, and Milan before finally making his way to Rome. There he decided that he wanted to live in France, and obtained authorization from the General of his Order (who tactfully overlooked his flight from Guatemala) to transfer to the Dominican friary at Orléans. But by the end of the year (1640), he had thrown over that plan, too, and was back in England, ready to take the next side-step in his already erratic career: on August 28, 1642, in the Gothic church of St. Paul's (the pre-Wren building which was destroyed in the Great Fire of London), Thomas Gage preached a sermon in which he renounced the Roman Catholic religion and entered the Church of England. Six weeks later the first battle of the Civil War was fought at Edgehill.

It was unlikely that religious motives had much to do with Gage's conversion to the Church of England. Naturally the convert himself made great play with "matters of conscience," claiming that he had wrestled with religious doubts even as a young novitiate friar, but this pious posturing was too shallow and too secondhand to carry much weight. Even the text of his recantation had a slightly overblown air, for it was entitled *The Tyranny of Satan, Discovered by the teares of a Converted Sinner. . . ."* Certainly Thomas Gage, with his gourmet palate and his light-fingered ways in the church offering, had little in common with the harsh austerity of the extreme Protestants.

Nevertheless, as time went on and England's religious center of gravity shifted further and further toward the left, Thomas Gage played the religious chameleon until he eventually became a "Preacher of the Word" in the parish of Acrise in Kent.

It would be pleasant to record that with this easygoing apostasy Thomas Gage harmed no one, and merely changed his religious hue in order to avoid the molestations of zealots. But this was far from being the case. As usual he had failed to ponder the implications of the changes he made; and as usual he suffered the consequences. After his recantation he found that he was expected to show how excellent a turncoat he was by giving evidence against his erstwhile colleagues who were working illegally as priests in England. As a result, three Roman Catholic priests, one of them a former schoolfellow from St. Omer and another the chaplain to Sir Henry Gage, were convicted and executed on the basis of testimony given against them by Thomas Gage. Even by the harsh standards of the day it was a shabby business, and Gage's own family was so shocked that they offered the renegade a thousand pounds to leave the country. When this bribe failed, Colonel Gage went so far as to send men across the Channel on an unsuccessful mission to abduct, or (according to Thomas's wild claim) assassinate, his errant brother.

Ironically, this bloodthirsty malevolence was misdirected. Thomas Gage had apostatized, not from religious conviction or from any wish to harm his former co-religionists, but because he was a worldly man with very human ambitions, who should never have been a priest in the first place. He was too frail a vessel to contain the privileged knowledge that he had acquired in the Antilles; he was bursting with self-importance and the need to tell the world of his adventures. He knew that if he adhered to the Catholic cause, he would be expected to serve it best by remaining silent about what he had seen in the New World. As a Catholic priest his task would be to work in the shadows, without recognition, like so many other Jesuits and Dominicans who were English by birth and who labored tirelessly for English Catholicism. But selflessness of this brand was utterly alien to the English American. Every fiber in his character ran counter to the self-effacing obedience expected of him. From the time when as a young man he had rejected the Society of Jesus in order to join the Dominicans, he had consistently chosen the unusual and the unexpected. A born maverick and malcontent, when Gage thought he saw his chance to make a real mark in life, he plunged forward restlessly. Like Ralegh before him, he believed that he could acquire renown and high office by nudging England's destiny to a role in the Golden Antilles; and like Ralegh too, he pinned his hopes on the propaganda impact of a book. In 1648, therefore, Gage's magnum opus appeared under the informative, if slightly boastful title, *The English-American his Travail by Sea and Land . . . or* A NEW SURVEY *of the* WEST INDIES *containing a Journall of Three thousand and Three hundred miles within the main land of America.* The subtitle went on to lure readers with promises of the "true and painfull endevours" of the author; an account of "his strange and wonderful Converfion"; a brief grammar of the Indian tongue; and fascinating snippets concerning the "behaviour of Spaniards, Priests and Friers, Blackmores, Mulatto's, Meftifo's, Indians; and of their Feafts and Solemnities."

Gage's *Travels*, as his book may be more conveniently called, appeared in a parliamentarian England, shortly before the execution of Charles I and just when it was politic as well as fashionable to be anti-Catholic and anti-Spanish. Not only was its publication, therefore, shrewdly timed, but the *Travels* lived up to the puff on its title page. Its Protestant readers were thrilled and fascinated to learn of Mexican cities where wealthy merchants kept shoals of luscious mulatto mistresses, and where gay young friars strummed guitars and composed sonnets to their lady loves, who were, it was hinted, the not-so-shy occupants of neighboring nunneries. They read of mountain trails so narrow and treacherous that the traveler was obliged to crawl on hands and knees over the worst spots, and of convents whose high-born residents occupied special suites, which were sumptuously decorated and staffed by their less fortunate sisters. They learned of dissolute and unscrupulous priests who threw dice in the seclusion of their cloisters, fleeced their uncomplaining flocks in church, and sprinkled forty-year indulgences like fragrance from their censers. In Guatemala, according to the *Travels*, one notorious slaveowner was more beast than man. He shunned the company of the other colonists and kept to a little thatched encampment far in the countryside, where he could rule like a despot over more than a hundred slaves, and amuse himself with new ways of cruelty. His favorite entertainment, ran the tale, was to whip some unfortunate wretch until the blood spurted from his back and the flesh hung in ribbons. Then he would douse the man with boiling grease. Or he would stroke a white-hot branding iron against a slave's face, thighs, legs, body and arms, until the victim was a mass of livid weals and tried suicide as a relief from the torment. This same slavemaster, wrote Gage, refused to marry because he liked to sleep with the wives of his slaves so that he might fill his village "with bastards of all sorts and colours." When the supply of bedmates failed, he would take one of his rare trips into the nearest town and prowl the streets until a slave girl caught his fancy. This woman he would pur-chase at whatever price was asked, for he was a rich man, and would boast "that he would pull down her proud and haughty looks with one year's slavery under him." A less vicious and more imaginative voluptuary, by comparison, was a certain rich mer-chant of Mexico City whose remarkable hobby was to make a comprehensive tour of the city's brothels every night. At each bordello this conscientious libertine would carefully remove a bead from his rosary, so that, by morning, he had an exact memorandum of his prowess. Yet, as Gage pointed out, this painstaking record was not for the man's personal satisfaction: he kept the tally because he wanted to know precisely how much money he should donate to the church to atone for his sins of the previous night. This brazen reprobate, added Gage with covetous indignation, was entirely able to afford such lustful eccentricities because he was so wealthy that it was said he had one closet in his house laid with gold bars instead of bricks.

    Such tales were strong meat for Gage's Protestant readers. They were titillated by the delicious details; they enjoyed the author's sly digs against the Catholics (for example, Gage archly referred to friars of the Mercedarian Order as "Mercenarians"); and they were impressed by his frequent quotations and puns in Spanish. To them, Gage's *Travels* was a long-awaited exposé, written by a master of his subject, and they trusted this first and very racy account of Spanish Central America to be written in English by an Englishman. To pander to their tastes, the publishers of the *Travels* even provided them with a number of woodcuts to illustrate the fabulous wonders of America and show the English American surrounded by the strange and papist world he described.

Of course Gage's book was, first and foremost, arrant propaganda. He was not merely interested in scratching the curiosity of his readers; he was carefully dangling a succulent bait before their very susceptible appetites. According to his tale, Spanish America was a mouth-watering prize, weakly defended by a pack of poltroons. The Spanish colonists, he maintained, would never have the courage to resist a daring invader; at the first whiff of a cut-and-thrust engagement they would throw down their weapons and take to their heels. Their Creole population was of no consequence, for the Creoles were apathetic to Spanish rule. And as for the Indians and slaves, they would welcome the English in the role of liberators. This last point had a familar ring, for it echoed Ralegh's call for an alliance between the English and the Indians of the Orinoco. According to the *Travels*, the marauds of Pie de Palo, El Mulato, and the other pirates had already exposed the rottenness of Spain's position in the Antilles. Their civil government, he went on, was so cowardly that during a riot in Mexico City the mob had actually chased a craven viceroy into his palace. A hundred good English fighting men, Gage thundered, could pluck Chiapa from Spain's grasp. Over a score of other rich towns on the mainland had neither fortifications nor ordnance to defend themselves. And should the English time their invasion cunningly, they could carry off the assembled riches waiting to be collected by the Plate Fleet.

Gage's theme was remarkably similar to the arguments and promises of Ralegh's *Discovery*, though in his day Ralegh had scoffed at the notion that the Spaniards would be so stupid as to leave their American riches lying around on the wharves when an enemy force was in the area. Nevertheless, the *Travels*, like *The Discovery*, aimed at a deliberate overstatement of the case, with the English American seeking to win converts with his stridency rather than with any appeal to reason. Like Ralegh, too, Gage dedicated his book to a man of influence, in this case to Lord Fairfax, captain-general of the parliamentary army. Another leading parliamentarian (and future regicide), Thomas Chaloner, may also have had a hand in encouraging Gage to write his book—if the vainglorious priest needed any such prodding—and Chaloner contributed a scrap of doggerel for its introduction, including the ponderous lines:

> Your [Fairfax's] well-built ships, companions of the Sun,
> As they were chariots to his fiery beams,
> Which oft the Earth's circumference have run,
> And now lie moor'd in Severn, Trent and Thames,
> Shall plough the Ocean with their gilded stems,
> And in their hollow bottoms you convey,
> To lands enriched with gold, with pearls and gems,
> But above all where many thousands stay
> Of wronged Indians, whom you shall set free
> From Spanish yoke and Rome's idolatry. . . .

It was a strangely apt prologue to Gage's weird potpourri of wishful thinking and personal reminiscences, geography and history (some of it plagiarized from Spanish writers), scandal and propaganda. More prosaically, the publication of the book showed that Thomas Gage, Chaloner, and the growing anti-Spanish faction felt that the moment had again come for England to enlarge her place in the Golden Antilles.

Since the days of Ralegh, England had been able to snap up only a few crumbs from Spain's rich West Indian table—Barbados, Nevis, and St. Christopher (now St. Kitts), small islands which the lordly Spaniards found scarcely worth bothering about. Nevis, for example, was less than thirty-six square miles, a flyspeck alongside Barbados, which was in turn slightly larger than the Isle of Wight. In the opinion of many of Gage's contemporaries after they had read his book, these island fragments of the Antilles were little more than appetizers heralding the larger meal yet to come.

Six years after it was published the Travels helped to produce the desired effect. By that time King Charles had gone to his death on the scaffold; the Commonwealth was in existence; and

Lord Protector Cromwell, having peace at home, was able to turn his considerable energies to new ambitions overseas.

Cromwell was much attracted by the idea of a powerful military invasion of the Antilles. He hoped that it would not only strike a blow for the Protestant cause but also, and more germane to his immediate needs, bring some badly needed money into the depleted English exchequer. In 1654, therefore, at the conclusion of the Dutch war and with 160 fighting ships lying idle in his navy, Cromwell decided to act. That summer the Spanish ambassador was summoned to his presence and informed that future good relations between England and Spain would depend upon all Englishmen being given the right to trade and to practice their religion freely in Spanish America. As Cromwell well knew, such capitulations were utterly repugnant to his Catholic Majesty, and indeed it was reported that the Spanish ambassador was so surprised that he blurted out "that to ask for these concessions was to demand of his Master his two eyes." Nevertheless, the excuse for hostilities had been established, and Cromwell did not delay long before initiating an invasion of the Caribbean. This "Western Design," as it came to be called, aimed at no less than the seizure of Spain's possessions in the Golden Antilles. Logically enough, one of the experts called in to advise the Protector and his council was Thomas Gage, author.

Gage was delighted. At last he had achieved the recognition he craved, so now he jumped at the chance to prove his worth. As quickly as he could, he drew up a memorandum of advice, and posted it off to London where a copy was eventually to come to rest among the files of John Thurloe, Cromwell's influential and talented head of intelligence. In essence, Gage's memorandum was a repetition of the arguments already used in the *Travels*: he stressed the weakness of Spain's hold over her colonies, the extent of the Spaniard's military unpreparedness, and the possibility of invaders linking up with Indian and ex-slave guerrilla forces. Understandably too, since it was the area he knew best, he recommended Guatemala or Honduras as the most vulnerable target for an English attack. But Cromwell, eager though he was to thrust into the heart of Spain's American territories, was too canny to risk his forces in a land war at the most distant end of the Caribbean. He grasped the strategic fact that it was better tactics to begin his attack in the east, where the powerful English fleet would be used to the best advantage. There, he hoped, he would first overwhelm a small and isolated island, and then use it as a base from which to roll up the Spanish colonies farther west.

Gage's plan was not the only one to be considered by the English council, for they heard another scheme, put forward by Thomas Modyford, a planter and lawyer from Barbados, who advocated what was really a revival of Ralegh's old dream for the empire of Manoa. Modyford suggested that Cromwell should send an expedition to seize Trinidad and the lower Orinoco, because they lay to the windward of the other Spanish colonies and it would be extremely difficult for the Spaniards to send a relieving force from inside the Caribbean. Modyford argued that by the time the Spaniards had organized and equipped a relief force in the mother country and sent it out from Spain, the English would be so firmly established on the Orinoco that it would be difficult to dislodge them. His plan had its merits, but in the final analysis, both Modyford's and Gage's schemes were rejected in favor of a compromise: the first blow of Cromwell's Western Design was to fall upon Hispaniola (now Haiti and the Dominican Republic), an island reputedly fat and rich, and so weakly held that Sir Francis Drake had once captured its capital of Santo Domingo with a tiny landing force and held the place for a month until he was paid a ransom of twenty-five thousand pieces-of-eight. According to Gage, Hispaniola was "the chiefest of all the islands of the New World," and surpassed all the rest of America in the fineness of its gold, the great yield of its sugar fields, and the fertility of its soil. In short, it was an ideal starting point for the Puritan empire of the West.

Characteristically for a man who had risen to power with the help of the New Model Army, Oliver Cromwell decided that his Western Design should be entrusted to as formidable a strike force as possible. To this purpose and after considerable deliberation it was decided that no less than three thousand regular troops from England and another three thousand colonial volunteers from the English "Carribees," together with a full-scale invasion fleet, would be used in the operation. The task of recruiting the English contingent and of laying in the necessary stores was entrusted to Major-General Desborough, Cromwell's brother-in-law.

But in the weeks that followed the decision to attack Spain in the Antilles, a wide gap opened up between the Lord Protector's wishes and the actual material assembled for the Design. Originally the military calculations had been based on the assumption that the three thousand English soldiers accompanying the expedition would be the cream of the professional army, a hard core of well-trained men drawn from the standing regiments. There was even talk of recalling crack troops from the garrison in Ireland to add to the expedition. But as matters turned out, these calculations were wildly optimistic. Very few trained volunteers actually came forward for the venture, partly because the expedition's destination was kept secret and partly because a number of adverse rumors had sprung up, including one that the English authorities were hatching a sinister plot to raise money by hiring out volunteer troops to a foreign prince. To aggravate the situation still further, the colonels of the regular regiments refused to cooperate. They were reluctant to see their best men taken for the expedition and so, instead of sending volunteers, they instructed their color sergeants to select ne'er-do-wells from the ranks and send them to Portsmouth where the transports were assembling. When it became apparent that even these crude methods would fail to raise the number of men required for the expedition, General Desborough was obliged to authorize recruiting by beat of drum in London and elsewhere. Thus, instead of absorbing veteran regulars, the expedition's make-weight soon took on a distinctly third-rate atmosphere. Many of the levies, according to one eyewitness, were "hectors, knights of the blade, with common cheats, thieves, cut purses, and such like lewd persons, who had long time lived by sleight of hand, and dexterity of wit, and were now making a fair progress into Newgate, from whence they were to proceed towards Tyburne; . . . but considering the dangerousness of that passage, very politicly directed their course another way, and became soldiers for the state." It was apt criticism, for with only 2,500 men enrolled,

Desborough's cavalry had to be called out and sent down to the wharves in order to chase the reluctant heroes on board the ships.

But the poor quality of rank and file was nothing unusual for a seventeenth-century army. It was the caliber of their officers which normally sparked the difference between a rabble and an effective body of troops; and in this department, the Western Design seemed to be well served. Cromwell had decided that the supreme command should be shared between two experienced officers, Admiral Penn and General Venables, whose authority would extend to naval and army matters respectively. Both commanders were men of proved ability. Admiral William Penn, father of Pennsylvania's Quaker founder, was a thoroughgoing professional seaman. A round-faced, fair-haired, sociable man, who liked a glass of wine and a good company, he was the son of a West Country merchant captain, and had worked his way to his admiralcy. He had served with Blake and Monck, and recently he had been fighting creditably against the Dutch under their finest leaders. After the engagement in which Admiral Tromp was killed, he had been awarded a gold chain to the value of one hundred pounds in recognition for his services during that action. The Lord Protector placed the greatest confidence in him, and only the previous year he had been made the General of the Fleet (a misplaced appointment, as matters turned out, for Penn was secretly negotiating with the future Charles II, then an exile in Holland). On the other hand, Penn was a seaman's seaman, who had little rapport with the landgoing military. Moreover, he did not feel intimately concerned with the success or failure of the total operation, believing that his only job was to deliver the troops to their landing beaches and no more. At times, too, he could be tetchy and high-handed, an attitude which probably resulted from his position as a self-made senior officer in a navy riddled with patronage. Pepys, who was later his subordinate, called Penn "a counterfeit rogue" and "as false a fellow as ever was born," though Pepys was seldom polite about any man in a position to interfere with the indefatigable diarist's own peculations.

In the final count, however, it was General Robert Venables, as commander of the land forces, who bore the chief responsibil-

ity for the Caribbean campaign. He was in later years to excuse
his fumbled generalship with an endearing *Narrative of the
Design*, which began with the charmingly apologetic line: "It
being the usual course of such persons whose Pikes prove too
short, to make use of their Pens to supply that defect, . . . I
should have wav'd anything in this nature." Fortunately for
posterity, however, General Venables did succumb to the temptation of setting pen to paper, and it was largely in his *Narrative*
that the story of the West Indian campaign survived. Certainly,
when Cromwell's expedition sailed for the Caribbean, there was
little reason to suspect that its military commander would ever
have to scratch around for excuses, for General Venables, at
forty-one years of age, already had an excellent record as a sober
and competent soldier. Steadily advancing to his colonelcy, he
had fought in many of the battles of the Civil War and finished as
commander of the parliamentarian forces in Ulster (it was his
suggestion that the expedition should include drafts from the
Irish garrison). It was true that as a commanding officer, he was
not good at gaining the confidence of his men, but this was a
minor flaw, and the only slightly suspect note about General
Venables prior to his sailing on the Western Design expedition
was that he refused pointblank to accept command of the expedition, until his back pay, which was considerably in arrears, had
been settled. By coincidence, it was precisely this embarrassing
lack of hard cash that Cromwell expected to alleviate with his
venture to the Antilles.

In addition to Penn and Venables, the conduct of the Design
was entrusted to three other "commissioners," as they were
labeled in true parliamentarian style. Two of these commissioners
were men of considerable distinction: Edward Winslow, now on
a commissioner's salary of one thousand pounds a year, had been
one of the passengers aboard the *Mayflower* in 1620 and three
times governor of the colony of New Plymouth; while Daniel
Searle, governor of Barbados, was an invaluable adviser on West
Indian conditions, although he did not actually accompany the
expedition to Hispaniola. Captain Gregory Butler, the fifth and
last commissioner, was the odd man out. Indeed, he was so
unsuited for his post that it is difficult to know why Cromwell

appointed him at all, unless it was that, like Searle, Butler had some knowledge of the Caribbean. In every other respect he was a pest. He drank. He was a buffoon and a bore. He was quarrelsome by nature and got on badly with the other commissioners. In the end he was to abandon his colleagues when he was most needed, and sail back to England. Yet since the three "civil" commissioners were expected to restrict their attention to non-military matters, their capabilities were only of secondary importance. The real weight of the expedition fell upon the fighting men, on William Penn and especially on General Venables.

Strangely enough, once Cromwell had picked his commissioners, he was content to retire to the sidelines and leave the conduct of the expedition entirely to his chosen commanders. Venables, in particular, was given almost a free hand in the management of the campaign. He had specifically requested that his official orders should not bind him too closely to any particular plan of action, and because there was still some doubt about how fiercely the Spanish garrison would defend Hispaniola, he was told that he could switch the attack to another island if the conditions warranted. It was clearly understood that Hispaniola was to remain the prime target, but Venables also had the choice of invading Cuba, Puerto Rico, or the Spanish Main itself. Such operational flexibility would have been admirable if the expedition had been commanded by a single, incisive leader. But Cromwell and his council, having given Venables freedom of action with one hand, in effect took it away with the other; according to Venables' orders he was not to make any major change of policy unless he first obtained the agreement of his fellow commissioners. Unhappily there was little chance that all five men would ever be able to agree on anything, and in the event of a deadlock, neither Venables nor Admiral Penn had been given a deciding vote.

Nor had anyone been given a clear-cut ruling on the different areas of responsibility for the various commissioners. It was taken for granted that the civilians would attend to matters of general policy and civil questions, but, by some extraordinary oversight, no definite separation of powers was set up between Venables and Penn. In their orders it was airily decreed that the admiral should have charge of the naval forces and the general would command the landsmen. But in what was essentially an amphibious operation, Cromwell should have known that an overall commander was a crucial appointment. Without this supreme authority, it was unlikely that the Western Design would ever fulfill the saber-rattling prose of Venables's official instructions, which called on him to set upon the Spaniards, "surprise their forts, take or beate down their Castles and Places of strength, and to pursue, kill, and destroy by al meanes whatsoeuer al those who shall oppose or resist you there-in. . . ."

The fabric of this unwisely split command began to tear even before the expeditionary fleet sailed from England. It had been planned that the ships should assemble in the southern ports as quickly as possible, load their stores and men, and then hurry off to Barbados and the Caribbees before the Spaniards got wind of the affair and reinforced their Caribbean defenses. But as matters turned out, the expedition's shaky administration soon collapsed under the pace. Venables, worrying about the sluggish recruitment of his troops, was distraught when the levies arrived at Portsmouth so late that the naval authorities insisted on shepherding them on to the transports without even allowing time for a general muster. The general promptly complained to the council that he could not be expected to go to war without the opportunity to train or review his men and that the navy was deliberately undermining his authority. Penn, whose irascibility did not need much excuse for a quarrel, then had a blazing row with the general over the distribution of the expedition's stores, with each party accusing the other of keeping back supplies and weapons for its own men; their accusations were made all the more bitter because Desborough had failed to deliver a sufficient quantity of munitions. It took Cromwell's personal intervention to put a temporary halt to the bickering, although in the long run the navy won the argument, since the sailors took care to stow the bulk of the equipment in such a way that they had first access to it. Months later General Venables would be complaining petulantly that his land forces never saw half the military stores that had been allocated to them in England.

The general's personal behavior also aroused some adverse

muttering. Venables had married (for the second time) during the previous summer, and now he insisted on bringing his wife along with him on the somewhat flimsy excuse that she might prove useful as a nurse. This blatant uxoriousness led to the inevitable criticism that Elizabeth Venables had far too much say in her husband's affairs, "petticoat over topsail" as one commentator sourly put it, and it was not long before these high-level squabbles began to percolate downward. By the time the fleet sailed, the Western Design was not only split horizontally, between officers and men, but vertically between landsmen and sailors, neither of whom had much time for the other.

Admiral Penn, at least, had little cause for complaint. Cromwell had been exceptionally generous with his allocation of naval forces, and Penn had been authorized to take fourteen ships-of-the-line and as many transports as he needed. By the time the invasion force actually sailed, its full strength had been increased to thirty-six vessels, most of them moderately large ships of up to nine hundred tons, and their combined firepower exceeded a thousand cannon, a fact which made Penn's command one of the most formidable fleets ever to have sailed for the Antilles. For administrative purposes the fleet was divided into three squadrons under Admiral Penn, Vice-Admiral Goodson, and Rear-Admiral Dakins, although the ships actually sailed in two groups, the first leaving Portsmouth on December 20, 1654, and the second setting out on Christmas Day after General Desborough had paid a personal visit to Penn aboard his flagship, the *Swiftsure,* to wish the commanders good luck. Shortly before the fleet weighed anchor a brand-new frigate, the *Fagons,* arrived at Spithead under special orders from the Admiralty. She had come from Deal, where she had picked up Thomas Gage, preacher, now assigned as chaplain and adviser to General Venables. It was the zenith of Gage's career. His *Travels* had made its mark and Thurloe had apparently taken heed of his memorandum. Now Thomas Gage had decided to show his confidence in the Western Design by joining the expedition. It was to be his last trip to the Golden Antilles.

Although Cromwell's expedition was intended as a surprise attack against the Spaniards in the West Indies, the Madrid authorities were not taken completely unawares. Cromwell's brusque demands of their ambassador in London had been a clear indication that something was afoot, and it had not been difficult to guess that a Caribbean raid was being contemplated. Through inspired intelligence work, the Spaniards even gained some inkling that Hispaniola was one of the places that was threatened, and they tried anxiously to protect the island as best they could. However, as with Ralegh's Guiana ventures a half-century earlier, the Council of the Indies found it extremely difficult to coordinate their Caribbean defenses. They would have preferred to have moved colonial troops from within the Antilles to the danger point, but their Caribbean forces were already so thinly spread that it would have been rash to reallocate troops who were guarding the coasts against Dutch raiding ships and the ever-increasing number of pirates. So in the end, they found that there was very little that they could do, besides sending out to Hispaniola a new governor, the Count of Peñalva, with two hundred arquebusiers and authority to take over the island's defenses. It was an impotent gesture, and the harassed Peñalva arrived in Hispaniola to find that the island was in a far worse state than the home government had imagined. Santo Domingo, the capital and only place of any consequence on the island, was the obvious target for any attack, and there the regular garrison of three hundred men was reduced by sickness to 170 effectives. The city's fortifications were half tumbled down; there were large gaps where the city wall had never got beyond the drawing board of the military engineers; and there was a chronic shortage of gunpowder, shot, and all other munitions. It was a bleak prospect, but Peñalva bravely set about shoring up the walls, placing temporary fascines in the gaps, and organizing a local militia force composed of farmers and planters from the neighboring countryside. He also sent urgent appeals for reinforcements to the other colonial governors, but, typically, these requests went unanswered. In the final count the new commandant of Santo Domingo found that he could muster some six or seven hundred men, professional or part-trained, to face the anticipated English onslaught.

Moreover, Peñalva had very little time to prepare his defenses. Due to poor sailing conditions he had taken fifty-four days to cross from Spain to Hispaniola. Thus he arrived in the Antilles only a few days ahead of Penn, Venables, and the men of the Western Design. Superficially, too, the balance of power swung even more heavily in favor of the English interlopers, because Admiral Penn had accomplished what Ralegh had failed to do—the English admiral had safely delivered a major English expeditionary force, healthy and in good order, to the other side of the Atlantic. Only two English ships were lost on the outward voyage: the *Great Charity*, which foundered with all hands in heavy weather, and the little twenty-gun *Pelican*, which had sprung so badly during the voyage that she was pronounced unseaworthy and turned adrift after her crew had been taken off. Apart from these losses, only twenty men had died of illness during the passage, and two other storeships, including the one carrying the cavalry mounts, had to be left behind in England owing to last-minute administrative problems. Otherwise, Admiral Penn had successfully transported to the Antilles five regiments of five hundred men each, a small artillery train, a company of scouts, a company of arquebusiers, and the "reformados," an irregular formation of about one hundred veteran officers who had no troops of their own, but who had banded together to fight as a unit. In addition, Vice-Admiral Goodson was about to raise and command a "sea-regiment" or naval brigade drawn from the sailors of the fleet. It was more than enough to crush Peñalva's garrison to powder, but Venables, not knowing Hispaniola's enfeebled condition, decided to play safe and recruit additional men from Barbados and the neighboring islands. These new recruits, supposedly acclimatized reinforcements who would perform well under local conditions, would soon be Venable's undoing.

Barbados in the mid-seventeenth century was less than glamorous. Originally included in conflicting patents issued to the Earl of Carlisle and the Earl of Pembroke, the island had quickly acquired a reputation as a convenient dumping ground for undesirables. It was the terminus for a steady influx of indentured laborers, part-time pirates, seamen deserters, remittance men, contraband traders, and Royalist exiles from the Civil War who had been "barbadosed," that is, banished to the island. Naturally there was also a leavening of decent, hard-working settlers, but at the time Penn and his fleet arrived there, Barbados society was chiefly renowned for its turbulent politics, its *nouveau riche* plantocracy, and the heavy drinking of everyone with enough money to buy rumbullion or "kill-divill." According to the diary of one Mr. Whistler, sailing master of the *Swiftsure* and one of the shrewdest observers of the entire venture, Barbados was "the Dunghill whereone England doth cast forth its rubidg: Rodgs and hors and such like peopel are those which are gennerally brought heare. A rodge in England will hardly make a cheater here: a Bawd borught over puts one a demour comportment, a whore if handsume makes a wife for sume rich-planter. . . ." It was from such poor timber that Venables hoped to recruit the extra men for his expeditionary force. In the meantime his own shabby English infantry were put through their drills twice a week to shake off the effects of the sea voyage, and the army quartermasters made a despairing inventory of the expedition's equipment.

Almost at once it was discovered that Desborough's promised stores were either substandard or had never been shipped. During the scrambled embarkation at Portsmouth there had been little time to check the quantity and quality of the equipment; at Barbados the supply officers found to their dismay that many items had either been mislaid or simply left behind on the docks. Although a number of the storeships had not yet arrived, the army immediately began to suspect that Penn's sailors had appropriated more than their fair share of the stores, and that Desborough and his friends had turned a dishonest penny on several of the victualing contracts. A shortage of weapons was the worst problem. It was so serious that the senior army officers at once called a council of war, after which they sent an appeal to the navy for two thousand firearms, six hundred pikes, two hundred half-pikes, and a quantity of pistols, carbine, and ball. Whether or not the navy had hidden the missing weapons, the army received only a fraction of what they asked for, and Venables was obliged to set every blacksmith on the island to hammering out makeshift equipment for his infantry. In this gimcrack fashion 2,500 heads for half-pikes were forged, and then fitted to what one observer scathingly called "cabbage stalks," a description which probably referred to pike-staffs whittled from the stems of a tree known as the cabbage tree. These substitute half-pikes were sorry weapons, top-heavy, cumbersome, and liable to snap. Fifteen hundred matchlocks were also rounded up from the island's train bands, and a number of better-quality sporting guns were brusquely commandeered from the wealthier planters. Some additional gunpowder and shot were also collected, but even so, the total supply of gunpowder remained a matter of grave concern, as the expedition was at least ten tons short of its estimated requirement. Eventually Venables wrote home to England, asking that saltpeter, a mill, and gunpowder makers to be sent out to remedy the deficiency. Furthermore, he complained, the English gunpowder had a poor reputation in the West Indies. Under tropical conditions it deteriorated beyond use inside nine months, whereas the French and Spanish gunpowder lasted in good condition for many years. The only way of overcoming the problem, he said, was to send out the powder uncompounded, to be mixed and bagged as needed. The artillery officers had other worries. Part of their artillery train had been left behind in England, and much of the remainder had gone down with the *Great Charity*. Now the only serviceable guns they had were two "drakes," a type of light field ordnance small enough to be manhandled ashore onto a landing beach. To remedy this deficiency the artillerymen borrowed a mortar from the Barbadian garrison, and one ingenious individual even attempted to devise home-made mortars with wooden barrels. Luckily for the gunners, these dangerous contraptions were never actually fired.

While these last-minute improvisations were in progress, Venables and his senior officers had been signing on their additional troops. To their surprise and gratification, the army's appeal for Barbadian volunteers produced an absolute deluge of eager recruits. These men were being blithely welcomed into the ranks when it was suddenly discovered, to everyone's embarrassment, that a good proportion of the new recruits were runaway indentured servants, fugitive apprentices, or undischarged debtors. Of course the planters were dismayed to see these laborers disappearing into the clutches of the military, and to make amends for this error the commissioners had to post an order that only men with less than nine months left to serve in their indentures would be eligible for the expedition. Despite these precautions, however, many rascals still managed to slip through the net, and Venables' already third-rate regiments were further swollen with a motley collection of rogues and failures who saw the Western Design as a heaven-sent opportunity to escape the detested island. Virtually the only respectable drafts were a handful of Barbadian freemen and yeoman farmers. They had found it difficult to farm on the island without the necessary capital to invest in slaves and decided to join up with the expedition rather than wear themselves out on their small-holdings. But on balance Venables's newcomers were a contemptible lot. There were three or four thousand of them, or about half the total expeditionary force, and in one opinion they were nothing but "old beaten runaways." Venables himself was to describe them in his apologetic *Narrative* as the "most prophane debauch'd persons that we ever saw, scorners of Religion, and indeed men kept so loose as not to be kept under discipline, and so cowardly as not to be made to fight." Nor were their Barbadian officers much better. One group came prancing in, cavalier-fashion, with their horses and servants, and grandly volunteered to act as the general's lifeguard. And one of the new planter-colonels actually insisted that he would not go on any campaign unless the commissioners first settled his outstanding debts on the island. When this brazen demand was flatly rejected by the army, the new colonel dismissed himself forthwith, though not before his regiment of Barbadians had been securely cooped up on board the fleet in case they tried to follow their colonel's example.

For ten weeks the expedition lingered in Barbados, and during that time so many extra recruits were signed on that the army's logistical structure, already tottering, was overloaded beyond endurance. Cromwell's army for the Western Design had been one of the worst-equipped and most poorly planned military adventures ever to have left the shores of England. The visit to England's "rubidg heap" only served to accentuate its shortcom-

ings. The missing storeships failed to show up; too many indifferent recruits bloated the land forces; and even as Venables sailed
forth to the battlefield, his quartermasters were issuing instructions that the soldiers were to receive only a two-thirds ration of
food until additional supplies were obtained or further reductions
became necessary.

At Barbados, too, it was decided that Hispaniola was definitely to be the point of attack, and so, when the fleet set sail on
March 31, it moved to the north along the arc of the Caribbee
islands. For two happy days the ships stopped in the enormous,
almost landlocked harbor of St. Lucia Island, where the sailors
filled water casks and the commissioners went ashore to the un-
spoiled idyll to amuse themselves by knocking down lumbering
pelicans with their fowling pieces. Soon the ships plowed north
again, making their way past Dominica near where Thomas Gage
had first set foot in the Antilles some thirty years earlier, and the
Caribs, still ripe for mischief, paddled out to greet the newcomers
with a salvo of arrows that wounded five soldiers. Then the
convoy bore away to their next port of call, the insignificant
English colony at St. Christopher's, in order to pick up Commissioner Butler, who had gone ahead with the thoroughly Crom-
wellian-sounding vessels *Marston Moor* and *Selby* in order to
enlist yet more colonial troops.

The island of St. Christopher was at that time a political freak.
Both England and France laid claim to the tiny place, and by a
bizarre and singularly unworkable diplomatic arrangement, they
had agreed to turn it into an international sandwich, with the
English holding the central slice of the island and the French
settlers occupying the two ends. Under the circumstances it
would not have been tactful if Commissioner Butler had arrived
to raise a large body of armed men among the English settlers
without first paying a courtesy call on the French authorities to
explain his reasons. But Butler was a bungling sot, it being said
that he had been packed off to St. Christopher because he had got
so drunk one day in Barbados that he had shocked even that rum-
sodden community. On St. Christopher, moreover, Commissioner
Butler had refused to mend his ways. When he arrived at his

meeting with the French representatives, the pot-valiant commissioner was so gloriously drunk that he tumbled from his saddle and, to undisguised Gallic delight, vomited copiously on the ground. After this lurid performance it was something of an achievement that by the time the main fleet arrived, Butler had managed to collect together eight hundred men to be signed on. With these reinforcements and another 380 volunteers from Montserrat and Nevis, Venables now had between eight and nine thousand alleged fighting men under his command, the exact figure being obscured in the mists of the expeditionary paymaster's poor mathematics. But whatever their precise strength, the English now massively outnumbered the Spaniards on Hispaniola. By the same token, they far exceeded the capacity of their own supplies. It remained to be seen which imbalance was the more important.

Count Peñalva had not been idle while the English expedition was ponderously working up substance for its attack on Hispaniola. His position at Santo Domingo was by no means easy to defend. The town stood in the right angle between the mouth of a small river and the seashore, and was dangerously exposed on two sides to bombardment from Penn's heavily gunned fleet. To prevent Penn from sailing directly into the mouth of the river and forcing Santo Domingo's quays, Peñalva placed two block ships at the entrance to the river with orders that they should be sunk if the English fleet made a direct assault. Behind these blockships, Peñalva reinforced his usual shore batteries with a new gun platform mounting several recently acquired brass cannon, of which the Spanish garrison was inordinately proud. But Peñalva's real worry concerned the landward defenses of the city. There the city wall was so sadly neglected along much of its length that in some places there was little more than a thick hedge to deter an attacker. Peñalva made some attempt to close the worst gaps, but with great presence of mind he decided that his best strategy would be to concentrate on the main approaches to the city. To this end the main gate was strengthened; the small forts and gun emplacements along the line of the wall were cleared for action; any shrubs which might provide cover for the attackers were cut back; and a number of trenches were hastily dug so that his arquebusiers would be able to provide enfilading fire.

Peñalva's real stroke of genius, however, was to send his men out into the countryside with orders to barricade the smaller country lanes and to prepare camouflaged redoubts and ambuscades overlooking the main road leading into the city. He calculated that since most of the countryside around Santo Domingo was covered with thick, thorny brush, it would be extremely unlikely that the English would choose to attack across such forbidding terrain. The core of his plan of defense was to divert the English troops into the long narrow road leading up to the city where their numbers would hamper their movement and his own sharpshooters and cavalry could pick them off at leisure.

His troops were still feverishly digging in when, at noon on April 13, the English fleet was reported on the horizon.

10-

Debacle at Hispaniola

BY THE TIME THE ENGLISH FLEET SIGHTED HISPANIOLA, relations between Penn and Venables, already strained, had
broken down still further. Both men had an unfortunate habit of
retreating into fits of sulks whenever they felt they had been
snubbed by the other, and since neither was prepared to compromise on the least point of disagreement, the atmosphere was
tense and lowering. This bickering at the very peak of the expedition's organization had spread down to the other officers.
They took sides in support of their respective commanders, and
even prior to the fleet's departure from Barbados there was so little
trust left between the two factions that it was necessary for the
senior officers to sign a joint resolution pledging that "the land
forces do promise never to desert the Fleet" and that the sea
officers would not sail off and abandon the army once it was
landed. It was hardly an auspicious beginning to a campaign
which clearly required the closest cooperation between both arms
of the service, and it should have been obvious to all concerned in
the affair that the two factions would have to stick to the spirit
of the resolution if their attack on the Spanish Antilles was to be
successful. But Penn soon dragged his feet. At the council of war
on the voyage to Hispaniola the army proposed that an all-out

frontal assault should be launched against Santo Domingo with both land and sea forces throwing their full weight simultaneously against the Spaniard. Penn immediately objected. He claimed (erroneously, as it turned out) that the Spanish garrison had floated a defensive boom across the mouth of the harbor and that his ships would be at too great risk if they did not go in very cautiously, sounding the channel as they advanced. He was only a little less critical of the alternate plan, which was that the English fleet should divide, and while the transports set the infantry ashore at the mouth of the Rio Jaina a few miles to the west of Santo Domingo, his warships would take up bombardment stations opposite the city and distract the Spaniards's attention by shelling their outworks and disembarking a small diversionary force to the east. The main body of the English infantry would then advance from the landward side, knock down the city wall with their drakes and the mortar, and rush in with the sword. This plan was adopted, but it was ponderous and notably uninspired. Yet given a fair measure of cooperation, there was no reason why the English should not have overwhelmed Peñalva's outnumbered and by now dispirited garrison.

But as matters turned out, everything went disastrously wrong. Penn himself elected to stay with the bombarding squadron, and so it was Vice-Admiral Goodson who was entrusted with the task of taking Venables, five regiments of foot, the artillery, the troop of horse, and the reformado company, and landing them near the mouth of the Rio Jaina, about six miles to the west of the city. Clearly the timing of the operation was critical; it was calculated that the main infantry force would need only a few hours to move from their disembarkation point to the city wall in order to arrive there soon after the fleet had softened up the defenses with their big guns. At the same time the diversionary landing on the east should have drawn off most of Peñalva's men. But by an appalling oversight Goodson and General Venables managed to sail blithely off on the vice-admiral's *Paragon* without taking on board the pilot whose job was to identify the correct landing beach at the mouth of the Jaina. So the transports wallowed merrily downwind and well past their destination while Goodson blandly waited for the absent pilot to tell him where to disembark the troops. When at last Venables noticed that the pilot was not on board and that something had gone gravely wrong, the transports were too far downwind to work their way back to the Jaina, and the invading troops were dumped ashore more than thirty miles from their target. There, at least, the English infantry had an unopposed landing, for Peñalva had never dreamed that his enemy would wander so far away before coming ashore, and he had no one on the beach to contest the disembarkation. But from the Spaniard's point of view, Goodson's mistake was worth a regiment of skirmishers, for the raw, under-trained English foot-soldiers now had a grueling two-day march under a scorching sun before they came within arquebus shot of his defenses. As an exercise in military tactics the English landing was a catastrophe. Poor liaison between land and sea forces, exacerbated by halfhearted collaboration between Venables and Penn (the missing pilot was in fact on an errand for the admiral when Goodson sailed off), had squandered the attacker's advantage of mobility in the face of static defense. And of course the carefully arranged English battle plan with its neat dovetailing of bombardment, feint, and major assault was now fallen to the ground.

The condition of Venables's land force, once it got ashore, was a stark example of the ill-contrived fabric of most seventeenth-century armies. The five infantry regiments and their auxiliaries, so casually off-loaded onto a hostile coast, possessed no maps of the area, had no guides, only a handful of tents, shoddy weapons, less than two days' marching rations, and no gunsmith's tools. There was such a shortage of clothing that the soldiers had already been borrowing from the seamen's slop chests, and they had been given less than half the allotment of powder, match, and shot. Their bread was moldy and rotten; the cured meats were oversalted; and, worst of all, they had no blackjacks, as the leather army water bottles were called. Even as they waded ashore, some of the foot-soldiers were in such bad physical shape that they stumbled and fell in the water and had to be rescued by their comrades. Before the column was half way to Santo Domingo the combined effects of heat, poor food, and drinking water scooped from ditches produced an outbreak of "the bloody flux," dysentery. The standard medicine for this, and indeed any other, sickness was a stiff dose of brandy, but all the brandy supplies and most of the other medicines had been accidentally left behind with the fleet. Furthermore, the normal quota of one surgeon and two amateur assistants per regiment was utterly inadequate to handle the emergency.

Poorly served, the troops were as badly led. Their regimental officers paid virtually no attention to their men's welfare and were heedless of their general's instructions concerning the line of march. The officers, it seemed, were more interested in discussing how they would divide up the anticipated booty of Santo Domingo, "asharing the skin before wee had Cached the foxx" as Sailing Master Whistler caustically put it in his diary. The various colonels of foot behaved exactly as though their regiments were personal property rather than units within a larger task force; it was a measure of their incompetence that when planning disembarkation, they merely drew lots among themselves to decide whose regiment would have the honor of being first ashore. Once on land, the various detachments then took up their positions in much the same manner, social etiquette being more important than military good sense. In the vanguard came the glory-seeking reformados; behind them, Venables's own regiment by virtue of its commander's seniority; and then the other units straggling along in a haphazard muddle. The troop of horse, which should have been scouting ahead for ambushes, had been held up in disembarkation and was nowhere to be seen; not until evening did it put in an appearance. Indeed, the only firm arrangement on which the army's high command was able to agree was that the sea regiment should be placed at the tail of the column. The sailors, it turned out, had been grumbling about an order regulating the seizure of booty and had pointedly asked why they should risk their lives on land service when there was no profit to be gained.

Opposing this rag-bag collection of soldiery, Count Peñalva disposed his city garrison, his trained Spanish arquebusiers, and the country levies. The morale of the Santo Domingo's garrison was, if anything, as dismal as that of the invaders. Had Penn's broadsides had come crashing into the city with any degree of

accuracy, it was likely the garrison men would have evacuated
the town and hidden in the hills. But Admiral Penn did nothing
useful. His fleet tacked gently up and down in front of Santo
Domingo, loosed off a few desultory rounds, and then cautiously
"scouted." The English admiral may have been waiting for
Venables and his men to appear on the landward side, but by then
the English land forces had their hands full, for they had run into
the finest of Peñalva's troops—his arquebusiers and his irregulars.

According to the official Spanish records of the campaign, the
detachment of arquebusiers performed steadily and accurately
throughout, and were competently backed up by the gunlayers
of the defensive batteries stationed on the city wall. But from the
English point of view it was the Spanish irregular forces which
did the real damage. They were a scratch group of cavalry drawn
from the local officers and planters, and a body of redoubtable
pikemen known as "cowkillers." The latter were a fearsome
group of men. Composed of a few Spaniards, Negro slaves, and
Creoles, but mostly of mestizos and mulatto slaves, they made
their living in peacetime by hunting the wild cattle which
infested the island. Their frivolous-sounding nickname, given
them by the English troops, was not meant with disrespect, for
their trade made them formidable warriors. Peñalva had offered
the "cowkillers" a special bounty to hunt Englishmen instead of
wild cattle, and now they responded with a will. They were
familiar with every copse and gully suitable for an ambush, and
their customary hunting weapon, a long and well-honed lance,
was a terrible engine in the hands of an expert. It was said (and
all the English accounts spoke with awe of these guerrilla forces)
that no one ever survived a thrust from a cowkiller's lance; it tore
a gaping hole right through a man, leaving as big a wound at the
back as at the front. In Sailing Master Whistler's opinion, it was
futile to try to shoot a cowkiller as he came at you, for he would
coolly anticipate the volley, and drop down on one knee so that
the bullet flew overhead. The next instant, however, he would be
back on his feet and come charging down on the helpless
musketeer as he fumbled to reload his unwieldy firelock.
Whistler claimed that the only way to deal with these ferocious
fighters was to hold them off at pike's length, taking advantage of

the fact that a cowkiller's lance was a trifle shorter than the standard sixteen-foot English weapon. But should the cowkiller slip under the pikeman's guard or should the notorious "cabbage stalk" snap, then, said Whistler, "stand clear!"

For their first three days on Hispaniola, the English soldiers had no notion what was in store for them. Peñalva had ordered his scouts to fall back without offering battle, and the English soldiers were entirely occupied with the immediate problem of finding their way to Santo Domingo in fit condition for a fight. Their chief concern was water. Always there seemed to be either too much or too little of it. Part of the time the infantry found themselves trudging along with a raging thirst, and part of the time they were on the bank of some stream or river, disconsolately trying to find a way of crossing to the other side. If the Barbadians had kept their wits about them, they would have known from experience that there are sandbars across the mouths of most Caribbean rivers, where one can ford them almost dryshod. But stupidly they did not use their local knowledge, and Venables, like the duke in the rhyme, wasted much time and effort in sending his men tramping up and down the rivers looking for crossings. Had the English brought maps or a guide with them, this difficulty would have been solved; but the army's only chance of obtaining a guide, an Irishman whom they picked up at an abandoned farmhouse, was thrown away when Venables suspected the man of treachery (perhaps remembering his days in Cromwellian Ireland) and hanged the fellow out of hand. Otherwise, the advancing soldiers only came across castoff slaves, the diseased and the dimwitted, whom the Spanish planters had left behind as they evacuated their farms and withdrew into Santo Domingo. The planters had also burned the crops standing in the fields, emptied the granaries, and stopped up the wells with rubbish, so that the English army, without supply wagons and already reduced to one biscuit per man each day, was hard put to it to scavenge successfully. Occasionally the men were able to round up stray pigs and chickens, and in the citrus orchards of the plantations they stripped the orange trees. But these were meager spoils, and the unripe fruit brought on diarrhea.

The thirty-mile march from the disembarkation point to the

walls of Santo Domingo would have presented no difficulties to a
first-line unit of the New Model Army, but those thirty miles
shattered Venables's rejects and third-raters. They moaned about
the heat, complained that the rocks and gravel of the road hurt
their feet, discarded equipment and all sense of discipline and
purpose, and cursed as wickedly untrue the myth that nature
smiled on man in the Golden Antilles. In those thirty miles
Venables's column stretched out into an elongated rabble; the
weak-spirited and the cripples dropped to the back of the line;
and the various segments of the column fell away from one
another like beads from a snapped necklace.

On the second day a group of foragers turned up a tarnished
statue of the Madonna on a deserted farm, and the hooting troops
battered this "Popish trumperie" to pieces with a hail of oranges.
But it was poor sport, since there was no real loot; the Spaniards
had in fact carried off every single article of any value. The next
afternoon there was a brief scare that the Spanish had decided to
stand their ground after all, when the English vanguard saw a lone
soldier ahead. The alarm was given, but on closer inspection, the
stranger was recognized by the colors on his pike as a member of
the regiment that was supposed to have launched the diversionary
attack on the east side of Santo Domingo. Venables went forward
to investigate and learned that the feint had also been a fiasco.
The navy had not been able to find a suitable landing beach to the
east of the city, and had therefore taken the diversionary troops
back to the western approaches and deposited them at the mouth
of the Rio Jaina, precisely where Venables should have landed
two days before. The English attack had now lost all resemblance
to the original campaign plan, and without the advantages of
surprise or feint, Venables's column was blundering toward the
entrenched Spaniards.

The skirmish that took place on the 17th was the direct fault
of Colonel Buller, commander of the diversionary force. He had
been ordered by Penn to wait with his regiment until Venables
and the main English strength came up with him. But Colonel
Buller, crass and self-important like so many of the officers, took
it into his head to start his troops marching toward Santo
Domingo before Venables had put in an appearance. By the time

the English general arrived on the scene, Buller's advance guard was on the brink of making contact with Peñalva's defenses around the city. And, as luck would have it, they stumbled directly onto one of the strongest Spanish redoubts, the fortress of San Geronimo, which marked the seaward end of the city wall. Thus Venables and his staff officers, elegantly strolling forward to inspect Buller's dispositions, suddenly found themselves in the thick of a fierce and quite unlooked-for fight, and the English attack developed into the same confused and useless affair as Wat Ralegh's charge against St. Thomé.

Buller's advance troops first sprang one of Peñalva's carefully planned ambushes. The Spaniards fired a single volley from their slow-loading arquebuses and then ran back toward the city wall. The English, thinking they had victory within their grasp, rushed forward unsupported into withering crossfire from the guns of the San Geronimo redoubt. A few of Buller's men actually succeeded in reaching the base of the new fortress wall, but it was a pointless maneuver for there was no breach and they had no scaling ladders. Instead, they were raked by Spanish musketry as they stood there wondering what to do next. As the English turned to withdraw, they were promptly set upon by the Spaniards courageously sallying from their positions. The retreat became a rout; and the unfortunate Venables, who had been looking forward to a gentlemanly discussion of tactics with Colonel Buller, found himself first deafened by the booming of the Spanish batteries, and then surrounded by a wild-eyed mob of panic-stricken Englishmen throwing away their equipment as they scampered helter-skelter for safety. It was so upsetting for the English general that, according to Whistler (who never lost a chance to poke fun at him), Venables completely lost his nerve and bolted, hiding himself behind a large tree. When the panic subsided, he emerged, full of shame-faced excuses and "so prosesed [sic] with terror that he could hardly spake."

This ridiculous and botched engagement set the tone for the rest of the catastrophic Hispaniola campaign. The skirmish had cost the English some twenty dead and the last tatters of their self-respect. Now, brought face to face with the realities of a nasty colonial war, the broken-down English contingents and the untrained West Indian levies decided that they did not like the prospect. In fact, for the next week they kept to camp, strangely dazed and not a little ashamed of themselves. Naturally Venables had lost face because of his behavior during the skirmish, and he proceeded to make matters worse by stumping off in a huff to rejoin the fleet. He claimed that he went to consult with Admiral Penn, but popular opinion had it that he was more interested in seeking the battlefield's lost glory in the accommodating arms of his wife.

With their general gone, the condition of the land forces deteriorated still further. They had withdrawn to a ramshackle encampment on Jaina beach in order to be closer to the supply ships. But to their disgust the rations sent ashore to them were inedible. The fault, it soon came out, lay with the commissioners. They had instructed the quartermasters to buy up additional supplies of food on Barbados in order to supplement the inadequate rations that had been carried out from England. But exorbitant profiteering by the Barbadian merchants had driven prices so high that the quartermasters had been forced to purchase their requirements from stocks of food held on Babados by the navy. For years the victuallers to the navy had quietly been using Barbados as a dumping ground for condemned stores and shoddy contract supplies; and now the barrels of biscuit and meat sent to the land forces as the mainstay of their diet were so decomposed that many of the men refused to eat the revolting stuff. Some of the soldiers preferred to starve and fell sick; others ate and died of food poisoning; and those who went foraging were in constant danger of being spitted by the cowkillers, who began to lurk around the camp. Dogs and cats were killed by the English and eaten, and it was said that a cavalryman had to keep a sharp lookout when he went off into the bushes to relieve himself. If not, he was likely to return and find that his horse had been spirited away to the stew pot.

Clearly, the army was about to disintegrate entirely. Yet for seven days General Venables, snug in his great cabin aboard the *Swiftsure*, frittered away time, while dysentery ravaged the poor wretches on shore and the Santo Domingo garrison gained strength as Peñalva frantically called in reinforcements from the other Spanish settlements on the island. As usual, Sailing Master Whistler caught the flavor of the situation with his characteristically earthy prose. "Gennerall Venabelles," he wrote, "Being aboard of our ship, and haueing a good ship vnder him and his wife to lie by his side, did not feel the hardship of the Souldgers that did lie on the sand vntell the Raine did waish it from vnder them, and haueing littell or noe vitelles, and nothing to drink but water. . . . and the abundant of frute that they did eate, and lieing in the raine did case most of them to haue the Bluddie-flux, and now thayer harts wore got out of thayer Dublates into thayer Breches, and wos nothing but Shiting, for thay wose in a very sad condichon, 50 or 60 stouls in a day, . . ."

The navy made an attempt to relieve the distress of the land forces when Penn informed Venables that he could set his sailors to boiling meat on board the ships and then ferrying it ashore to the troops. Similarly, it would have been an easy matter to land casks of water for them. But these arrangements ran aground on the reefs of incompetence and poor organization, and when Penn offered to send a few ships-of-the-line and land a storming party "on the town quay" if it would help the army, Venables snapped back at him. The army, he haughtily informed Penn, did not want the San Geronimo fort to be harmed, because an undamaged fort would be more useful to his infantry once they had taken and occupied the city. The English general, it was clear, sought help from no one. Brooding on the sting of his disgraceful defeat, he was quite ready to turn on those around him. Venables had never been the sort of officer to consult with his juniors very closely, and now he ignored them so completely that henceforth his staff officers had very little idea of what was in their general's mind. So it came as something of a surprise when on April 24, eight days after his first abortive attack, Venables summarily reappeared on the beach and told his lackluster troops that he had decided on a frontal attack on Santo Domingo. This time, instead of advancing against San Geronimo, the army would assault a section of the wall slightly to the left of the fort, breach the Spanish defenses with the drakes and the mortar, and carry the gap with cold steel. Had Venables taken the trouble to scout the entire Spanish perimeter, he would soon have discovered those weak sectors which were defended only by trenches and a hedge. But, neglecting this elementary precaution, he had chosen to send his bedraggled column blindly down the main road leading to the city, precisely where Peñalva had hidden his best-laid ambushes and deployed his most effective firepower.

Perhaps two thirds of the English army, if not exactly fighting fit, was at least in a condition to advance, and after bivouacking on the road during the night of the 24th, they set out the following dawn on their second attempt to capture Santo Domingo. The "forelorn," or forelorn hope," as the vanguard was suitably called, was entrusted to Adjutant-General Jackson. He was an officer, according to later reports, who was an out-and-out incompetent with a fine regard for the safety of his own skin. With a notable mixture of negligence and forethought, Jackson failed to deploy scouts to search the woods on each side of the road ahead of his unit. Instead, he placed his pikemen at the back of the vanguard, where they would be useless against the cow-killers. Then he cautiously took up his own position at the extreme rear of his command, where he had a line of escape if anything went wrong. Behind him marched the company of firelocks, then the officers of the reformado company, and the troop of horse. After them, four abreast, came Venables's regiment (though without its commander, who was farther down the line), a regiment led by Major-General Heane, and the sailors of the sea regiment under Vice-Admiral Goodson. The artillery was laboriously hauled along by teams of men harnessed to the gun carriages, and the musketeers had strict orders to conserve their match, which was already down to three or four inches a man and would not last out a prolonged engagement. Thus the whole column resembled nothing so much as a grotesque, blind worm clumsily groping its way down the long, narrow, sunbaked road to Santo Domingo. The day was furnacelike, and the heat, accentuated by the clouds of dust kicked up by the men, throbbed back from the scrubby woods lining each side of the road like a tall hedge. When the column had tramped six of the eight miles to Santo Domingo, many of the foot-soldiers were tripping over themselves with exhaustion and thirst, and at the front Adjutant-General Jackson, unscouted and nobly disinterested, led the worm's head into the jaws of Peñalva's trap.

The Spanish troops waited until the slovenly English forelorn was well into their main ambush. In fact many of their victims were gaping open-mouthed at the smoke from the San Geronimo battery which had begun shelling them at long range with round shot and case, when the ambush erupted. After a point-blank volley from the hidden arquebusiers, Peñalva's cavalry and cow-killers came bursting out of the thickets, yelling their battle cries and brandishing swords and lances. For a moment the front rank of the forelorn stood firm and actually loosed off a single volley ("over nimbly," according to Venables's subsequent apologia). But then, terrified by the spectacle of the dreaded cowkillers careering down on them, the forelorn broke into fragments and ran. Behind them, it was said, Adjutant-General Jackson took one swift look at the situation and was the first to take to his heels, cleaving a path through the ranks behind him as he bolted for safety in the rear. As the Spaniards tore great holes in their line, one English unit after another wavered and turned back on their comrades as they fought to escape the jabbing lances. Only the reformados and Major-General Heane stopped long enough for a fight. Heane and two courageous officers with him threatened to kill any runaway who fled past them, but they were ignored and the Spanish cavalry rode them down in a trice. The refor-mados also tried desperately to make a stand and were cut to pieces, only seventeen out of fifty-five of them surviving. Else-where it was total debacle, with the English column telescoping into a jam-packed rabble as the men struggled to claw their way out of the death-trap in the lane. Scarcely one soldier in fifty actually faced the Spaniards. Most of them were routed by their own comrades blundering back in complete panic. But utter terror had convulsed the column, and Peñalva's men, who numbered less than two hundred, ran whooping up and down the mob, casually spearing every back they could reach, until they were weary of the killing and drew off. Eventually it was the despised sea regiment toward the rear who staved off entire collapse. With

Venables at their head, the sailors opened up to left and right to let the runaways stream through, and then, closing ranks and threatening to cut down anyone who broke formation, they moved forward, only to find that the Spaniards were too exhausted by the slaughter to put up a resistance and had already withdrawn. Peñalva's irregulars had scored a crushing victory. They had killed between three and four hundred of the enemy, including a major-general, a lieutenant-colonel, a major, and four captains; they had carried off English battle standards like poppies from the field; and they had earned every penny of Peñalva's English-killing bonus.

But the second engagement of the Santo Domingo campaign was not yet over, for Venables, who had earlier procrastinated when he should have attacked, now plunged forward when he should have held back. His newfound recklessness may have had something to do with the fact that he, like many of his troops, was being racked by spasms of dysentery. (Indeed, he was in such bad condition that he had to be carried about on the shoulders of two men.) In this distressed condition the English commander appeared to lose all grasp of military tactics. Instead of ordering his men to fall back and regroup, he sent the sea regiment pressing forward against the Spaniard. And incredibly, he once again did not trouble to scout the ground that lay immediately ahead of them. So it was that the sailors, unsupported by any other units of the English force, marched forward and emerged from the shelter of the woods straight onto open ground commanded by the guns of the San Geronimo fort and by a neighboring redoubt aptly called the "slaughterhouse fort." These two batteries promptly opened up with murderous effect, raking the English troops as they stood there, like toy soldiers in a child's playset, waiting for the order to launch a final assault. But no order came, for Venables, the only man who knew the English plan, if there was any plan at all, was a broken reed. In pain and dazed by the clamor of battle, he seemed lost in admiration at the way the troops stood firm "though the Enemy's cannon from the Fort[s] swept away our men by eight or nine a shot." While he dithered, the English began to fall back, and by the time Venables had gathered his wits about him and ordered the mortar to be brought forward to play on the walls of the city, there was not a man in his battered force who would even volunteer to drag the gun into position. The entire English attack had lost its direction, and as the spirit of indecision spread, Venables's officers found it necessary to intervene and order a retreat lest the withdrawal became a headlong flight. The mortar was hauled out of cannon range, and all the officers who could be found met in an acrimonious council of war. They were stunned by the panache and vigor of the Spanish defense, and they knew that their own authority over the troops was in doubt. If they ordered another advance, they were not at all sure that the troops would obey them; and in front of them still stood the undamaged walls of Santo Domingo, manned by apparently resolute Spaniards who fought like tigers. There seemed to be no choice but to order the army back to the beach; as a gesture, they first arranged that the mortar should be buried where it stood, so that it could be used in the next attack. Yet neither Venables, when he regained his composure, nor his officers believed there could be another attack. The English infantry were too disheartened; the battlefield was littered with broken and abandoned equipment which could not be replaced; and every officer was seething with recrimination. In effect, Peñalva's small garrison had gallantly brought Cromwell's Western Design to a bloody halt.

Back on the beach, the inevitable spate of accusations and counteraccusations began. Not unnaturally, the chief scapegoat for the English disgrace was Adjutant-General Jackson. With all solemnity he was court-martialed, found guilty, and his sword snapped over his head. Then he was put to swabbing the decks of the expedition's hospital ship. He was lucky. A sergeant of the forelorn, accused of precipitating the retreat by shouting, "Gentlemen, fend for yourselves, we are all lost," was hanged, and a notice stating his crime was pinned on his chest. In reality neither man had behaved very differently from the majority of their fellows, and Jackson was certainly no more deserving of blame than many of the other officers, who, Venables pointed out, had come "in hopes of Pillage into a country where they conceived Gold as plentiful as stones." Jackson's real mistake, it seemed, was that he had been discovered during the height of the battle lying on the ground well to the rear of the engagement, having his back massaged by a camp-follower. To make matters worse, he was rumored to have had a bigamous affair in England before he left on the Design.

Commissioners Penn, Winslow, and Butler aboard the fleet were incensed by the outcome of the attack. In their anger they fired off a letter to the unfortunate governor of Barbados who had sent them off so ill-provided. "Your men," they fumed, "and the men of St. Christopher's lead all the disorder and confusion." The colonial levies were so bad that the officers refused to lead them in another attack, and had volunteered instead to form a special regiment composed only of officers in order to launch another assault and try to retrieve the affair. Of course this idea was too risky to be entertained, and "to our great grief and anguish" the commissioners announced that they had decided to withdraw the expeditionary force from Hispaniola altogether. Instead they would use the discretionary powers vested in them by Cromwell and redirect the Design against Jamaica, an island which they hoped would prove to be a less prickly target than Hispaniola and more suited to the capabilities of the crestfallen troops under their command. "Thus," they concluded, "you see our sad condition."

The army's condition was indeed appalling. After the disastrous events of the second attack on Santo Domingo, the English troops had gone to pieces so completely that they imagined an invincible Spaniard lurking in every bush and shadow. Nightly on the beach there were false alarms as the English pickets fired blindly into the darkness, mistaking the clacking scuttle of the land crabs and the zig-zag flight of fireflies for the rattle of Spanish bandoliers and the glow of lighted arquebus match. In twenty calamitous days on Hispaniola nearly a thousand English troops had died, over half of them from disease. Two thirds of the remainder were sick. They had lost between two and three thousand weapons to the enemy, and most of their powder had been used up. The supply of food and medicine was still precarious, and many of the wounded, after being ferried out to the ships, were then left on deck for forty-eight hours while their wounds turned gangrenous. More depressing yet, the army's morale was in a shambles. The debacle at Hispaniola had brought out the worst in the officers and men, and Cromwell's bold Design was now in the fumbling care of an army so cowed that they shot their horses rather than take the trouble to load them on ships again. As a final insult to the long-suffering sailors, the infantry then demanded that the sea regiment should be the last unit to re-embark. Otherwise, they claimed, there was no guarantee that the navy would not sail away and leave the army to rot. So, in dribbles of men and equipment, the re-embarkation was carried out, and by May 3 the entire expedition was aboard the fleet. The following morning the English sailed away.

Behind them there was wild rejoicing. On Hispaniola the notaries of Santo Domingo dashed off a stream of enthusiastic letters to Spain, describing in glowing terms the great and glorious valor of the defenders and the utter defeat of the "belligerent English warriors" who had descended on their coasts. The buried mortar was dug up and put on parade; the captured English weapons were heaped into a celebration bonfire; and an annual holiday was proclaimed in honor of a famous victory in which, it was said, enormous numbers of English were slain. So that everyone in the city should have excuse for thanksgiving, the somewhat stingy sum of five hundred pesos was distributed to the poor, while a more substantial bonus was handed over to the cavalrymen and cowkillers who had borne the brunt of the fighting. Various high-ranking officers were also honored, and the wives and families of the Spanish dead—about forty men had been killed—were given pensions. However, not all these rewards were quite so generous as it at first seemed: several of the recipients later discovered that they had been honored with land grants far away in the backlands of Venezuela where the Indians were untamable, and those who received more immediate bounties often waited in vain for their promised rewards, which were smothered beneath the weight of Spanish bureaucracy. But these disappointments were as yet in the future, and for the moment the citizens of Santo Domingo were in a blaze of delight as they danced around the burning "cabbage stalks" and indulged in torrents of mutual congratulation. Amid all this jubilation, Peñalva and his advisers had learned from captured English prisoners that the Design was now headed for Jamaica. But in their excitement and with their own danger successfully rebuffed, they saw no reason why they should make more than a halfhearted attempt to warn their Jamaican colleagues that the next blow from the English would fall on them.

11.

The Capture of Jamaica

Of all the islands of the Golden Antilles, perhaps Jamaica most deserved the comparison with an earthly paradise. The soldiers of Cromwell's Design, sailing along the south coast of the island, would have leaned over the bulwarks of their transports and peered down through waters so clear that brilliant tropical fish swimming at five fathoms over a backdrop of coral and white sand seemed close enough to touch. Off the starboard bow rose the magnificent bulk of the Blue Mountains, rank upon rank of sage-green hills leading up to a central massif that stood sharp and clear against the tropical sky. White plumes of cumulus cloud streamed like banners from the higher peaks where the trade winds brushed them. In these mountains the soldiers would soon find spectacular gorges where rivers had cut through, exposing on each flank the fossil shells and sponges of age-old coral reefs whose bones were now embedded in the mainland. Smaller rivulets ran through miniature valleys filled with delicate traceries of ferns or overhung with vines and lianas clinging to huge trees whose succulent leaves glistened like polished green leather. "This isle," an English visitor in Ralegh's day had written, "is a marvellous fertile isle, & is as a garden or store house for divers parts of the maine. It is full of plaine champion ground, which in the rest of the Indies we have not seene; it aboundeth with beeves and cassavi, besides most pleasant fruit of divers sorts. We have not found in the Indies a more pleasant and holsome place." The climate was the main reason for this excellent fertility. The growing season lasted twelve months in the year, and native plants shed their leaves and sprouted again with extraordinary profusion. Day after day the sun shone bright and warm and, although there was a pronounced dry season, many regions of the island were relieved by summer rains which fell with almost magical precision—thirty minutes every afternoon, settling the dust and cooling the air. Then the shower would cease as miraculously as it had begun, the sun would re-emerge to dry off the newly washed vegetation—and life went on with increased vigor. Even the hurricanes, the scourge of the Antilles, seemed to respect Jamaica's tranquillity. Every year as they flailed the other islands, the hurricanes would approach menacingly toward Jamaica, but nearly always they veered away at the last moment and spun off to torment other, less fortunate, places, leaving Jamaica to her unscathed calm.

Yet, beneath its iridescent crust, this Jamaican idyll had treacherous flaws. The gorgeous mountains were too steep and too thickly forested to be used for farming, and so the only agricultural land was concentrated in the lowland pockets near the coast. But these lowlands at times could be infernally hot and parched. They lay in the rain shadow of the mountains and in bad years were afflicted with terrible droughts. Their virgin soil was difficult to break; communications between one lowland basin and the next were extremely difficult; and the heavily clad northern Europeans would soon find that the sultry summer days of the plains were extremely enervating. Then there were the local diseases, particularly malaria and yellow fever, usually diagnosed in those early days as dropsy and the ague, and considerably aggravated by the heavy drinking and incontinent habits of the settlers. Equally, it was essential to know and compensate for the regional peculiarities of the island: one spot in the upland might receive as much as ninety inches of rain in the year, while another place in a valley only ten miles away had less than five inches. Some localities were sun traps where crops ripened early and the tree fruits were ready for picking when the rest of the island was still several months from harvest. One locality might be excellent for pineapples, but would not grow cassava. In another place any citrus orchard would be decimated by insect pests, but sugar cane sprouted marvelously. It was all very confusing; and if Jamaica was indeed some sort of earthly paradise, it was also true to say that special knowledge and much experience were necessary before this bounty could be enjoyed.

As a target for their next attack, however, Jamaica was an excellent choice by the English commissioners. After the rebuff at Hispaniola, the island was a consolation prize, but it was not to be sneered at. Supposedly named by the Caribs "the land of wood and water," Jamaica lay in the underbelly of the rich arc of the Spanish Antilles, and was a superb base for any sea power that wished to rake Spain's colonies and Plate Fleets. The island did not offer Cromwell the rich mines and plantations he had hoped for, but if the English took Jamaica, they would have moved at a single leap one thousand miles westward from their fringe position on the margins of the Antilles to land at the very hub of the Caribbean. In the strategic sense, therefore, Jamaica was perhaps the most important Caribbean island of all.

And Spain had neglected her. Smaller than nearby Cuba and Hispaniola, she had been a Cinderella, passed over while Spain's larger colonies absorbed the attentions and money of the mother country. Since the early, enthusiastic days of Jamaica's colonization by the Spaniards, many of the original settler families had grown disgusted and re-emigrated to the greater opportunities of mainland America. By 1655 the island was once again a backwater. Her poverty-stricken population did not exceed 2,500 souls, and it was clustered in and around Villa de la Vega (also called St. Iago de la Vega and later renamed Spanish Town by the English), the only town on the island. There were not even enough people in the countryside to exploit the island's agricultural potential. In theory the lowland had been shared out to Spanish landowners, but they had done so little to cultivate their semifeudal domains that these were left to herds of wild cattle and their attendant cowkillers. As usual, Sailing Master Whistler reached the pith of the matter when he noted that Jamaica "may be made one of the riches spots in the wordell; the Spaniards doth call it the Garden of the Indges. But this I will say, the Gardeners have bin very bad, for heare is very litell more than that which groweth naterallie."

In fact the Spanish colonists on Jamaica had been handicapped by a peculiar problem. Columbus's descendants insisted in the law courts that their Catholic Majesties had given Jamaica to Columbus as his personal fief and that it should therefore devolve to his descendants. This extraordinary claim, based on dubious legality, had created such confusion that the settlers could never be quite sure whether they held their lands from the Spanish Crown or the Columbus family. In the litigious atmosphere of Spanish colonial politics this uncertainty had deterred all but the most optimistic farmers from settlement. In the 161 years since Columbus had claimed the place for Ferdinand and Isabella, the colony had done so poorly that the English invaders found it difficult to distinguish between the richest planter on Jamaica and the poorest artisan. Neither class lived very grandly. Both dressed in workaday clothing, ate the same monotonous food, and lived in humble single-story houses made of dried mortar packed around a framework of upright posts. Many of the colonial families were intermarried, and very few of them were wealthy enough to afford large numbers of slaves. After more than a century of toil, the Spanish settlers still lived in a frontier atmosphere, frugally scratching together their annual production of hides, lard, tallow, and spices, and hopefully awaiting the day when the Council of the Indies would decide to develop their island properly. The great event of the year was the arrival of the ship from Spain, bringing news from the homeland, manufactured wares, and perhaps a collection of new government functionaries. Otherwise, Jamaica might well have been the far side of the world; it was so isolated and neglected. Villa de la Vega, only six miles inland from the huge natural harbor on which Kingston was later to be built, was perched halfheartedly on the very rim of the island, and most of the Spanish colonists looked backward to their landing beach as their only link with the outside world, rather than forward to the undeveloped interior of their island.

Penn and Venables were not entirely ignorant about conditions on Jamaica. English ships had often careened in the island's sheltered coves, and in the past the Spanish settlers on Jamaica had been only too glad to do business with an occasional English contrabandeer supplying them with goods which Spain either neglected to send or sold at an outrageous price. Twelve years earlier, too, a large band of English privateersmen had boldly landed on the island, seized Villa de la Vega and held it to ransom. Several of the men who had taken part in that raid were now with Penn's fleet to advise the commissioners on the best way of overrunning the Spanish positions. Indeed the Spaniards of Jamaica had become so depressingly familiar with the attacks of pirates and other predators that they had developed a healthy respect for raiders of any sort. They knew that their position was too weak to sustain a prolonged resistance, and so at the first glimpse of unfriendly sails on the horizon, the Spanish Jamaicans customarily bowed to the inevitable. They packed their belongings on carts, evacuated their families, and fled into the mountains to wait there until the raiders lost interest and went away. This was their initial reaction when, on May 9, 1655, the Spanish lookout on the watchtower at the landing place on the bay reported that a powerful English fleet was heading straight for the anchorage.

The day the English fleet sighted Jamaica, "very high land afarr off," Commissioner Winslow, the veteran of New Plymouth, died. It was said that he succumbed to a broken heart, his spirit crushed by the disgraceful affair at Santo Domingo; but more probably he was killed by fever, inadequate medical attention, and the effects of an overstrenuous life. He was sixty-seven. His body was nailed up in a coffin with two-round shot at his feet and hung on ropes over the side of the *Swiftsure* while the burial service was read. Then, at the last Amen, the ropes were loosed off and the coffin splashed into the clear Caribbean water while Penn's ships began to thud out a forty-two-gun salute over the commissioner's grave. Winslow's death set the mood of the new campaign, and as the fleet maneuvered into what would later be called Kingston Bay, the English troops bore little resemblance to the cocksure opportunists who had gone ashore on Hispaniola so confidently. Now they were somber, sickly, and nervous. Venables too was affected by the general depression. As the ships dropped anchor off the Jamaican coast, he paced morosely up and down the deck of his ship, his head thrust forward into the collar of his cloak and a hat drawn low over his eyes. He would not even raise his head to acknowledge the halfhearted cheers of his men as they were rowed past in the ships's boats on their way to the landing beach. A few hours earlier he had specifically warned them that any man who turned his back on the enemy during the Jamaica campaign was to be killed instantly by the soldier standing next to him; otherwise, both men would be executed as cowards. With this gloomy thought in their minds, the soldiers, aided by a smart breeze, swiftly neared the Spanish landing beach. Already they could make out a small defensive breastwork and could see the puffs of gunsmoke as the defenders opened fire.

Venables was being overpessimistic. The military position on Jamaica had little in common with the conditions he had encountered so disastrously on Hispaniola. The Spanish population on Jamiaca was too small and too poorly armed to mount the type of defense that the Count of Peñalva had used. Villa de la Vega had no fortifications worth the name; and there were no country levies who could be called in to strengthen the garrison. The Jamaican Spaniards were as plucky as the men who had fought under Peñalva, but they were not so foolish as to think that they could throw back seven or eight thousand Englishmen, however sorry-looking the raiders appeared to be. For the moment, indeed, the Spaniards were not even sure of the invaders's intentions, and they were chiefly interested in finding out exactly what this ponderous attack was all about. No European power, Spain included, had ever before considered that lowly Jamaica warranted such a massive onslaught. Jamaica's Spanish population was hoping that the English had either made some sort of navigational mistake or that they had come only to pick up supplies en route to more important targets elsewhere. Cautiously, therefore, the 180 men of the colony's tiny militia force took up position near the landing place.

They were led by their governor, Don Juan Ramírez de Orellana, an unhappy figure so tormented by the sores and fistulae of an incurable skin disease covering his body that he had to be carried everywhere in a padded litter and swaddled like a baby. At the landing place only three guns were mounted within the breastwork and ready for use, and the militiamen could have done very little harm with their miniature broadside even if their aim had been good, which it was not. But they banged off about twenty rounds, concentrating their fire on the leading English vessel, the galley *Martin*, as she nosed her way into the shallows, her guns returning the Spaniards' shot with an equal lack of success. Then, as soon as the English started coming ashore in earnest, the Spaniards discreetly abandoned their positions and hurried back to the town without having lost a man. There they supervised the customary evacuation of their families and the flight to the hills, while a handful of their scouts glumly watched as regiment upon regiment of English foot-soldiers landed and proceeded to set up camp on the beach with an ominous lack of haste. Next morning, when the English column began to trudge purposefully inland, the Spaniards could bear the suspense no longer. They sent forward two messengers under a flag of truce to see the English commander, and when the messengers were taken before Venables, they hopefully informed him that if he had come to find food for his men, the Spanish colonists on the island would be happy to supply the English army with as much beef and cassava bread as they could spare so that his expedition could be on its way again. Venables's harsh answer confirmed their worst fears. He came, he told them bluntly, "not to pillage, but to plant," and he intended to take permanent possession of the entire island in the name of the Commonwealth. At two o'clock the same afternoon the English infantry marched un-opposed into an abandoned Villa de la Vega.

The Spanish leaders now found themselves in a dilemma. For the first time in the history of their colony, it was no use waiting for the invaders to go away of their own accord. If Venables had meant what he said—and there was every indication that he did—it was necessary to take more active steps to dislodge the English. Furthermore, the Spaniards knew from experience that the next two or three months would provide their best chance of re-pulsing the occupying force. The worst part of the dry season

would soon be on them, and, if there was a drought, the
newcomers would find it exceptionally difficult to hunt or raise
enough food to sustain themselves. It was just possible that by
withdrawing into the central fastnesses, the Spanish could keep
up military pressure against the invaders until the natural conditions of Jamaica had disheartened the English army. The Spanish
colonists were well aware that Jamaica's nascent economy was
geared to sustain three thousand colonists, and that the arrival of
another six or seven thousand mouths would place an intolerable
strain on it. In this event, starvation would be Spain's ally. For
the next few days, however, the Spaniards needed the extra time
to allow their slow-moving refugee column to plod into the hills
and disperse into their customary safe hiding places. In a bold
effort to gain this breathing space a small deputation of settlers
rode back into the capital and asked for a parley with the English
commanders.

In Villa de la Vega, General Venables and his staff officers
were in high spirits. Glad to be rid of the naval men at last, they
boasted that the army now had a free hand to show just how well
it could perform on its own. They had been completely misled
by the ease of their advance on the Spanish capital, and, with
quite staggering self-delusion, they congratulated themselves on
the significance of their conquest. Villa de la Vega, they claimed,
was a splendid trophy. In reality, of course, it was of little
military or financial importance, a shabby provincial capital that
the Spaniards had evacuated many times before in the face of far
less formidable invaders. Even while Venables and his staff were
magnifying the importance of their achievements, the English
soldiers, disregarding the prohibition against looting, had gone
wandering through the deserted streets, breaking down doors,
desecrating churches, and ransacking every private house to see
what they could find. Their haul was a disappointment. The
Spaniards had picked the place clean before they left, and every
article of value was now trundling off on the refugee carts. Only
a few broken-down beds, chairs, and tables had been left behind.
The scavenging English soldiery scrabbled at these pathetic
spoils, even pulling up the bald and greasy cowhides that lined
the floors of the slave huts. These cowhides were eventually

shipped to New England, where they were exchanged for a cargo of biscuit, pease, and meal. Suitably, it was the only profit that Venables and his men managed to squeeze from their unearned capture of the Jamaican capital.

By the time the Spanish deputation arrived in the town, Venables, Commissioner Butler, and the other senior army officers had established themselves in the municipal building overlooking the main square, in offices that had formerly been occupied by the town council. So it was to familiar surroundings that the Spanish envoys were led for the first in a series of meetings which was to illustrate the dullwittedness of the English leaders and the comparative astuteness of their Spanish adversaries. The chief negotiators for the English were Venables, Major-General Fortescue (his second-in-command), several of the other senior land officers, and Commissioner Butler. As their adviser and interpreter they had Thomas Gage, self-styled expert in American affairs. The Spanish delegation was led, oddly enough, by a Portuguese, Francisco de Carvajal. He was acting as a deputy for their Sargento Mayor, or senior officer of militia, who was then occupied in the much more urgent task of shepherding the refugees to safety. The Spanish delegation, of course, had only one aim: to drag out the proceedings for as long as possible while their forces made ready for war. And to win this respite, they came prepared to dissimulate behind an air of deep humility and politeness. By contrast, the English thought only of negotiating the terms of the Spanish surrender; they were so confident they held the Spanish Jamaicans at their mercy that they behaved like bullies and, in the end, were duped.

Venables opened the first meeting in characteristically high-handed fashion by refusing to discuss anything of importance until the Spaniards first agreed to supply the English army with a daily quota of beef cattle, milch cows, sheep, and cassava bread. His troops, he announced grandly, had been long at sea and needed fresh meat, and this food should now be delivered by the Spaniards. He omitted to mention that even then the improvident English soldiery were in the process of rounding up and wantonly slaughtering every living creature, draft animals included, that they could lay their hands on, and that very soon there would be no fresh meat at all in Villa de la Vega. Carvajal was shrewd enough to see immediately that Venables had given him an ideal opportunity to stall the negotiations before they had even begun, and very tactfully he broke off the meeting on the excuse that he needed to return at once to the Spanish encampment in order to make the necessary arrangements to comply with the wishes of the English general.

At the meeting on the following day, Venables was in a towering rage. He had asked, he told Carvajal, for at least three hundred cattle and a large quantity of cassava bread to be delivered to his hungry men—but his quartermasters reported that the Spanish herdsmen had only shown up with thirty scrawny cows and no cassava bread whatsoever. He did not intend to be trifled with, and he had not expected the Spaniards to break their word. Unruffled, Carvajal answered this outburst with smooth assurances that, although cassava bread had regrettably proved to be unobtainable due to a shortage throughout the island, the full quota of cattle would have been delivered but for unforeseen difficulties. Unfortunately, the Spanish camp was far away and it was difficult to herd the half-wild animals into town. But, he promised, the Spaniards would do better next day. Very courteously, he then begged leave to inquire by what right the English had decided to lay claim to Jamaica, when the island had been in Spanish hands for over a century and had been granted to the Spanish nation by Papal Bull. To this question Gage promptly retorted that the English intended to take the island from the Spaniards just as the Spaniards had once taken it from the Indians. As for the Pope, he quipped, his grant of Jamaica had nothing to do with the matter, for in the days of Henry VIII the Pope had made a gift of England to any prince who cared to seize the realm, but no one had accepted the challenge. At this sally, noted one of the Spanish delegation, "the Parliamentarians had laughed long and heartily." Venables next turned his attention to the terms under which the Spanish were expected to surrender the island and began to read out a long and detailed list of conditions, only to have Carvajal tell him very politely that the Spanish delegation was not empowered to discuss surrender terms without referring the matter back to their governor and his council. At

this point Venables became so exasperated that he flatly refused
to deal any longer with the Spaniards unless their governor
himself put in an appearance. Once again Carvajal took his cue,
and made Venables's outburst an excuse to withdraw.

For two more days the negotiations dragged on; this time
with Governor Ramírez leading the Spanish deputation, much to
the dismay of the English negotiators, who were appalled and
disgusted by the wretched appearance of the pox-ridden invalid
whom the English surgeons refused even to touch. Meanwhile,
with each extra day, the Spanish evacuation continued swiftly
and efficiently, and the refugees' morale rose higher and higher
as they began to realize the ineptitude of their opponents. Eventually Ramírez did agree to Venables's terms, but it was the
gesture of a sick and weary man, for when the news was taken
back to the Spanish camp, there was a public meeting at which
both the capitulations and the governor himself were vehemently
denounced by the majority of the colonists. The Spanish settlers were not prepared to give up their lands as meekly as
Venables's clumsy and impossibly harsh terms of surrender demanded. According to his draft capitulations, all hostiles under
arms, all Spanish forts, munitions, instruments of war, and ships
in port were to be handed over to the English within ten days.
The English commissioners promised that the Spanish colonists
would not be harmed in any way, but they were to be disarmed
and only their officers allowed to carry swords and daggers. Any
Spaniard wishing to leave the island would be permitted to do so,
and transport would be provided. However, the evacuees could
take with them only the clothes they wore, their books, and any
written work they wished to retain. All other valuables, goods,
and chattels improperly removed from their usual places by the
refugee column were to be returned forthwith. There was also a
clause offering special incentives to any artisan or craftsman who
elected to live under English law, and another clause which
informed the slaves that they would soon receive their freedom.
To ensure the implementation of these capitulations, the commissioners demanded a census of all persons wishing to remain on
Jamaica and stipulated that the Spanish authorities were to hand

over an adequate number of hostages. In short, Jamaica was now to be regarded as the absolute property of the English nation; and the previous Spanish occupants could either stay on as second-class citizens or go elsewhere.

Not surprisingly, the Spaniards decided to stay and fight. Governor Ramírez, feeling that he had pledged his honor when agreeing to the capitulations and that he was in no fit state to go campaigning, surrendered to the English along with several of his senior officers. Command of the Spanish forces therefore passed to younger and more daring leaders, several of whom quickly proved to be superb guerrilla fighters. Under them the Spaniards began the hard-fought campaign that was to last another three years and cause the English much grief. Typically, the first casualty of this campaign was an innocent noncombatant. He was a Negro slave who had been sent by his master, one of the Spanish hostages held in Villa de la Vega, to take a letter to the Spanish camp. He was immediately arrested by a Spanish picket, and, thinking that the Negro had come as a spy for the English, the Spanish garrotted him without asking for explanations.

Yet it took more than the death of an obscure Negro slave to shatter the fool's paradise in which Venables and his staff were living. They were so confident the Spaniards would not dare to resist the enormously superior English force that they scarcely took the trouble to post guards or scout the enemy's position. Instead they spent their time taking an inflated inventory of this alleged treasure store of the Antilles which they intended to present to a delighted Lord Protector. They drew up a list of the number and worth of the sugar mills and plantations on the island, made wild guesses at the value of the slaves they expected to defect from the Spaniards (and had little intention of setting free), speculated about the existence of yet-undiscovered gold and silver mines in the interior, and even began to lay plans for making beer and ale on Jamaica. They were still day-dreaming when the first signs of trouble began to show. A party of men who had gone out to shoot guinea fowl failed to return. The daily delivery of the Spanish beef cattle mysteriously dried up. Then came reports that an English foraging party had been ambushed by unidentified assailants, and that several of the Spanish hostages had slipped out of Villa de la Vega and disappeared. Too late, Venables realized that he had been tricked.

He reacted with unusual speed. The infantry were rousted out of their billets and sent hurrying after the Spanish refugees, and a seaborne force was taken aboard the navy's light boats and rushed down the coast in an attempt to cut off the Spanish escape route. But it was much too late. The Spaniards were already well clear, and had protected their line of march cleverly. In a few days Venables's men returned empty-handed and sullen, having lost several men to brilliant rearguard actions by the Spanish irregular cavalry.

Now, in all its tragedy, began the Englishmen's long, hard apprenticeship in the ways of guerrilla warfare in the tropics. It was to their eventual credit that, although they learned only with painful slowness, they did finally grasp the ground rules of the campaign and in the end came to be as effective in the tangled woodlands as the dreaded cowkillers who had terrified them so unspeakably on Hispaniola. But at first it was the bitterness of Santo Domingo all over again. The Spaniards knew every inch of the country; the English foot-soldiers unwarily blundered into traps and were badly mauled; and even after the enemy had shown himself, Venables's officers had no idea of how to come to grips with their fast-moving opponents. In a series of small actions, English watering parties and forward patrols were ambushed; hunting groups and wood-cutting details were surprised and cut to ribbons. Sometimes a single terrified trooper would come stumbling back to blurt out the news of the massacre, but more often the Spaniards systematically killed all the soldiers in the trapped unit and left their bodies lying in the open as a warning. The guerrillas could not take prisoners, for they had little enough food for themselves and their families, and they did not want an escaped prisoner to inform the English staff of how precariously they were surviving in their forest camps in the mountains. But as the months passed and the guerrillas failed to receive adequate reinforcements from the other Spanish islands in the Antilles, the balance of warfare slowly tipped against them. The English adopted new and more ruthless tactics. They "famined" their enemy by burning the standing crops and they razed every humble cabin they found in the woods. Venables's troops planted counterambushes on the mountain trails; they mounted patrols on captured Spanish horses and occasionally managed to catch the raiding parties before they could fade away into the interior. And, with a well-planned series of surprise landings along the coasts, they gradually whittled away at the enemy-held territory. When the rainy season arrived, several guerrilla bands found life too difficult in the rain-sodden mountains and came down to the capital to give themselves up. Other Spaniards dribbled away to Cuba, bravely making the ninety-mile crossing in cottonwood dugout canoes, until there was only a hard core of resistance left on the island. This last handful hung on tenaciously, but finally the English located their one remaining stockade on the north coast, stormed it, and drove the last hostile Spaniard from Jamaica.

Yet, all this time, the real battle for Jamaica was not being fought with guns and lances in the mountains. It was waged with pickaxes and hoes on the plains around Villa de la Vega. There it was that the English learned the ironic lessons of survival in the Golden Antilles. The Design had arrived on the shores of this alleged paradise with a scanty reserve of food supplies, and the commissioners knew that it was a life-and-death matter for the army to clear the land and learn to feed itself. Emergency shipments from England and Barbados, erratic at the best of times, could not be sustained indefinitely, and the expedition had perhaps five or six months in which to expand Jamaica's agriculture into an adequate base for the colony. So, pathetically, they tried to turn the soldiers into farmers on a regimental basis. Each regiment was allocated a specific area of the lowland and ordered to cultivate it under the supervision of the officers. It was a likely theory and commended itself to the colonels, who wanted to keep their military formation together in case they were needed in a hurry to repel a Spanish relief force. But in practice the scheme foundered disastrously, for the commissioners failed to realize that soldiers did not necessarily turn farmers at a given command, and that those enlisted men who had come to Jamaica with dreams of a lotus life in the Antilles were not prepared to become drudges for the benefit of their officers. To exacerbate this feeling, the officers then proceeded to treat the land grants as their own private estates, and with tactless disdain asked for Scots and Irish beggars and other destitutes to be shipped out to work alongside the common soldiers. Resentment between officers and men blighted the whole project from the start, and mutiny was very near the surface. Finally, even the landless subalterns threw in their lot with the enlisted men and began to demand a greater share of the spoils of Jamaica.

But there were very few spoils to be distributed, for the cultivation of Sailing Master Whistler's "Garden of the Indges" went desperately slowly. The man lacked proper tools to work the land; the tropical soils seemed to be sadly infertile; and not even the levies from St. Christopher's and Nevis knew what and when to plant. The soldiers were so discouraged that they neglected to weed patches of land which they had already cleared; and with their issue of rations necessitating three meat-less days a week and permitting only three biscuits every seventeen days, they were too weak to tackle virgin-forest cover. Life became so hard that several of the runaway apprentices and indentured men from Barbados began to ask if they could not be shipped back to their former masters to face punishment and the rest of their time, rather than stay on Jamaica. One Barbadian officer, it was true, seemed to be doing well at the new trade of planter. But he was found to be embezzling his troops' pay as a sideline, and it was necessary to have him cashiered and deported.

Often, the soldiers-turned-farmers did more harm than good. They chopped down fruit-bearing trees, trampled down fields of cassava planted by the Spanish, and scared away the wild cattle. During the reckless days immediately after disembarkation in Jamaica, the soldiers had not been too squeamish to slaughter dogs, donkeys, cats, snakes, and rodents for food. But this killing had dangerously reduced the supply of livestock, and now the soldiers were obliged to try their hand at herding the wild cattle on the savannahs. But they made indifferent cowboys, and in their annoyance tried to shoot the beasts with their arquebuses. This was a mistake, because the herds that had once swarmed on the lowland took fright and migrated into the woods where they were almost impossible to track down. One English hunting party, even more poorly managed than most, surrounded a small drove of cattle, opened fire from all sides and failed to hit a single cow, but killed several of its own men. Even when an arquebusier was lucky enough to hit his mark, a ball from his gun was seldom enough to drop a cow in its tracks, and the wounded beast usually ran off to die in the undergrowth where its carcass could not be found. One English officer claimed that during a short ride through the woods he came across the putrefying bodies of eighty dead cattle, rotting uselessly in the sun; and Major-General Sedgewicke, writing to Cromwell about conditions on the island, glumly informed him: "Our soldiers have destroyed all sorts of provisions and cattle. Nothing but ruin attends them wherever they go. Dig or plant they neither will nor can, but are determined rather to starve than work."

Underpinning this appalling record of waste, incompetence, and idleness was the gnawing quarrel between the land and sea which had not abated since the first day on shore. General Venables was still scarcely on speaking terms with Penn, and had so little trust in the admiral's intentions that he had started keeping a dossier of all Penn's imagined misdeeds. He was sure that the navy was deliberately underestimating the true quantity of stores aboard the fleet, and that the sailors were maliciously refusing to land food and munitions which rightfully belonged to the land forces. He also suspected that Penn was permitting his naval officers to divert prize money, belonging to the expedition as a whole, into their pockets. This last assertion may have had some truth, for Penn had somehow engineered the appointment of his own nephew to the post of expedition prize officer, and when the time came for the nephew to relinquish his position, he would neither produce the original documents relating to his handling of the sale of prizes nor allow a proper audit of his accounts.

But this internecine wrangling was by no means confined to accusations and counteraccusations between the two services. The army itself was badly split. Many officers were incensed with Venables for what they considered to be an incompetent handling of the capture of Villa de la Vega. In their opinion he should have moved against the Jamaican capital more quickly and caught the Spaniards before they stripped the town of plunder. Colonel Buller was the natural focus for these malcontents, for the colonel had already proved with his mismanagement of the diversionary force before Santo Domingo that he was an independent-minded and pompous troublemaker. Thus when Venables fell sick under the strain of managing his ramshackle army on Jamaica, Buller actually went so far as to convene his own council of war and issue orders as though the expedition were his own command. When Venables recovered, he stormed back at the insubordinate faction, who were, in his phrase, "Lazy dull officers that have a large Portion of Pride, but not of Wit, Valour, or Activity." Commissioner Butler, too, had been making a pest of himself, and when Venables eventually could contain himself no longer and called Butler a "drunken sot," the commissioner took umbrage and, much to everyone's relief, decided to leave for England.

In Kingston Bay the navy was having an equally miserable time. The sailors were on half allowance of meat and drink, and, instead of scouring the island for loot as they had anticipated, they found themselves hard at work careening their vessels to rid hulls of fouling. During the careening, the *Discovery,* one of the storeships, caught fire in her bread room, and, since she was carrying a cargo of brandy, bosun's and carpenter's stores, and 120 barrels of gunpowder, she blazed famously. In fact she endangered the rest of the fleet anchored around her, and a number of cockboats had to go over to her and tow her off to a sandbar. There she was beached and left to burn herself out. But as she burned, the *Discovery* lightened, and with a change in the wind she came swaying wildly down on the fleet like a great, floating bomb, until she blew up less than a carbine shot from the awed gaze of Sailing Master Whistler, who was busily recording the alarums and excursions of the night in his diary.

Despite their troubles, the English somehow held on. There were, perhaps, too many of them for every man to be broken, and a tiny minority actually found Jamaica very much to its liking. "'Tis not soe hot as Italy by day and cooler by nights and mornings," commented one soldier; and another, obviously prone to overweight, wrote home delightedly to his friends that due to the shortage of food and "much sweating," he had "fallen away 4 fingers about the waist." Badly needed equipment also began to reach the island. Gradually there arrived, in reply to Venables's urgent requests, water bottles, iron, steel, flint, shoes, linen, tents, new swords, and even a new constitution for ruling the island. Discipline too began to take hold once again. Skirmishers were warned that if they shot at the wild cattle they would be imprisoned or made "to ride the wooden horse," an excruciating punishment which combined physical torture with the ignominy of the public pillory. Two inveterate "swearers" were whipped and then burned through the tongue. Reinforcements arrived, eight hundred fresh troops from England brought in to replace the sick and repel any Spanish counteroffensive. "Poor men," wrote one observer watching them come ashore, "I pitty them at heart, all their imagined mountaines are turned into dross."

Disappointment in the harsh reality of the Antilles was by no means confined to Jamaica, for in England Cromwell was aghast at the poor success of his colonial schemes. Having believed in the myth of the Antilles, he had poured vast amounts of men and material into the Design. Now, it seemed, his commanders had failed him and squandered the golden chance. They were a pair of nincompoops, who did nothing but write to London asking for more and more aid while their mismanaged colony tried to strike root. His splendid tributary to the Protectorate had turned into an open-ended drain insatiably swallowing funds and men. Even at a five-thousand-mile distance, Penn and Venables could feel the Protector's anger, and they caught more than a whiff of his irritation in the curt denials which he sent to their pleas for help. Finally Penn grew so worried that he made up his mind to return to England and personally explain the situation. His ships, he claimed, needed to refit and he felt that there was little prospect of a Spanish counterattack. So, leaving twelve frigates under Goodson to nurse the infant colony, he sailed for home. General Venables, terrified that the admiral would shift the entire blame for the expedition's unhappy performance onto the land forces, followed him soon afterward. Cromwell had little sympathy for either of them. They were summoned to London, given a blistering dressing-down for deserting their posts on Jamaica, and thrown into the Tower of London. Both men were later released after they had delivered an abject apology to the Protector, but neither was ever employed by Cromwell again.

After his release from the Tower, Venables, still smarting from the disgrace of Santo Domingo, went off to write his *Narrative* in reply to certain scurrilous broadsheets which had begun to be circulated in England, accusing him of cowardice and incompetence. Somewhat pathetically he attempted to dispel the rumors by reciting long-winded testimonials to his own skill as a military commander. But it was clear that he had had his fill of soldiering, and soon afterward he went into semiretirement, where he could devote time to his favorite hobby of fishing. In 1662 he took to print again, but this time it was in happier circumstances, as he wished to publish "*The Experienced Angler or Angling Improved*, being a general discourse of angling, imparting many of the aptest ways and choicest experiments for the taking of most sorts of fish in pond or river." The quondam general was evidently a better fisherman than warrior, for Izaak Walton gave high praise to Venables's hints to the angler. "I have read and practiced many books of this kind," he wrote generously to Venables, "yet I could never find in them that height of judgement and reasoned which you have manifested in this [book]."

Admiral Penn, on the other hand, still had a long and active career ahead of him. Showing more good sense than he had formerly used in the Antilles, he switched to the Royalist side shortly before the Restoration, and in consequence he prospered excellently. He received his knighthood and was to remain for several years a senior flag officer in Charles II's navy, in which role he was to be a thorn in the flesh of the ambitious and conniving Pepys.

Thomas Gage, the third main figure in the drama and the man who had helped to usher in the Design, was the only one to remain in Jamaica. There he suffered the penalty for his earlier optimism. Within ten months of seeing his dream fulfilled and the English nation take its place in the Golden Antilles, Thomas Gage was dead. Yet his passing was scarcely remarked, for he was only one of some five thousand casualties during that tragic year on Jamaica. He left behind a wife and children to be supported by a not-over-grateful English government, his now-famous *Travels*, and the grim reality of the English colony he had promoted so strenuously. There the garbage was piled so high in the English lines that whole streets were rendered impassable by the stench, and the medical officers dreaded an outbreak of bubonic plague. Not even the dead were left in peace. Their graves were too shallow and, as the summer heat increased, their bodies putrefied and swelled until they broke through the crust of the earth. Spanish pariah dogs, emerging after dark from the bush, gnawed on their bones and dug up the graves with their paws. There were no English dogs to help with the disinterment because every English dog had long since been eaten by the soldiers who had brought them to the Golden Antilles.

12.

The Legend of the Buccaneers

THUS, ON JAMAICA, THE SLAP OF HARSH REALITY once again interrupted the dream of the Golden Antilles. And just as Ralegh's fiasco in search of El Dorado had sent its martyr to the headsman's block, so too did Cromwell's lame-footed Western Design punish the five or six thousand English soldiers left to rot in semistarvation under a West Indian sun. The army's letters plumbed the abyss of despair. The soldiers wrote home only to complain and wallow in self-pity. They cursed the climate, blamed their officers, and hated the grudging land. A few snarled at their shattered hopes, and not a ship sailed for England without first being besieged by a horde of disheartened men who clamored to be taken away from the dreary island. Even the highest-ranking officers, who at least had enough to fill their bellies, devoted their energies to devising ways of resigning their commissions and leaving the flawed jewel which had snared them. This demoralization was so abject and so widespread that the early governors of the island, hopefully sent out from England to repair the damage, were at a loss to know how to put the place in order, and they too swiftly joined the lines of supplicants who begged to be relieved of their appointments. Several of the governors in fact died in harness, overwhelmed by the chaos they had come so confidently to disentangle. With their deaths the colony's evil reputation began to spread. Like plague germs it was carried to the mother country in the army's dispatches and the administrator's official reports. It went to the American mainland colonies aboard small merchant vessels that came sniffing down in hopes of trade with the new settlement and went away sharply disappointed. And it reached the other Caribbean islands by the returning supply ships that brought seedlings of useful plants, inadequate quantities of food, and much useless advice. Everywhere the rumor was the same: Jamaica was an ill-favored pesthole from which few people ever escaped, and those who survived the ordeal always swore that they would never go back. On Barbados these gloomy reports met with smug satisfaction, since the Barbadian planters had never really forgiven Penn and Venables for the high-handed way they had siphoned off many of the laborers and indentured men. Now the Barbadians were quietly pleased that the Design had gone off so shabbily. Venables's failure meant that Jamaica was less likely to be a rival to the older colony, and in an uncharitable attempt to hasten Jamaica's decline the Barbadian planters actively discouraged further emigration from their own island to the stricken conquest. Jamaica, they let it be rumored, was an open grave which beckoned any laboring man so foolish as to try his luck there. Moreover, the army authorities on the island would enslave any new arrival until he was utterly worn out. Their campaign of slander was so effective that for a time virtually all movement of settlers to Jamaica from the Caribbees dried up, and even the most miserable wretch on Barbados preferred to serve out his apparently endless indentures rather than risk the thrice-told horrors of Jamaica.

Even more pathetic was the plight of the families of those soldiers who had gone on the Design with Venables. When the wives in England heard reports of the capture of Jamaica, they took their children and made arrangements to follow their husbands and settle the new colony. But they arrived at Jamaica to find conditions worse than anything they had left behind. Often they learned that their menfolk were already dead and buried. So, to the ill-concealed satisfaction of the Barbadian planters, these

distressed women insisted on being shipped across to the Caribbees, where they sold themselves as servants into the islands
rather than stay and live under army rule on Jamaica.

Among the American colonies to the north, a similar catastrophe was only just averted. Cromwell had decided that the
experienced colonists of North America might survive Jamaican
hardships more stoutly than his own Englishmen, and so he tried
to recruit volunteers from the seaboard colonies of America. His
agent, Nathaniel Gookin, attempted to persuade some of the
New England men that they should "remove" themselves and
their families to the sunnier climes and more fecund soils of
England's latest territorial acquisition. But Gookin's blandish-
ments fell on stony ground. The citizens of New England
retorted that they preferred their bleaker shores to a land that
was widely known, as they primly put it, for "the prophaneness
of the soldiery; the great mortality in the island; and the continued hazard to the lives of any peaceable settlers there from the
skulking Negroes and Spaniards." Nor would the New England
merchants, a group less concerned with the morals of the army
and the habits of the Spaniards, agree to continue supplying
shipments of food to Jamaica. They disliked payment by army
and navy bills, and cannily looked to more lucrative and reliable
profits from this alleged emporium of the tropics.

So, to all appearances, the infant settlement of Jamaica was
doomed to languish, as one by one her colonial cousins turned
their backs on her. Yet Cromwell played the fairy godmother and
saved Jamaica. He had inaugurated the unhappy venture and now
he refused to let it perish, continuing to support his project with
men, money, and material. His Council of State was prodded into
voting that a thousand girls and as many young men should be
"listed" in Ireland and sent out to work on the half-completed
plantations of Jamaica. And in Scotland, that other unruly ap-
pendage of the Protectorate, the sheriffs of counties and the
commissioners of parishes were asked to "apprehend all known,
idle, masterless robbers and vagabonds, male and female, and
transport them to that island." These undesirables were indifferent recruits for a struggling colony, but the government in its
forthright way was sublimely confident that an arduous life,

short rations, and the rigors of colonial existence were ideal therapy for the most idle rogue, who would soon be transmuted into a pillar of God-fearing rectitude. The Lord Protector also arranged for another string of supply ships to sail from England, and when it was found that the first season's planting on Jamaica had been so badly bungled that most of the crop had died, a fresh batch of seeds and young plants was sent across from the Caribbees.

Thus coaxed into motion by the efforts of the home government, Jamaica's economy slowly began to move. Like the fly-wheel of some gigantic engine it turned hesitantly at first, with a heartstopping pause every year as the summer drought reduced all progress to a halt. Then it gathered momentum as the summer swung into autumn, the rains came, and the land gave a little more generously. With each succeeding year the tempo of the economy picked up speed and rhythm; the planters learned more skills, and the prospects improved. By the end of the first ten years, Jamaica's continued progress was assured, for by then she was progressing without the need for an annual influx of help from England. Fields had been laid out; the colonists had moved from their tents and shacks into more substantial dwellings; a brace of forts, one with twenty-one pieces of ordnance in it, had been built on the two headlands commanding the entrance to Kingston harbor, and under their shelter trading ships were beginning to gather where Penn had once put his naval storehouses. There began the first embryonic stirrings of Port Royal, later to be notorious for its stews and brothels, and where even in those early days salvage men made their living by locating and picking over the wrecks of Spanish ships which had foundered on nearby reefs. Each year, too, Jamaica's population increased. They came in odd lots, a boatload of Quakers from the Caribbees, and a group from the Bermudas who were unwanted in the older colony. They were joined by political refugees from England, where the Protectorate's stability did not look so stable after all. Even righteous New England forgot its anathema of godless Jamaica and set three hundred recruits to take the opportunity of moving into a new and untried colony. Their enterprise was soon rewarded. The island's rich soil repaid skilled attention, and

Venables's once lackluster troops began to farm more willingly when they were given their own plots of land and saw the profits that could be made. "The activity of the officers," drily commented Henry Long, an eighteenth-century Jamaican historian and himself a landowner, "now seemed to form a perfect contrast to their past indolences; they were to become, in the phrase of the West-Indies, red-hot planters."

The importation of Negro slaves had much to do with this growing prosperity and the increase in population. By 1673 there were more than seventeen thousand inhabitants in Jamaica, and twelve years later the number of Negroes was large enough for the first slave revolt to take place. But by that time the planters were doing so well that they refused to curb the number of slaves landed each year on the island. The richer colonists had learned to concentrate their efforts on the production of sugar, where the profits were enormous, and they were labor short and land hungry. Soon the half-empty Jamaica of Spanish days was a thing of the past, as English landholders gobbled up their prize in the Antilles, and their dreams of wealth began to materialize. Within two generations the plutocracy of Jamaica would be synonymous with extraordinary wealth and ostentation, and the tale would be told of the rich duchess whose husband, a much depleted and spendthrift duke, had been bundled off to govern Jamaica on the understanding that he was to recoup his fortunes at the same time. The duke seized his opportunity with a powerful grasp, and not only rebuilt his private finances through the usual speculation, but even entered into partnership with some of the salvage men of Port Royal. When they had the good fortune to find and recover the cargo of a well-laden Spanish merchant ship, the duke then used his authority to swindle his partners and make off with the lion's share of the spoils. But he died a short time later, and his widow, left to face the wrath of the salvage men, had to be smuggled off the island aboard an English warship. Arriving home fabulously wealthy and in a state of mild delusion, Her Grace was convinced that the Emperor of China had heard of her wealth and wished to marry her. According to the historian Bryan Edwards, who recounted this tale in the 1790's, "as she [the Duchess] was perfectly gentle and good-humoured in her lunacy, her attendants not only encouraged her in her folly but contrived also to turn it to good account by persuading a needy peer (the first duke of Montague) to personate his Chinese Majesty, and deceive her into wedlock, which he actually did; and with greater success than honesty, or, I should imagine, even the law would warrant, got possession by this means of her wealth, and then confined her as a lunatick." Happily the duchess had the last victory, for Edwards added "her grace survived her husband, the pretended emperor, for many years, and died in 1734, at the great age of 98. Her frenzy remained however to the last, and she was served on the knee as Empress of China to the day of her death."

Curiously enough, although the strange habits of such luminaries as Her Grace gave much added splendor to the legend of the Golden Antilles during the closing years of the seventeenth century, these gorgeous blooms were grafts onto an already flourishing stock of the legend. Against all expectation, the myth of the Golden Antilles not only survived Cromwell's Western Design, but actually took sustenance from it. Within a generation of Thomas Gage's death the legend of the Antilles was in full flower once again, thanks to another propagandist—Alexander Oliver Oexmelin, known to the English as John Esquemeling, author of a book entitled (in English) *The History of the Bucaniers of America*. His volume was so popular and so readable that it was reissued, re-edited, plagiarized, translated, and imitated almost without a break for the next century.

Paradoxically it was the decline of Spain's American grandeur which gave Esquemeling the excuse for his popular yarns. Throughout the second half of the seventeenth century Spain's position in the world had slumped spectacularly. On the mainland of America she remained, in form at least, an imperial power of sprawling proportions. But in Europe she had faded to a parody of her former self. She still observed the pomp and circumstance of the world's most powerful state, but in reality she was obliged to negotiate with upstart nations she would once have scorned or crushed; her armies and navies were financed by money-lenders who constantly dunned her for repayment; and she was ruled for a good part of this time by a royal halfwit, aptly nicknamed "Charles the Bewitched." Against the Caribbean possessions of this enfeebled giant, the boisterous English and French had thrown their weight and forcibly broken through the magic ring of West Indian islands which had once formed the defensive perimeter of Spain's American holdings. In consequence the Antilles were in uproar. The Spaniards, without their aura of invincibility, were desperately trying to shore up their defenses on the mainland and the islands they still held; the English and French were consolidating their recent gains and looking around for fresh spoils; and to compound the general sense of confusion, organized gangs of freebooters mushroomed among the rubble of the old order and joined in the fray to seize what riches they could.

The flamboyant behavior of these freebooters was the very stuff of legend, and within a few years their lurid adventures and extravagant personalities had struck a deep and lasting stamp upon the entire mythology of the Caribbean. They even changed the language of romance itself, minting new words such as *buccaneer*, *filibuster*, and *zeeräuber* or sea-rover. The Spaniards, however, continued to describe them more sourly as pirates, and treated them accordingly.

Yet even here the contradiction of the legend still persisted, for the buccaneers, to use the name by which they were best known in English, were both victims as well as heroes of the myth of the Golden Antilles. Despite their grand reputations and apparently insatiable hopes of instant wealth, very few of them ever won fortunes with the sword and carronade. Most finished up in obscure retirement, fever graves, or at the bottom of the sea. But this ill success was alien to the legend, and therefore it escaped the attention of the credulous public, which, in the fifty years following the capture of Jamaica, came to think of the Caribbean as much for its larger-than-life desperadoes as for the rich sugar planters and their antics. And for the most part this new reputation was drawn from the tales of Alexander Oexmelin.

There was nothing very new about the buccaneers and their marauds. As early as 1568, a Spanish official at Rio de la Hacha (now within Colombia) had wanly reported to his superiors that "for every two ships that come hither from Spain, twenty corsairs appear. For this reason not a town on this coast is safe;

for wherever they please to do so, they take and plunder these settlements. They go so far as to boast that they are lords of the sea and land. . . ." His lament was to be echoed by generation upon generation of colonial functionaries suffering from the greed of opportunist nations who claimed there was "no peace beyond the line," that convenient boundary of European affairs which ran down the meridian of Ferro (Hierro) in the Azores and turned westward along the Tropic of Capricorn. Beyond this huge right angle lay a Tom Tiddler's ground where, it was held, no European treaty was valid and no rules of war or diplomacy applied. For more than 150 years ships of Holland, France, England, and even Algiers had crossed the "line" to raid or trade, occasionally bringing back spectacular rewards. In 1523 a portion of the loot which Cortés had stripped from Montezuma's palace was in turn stolen by French privateers operating in the Atlantic, and in 1628 Spain's entire American convoy was lost to enemy action. Both Ralegh and Gage—the former taking valuable intelligence from papers captured by an English privateer; the latter to his own disgruntlement, meeting up with Diego el Mulato—had experienced the Caribbean sea robbers. Now with Spain's decline the situation became much worse. The Spanish cruisers, the famed *guarda costas* which policed the Caribbean basin from strategic bases around its rim, were no longer adequate to keep down the menace of the pirates, who swarmed to new nests and multiplied like wasps that have discovered rich feeding grounds. The Caribbean sea robbers became bolder and better organized, and as a result they were more successful. But like the previous manifestations of the legend of the Golden Antilles, it took the skill of widely read propagandists to mix fact and fiction until the legend of the buccaneers had blended into the fabric of the Golden Antilles itself.

Even in his own day the precise identity of Alexander Oliver Oexmelin (or John Esquemeling) was a mystery. The name itself was possibly a convenient fiction, for the man who wrote *The History of the Bucaniers* claimed that he had taken part in several of the piratical and gory actions which he described so vividly, and it was only natural that he should have taken steps to conceal his own identity. In fact the only information known about

Esquemeling was the smattering of detail which he provided in his own book. According to his account, he first went to the Antilles in 1666 aboard a French ship (eleven years after the Western Design). Apparently, too, he paid for his passage in the manner usually adopted by impoverished emigrants who could not raise the fare—by agreeing with the captain of the ship that when they reached the West Indies, the captain could then sell Esquemeling as an indentured servant to a planter. Unfortunately for Esquemeling, however, he found himself auctioned off to a particularly hard and stingy master on the French-held island of Tortuga. This man fed him so badly and treated him so harshly that he fell dangerously ill. In this dilapidated condition Esquemeling was of little use to his employer, who then disposed of the remainder of his indenture to a surgeon for the sum of seventy pieces-of-eight. Luckily the surgeon proved to be a decent master who restored Esquemeling to health and used him kindly. After a year's service the surgeon even offered Esquemeling his freedom on the understanding that the former servant would pay him a hundred pieces-of-eight when he could do so. Since the only quick method of raising the money was to seize it as a buccaneer, Esquemeling promptly enrolled himself in "the wicked order of the Pirates, or Robbers at Sea" as he called them; and set out to win his fortune as a surgeon to the buccaneers, presumably using the medical knowledge he had picked up from his former master. Curiously enough, the name of a certain Esquemeling was to appear some years later in the record books of the Dutch Surgeons' Guild, and it is quite possible that the quondam buccaneer eventually went home, and became a respectable practitioner. But the evidence is not conclusive, since the author of *The History of the Bucaniers* may have been clever enough to adopt the name of a real surgeon in order to conceal his own identity all the better.

But whether Esquemeling was Dutch or French (as some claimed) or plain bogus, he was without doubt a most gifted storyteller, and his book was a publishing sensation. It first appeared in Holland in 1678 under the title *De Americaensche Zee-Rovers*, and was such a *cause célèbre* that six years later the translator of the first English edition could write in his Preface:

"The present volume, both for its curiosity and ingenuity, I dare recommend to the perusal of the English nation. . . . [The book] was no sooner published in the Dutch original than it was snatched up for the most curious libraries in Holland; it was translated into Spanish (two impressions thereof being sent into Spain in one year); it was taken notice of by the learned Academy of Paris; and finally recommended as worthy of our esteem by the ingenious [i.e., discerning] author of the Weekly Memorials for the Ingenious, printed here at London about two years ago." But the English translator was frankly puzzled about the identity of the author. "I take him to be Dutchman," he wrote "or at least born in Flanders, notwithstanding that the Spanish translation represents him to be native of the kingdom of France; his printing this history originally in Dutch, which doubtless must be his native tongue, who was otherwise but an illiterate man, convincing me thereunto. . . . For were he a Frenchman born, how came he to learn the Dutch language so perfectly as to prefer it to his own?"

Events soon proved the enthusiasm of the English translator to be well founded, for *The History of the Bucaniers* ran through more editions in England than anywhere else, despite the fact that the translation was taken from a Spanish version which made Esquemeling out as a raging Anglophobe who loathed the English above any other nation. Indeed the arch-villain of the entire Caribbean was said to be an Englishman, Sir Henry Morgan, described as a bloodthirsty, calculating, and unscrupulous blackguard who cheated his own comrades and allowed his men to commit atrocities against women and priests. In fact Esquemeling had so low an opinion of Henry Morgan that the English editors of his book usually toned down his more vitriolic passages or attached apologetic prefaces to them. Two London publishers, who unwisely overlooked this precaution, were promptly sued by the redoubtable Morgan on the grounds that they were impugning his character. As Morgan was then officially a reformed character, and one of the richest and most influential planters on Jamaica, his complaint was taken seriously. At high levels it was considered impolitic to invoke the dubious past of a former privateersman whose subsequent offices had included

Governor-General, Admiral, Judge of the Vice-Admiralty Court, and, strangest of all, Custos Rotulorum or Principal Justice of the Peace. Morgan took his case to the Court of the King's Bench in London, and sued the two offending booksellers for ten thousand pounds in damages on the grounds that they were "cunningly contriving to injure his good name and fame by printing, spreading and publishing a certain false, malicious and famous libel entitled *A History of the Bucaniers.*" The irate poacher-turned-gamekeeper made his point successfully and was duly awarded two hundred pounds from each publisher, plus nine pounds in costs and a printed apology in subsequent editions. But the *History* itself continued to rattle off the presses, and the bulk of Esquemeling's sensational details were retained because his publishers were no fools and knew very well why the book sold so briskly.

As an exercise in the art of myth-making, *The History of the Bucaniers* was unrivaled. Wherever it appeared in translation, the editors in each country carefully "nationalized" the book to suit local tastes and expectations. To the Spanish, who changed the title to *Piratas de la América,* it was an indictment of the inhuman and illegal deeds of those godless outlaws who terrorized their peace-loving colonists in the West. In France, the editors seized on any section which dealt with French buccaneers and added much material of their own invention which glorified France. And in England this chauvinism went so far as to produce one contradictory edition whose title page extolled the "Unparalleled Exploits of SIR HENRY MORGAN, Our English Jamaican Hero, who sacked Porto Bello, burnt Panama, etc.," but whose unedited pages damned Morgan as a bloody pirate. Naturally this patriotic tinkering with Esquemeling's original text gave birth to several extravagant mutants, and many of those anecdotes that were tacked on had even less regard for the truth than the original. But European readers were avid for the picaresque, and they had an apparently insatiable appetite for these colorful tales which, beginning with Esquemeling's *History,* now emanated from the enchanted lands of the Golden Antilles.

Esquemeling, with his quick eye for interesting detail and a telling phrase, thoroughly deserved his literary success. His narrative had thrust and charm, and although he was by no means a polished stylist, the English translator was being less than fair when he described Esquemeling as an "illiterate man." Not only was Esquemeling's prose muscular and direct, as suited the topic, but he saw the advantage to be gained from building his own stories on the foundation of the existing Antillean myths of natural opulence and vegetable fertility. "Description of the island of Tortuga; of the fruits and flowers there growing" began the caption to his second chapter after the introduction had transported him briskly to his chosen locale in the Antilles. "Description of the Great and Famous Island of Hispaniola" (with a suitable picture over the text, showing the goddess Nature dropping largesse from the clouds to richly dressed planters), and again, "Of all sorts of animals and Birds that are found in this island" were the enticing titles of later sections of his book. Here, like a master showman, Esquemeling paraded the exotica of the Caribbean. For the diversion of the European reader there was an entire arboretum of strange trees: the candlewood, whose splinter burned like a wick dipped in oil; the wine palm, whose sap made excellent toddy but whose fruit was dangerous to the throat and caused malign quinsies; the prickle palm, the thorns of which the Indians stuck into the flesh of their prisoners "as thick as the bristles of any hedgehog" and then set them alight to see if their victims were brave enough to stifle their screams; and the strange genipa tree, which looked like an ordinary English cherry tree but provided a thick black sap that some people used as ink, though within nine days the marks of writing faded completely from the page. Most useful of the Caribbean trees, said Esquemeling, was the cabbage palm: its top, or cabbage, was a succulent vegetable to accompany a meat stew; its leaves made roofs for cabins better than any tile or could be stitched into satchels and buckets; and its inner skin was a substitute for parchment. Most dangerous, by contrast, was the *Manzanillo*, or dwarf apple tree. Its poisonous sap raised blisters on the skin, and any person who ate its fruit was seized by a raging thirst "as all the water of the Thames could not extinguish." The victim, said Esquemeling, would thrash in delirium until he died. "One day, being hugely tormented with mosquitos or gnats, and as yet unacquainted with the nature of this tree, I cut a branch thereof, to serve me instead of a fan, but all my face swelled all the next day and filled with blisters, as if it were burned to such a degree that I was blind for three days."

Matching this strange array of Antillean flora was an equally odd collection of birds, insects, and reptiles, which flew, crept, or slithered through the pages of the *History*. The Caribbean house snake, a clever rat-eating mimic, supposedly lured small rodents to their deaths by imitating their squeaks; sea turtles followed annual migration paths which were so regular that ships steered their courses at night by the sound of their swimming; talking parrots lived in tree holes conveniently picked out for them by obliging carpenter birds; mother crocodiles swallowed their young when there was danger about, and regurgitated them when the coast was clear; seventy-foot crocodiles filled their bellies with two hundredweight of stones so that their onslaught would be all the more formidable; and there was the West Indian tarantula, "very hairy" and "with four black teeth, like those of a rabbit." None of these creatures was any less plausible than the others, and the *History*'s readers could be forgiven if they believed in them all, especially as Esquemeling even played down some of the oddities like the West Indian tarantulas, which he firmly assured his readers were comparatively harmless, "although they can bite very sharply, and do use it very commonly."

Like Gage, John Esquemeling had been much impressed by the gnats, mosquitoes, and chiggers of the Antilles. These insects, he reported, were such torment to humans that the hunters on the islands constantly burned smudges of tobacco leaves in their cabins or smeared their faces with a primitive insect repellent made from hog's grease. Fireflies, on the other hand, were one of nature's true curiosities, and the buccaneer-surgeon was enough of an amateur naturalist to have taken the trouble of catching and examining them to find the "two little specks on their heads" which were the light source. Unfortunately, Esquemeling then rather spoiled the scientific effect of his observations by claiming that when two or three fireflies were together in a darkened room, one could read the smallest print by their light. On his return to Europe, he tried to carry back several live fireflies with him as specimens, "but as soon as they came into a colder climate," he noted sadly, "they died by the way. They lost also their shining on the change of air, even before their deaths."

Yet these wondrous creatures of Esquemeling's Caribbean bestiary were no more than the trimmings to his central theme. The pride of his collection was the extraordinary species of pirate-buccaneers, whose very name, according to the English translation, was "as yet known to but a few of the ingenious." Esquemeling devoted more than two thirds of the *History* to these buccaneers. Here, like a conducted tour through the carnivores's gallery, he displayed the great pirate figures: Pierre le Grand, believed to be the first true pirate on Tortuga; Bartholomew Portugues and Roche Braziliano; Lewis Scot; Mansvelt and his disciple Henry Morgan; John Davis who sacked Nicaragua and St. Augustine; and the bloodthirsty Francis L'Ollonais who, it was said, once cut the heart out of a Spanish prisoner and gnawed upon it in his fury, and was himself taken by the Indians of Darien and plucked limb from limb like a human fly. These monsters were the prize exhibits, the grand spectacles, of Esquemeling's *History of the Bucaniers*. Behind them he carefully arrayed a supporting cast of lesser figures, the rank and file of the pirate flotillas, the hangers-on and the "jolly lads," the grog-shop keepers who took their money, the corrupt government officials who connived or protected them, the part-time pirates who were farmers for ten months in the year and sea raiders when the Plate Fleet sailed by, the logwood cutters of the Mosquito coast, the salvage men, and the prostitutes. According to Esquemeling these outsized characters were the everyday denizens of the Golden Antilles, and it was largely from his *History* that there evolved the classic picture of the buccaneer who, with additions from later travel accounts, became a part of European lore.

According to Esquemeling, however, the genuine buccaneer was something very different from the later concept of a swash-buckling freebooter. He was, said Esquemeling, first and foremost a hunter of wild cattle. On Hispaniola, for example, the French settlers could choose among three ways of making a living, "either to hunt, or plant, or else to rove the sea in the quality of pirates."

Significantly it was the hunters who were "called buccaneers." In fact the name came from their *boucanes,* the little beehive-shaped huts in the woods where the hunters cooked the meat of the wild cattle they had killed. The meat was cut in strips and slow-cured on a lattice of green sticks over a fire. In this condition the *viande boucanée* kept in good condition for long periods and was much in demand by ships' crews and slave-owning planters. The "boucaniers" sold their product in bundles of a hundred strips, six pieces-of-eight per bundle, and it was not uncommon for a gang of hunters to have a regular contract with some rich planter to supply him with dried meat all year round at a fixed price. Having made this contract, the buccaneers would then disappear into the woods for months on end, only re-emerging to deliver the meat, accept payment, and immediately make their way to their favorite rendezvous, which in Esquemeling's day was the island of Tortuga. There they would stock up with a fresh supply of powder and shot for their hunting weapons—the favorite gun was a six-foot French-made musket that threw an extremely large ball with considerable accuracy—and then settle in to squander the rest of their earnings in an uproarious drinking binge. Brandy, wrote Esquemeling, was the favorite tipple, and "this they drink as liberally as the Spaniards do clear fountain water. Sometimes they buy together a pipe of wine; this they stave at the one end, and never cease drinking until they have made an end of it. Thus they celebrate the festivals of Bacchus so long as they have any money left." So was born the legend of the buccaneers' carouse.

But if Esquemeling's buccaneers were in reality the equivalents of those same cowkillers whom Sailing Master Whistler had described with such awe in his diary, it was by no means the only example of popular imagination distorting the original facts of the *History.* Another, equally inaccurate, misconception was the idea that these buccaneers were freedom-loving adventurers steeped in exuberant camaraderie. On the contrary, *The History of the Bucaniers* made it abundantly clear that the buccaneers were not so much seekers after freedom as misanthropes of frightening intensity. It was true that, while hunting, the buccaneers would work together in packs, helping one another as necessary; but these were fragile associations that broke up when they received their pay and culminated, as often as not, in bloody and bestial fights among the erstwhile partners. Nor, despite their much-boasted love of personal independence, were the buccaneers averse to the idea of keeping indentured servants of their own or carrying off unwary fishermen who were put to work for them as slaves. Occasionally, too, an indentured servant was loaned to a buccaneer gang by their contractor-planter, and in this case the poor wretch was appallingly badly treated. Esquemeling himself may well have been loaned out in this fashion by his first master, for he wrote of the buccaneer huntsmen with much bitterness. "The said buccaneers," he noted, "are hugely cruel and tyrannical towards their servants: insomuch that commonly these had rather be galley slaves in the Straits, or saw brazil-wood in the rasp-houses of Holland, than serve such barbarous masters."

In fact Esquemeling's spell as an indentured servant left several scars, for the author of the *History* returned again and again to the theme of the mistreated indentured man. According to him, white men who were serving out their indentures were bought and sold, whipped and overworked, with far more cruelty than any of the Negro slaves from Africa, even though the treatment of slaves in the West Indian islands was held to be far more severe than anywhere else in the Western hemisphere. The reason for the greater suffering of the indentured servant, Esquemeling took care to explain, was that an indentured man had sold himself for only three years (seven years in some of the English islands) and was therefore a short-term investment compared to a Negro slave with a whole lifetime of slavery ahead of him. Under the circumstances the employer had no reason to prolong the useful life of an indentured man, and strove to extract the maximum of work from him with the minimum of upkeep. In consequence an indentured servant was starved and left unattended at times when a slave would have been fed or clothed. This callousness, Esquemeling reported, was often fatal to delicate or educated white men who had fallen on hard times in Europe and believed in the tales of the Golden Antilles. They foolishly sold themselves to the recruiting agents of the colonizing companies and were transported to the West Indies, where they were so badly mistreated that many of them lapsed into a state of shock, a "coma" as Esquemeling called it, and eventually dropped dead in their tracks as they were working in the fields.

Antisocial by nature, a hunter-buccaneer also behaved in a way not calculated to endear him to his more civilized neighbors. While hunting in the woods, a buccaneer lived like a savage. Festooned with hatchet, bayonet, skinning knives, powder horn, bullet bag, and the other paraphernalia of his trade, he and his colleagues wore blood-stained linen or the skins of wild beasts, which they neither cured nor cleaned. As a result, they stank abominably. In place of shoes many of the hunters wore a crude boot made from the skin of a boar's foreleg, roughly trimmed, and gathered up round the ankle with a thong. Although cheap and very durable, this footwear was filthy and malodorous, and the only way to remove the stiffened pigskin was to carve it off with a knife. Equally offensive were the manners of the buccaneers. Esquemeling's first master, for example, had picked up several buccaneer habits. When he went into town, he would buy a pipe of beer or wine, and order that it be placed in the street. There he would mount guard with his pistol and demand that every passerby drink or be shot. After a while, when this simple-minded diversion had lost its sparkle, he would lurch around his barrel, drunkenly scooping up its contents in his hands and splashing the clothes of the pedestrians. In the end, Esquemeling noted with obvious relish, the riotous behavior of this bully brought him into such debt that, in the ultimate irony, he too was obliged to sell himself off as an indentured servant.

But Esquemeling's cattle-hunting, brandy-swilling buccaneers were milksops alongside his sea-going pirates. These maritime blackguards were for the most part former cowkillers who had taken to the sea after they had severely depleted the supply of wild cattle on the islands. Unfortunately, this enforced change of occupation only served to bring out the worst in an already unsavory gang of cutthroats. The author of the *History* was able to produce a long and detailed list of their grisly misdoings— ships boarded, women raped, men tortured, nuns and priests used as human shields against the Spaniards' bullets, prisoners hacked to death, and bloody mayhem stalking from one page of the *History* to the next. It was all most spectacular and, of course, precisely what Esquemeling intended, because he was writing specifically for those armchair adventurers who might drool over the pearl fisheries of Rancheria or take part, in their wildest dreams, in the sacking of Maracaibo and the wild rapine which was said to have followed Henry Morgan's capture of Panama.

Yet Esquemeling was not such a bore as to let his narrative degenerate into a clumsy surfeit of blood-and-guts, pieces-of-eight, and swashbuckling. He knew that his *History* would profit from the solid ballast of those daily minutiae which, as a sea-going surgeon, he would have seen in the Carribbean. So, to balance the huge exploits of Morgan, L'Ollonais, and the others, he drew on his intimate knowledge of the lesser folk of piracy to provide that air of authenticity which was so important to his ordinary readers. And here again the distorting lens of the Antilles myth later produced its deception, for Esquemeling's original, run-of-the-mill pirate was by no means that romantic daredevil of legend, who sailed a fine frigate against bullion-laden galleons, boarded foreign ships with a flash of white teeth against a black beard, and then sent his captives to walk the plank. In *The History of the Bucaniers* the usual Caribbean sea robber was much more likely to be a greedy and somewhat cowardly figure, mortally afraid of wild Indians on the Mosquito coast, mistrustful of his companions and his leaders. He sailed a stolen coastal smack or even a cottonwood dugout canoe, and his dream of wealth was a cargo of cocoa beans sold, with no questions asked, to an un-scrupulous merchant in Tortuga or Port Royal. Esquemeling did not belittle the pirates' sea skill or their courage in adversity, but there is no mistaking that in his own view the pirates were something lower than wild animals, a scabby lot who deserved to be stamped out as soon and as ruthlessly as possible.

Esquemeling backed up this thesis with damning evidence. The former cowkillers, he pointed out, grew so lazy that they no longer cured their own beef, but preferred to descend upon some isolated and defenseless swineherd whom they terrorized into giving up his beasts. If, on a raid, they caught a potential ransom victim, they would hang him from his testicles until he promised to hand over his money. One old man, suspected of hiding his wealth, was strung up by his thumbs and toes, and the cords were then thrashed with heavy sticks. When this cruelty failed to produce the desired confession, the pirates staked out their victim on the ground, half-crushed him beneath a rock weighing over three hundred pounds which they dropped on his belly, and then lit a fire of palm leaves under his head. As it happened, they had mistaken their victim, for the old man was a pauper, who only managed to obtain his release by promising to borrow money from his friends. An even worse beating was handed out to a man caught wearing a pair of rich taffeta breeches with a tempting silver key dangling from the drawstrings. The prisoner was a rich man's servant who had made off with his employer's clothing, but the pirates would not believe his excuses and went to work on him. They began by dislocating their victim's arms and legs, then cut off his nose and ears, singed his face to stop his screams, and finally twisted a cord around his forehead "which they wrung so hard that his eyes appeared big as eggs." The *History* ascribed most of these atrocities to ruffians operating under the command of Henry Morgan.

Tucked away among these yarns of torture and cruelty, Esquemeling's readers, if they looked carefully, could have learned that these supposedly carefree pirates were in fact as narrowly encompassed with rules, regulations, and ordinances as any shareholder in a London stock company. "Before the pirates go out to sea," wrote Esquemeling, "they give notice to everyone who goes upon the voyage, of the day on which they ought precisely to embark, intimating to them their obligation of bringing each man in particular so many pounds of powder and bullets as they think necessary for that expedition." When the recruits were assembled, they then swore to obey a formal set of Articles which laid down the rules of the venture and stipulated the exact division of prize money. The man who provided their ship was allocated an agreed bounty for his vessel; the shipwright who mended, careened, and rigged her received a bonus of between 100 and 150 pieces-of-eight; another 200 pieces-of-eight were set aside for the purchase of stores; and the surgeon (a matter of some interest to Esquemeling) was given a special bounty of 200 to 250 pieces-of-eight if he proved to be reasonably competent and brought along a well-stocked medicine chest. In addition, there was a rough-and-ready insurance policy to compensate the venturers against the surgeon's knife or the enemy's bullet. This policy valued a man's parts by their comparative usefulness in a fight. Thus the top price was paid out for the loss of a right arm, which was valued at 600 pieces-of-eight or six slaves. The loss of a left arm or right leg brought 500 pieces-of-eight (no exception being made for left-handers); a left leg went for 400 pieces-of-eight; and, strangely enough, an eye or a finger was each valued the same, each being worth 100 pieces-of-eight. All such bounties and insurance payments had prior call upon the common stock of the venture—Esquemeling even called it the "capital"—which was the sum of all loot taken on the trip. Only after these deductions had been made could the remainder of the profits be shared out among the pirates. Even then the subdivision was precise, with the captain usually receiving five or six portions, the master's mate two portions, common seamen one, and the sea boys one half. The sea boys were hard done by, because according to the *History* they were charged with the special duty of remaining aboard a condemned ship and setting her alight before being picked up by the pirate vessel.

This, then, was the world of the pirates as Esquemeling's readers saw it—a strange and wondrous place, fully in the tradition of everything they had read or heard about the fabulous Antilles, and naturally enough *The History of the Bucaniers* soon became gospel for the legend. Moreover, it opened the flood gates of a new publishing craze. In the years that followed the publication of Esquemeling's revelations, a host of retired ex-pirates brought out their own memoirs of life in the Caribbean. Several of these later authors were also one-time surgeons, presumably because they were the most literate element in the pirate gangs and best equipped to recount the adventures. Wielding pen instead of cutlass, they embellished Esquemeling's account or stole sections of it as their own, and took their readers to places Esquemeling had never sailed. Bit by bit the pirate tales grew more extravagant, the accompanying wood-cut illustrations more lurid, and Esquemeling's earlier distinctions between buccaneer and pirate were buried beneath an avalanche of synonym and euphemism. Once or twice through this shroud of invention there came a glimpse of proved fact, as for example when Hans Sloane, at that time a young physician in Jamaica, described a sick and aging Henry Morgan. Sloane had been avidly making a collection of West Indian fauna and flora and writing the journals which would one day form the basis of the British Museum's library, when he was asked to visit and examine the ex-pirate. He found Morgan to be "lean, sallow coloured, his eyes a little yellowish and belly jutting out or prominent." The old reprobate was complaining of the typical symptoms of the debauchee—loss of appetite, nausea, weakness, and diarrhea—and Sloane correctly diagnosed too much "drinking and sitting up late." He prescribed an alarming list of diuretics and purges, including gentian roots, linseed, and oil of scorpion. But Morgan was unwilling to give up his pleasures, and instead called in a Negro obeah man who, Sloane disapprovingly noted, "gave him Clysters of Urine, and plastered him all over with clay and water, and by it augmented his cough. So he left his Black Doctor and sent for another, who promised him cure, but he languished and his cough augmenting, died soon after." The year was 1688 and Esquemeling's *History* with its black legend of Morgan was already in its fifth edition. The age of the buccaneers was past its peak, but its effect on the myth of the Golden Antilles was not yet expended. One more great illusion would be conjured up out of the tales of men like Esquemeling, and on this occasion the dupes would be hard-headed Scots investors who dreamed of sun-washed riches in the warm Caribbean. The perpetrators of this time-worn illusion would be an unlikely congregation: an ex-pirate who had circum-navigated the world, another buccaneer surgeon who was also an Indian expert, and a company promoter who had helped found the Bank of England.

13.

The Adventures of a Buccaneer Surgeon

IN THE SUMMER OF 1681 A YOUNG BUCCANEER SURGEON named Lionel Wafer met with a near-fatal accident which was to have momentous consequences for the legend of the Golden Antilles. When the accident occurred, Wafer was with a band of some forty rather bedraggled English buccaneers marching through the dense, rain-sodden forests of the isthmus of Panama on their way back from a raid into the Pacific. The damp of the forest had affected the flasks of gunpowder that the adventurers were carrying, and one of the buccaneers was attempting to dry out his stock of powder on a silver plate held over the campfire, when he mismanaged the delicate operation and the gunpowder ignited. Lionel Wafer, who was sitting nearby, was caught by the full force of the explosion. The blast ripped the flesh from one knee, laying bare the bone, badly scorched the whole length of his thigh, and temporarily crippled its victim.

Originally the buccaneers had sworn to kill anyone who lagged behind the column, but they did not have the heart to kill the maimed surgeon. So Wafer was abandoned to his fate. Naturally the buccaneers did not expect ever to see Wafer alive again. Yet, by good luck and adapting to his surroundings, the injured surgeon was not only to survive his ordeal but even to flourish in the strange tropical world where he now found himself. More important, he was soon to glean various scraps of knowledge about the isthmus, which would have the same stimulating effect on the dream of the Golden Antilles as those half-crazed notions of El Dorado that the Spanish castaway Juan Martínez had brought out of the Venezuelan jungle more than a century earlier.

But unlike poor Martínez, Lionel Wafer was perfectly sane when he reappeared in the outside world, and his account of his experiences in the isthmus was largely truthful. For Lionel Wafer was one of those quiet and unassuming travelers which the seventeenth century brought forth in such profusion, and who, it seemed, went to great lengths to report their extraordinary adventures as soberly and sensibly as possible. Wafer, when cast up in a primitive land whose inhabitants were still living in the Stone Age, behaved with as much aplomb as if he had arrived in a drowsy English village in the shires. He remained poised and calm, interested in his surroundings yet seldom querulous, and never once did his scientific curiosity abandon him. Carefully he made notes about the strange aboriginal customs as he discovered them, experimented with the nostrums of the medicine men, compiled a vocabulary of the local Indian language, and made very sensible observations on every subject from meteorology to geology. He was, in short, the perfect traveler; and it was not his fault that his European audience later transmuted his largely accurate observations into a mirage of Antillean promise.

Lionel Wafer was a man stricken with a severe case of wanderlust. His first foreign trip had been as a "loblolly" boy aboard the East India Company's ship *Anne*, bound for Bantam in the Spice Islands. He was probably less than seventeen years old at the time, and his job was to serve loblolly, a kind of unappetizing gruel, to men in the ship's sick bay. It was a lowly task, but in the days when formal medical training was a rarity, it was often the first rung on the ladder to becoming a ship's surgeon. This first sea voyage turned out well enough for Wafer, though when he was in Bantam he somehow missed his ship, and the *Anne* sailed for home without him. Unperturbed, he found a berth for himself aboard another company vessel, the *Bombay Merchant,* and reached England safely after an absence of a little more than two years. A few months later he was off again, this time aboard a vessel bound for the West Indies and the new colony of Jamaica.

According to his own story of his adventures, published after his return from Panama, Wafer's chief reason for going to the Antilles was to visit a brother who was then employed at the "Angels," a large sugar estate a few miles outside Spanish Town. This brother had evidently reached a position of some responsibility, for when Lionel Wafer arrived in Jamaica, he was invited to stay at the plantation. His brother then furnished the capital for young Lionel to set himself up as a practicing surgeon in Port Royal. Just how skillful a surgeon Wafer would have been at that time is doubtful, for he had only his two years's experience of shipboard surgery to his credit. But in the event, his skill was not in question, for Lionel Wafer almost immediately turned buccaneer.

Port Royal, where Wafer had originally proposed to carry on his business, was much altered from the swashbuckling place of twenty years earlier. It was still one of the busiest ports in the Caribbean and its prosperity had increased considerably. The vast bay behind the curiously elongated Palisadoes sandspit was a haven for men-of-war, merchant ships, coasting sloops, and scows of every size and description. The grog shops did a roaring business; stone-built warehouses jostled for space in the limited area at the tip of the sandspit; and the harbor's defenses had been greatly strengthened. Port Royal's size and opulence reflected the increasing success of the Jamaica colony, and this success was quite astonishing when compared to the lean years which immediately followed Cromwell's Western Design. But Port Royal had changed in another, very important, respect: with increased prosperity the port's operations had been legitimized. Buccaneers and freebooters were no longer welcome there, at least, not overtly. The days of officially condoned buccaneering were gone, and now that Jamaica's existence was no longer in question, the ruling clique on the island wanted to reap the benefits of steady, legitimate trade. Buccaneers had become an embarrassment, and it did not need much imagination to see that they were just as likely to attack London-bound English bottoms, well ladened with sugar and the trade products of the Antilles, as Spanish galleons. So His Majesty's ships-of-the-line now patrolled against the buccaneers, just as the *guarda costa* had done; and in a crowning gesture, English warships were sometimes dispatched to convoy Spanish merchantmen and protect them from marauding freebooters.

Of course this swift somersault of official Jamaican policy had not changed matters overnight. There were still influential men on the island who practiced a little unobtrusive buccaneering on the side, and there were many more who made their living by selling supplies to the buccaneers and buying their booty in return. Others, who had founded their own fortunes as privateersmen, now looked leniently on the efforts of those adventurers who tried to follow their example. So an occasional buccaneer vessel still called at Port Royal, dressed up as a legitimate trading ship or perhaps with a captain who held a letter of reprisal permitting him to seize foreign ships as restitution for some past injury. And it was two such commanders, Captains Lynch and Cook, on a visit to Port Royal, who met up with the newly installed surgeon Wafer and suggested that he join them on a voyage toward the coast of Cartagena.

The coast of Cartagena was certainly not the two captains' real destination, and it was unlikely that Wafer really believed that he was associating himself with a straightforward trading venture. Privateer captains were notorious figures, and Lionel Wafer had already had enough seafaring experience to recognize a buccaneer when he met one. Thus, when he signed up for the voyage, it was almost certainly with the knowledge that he was throwing in his lot with a very dubious crew.

Lynch and Cook were headed, in fact, for a secret rendezvous off the Panamanian coast, where a combined squadron of English and French buccaneers was assembling for an unprecedented and extremely hazardous raid across the Panamanian isthmus. The master plan was that the adventurers would leave their own vessels in the Caribbean, march through the jungles of the isthmus, and suddenly appear in the Pacific. There they would seize enough Spanish ships to make themselves a seaborne force once again, and proceed to harry and loot Spanish settlements up and down the length of the coast. As an additional bait, they believed that they had a chance of intercepting the legendary Manila galleon as it brought the royal treasure of the Philippines for transshipment between Panama City and Portobelo. The potential reward was enormous, but the risks were equally great. The buccaneers did not know whether they would be able to find a way across the unexplored and mountainous isthmus; in the Pacific they would be sailing unknown waters and would not have the protection of their usual bases; and if they should be mauled by the Spanish defense forces in the Pacific, very few survivors would ever make their way back to their vessels in the Caribbean. Almost their only advantage was the element of surprise. The Spanish garrison on the Pacific, it was said, had been lulled into such a false sense of security that even the guns of Panama City were mounted to point inland down the road from Portobelo and not out across the harbor where the Spanish merchant ships lay at anchor. When Lynch, Cook, and Wafer reached the buccaneer rendezvous off the then-abandoned town of Nombre de Dios, the buccaneers were in the process of electing their leaders for the new venture. But before the combined raiding force left the beach, the French contingent quarreled with the English, and withdrew to their ships. Their departure left 336 men to attempt the epic march across the isthmus to the South Sea, as the Pacific was then called. With the raiders went Lionel Wafer and another traveler who was soon to achieve world renown—William Dampier, navigator, practical scientist, and later captain of a Royal Navy vessel on special exploration duties.

The story of the buccaneer invasion of the Pacific falls outside the scope of the Golden Antilles, and here it is enough to record that although the raiding force successfully found its way across the isthmus with the help of Indian guides, the buccaneers were disappointed in their rewards. They fought a succession of stiff engagements against Spanish patrol boats in the Pacific and captured several, which they then turned into raiding vessels. But the delay cost the raiders the advantage of surprise, and the entire coast was forewarned. As usual the Spanish-American colonists evacuated their towns, carried off their valuables into the hills, and waited for the buccaneers to lose patience and sail off. One half-empty town after another was captured, and several were burned to the ground when ransom demands were ignored, but the loot was meager. At sea it was much the same story. The Spanish shipping either stayed out of sight or the more valuable cargoes were carried ashore and cached in secret places. The Manila galleon was not intercepted. Thwarted and constantly short of supplies, the buccaneers began to bicker among themselves. Their numbers were whittled away by disease and battle casualties, and although this reduction meant that there was a richer division of booty for the survivors, the raiders also lost their best and most daring captains. Step by step the management of the venture deteriorated, and open quarrels began to split the buccaneer councils. Replacement leaders were elected by popular vote; and the choice was not always a good one. Finally, when a proven incompetent was elected to overall command, a sizable portion of the raiding party broke away in disgust. Leaving the main body to continue their campaign, this splinter group, William Dampier and Lionel Wafer among them, agreed to attempt the return crossing of the isthmus on their own.

It was a courageous decision, for they already knew that the isthmus of Panama was appallingly difficult terrain to cross. Now the journey would be made twice as arduous because the small group of buccaneers was tired and in retreat. They were short of food; many of them were wounded; and all of them were heavily loaded down with their loot. Several men, in fact, were later drowned in the forest streams when they slipped and were pulled underwater by the weight of their packs. Yet somehow this weary little band of fugitives evaded the Spanish cordon guarding the Pacific beaches, and vanished into the comforting mystery of scrub and forest that covered the mountainous spine of the cordillera. There, in the dense, unexplored forest high among the mountains, Lionel Wafer was crippled by the unlucky gunpowder explosion.

The accident was doubly serious because it had happened at a point well outside the usual sphere of buccaneer operations.

The isthmus of Panama was a wild region, known only as the home of strange and primitive Indians who had seldom been seen by white men. The Englishmen had no idea whether these natives might not ambush their small and weakened force; and, further, there was the constant risk that a Spanish patrol had already picked up the buccaneers' trail and was closing in on the raiders. To make the situation even more dangerous, the buccaneers were reduced to the last scraps of their marching rations, and the summer rains were about to break. In a few weeks the swollen, turbulent streams of the isthmus would make all traveling across the territory impossible, and unless the travelers made forced marches day after day, they would never reach their ships, which were anchored under skeleton crews off the Caribbean coast. Under the circumstances, it was out of the question that the raiding party should slow its pace for the sake of the injured surgeon.

For five days Lionel Wafer, in great pain, tried to keep up with his comrades. But then the Negro slave who was carrying the surgeon's chest ran off into the woods one night, and took with him the entire stock of medicines. Wafer was greatly discouraged. With no way of treating his gaping wound he gave up the hopeless attempt. He told his comrades that he preferred to drop out of the line of march and throw himself on the mercy of the Indians.

Typically, Wafer did not panic. Although he knew his situation was desperate, he was not alone. He had with him two other buccaneers who had elected to stay behind because they were too exhausted to continue. These men, Richard Gopson and John Hingson, both turned out to be the staunchest of companions. Gopson, once a druggist's apprentice in London, had run away to turn buccaneer. He was, said Wafer, "an ingenious man and a good Scholar," who tried to cheer up his companions during the darker days of their escapade by reading them passages from a Greek Bible which he had somehow managed to keep with him during his travels. This Greek text, said Wafer, he would translate "ex tempore into English for such of the company that were dispos'd to hear him." John Hingson, though only briefly described as a "mariner," was to strike up such a close friendship with Wafer during their time in the isthmus that the two men would remain together for at least the next nine years, sharing a long succession of adventures and finishing up together in a Jamestown jail, from where they finally returned home to England in company. In addition to this pair of admirable companions, Wafer was soon joined by two more of the buccaneer party, Robert Spratlin and William Bowman, who had earlier got lost and were floundering through the woods trying to catch up with the main group. When Spratlin and Bowman came upon Wafer and the others, the three castaways were resting in a village of forest Indians until they would be strong enough to continue their trek to the Caribbean coast.

Although Wafer and his companions did not know it then, the five buccaneers were still on the Pacific slope of the cordillera. Between them and the safety of the Caribbean beaches ran an almost impenetrable barrier, formed by two upland ranges extending lengthwise along the spine of the isthmus. Short, swift rivers had sliced the cordillera into a tangle of deep valleys and sharp ridges. Here and there an Indian foot trail snaked through the wilderness, but it took the trained eye of a forest tracker to detect the path, and a stranger was certain to lose his bearings in a few minutes. The Indian trails wandered back and forth with an apparent disregard to direction, and when the tropical rainbelt hung over the isthmus and the torrential downpours fell with monotonous regularity each day, all movement was impossible. A muddy slime made it difficult to keep one's footing; tiny rivulets rushed across the trails, turning footpaths into streambeds. Even when the rain stopped, the trees continued to drip their loads of catchwater on the traveler. On all sides there were enormous trees, standing eighty to a hundred feet above the ground, their tops high above a lower layer of secondary underbrush that ran riot in a tangled, almost impenetrable, carpet around the contorted trunks of the forest giants. Flowers of blue, gold, and red twined about the larger shrubs and blossomed as parasites in the branches of the greater trees, but their splashes of color were a delusion in a landscape that was basically inimical to the intruder.

Through this tangled vegetation the Spanish conquistadors had once hacked and slashed a way from the Caribbean to the Pacific and planted a handful of cities on each coast. They called the land "Darien" and had high hopes of it. But their cities were ephemeral creations. Some had already faded away; others had lingered on for years in defiance of natural disasters; and a few, like Panama City itself, flourished only because it was essential that there be a port to handle the transshipment of goods between Spain and her Pacific empire. Several times the Spaniards had tried to fly in the face of nature and settle the interior of Darien, but every attempt had failed, and finally they had learned to keep to the coasts. Even the rumors of gold mines in the inland gorges were not enough to tempt the Spaniards into the hinterland permanently. The miners climbed into the cordillera to pay fleeting visits to the rivers, panned for gold when the weather was favorable, and hurriedly retreated to the coast when the rains closed in.

Only the Indians managed to live all year round in the interior of Darien. Most of them lived on the north, or Caribbean, side of the cordillera and were called "Cuna" by the white men, a name probably given them when the first Europeans visited the area and asked "Who are you?" and were told, "*Quyni*," meaning "a grown up man" in the native tongue. They, in a sense, took profit from the disadvantages of their environment. The forests, the cordillera, and the tropical diseases shielded them from the outsiders, and apart from an occasional missionary priest—who usually gave up in despair or died of fever—the Indians were left very much alone. Certainly they had no reason to encourage intruders, for they were a proud people who placed great importance on racial purity and discouraged their womenfolk from any contact with strangers who happened to stumble into their isolated retreats. Like the shy river folk whom Ralegh had met in Guiana, these Cuna lived in huts of cane and leaf thatch and went near-naked. They used hammocks for sleeping and dugout canoes for fishing, and hunted with bows and arrows in the woods. Plantains grew in untidy plots near their villages, and they gathered wild fruit in the forests. They also knew the use of tobacco—though they sniffed the smoke rather than taking it into their lungs.

To Lionel Wafer and his companions, the outlandish Cuna were a frightening puzzle. The buccaneers had no experience of

the timid forest Indians apart from an occasional brief encounter
with the Cuna clans when the raiding party had been on its way
westward toward the Pacific, and it was unlikely that the Cuna
would have dared to attack such a strong and well-equipped
column. Now, however, Wafer and his friends were entirely at
the mercy of the aborigines, and to make matters worse, their
colleagues in the main buccaneer party had pressganged several
Cuna villagers into acting as guides for them on the way to the
coast. Understandably, the Cuna had not wanted to leave their
village so soon before the onset of the rainy season, and the
buccaneers had overcome their reluctance by dragging off their
guides by force. This high-handed action left Wafer and his
friends in grave jeopardy. They had every reason to worry that
the remaining Cuna might decide to take revenge on the castaways. It was a gruesome prospect because it was rumored that
the Cuna had an aversion to spilling blood and therefore put their
prisoners to death by suffocating them over a slow fire.

But as matters turned out, the Cuna were too cautious to
slaughter the white men out of hand. A few of the more hot-
headed young warriors in the village loudly demanded that the
stranded foreigners should be killed because they had trespassed
on tribal territory, but the council of village elders urged re-
straint and pointed out that it would be wiser to see if the
kidnapped guides returned safely. Thus for ten days Wafer and
his colleagues, stranded in the Cuna village, waited in an agony of
suspense, fervently hoping that the buccaneers would have the
good sense to treat their Cuna guides handsomely and send them
back to their village before their clansmen lost patience. In the
meantime, the five castaways had a hard time of it. With ill-
concealed disdain the Cuna allocated them to the care of one
warrior whose palm-thatch hut gave them a degree of shelter
against the torrential weather. But the village as a whole deliberately made little or no attempt to feed them. Instead, wrote
Wafer, the white men were obliged to cringe and beg like dogs
before the Indians, gratefully snatching up any morsel of food
contemptuously thrown their way. And, as most of their food
was the unripe fruit of the plantain, the Cuna seemed to take a

malicious delight in knowing that the white men were suffering from stomach cramps.

Luckily the five buccaneers were resilient, and they managed to scrape by until they found a villager who took pity on them. He was an Indian who had been captured as a boy by the Spaniards and had spent some time in the house of the Bishop of Panama before rejoining his tribe. In consequence he spoke some Spanish,* and could act as interpreter and tutor to the castaways. He was also kindhearted enough to risk the anger of his fellow tribesmen by surreptitiously going out after dark to raid the communal plantain trees near the village and bring back handfuls of ripe fruit, which he distributed to the grateful Englishmen.

Yes, despite their deep mistrust of the white men, the Cuna villagers could not bring themselves to neglect Lionel Wafer's wounded leg, which was giving him much distress. The aborigines had evolved a remarkably effective system of medicine based on herbs and plants gathered in the forest, and it was little short of miraculous how quickly the English surgeon's wound healed under their treatment. The Cuna doctors chewed up a paste of medicinal herbs in their mouths which they then spread over the lacerated knee, covering the mixture with a large banana leaf to serve as a bandage. This treatment, wrote Wafer wonderingly, "prov'd so effectual that in about 20 days use of this Poultess which they applied fresh every Day, I was perfectly cured; except only a Weakness in that Knee, which remained long after, and a Benummedness which I find to this Day."

Unfortunately any cheerfulness which might have been aroused by the rapid improvement in Wafer's condition was more than dampened by the increasing hostility of the Cuna. The return of the guides from the coast was now long overdue, and as each day passed, the Englishmen were treated with less and less civility. Whenever they appeared in public in the village they were the target of a barrage of scowls, kicks, curses, and unpleasant gestures. Their impending fate became all too obvious when they saw that the Cuna had begun to heap up an execution bonfire.

---

* *Spanish was by far the most widely spoken language of the Antilles.*

Luckily for them, the village was visited at this crucial juncture by Lacenta, paramount chief of the Cuna.

Chief Lacenta, whose name Wafer may or may not have rendered correctly, was a remarkable individual. He had managed to achieve a position of overall authority in a society which was organized as a number of very loosely knit village communities scattered throughout the forest, and he maintained his authority by sheer force of character rather than by open warfare. He also lived, as Wafer soon learned, in considerable style. He had built a fortified village of his own, which was strategically located on a promontory between two rivers and protected on its landward side by a thick cactus hedge. Here he held a primitive court, surrounded by his advisers and an adoring flock of concubines which, rumor had it, numbered more than fifty attractive women recruited and dismissed by their lord with airy grandeur and immediate effect.

When Lacenta heard of the five stranded buccaneers, he promptly came to inspect them. And realizing that these white men and their friends could perhaps assist him against his traditional enemies, the Spanish, he immediately ordered that Wafer and his companions should be allowed to leave the village and be given guides to help them through the forest. By now Wafer felt well enough to move, so he and his four companions set out at once, vainly hoping that they would be able to catch up with the main buccaneer party before it reached the coast. But in their haste the only food they took with them was a small quantity of dried maize, and within three days these meager rations had been eaten up. At that point their Indian guides casually pointed out the correct path through the forest, and turned back to their own village, leaving the Englishmen marooned once again in the perplexing maze of underbrush.

At first all seemed to go well, for the travelers followed what they thought was the path earlier hacked out by the main body of buccaneers. They proceeded as fast as they could along this trail until it unexpectedly petered out. Then, however, they were at a loss. The twists and turns of their route, the dense undergrowth on each side, the succession of ridges, and the doubling back and forth of the rivers and streams had confused them

utterly. Without a compass to guide them and with the angle of
the sun constantly obscured by the thick canopy of forest over
their heads, they did not even know which direction they were
facing. More worrying, they were dizzy with hunger and fatigue,
as they had found nothing to eat beyond a few strange berries
tentatively plucked from the bushes. With neither tents nor
hammocks, they had spent the nights stretched out on the forest
floor, drenched by the frequent showers or soaked with their
own sweat in the fetid air.

Casting around for some sign of the trail, the five Englishmen
were briefly heartened by the discovery of a river running across
their path and a large tree which had been recently felled so that
it lay like a bridge across the river. Thinking that they were still
on the route of the main party, the buccaneers were halfway
across the tree, straddling its rain-soaked length like a hobby
horse, when Bowman lost his grip on the slippery trunk and
tumbled down into the racing water. He was a weak, slight man
and had been in difficulty ever since the day he dropped behind
the main party because he stubbornly refused to give up any of
his loot, four hundred pieces-of-eight that he carried in a bag
strapped to his back. Now, as he plummeted into the water and
was swept away out of sight, Wafer and his companions were
sure that the little man was lost. Scrambling to the far bank, they
tried to run down the riverbank to rescue him, but were stopped
by mud and swamp. Recrossing the river, they made their
way along the opposite bank, looking for his body. To their
amazement, they found Bowman safe and sound, still defiantly
clutching his swag. A freak eddy had swept him under a conveniently overhanging branch and he had been able to haul himself
back to safety.

Bowman's narrow escape convinced the travelers that their
overland route was too difficult for them in their weakened
condition. After one more day spent futilely hacking through the
ever-thickening bush, they decided to try their luck on the river.
They calculated, incorrectly as it turned out, that their trail had
brought them across the watershed dividing the northward flowing waters of the isthmus from the rivers, which empty south-
ward into the Pacific. So they planned to build a raft and float

downriver until they reached the Caribbean, where they might be picked up by a passing logwood cutter or buccaneer ship. The five men set about hacking down lengths of bamboo and lashing the pieces together with lianas to make two fragile rafts, but their only tool was an old, blunt machete, so it was slow work and dusk had fallen before the two rafts were ready. Tying their craft to the bank, the adventurers decided to rest for the night on a small knoll overlooking the river.

Wafer had scarcely settled himself down to sleep when he was treated to the full majesty of a tropical storm. "A little after sunset," he wrote, "It fell a Raining as if Heaven and Earth would meet; which Storm was accompanied by horrid Claps of Thunder, and such flashes of Lightining, of a Sulpherous Smell, that we were almost stifled in the open Air. . . ." The storm rolled over them for hours, and the rainwater cascading off the surrounding hills swelled the river until suddenly it overtopped its banks and came sweeping across the travelers's campsite. The knoll was turned into a rapidly diminishing islet, and the water quenched the campfire. In pitch darkness, broken only by the jagged tongues of lightning, the Englishmen thought that their last hour had come. Deafened by the constant peals of thunder, all five lost their nerve and scrambled for safety. Losing contact with one another, they splashed off in different directions, desperately hunting for trees, that they might climb out of reach of the flood. But most of the trees in the vicinity were giant cottonwoods, whose trunks rose tall and straight without a handhold for the climber. "I was in great Consternation," confessed Wafer, "and running to save my Life," when he found a dead cottonwood whose heart had rotted out, leaving a hole in its side some four feet off the ground. Taking a flying leap, he skipped up into this refuge and dropped into the hollow trunk like a squirrel skittering for home. There he crouched all night "almost Head and Heels together, not having room enough to stand or sit upright" while the swirling waters mischievously bumped driftwood against his perch, until the surgeon fell asleep from sheer exhaustion. When he awoke to see daylight, Wafer found himself knee-deep in water. Fortunately the rain and lightning had ceased at dawn, and as the floodwater subsided, the terrors of the night faded away. Wafer uncurled, clambered down, and made his way back to the soggy and deserted campsite. Calling and hallooing for his companions, he heard no answer; and finally the seven days without food and the terrifying events of the night overcame him. Overwhelmed by a sense of complete loneliness and defeat, Lionel Wafer sat down on the ground in black despair.

It was here that his companions discovered him, for they too had eventually found trees that they could climb to escape the flood. And now, returning wet and hungry to the campsite, they embraced each other with tears in their eyes, and gave thanks to God for their deliverance. A few moments later, however, their jubilation was cut short, for, on going down to the riverbank, they found that their precious rafts had not survived the deluge. The water had penetrated the hollow bamboo tubes, and the rafts now hung half-submerged at the end of their vine hawsers. All hope of taking the river route was gone.

At this stage in their wanderings the buccaneers were so dejected that they actually considered turning back the way they had come and attempting to reach the same Indian village where they had been so badly treated. But they could not even do this until they had found some food. Therefore, while groping through the brushwood which covered the riverbank, they became greatly excited when one of them caught sight of a small deer fast asleep in the forest. Quivering with anticipation, the half-starved men crept up on their quarry until they were nearly close enough to touch it. One of the buccaneers then placed the muzzle of his weapon almost against the animal's hide and pulled the trigger. But in the excitement the unfortunate man had forgotten to wad home the shot, and even as he fired, the musket bullet rolled gently out of the barrel and dropped to the ground. The gun exploded harmlessly, and the deer, awakened by the detonation, started to its feet and bounded away. Jumping into the river, it swam off to safety on the far bank, leaving the disconsolate buccaneers to take the edge off their hunger with morsels of the pithy heart of the edible palm, scooped out on the tip of their cutlass.

Wafer and his companions had reached the limit of their endurance. They were now so far from their original path that they realized they would never find the way back to the Cuna village; the recent episode with the escaped deer only served to remind them how exhausted and helpless they were in the inscrutable anonymity of the forest. They had not seen a single human since the day their Cuna guides had left them, and they knew that unless they found help very quickly they would die in the wilderness. In these straits, Wafer and his companions wisely decided to follow the trails left by the herds of peccaries, or wild pigs, as they moved through the forest. During their time in the Cuna village, the Englishmen had observed that the peccaries often raided the Cuna plantain patches and now they hoped that the pig tracks would eventually lead them to a village where they could beg for food.

Gopson, the weakest member of the party, was already in such poor state that he had been lagging behind the others and delaying their progress. Now, however, his companions could no longer wait for him because it was essential that help be found before the entire group perished. So, leaving him to follow as best he could, the buccaneers summoned up their last reserves of strength and stumbled forward, pushing their way through the undergrowth that arched over the peccary track. At last their luck had turned, for the trail quickly brought them to an old, abandoned plaintain patch, a sure sign that there was a Cuna village nearby. And here, at the fringe of rescue, the castaways's dormant fear of the aborigines surged up for the last time. For one heart-pounding moment of indecision the Englishmen hung back, debating whether or not they should make their presence known to the Cuna. But hunger got the upper hand, and it was Wafer who went forward to contact the Indians. His shocking appearance, bearded and dirty, as he staggered out of the forest caused a sensation in the village. Chattering tribesmen came forward to poke and examine the strange apparition with its matted hair and pale skin, and Wafer was bombarded with questions about where he had come from, and how he had managed to find the secluded village deep in the forest. The weary surgeon, unable to understand their excited language and stifled by the press of bodies around him, was swaying with exhaustion.

Then a whiff of the bubbling stewpot came to him, and spectacularly he fell to the ground in a dead faint.

For a full week the travelers, including Gopson who rejoined them, recuperated in the Indian village. And this time they found that they were treated with great kindness, being fed and housed with complete generosity and friendliness. The reason for the sudden change of heart was that the missing Cuna guides from the other village had finally returned home, gleefully displaying a collection of beads, mirrors, knives, and scissors which the main party of buccaneers had been able to buy from a French privateer vessel lying off the coast at the very point where the buccaneers emerged on the shore. The news of these lavish presents, plus the bonus of a half-dollar from every man in the buccaneer party, had spread among the Cuna clans, and they were behaving like children who had found a new and overgenerous uncle. Where formerly they had been surly and scowling, they now clustered round Wafer and his friends, eagerly offering to assist them and guide the stranded travelers to the coast. From them the Englishmen learned that the sinking of their bamboo rafts had been a blessing in disguise, for the castaways were still on the Pacific side of the isthmian watershed, and if they had floated downriver as they had planned, they would almost certainly have fallen into the hands of the Spanish and been imprisoned or executed as pirates. Instead, the Cuna were now happy to provide four strapping young warriors to lead Wafer and his companions across the central cordillera in the right direction. Retracing their steps to the river, the Englishmen were politely embarked upon a large dugout canoe and paddled briskly upstream. "Our condition," Wafer observed with considerable satisfaction, "was now well altered," and he and his friends sat back comfortably in the canoe, as relays of Indians paddled them swiftly to Lacenta's village, which was located almost exactly halfway across the isthmus of Panama.

At Lacenta's village, there was an unforeseen hitch. The paramount chief had not lost interest in the five castaways, and when they were brought to his village he decided to examine them a little more closely in order to see what manner of people they were. Blandly he claimed that the summer rains had made it impossible to traverse the north slope of the isthmus, and he insisted that the five buccaneers should stay in his village until the weather improved. It was this enforced sojourn among the then scarcely known Cuna that gave Lionel Wafer the wealth of detail which he later put into his account of the bizarre life and ways of the wild Indians of the isthmus of Panama.

14.

Life with the Cuna

WAFER'S STAY WITH THE CUNA BEGAN WITH a dramatic episode that had all the flavor of a schoolboy romance. Soon after the Englishmen arrived at Lacenta's village, the chief's favorite wife was taken ill, and the local medicine men tried to cure her. Their treatment, according to Wafer, was a crude form of blood-letting. The patient was stripped naked and seated upon a stone in the river. Then, using a small specially constructed bow and a set of miniature arrows, the native doctors began to shoot these little arrows from close range as fast as possible into her body. The force of the arrows was nicely gauged so that they penetrated only a half inch or so into the flesh, "and if by chance they hit a vein which is full of Wind, and the Blood spurts out a little, they [the medicine men] will leap and skip about, shewing many Antick Gestures, by way of rejoycing and triumph." The treatment was obviously very painful for the poor woman, and Wafer, who was looking on, decided that he could do a gentler and more efficient job with his lancet which, despite all his adventures, he still carried wrapped in an oilskin in his pocket. Offering his services to Lacenta, the buccaneer surgeon was somewhat taken aback at Lacenta's great enthusiasm to witness the white man's skill and the chief's insistence that Wafer perform his operation immediately. Wafer therefore applied a tourniquet of bark to the woman's arm and bravely punctured a vein with his lancet. Unfortunately the blood gushed out so strongly that his medical career almost ended, for Lacenta was greatly agitated and swore to put the surgeon to death if the woman failed to recover. Undaunted, Wafer drew off a full twelve ounces of blood, bandaged the arm, and boldly pronounced that his patient would begin to recover her health the next day. To his considerable relief, his prediction was entirely accurate, and of course his reputation was made. The chief himself came to him and publicly bowed and kissed his hand in gratitude. The enthusiastic populace insisted on carrying Wafer on a circuit of the nearby villages, where he was exhorted to undertake all the blood-letting he wanted or his patients thought was needed. His new prestige and these frequent medical tours gave Wafer access to all but the most closely guarded secrets of the Cuna.

The English surgeon frankly enjoyed his newly acquired eminence, and as he held a privileged position among the Indians, it was not surprising that he soon overcame his earlier fears and began to like and admire them. They were, he wrote, a tall, straight, clean-limbed people, big boned and well formed. Superbly fit and active, the Cuna menfolk normally went naked, wearing only a penis holder of gold or silver, shaped like a cone and held up by a string around their waists. The women normally wore a single breech cloth, but on festivals and great occasions both sexes would deck themselves out in long cotton or grass-cloth shifts or perhaps a cast-off European shirt. Both men and women were inordinately proud of their hair, which hung long, straight, and raven black, and they considered the length of hair a mark of great personal beauty. Every Cuna, man or woman, spent many hours combing, dressing, and oiling his or her coiffure. All other hair, except for eyebrows and eyelids, was removed, and the menfolk in particular had to endure the torment of having their beards plucked out by the roots, a task performed by their wives wielding specially made wooden tweezers. Body paint was also popular, and a fully decorated Cuna warrior was a dazzling sight. From head to toe he would be covered with the figures of birds, beasts, men, and trees, all drawn on his well-oiled skin with vegetable dyes of brilliant red, yellow, and purple. The womenfolk were the artists, and would lavish immense care on the display, squatting down in front of their men, surrounded by calabashes filled with the raw paint, and using the tip of a chewed twig as their brush. A few Cuna warriors also wore tattoos to enhance the paint work, but Wafer noticed that this fashion was comparatively rare because the Cuna dandies preferred to change their color schemes as the fancy took them, and had little patience for the slow and painful process of tattooing, done with a sharp thorn. At the request of one of the natives, Wafer once attempted to remove an unwanted tattoo, and was surprised to discover that although he stripped away most of the skin, the design still showed. He himself was so taken with the notion of body painting that it was not long before the English surgeon had entirely abandoned his European clothing and was as naked as the Cuna. He then persuaded a Cuna woman to cover him with the same gaudy and elaborate designs, and in this peacock state strutted about the Cuna village.

Wafer also adopted the other characteristic ornament of the Cuna, the lip plate. A small flat piece of metal, the lip plate was oval in shape and made of hammered gold or silver with a notch cut into one edge. The notch fitted over the central cartilage of the nose, pinching it gently, so that the plate hung downward over the mouth and rested on the lower lip. Only the Cuna men used these lip plates (the women wore heavy gold earrings in pierced ears), and as it was considered extremely important to keep the lip plates spotlessly clean, they were often scoured with sand. On hunting trips, a small and less cumbersome plate would be substituted, and when eating and drinking the plate was either removed entirely or held up out of the way with one hand. But, as Wafer remarked, "neither the plates nor Rings hinder much their speaking tho' they lie bobbing upon their lips."

Cuna feasts, much favored by Chief Lacenta, always followed the same pattern. First would come the formal arrival of the guests, each deputation entering the village separately, with the menfolk marching proudly at the head of the group. Behind the men came a file of their women, laden with panniers of essential festival equipment, necklaces, beads, shirts, cups, and spare provisions. After changing into their finery, the guests would assemble in the village longhouse, a communal building which served as a refuge in time of war or as a banquet hall in peace time. Inside the longhouse and in the village square there would be dancing to the sound of flutes and drums, followed by a grand barbecue, usually of a wild pig. And finally, when the eating and dancing were done, the drinking would begin. The longhouse was closed; weapons were hung up out of reach in case a drunken fight started; and the women were ordered off to one corner of the longhouse, where their duty was to peer out at their menfolk and refill any empty cup. Then, belching copiously, the Cuna men would swill down endless toasts to one another, always dashing out the last dregs in the cup after each toast and loudly calling for a refill. Astonishing quantities of palm liquor and corn beer were consumed in this way, and when the liquor began to have its effect, one by one the men would fall drunkenly to the floor and lie helpless. Then the women would come forward, pick up their fallen heroes, and hoist them into their hammocks, where the Cuna men slept off their excesses, snoring like pigs while the women sponged their bodies with water to keep them cool.

With its drinking bouts, feasts, and hunts, the daily life of the Cuna was a relaxed affair. In Wafer's opinion the Indians never really lacked anything, except for a reliable supply of salt, which was hard to come by in the forest. The surrounding woods and their plantain patches provided the Cuna with ample food; their houses were easily made from local materials; and they were so isolated that they had few enemies. In fact the Darien Indians led a very gentle existence. The men did not beat their wives; the Cuna children were well treated, if not downright spoiled; and entire families would spend the whole day doing nothing more arduous than gaily splashing about in the river or stream that ran beside every village.

In order to help him understand the ways of the Cuna better, Wafer doggedly undertook to learn their language. It was a formidable task, for the Cuna tongue was extremely awkward to imitate, being sounded deep in the throat with frequent aspirates and a circumflex tang. Curiously enough, Wafer managed quite well, for he found that it reminded him of Gaelic, which he had learned as a boy, and he was therefore able to pick up the pronunciation fairly quickly. The Cuna, of course, were vastly amused by the notion of a white man wanting to learn their speech and were prepared to spend hours with their pupil, teaching him and teasing him mercilessly about his mispronunciation. Years afterward, when Wafer wrote his description of the Cuna, he was able to provide a basic vocabulary of Cuna language that was to interest anthropologists two centuries later.

Indeed, very little escaped the English surgeon's curiosity. He described a Cuna marriage feast, which ended with the entire wedding party running out of the village into the nearby forest to clear a plantain patch for the newly married couple; and he examined the intricately-made Cuna basketwork, which was so closely woven that watertight cups were made of it. He watched Cuna children practicing with their bows and arrows until they were accurate enough to split bamboo canes at twenty paces, and he made notes on the potions used by the medicine men. The bitter gourd, for example, was a cure for tertian fever and constipation. And like Dick Whittington, he wanted to introduce cats to the Cuna villages in order to rid them of the rats and mice which plagued their huts.

Thus for three months Lionel Wafer lived among the Indians of Panama, and at the end of that time, though homesick, he was so popular with the Cuna that the easygoing surgeon began to have serious doubts whether Lacenta would ever allow him to leave. To add to his discomfort, his four companions had begun to make it clear that they did not share the surgeon's liking for the native way of life and that they were desperate to return to their own people. Wafer, of course, was the only one of the white men with sufficient status and a good enough knowledge of the Cuna language to broach the subject tactfully to Lacenta. His opportunity to raise the matter with the paramount chief finally came during one of the grand hunts that Lacenta held from time to time. These hunts were massive, almost medieval, affairs, when the entire male population of the area would form a cordon in the forest and begin to drive the game before them. In theory the Cuna dogs then ran down the wild pig (deer were not harmed, as the Cuna had a taboo against eating venison) and held them at bay until the Cuna bowmen arrived. But the Cuna hunting dogs, according to Wafer, were "mere whiffling curs," and the wild pig usually escaped. "I have seen about 1000 [pigs] started in a Day, in several droves," he wrote scathingly, "when I was hunting them; of which we kill'd but two, as I remember." On this occasion, as it happened, the Cuna dogs were even less effective than usual, and Lacenta and his men had spent the whole day running after their yelping hounds without killing a single pig. The chief was exasperated, and Wafer tactfully suggested to him that if he would allow the Englishmen to return to their own country, he himself could bring back a pack of good English dogs. At first Lacenta would not hear of the suggestion, insisting that Wafer was too valuable to be spared. But then he changed his mind and abruptly gave Wafer permission to leave on condition that he promised to return as soon as possible and spend the rest of his life among the Cuna. In what was probably a happy fiction, Wafer also added that the chief promised to give the surgeon one of his own daughters as a wife if he came back to the tribe.

Leaving Lacenta to continue with his hunt, Wafer hurried back to the village to tell his companions the good news. The following day the five travelers set out for the Caribbean coast. They were escorted by seven Cuna warriors and a pack-train of four Cuna women carrying panniers of food, the hammocks which the buccaneers had taken to using, and a bundle of Wafer's European clothing, carefully wrapped up against the time when the naked and painted surgeon with his bobbing lip plate would need them again.

The worst of the rainy season was over, but the trek to the coast was still not easy. At one point during the crossing of the cordillera, said Wafer, "The Indians carried us over a Ridge so narrow that we were forced to straddle over on our Britches; and the Indians took the same care of themselves, handling their Bows, Arrows, and Luggage, from one to another." At another place where the path ran along the edge of a precipice, the indefatigably curious Wafer could not see what was down below, so lay down on the ground and stuck his head out over the abyss while two of his companions sat on his legs to prevent his tumbling over. But below him the clouds obscured his view, and he had to content himself with taking notes on the giddiness brought on by the sudden change from the steaming lowland forests to the thinner air of the cordillera.

WHILE WAFER AND HIS FOUR COMRADES had been living with the Cuna, their companions from the large buccaneer party had also been kept busy. After they had reached the Caribbean and dismissed their guides, the buccaneers had been taken aboard a French privateer. Sailing north on her, they encountered an English ship and transferred to her. Shortly afterward, they had overtaken a Spanish coaster, boarded her, and turned her into a buccaneer ship. Then their luck changed. A storm parted them from the other English ship, and a powerful squadron of Spanish *guarda costa* cruising against freebooters had forced them to run south again. By August the buccaneers found themselves once more off the same stretch of coast where they had been picked up. Naturally, they were curious about the fate of the men they had left behind on their march through the forest, and so the buccaneers fired a gun to attract the attention of the coastal Indians. Several canoes immediately put out from shore, and to the buccaneers' delight, the first people to climb aboard the vessel were four of the five men they had left behind for dead. But of surgeon Wafer there was no sign, until one of the buccaneers took a closer look at the band of Indians who had come on board with the castaways. There "cringing upon my Hams among the Indians, after their fashion, painted as they were, and all naked but only about the waist, and with my Nose piece hanging over my Mouth" was Lionel Wafer, surgeon, enjoying the deception hugely.

Poor, scholarly Gopson with his Greek texts and his biblical consolations did not long survive his rescue. Only three days after rejoining his countrymen, the former druggist's apprentice died and was buried at sea, still in sight of the coast he had struggled so hard to reach. Spratlin and Bowman presumably took up their old life where it had left off, and went raiding and trading until they were killed or had accumulated enough loot to retire, though nothing more was heard of them. Wafer and

Hingson, on the other hand, both stayed well in the limelight. After a year of buccaneering in the Caribbean they signed on for a second raid into the Pacific. This time, instead of trudging across the isthmus, they sailed round Cape Horn aboard the notorious raider *Batchelor's Delight*, which appeared off the towns of Spanish America's Pacific coast, and in consort with other buccaneer ships had the audacity to molest the Manila galleons. Here, once more, William Dampier and Lionel Wafer crossed paths, for Dampier and Wafer shared those four years of fighting, raiding, and running which marked the progress of the second "South Sea" raid. But then Dampier decided to continue on westward, and sailed across the Pacific to the East Indies. On the way he was involved in a series of extravagant adventures which ranged from imprisonment to shipwreck to nearly being eaten by hungry shipmates. Having circumnavigated the globe, he finally made his way home to England. Wafer and Hingson meanwhile had gone in the opposite direction. They redoubled Cape Horn and came back to the Caribbean, bearing with them a substantial, if not spectacular, haul of booty.

But the Golden Antilles was no longer a refuge for buccaneers. During the four and a half years of the second South Sea raid the English authorities had initiated a vigorous policy of armed suppression to wipe out the last buccaneers in the Caribbean and the Atlantic. The English government had offered a period of grace, during which any buccaneer who gave himself up received a royal pardon, and then dispatched a powerful squadron of warships to blockade the favorite buccaneer haunts, arrest and interrogate suspicious vessels, and hunt down any unrepentant buccaneers. So when Wafer and Hingson arrived back from the Pacific, they found that they had dropped straight into a hornets's nest, and very wisely they decided to make themselves scarce. In company with Captain Edward Davis, the commander of the *Batchelor's Delight*, they concealed their identities and at the first opportunity took passage aboard a merchant vessel bound for the North American colonies. There they intended to vanish into the welcoming complaisance of Virginia, a colony widely recommended as a place where the authorities did not pry too closely into the affairs of visiting seamen so long as they had ample money to spend. But the Virginian bolt-hole was closed. The Virginia government was continually being harassed by English naval officers and their shore agents, whose eagerness to catch buccaneers was ensured by the fact that they received a share of any loot which they recovered. The navy was guarding the bays and inlets of Virginia, and Wafer, Hingson, and Captain Davis blundered unwittingly into the trap. They tried to slip through the waiting cordon of guard vessels by leaving the merchantman which had brought them from the Caribbean, and were working their way along the coast in a tiny rowing boat when they ran straight into a patrol from H.M.S. *Quaker.*

When they were caught, the three buccaneers had with them in the boat the incriminating evidence of the loot they had collected during the years in the Antilles and the South Sea. Worse still, Davis was accompanied by a Negro slave who could not be relied upon to support his master's story that they were all honest seamen returning from a lifetime of decent trading in the Caribbean. Eager to see its share of the proceeds, the navy drew up a careful inventory of the contents of the rowing boat. And, like the inventory of Ralegh's personal possessions when he went to the scaffold, the buccaneers' luggage was a microcosm of their lives. According to the official notary, Wafer's share consisted of: "In one Bagg, 37 silver plates; two scollops; seaven dishes, silver Lace, some cupps broken. Plate weighing bagg, string and all, 74 lb.

"Three baggs of Spanish money marked L.W., containing 1100 dollars or thereabouts.

"In a chest marked L.W., a peece of cloth and some old things, with old broken Plate and some little Basons, weighing in all 84 lb."

Hingson had a similar haul, including eight hundred pieces-of-eight; while Davis was credited with three bags of Spanish money, a chest full of broken silver, and some fine clothes. Precise to the last detail, the navy scribe carefully noted that Davis's seabag also contained a quantity of "fowle lynnen" and "two paper bookes very materiall to ye matter." This last entry was particularly damning for the captured men, as the books were probably the logbooks of the *Batchelor's Delight*.

The buccaneers' excuses when they were duly brought before a Virginia court of inquiry were laughably flimsy. Striking an air of injured innocence, Wafer lamely pleaded that Captain Davis was a total stranger whom he had never seen until the day they had been traveling together in the rowing boat. He admitted that he had known Hingson for some time, but only because they had both been engaged in the same line of business in the West Indies. There they had been legitimate merchants for several years, and it was because most of their customers had been Spaniards or buccaneers that they had accumulated the Spanish silver and the pieces-of-eight. Moreover, a good part of his property had been left to him by a deceased friend. Under the circumstances, the navy should return his goods forthwith.

Naturally Wafer's cock-and-bull story did not stand the slightest chance of acceptance, and his last hope of acquittal was blown to pieces when Davis's slave turned king's evidence and swore under oath that Davis had led the famous buccaneer expedition into the South Sea and that Wafer and Hingson had both been members of his crew. The gallows seemed uncomfortably close for the surgeon and his companions, especially as the navy was clamoring for quick justice and a rapid division of the spoils. But fortunately for the miscreants, the Virginia courts were tired of being hectored by the officers of the blockading squadron, and they deliberately dragged their feet. Instead of executing the prisoners as it had every right and ample evidence to do, the court of inquiry ordered that the three men should be imprisoned pending further investigations. This respite gave the buccaneers their chance to change their plea, and from Jamestown jail soon came a petition addressed to the King, in which the three men confessed that they were indeed former buccaneers, but that they had in fact surrendered to the Crown authorities earlier and had received the royal pardon. Somewhat impudently, the petitioners then concluded with a list of the goods taken from them on board the *Quaker* and a request that this property be returned forthwith. Apparently Wafer and his friends had found a shrewd lawyer, for in their petition they placed the confiscated goods at an even higher valuation than the navy's accountant had given.

For the next two years Wafer's career vanished into the tangled byways and back alleys of seventeenth-century litigation with its accusations, counteraccusations, and half-truths. From Jamestown two streams of letters went to the Virginia government and to the Lords of Trade and Plantations sitting in London who represented the King. In these letters the Virginian lawyers whitewashed their clients outrageously. The South Sea raid became: "for some years the prisoners were in the South Seas"; and their fat haul of stolen Spanish property was merely "a small quantity of plate." The navy, they said, had done three honest citizens a grievous injustice; Wafer and his friends had been wrongfully arrested and illegally imprisoned. In reply, the navy's lawyers grossly overplayed their hand, and further antagonized the colonial courts with their bullying tone. Then, as luck would have it, the naval captain who was a key witness against the buccaneers was drowned in an accident; and the Spanish ambassador, who had been collecting the evidence against the buccaneers as well as urging their prosecution, also died unexpectedly. Helped along by this mixture of good fortune and grinding legal tenacity, the three buccaneers began to wriggle free. At first, in early summer 1689, they were released from Jamestown jail on condition that they remain in Virginia as men under suspicion. Just over a year later they were cleared of the charges against them and provided with money to get them back to England. Finally, in the greatest victory of all, the three buccaneers battered away in the courts until eventually their ill-gotten gains were returned to them by order of the Crown. Curiously enough, though, a proportion of their coins and plate, worth some three hundred pounds, was kept back, and it was ordered that this money should be "applied to the building of a college in Virginia, or to such other charitable objects as the King shall direct." The ultimate beneficiary of this whim of royal generosity was, quite possibly, that college built on York River named "King William's and

Queen Mary's College" after its promoters. But by that time
Lionel Wafer was safely back in England, acting out that same
role which Thomas Gage had played before him. The surgeon
was writing a book about his adventures, and his fresh tales of the
Golden Antilles set in train yet another spasm of European
optimism about the Caribbean.

15.

The Company Promoter

LIONEL WAFER ARRIVED BACK IN ENGLAND IN 1690 after almost eleven years in the New World. While he had been away, James II had been replaced on the throne of England by William III, whose obsession with the balance of power in Europe had taken England back into the game of European politics. But while Dutch William labored unceasingly to check the power of Louis XIV of France, his subjects did not necessarily share his ambitions. Even as their king turned his attention more and more to affairs across the channel, many members of England's important merchant class were looking further afield, to the plantations in America and the Antilles, and to the trade with Africa. The enthusiasm of these merchants was aroused far more by the thought of new colonies than by the idea of military and diplomatic adventures in Europe. They wanted to foster trade, not finance war; and, in devoting their energies to finding new ways of expanding their overseas commercial empire, they examined once again the potential of the Golden Antilles.

But the merchants themselves were sharply divided. There were the lucky ones who sat on the boards of the existing trade companies, in particular the rich East India Company, and were, in consequence, eminently satisfied with the status quo. The

profit from a single voyage of one of their company ships could
be as much as 100 per cent; royal charters protected their privileges and their lucrative monopolies; and they wanted further
aggrandizement, rather than drastic change. Opposed to them
were those merchants who roamed on the fringes of the rich
mercantile preserves, and who were barred from sharing in the
really profitable areas of overseas commerce because they did not
belong to the monopoly companies. Some of these outsiders had
made money in small, independent trading ventures, yet they
resented being forced to remain on the periphery of the country's trade and were convinced that there was room for everyone
in overseas commerce. So they sought to break the monopoly of
their rivals. Undoubtedly the juiciest plum of all was the commerce with India and the Far East; but if the East Indies trade
should be denied them, the more ambitious entrepreneurs felt
that the West Indies offered a worthwhile substitute, and they
began to preach the doctrine that the potential wealth of the
Golden Antilles had scarcely been tapped. Pressure was beginning to mount against the old and constricting fabric of England's trade system, and the newcomers threatened to erupt
through the shattered pieces of the old framework. But in 1690
there was no way of knowing just when or where this explosion
would take place. The return of an obscure buccaneer surgeon
from the desolate Panama peninsula helped to decide the timing
and the location of the eruption.

Of course, these matters of high mercantile policy were of no
immediate concern to Lionel Wafer. His life had little to do with
the cliques of company promoters and merchants who endlessly
discussed their mercantile plans in London's coffeehouses. Rather,
he was fully occupied, with Hingson and Davis, in the immediate
problem of trying to recover his property from the hands of the
English authorities. When, after almost two years of constant
badgering and wheedling, the courts finally made restitution,
Wafer abruptly dropped out of sight. It was a tactful decision,
for he now had sufficient money on which to live in moderate
comfort, and there was no point in flaunting his success. The
navy did not enjoy being balked of its pickings, and Admiral Sir
Robert Holmes, commander of the antibuccaneer squadron, had

taken a personal interest in the case. The admiral had connections at court, and it was still possible that he might be piqued into reopening legal proceedings. Therefore Wafer kept in the background, and though it is not known exactly where he took up residence, it is probable that he went to live in or near Wapping, where many of the ex-buccaneers had congregated. This Wapping community was unusually colorful. It included retired seamen, former logwood cutters from the Campeche coast, buccaneers-turned-sailors, part-time contrabandeers, runaway indentured men who had sneaked home, ex-privateersmen, and an assortment of riff-raff who still hankered after their old life and would occasionally slip off to make a voyage of piracy or smuggling. Wapping, in fact, was a repository for the more romantic side of English overseas expansion, and it was only natural that London's publishers should soon have ferreted out this extraordinary lode of experience.

It was a time when Esquemeling's *History* was in its full flush of popularity, and the publishers were quick to seize on their opportunity. In Wapping and the other haunts of the returned buccaneers, the editors and the note-takers set about digging into this rich source of raw material, which the ex-buccaneers were only too delighted to provide. Their tales brought in a little extra money for the ex-buccaneers, and they were so flattered to find that publishers were interested in them that they usually adopted a note of slightly strained self-importance in recounting their adventures. Understandably, too, one of their favorite topics was the story of the first trans-isthmian raid in the Pacific, and at least seven accounts of that venture were written down. Some were dashed off with an eye to quick sales; others were little more than the emended journals of men who had taken part; and one, the most popular version, appeared as an addendum, tacked onto the end of Esquemeling's book as a sort of case history in buccaneering. Yet the most widely read account was to be found in a book that dealt only marginally with the raid, in a work entitled *A Voyage Round the World*, written by Wafer's old-time acquaintance, William Dampier.

Wafer, it will be remembered, had last seen Dampier in the Pacific when both men had sailed aboard the *Batchelor's Delight*.

They had parted company at the conclusion of that ship's raid into the Pacific, and it was a measure of the extraordinary compactness of the society of seventeenth-century English travelers that these same two men should then have met again in London four years later. By that time Wafer had sailed eastward around Cape Horn and also had spent time in a Virginia jail, while Dampier had made his way home around the world in the opposite direction. Both men arrived back in England within a year of one another.

There were other, rather odd, similarities between Lionel Wafer and the much better known William Dampier, and these likenesses were important to the story of the Golden Antilles. Both men were insatiable travelers, and their paths crossed surprisingly often—in Virginia, in Jamaica where they had worked on neighboring plantations, in the Pacific, and in the isthmus of Darien. More important, both men came back from their travels with much the same impressions of the Antilles. For this reason their accounts of the West Indies, when they were published in England, reinforced each other with startling accuracy, and therefore carried added weight. This similarity between their writings was something more than a simple reflection of the fact that they both wrote on the same topics. Rather, it resulted from a curious parallel of temperament between the two travelers. Both Dampier and Wafer were men of remarkably phlegmatic character, and they shared that same down-to-earth point of view which somehow gave additional substance to the exotic places they visited and described. If anything, Dampier was a trifle more the romantic and the dreamer; yet both he and Wafer saw the Golden Antilles in the same way and represented the area in their writings as a place that had solid, worthwhile potential for commerce.

Dampier, however, displayed a sense of purpose that Wafer lacked. The latter was content to drift as events took him, until he was finally cast up on whatever shore fate had selected for him. Dampier, though he allowed himself to be carried along by the flow of events and made judicious observations on everything he saw, always tried to influence his own career by deliberately picking the course that led him furthest into the unknown. His decision to continue across the Pacific and around the world to England, rather than returning with Wafer via Cape Horn, was a good example of this calculated adventuring. More important, Dampier always carried with him the unquenchable conviction that during his travels he was acquiring useful knowledge which was unique to his own experiences and denied to other men. This attitude smacked of arrogance, since it went hand in hand with the feeling that he, Dampier, was somehow better qualified to learn these revelations than any other traveler. Dampier was a morose, sardonic creature who, in later years, proved to be a singularly poor leader of men; but he did possess a remarkable mind, capable of absorbing, sifting, and correlating the enormous masses of information he fed into it on his travels, and yet constantly hungering for more data. In short, William Dampier intended to make some sort of an impact on the world and believed that he had the talent to do so, whereas Lionel Wafer lacked the vital spark of ambition.

This crucial difference between the two men was well illustrated by their actions when they returned to England. Dampier landed on September 18, 1691. With him he had a bulky, carefully preserved journal, describing his experiences during the circumnavigation. He had nursed this document with almost fanatical zeal. On the Panama crossing, for example, he had protected his manuscript by rolling it up and inserting it into a length of bamboo stoppered at each end with wax to prevent water entering and ruining the parchment. Dampier also brought back with him a South Sea Islander, a luckless wretch nicknamed "Prince Jeoly," whose chief attraction was that his body was entirely covered with a splendid panorama of tattoos. Dampier had seen Jeoly at Mindanao in the Philippines, bought a share in him with a shipmate, and dragged the native back to England as a "curiosity." Dampier's idea was to trundle Jeoly around the country, putting him on show to fee-paying audiences and reaping the benefits in cash and publicity. But when Dampier actually reached England, he was so short of funds that he was obliged to dispose of his share in the transplanted South Sea Islander, and never profited from his scheme. Jeoly was duly put on exhibition in London by his new owner, and the broadsheets puffed that "The Painted Prince is the Just Wonder of the Age, his whole Body (except Face, Hands and Feet) is curiously and most exquisitely *painted* and *stain'd* full of variety of Invention, with prodigious Art and Skill perform'd. In so much, that the ancient and noble Mystery of Painting or Staining upon Human Bodies seems to be comprised in this one stately Piece." The painted prince's "Back Parts," added the promoter with un-fettered imagination, "afford us a lively Representation of one quarter of the World upon and betwixt his shoulders, where the Arcktick and Tropick Circles center in the North Pole on his Neck." Jeoly was on display every day at the Blue Boar's Head in Fleet Street, though "Persons of Quality" might particularly request to have him delivered by coach or chair to their door-steps for private inspection. In the end, however, the hapless South Sea Islander was a short-lived wonder. On tour in the provinces he contracted smallpox and died at Oxford.

Thwarted of his money-making scheme with Jeoly, Dampier, like Wafer, dropped out of sight. But Dampier had no intention of going into permanent retirement. At some time during this period of obscurity he made contact with James Knapton, one of the London publishers who were so eager to print the ex-periences of the buccaneers. Dampier's manuscript account of his incident-filled circumnavigation was a publisher's dream. Much impressed, Knapton set the traveler to work on the la-borious chore of correcting, polishing, and rewriting the mass of material, a task which Dampier undertook with tremendous care, because he realized that he was at last within striking distance of his ambition. He revised and corrected his diary to give it as authoritative a tone as possible, researched and inserted extra background details, particularly if they were of a scientific nature, composed a preface, and astutely dedicated the book to Charles Montagu, then president of the Royal Society and a man of influence in learned circles. Finally, in 1697, Knapton brought out the finished product under the title *A Voyage Around the World.*

Dampier's *Voyage* was a sensation. As the successor to Es-quemeling's *History* it was a brilliant stroke of publishing. It capitalized on the interest created by the earlier work, and it offered all the ingredients for success: adventure, exotic description, travelogue, and scientific revelations. Within a few months the *Voyage* had run into its third edition, and soon it was appearing in Dutch and German translations. During the following century it was to be reprinted or excerpted at least nine times. Dampier was swept into high society on the wings of this literary success. Charles Montagu took him up; he dined with Pepys; the diarist Evelyn met him and thought the occasion worth noting down in his journal of events; scientists and men of letters like Sir Robert Southwell and Sir Hans Sloane (the latter now much more august than the mere physician who had traveled to Jamaica, but still deeply interested in the buccaneers) consulted him for his opinions. Dampier thrived. Initially he was rewarded with a sinecure in the customs service, but it was not long before the recommendations of his enthusiastic sponsors brought him an offer from an overimpressed government that the ex-buccaneer take one of His Majesty's ships on a voyage of exploration into the South Pacific. Dampier leaped at the chance. It was a personal triumph and the embodiment of his ambition. He was confident of his own peculiar ability for the task; he had already finished the draft of a *Supplement* to the *Voyage;* and this new publication together with other manuscripts was in Knapton's hands. There was nothing to stop him from pursuing his career to whatever heights he could attain.

In the meantime, the shock waves of Dampier's phenomenal success had dislodged Lionel Wafer from his quiet retreat. In his *Voyage,* Dampier had described the strange story of how "Chirurgeon Wafer" had been injured on the march across the isthmus and had been left behind with the Indians, only to reappear some months later, resplendently savage in body paint and lip plate. Such a tantalizing snippet bore the strong scent of a good story and publisher's profits, and was not the sort of detail which would slip by James Knapton. So Knapton, or possibly Dampier himself, successfully tracked down Wafer in his retirement and persuaded the surgeon to write his experiences for publication. Thus, two years after Dampier's *Voyage Around the World* had come out and just as Dampier was sailing off with government backing on his voyage of exploration, there appeared from Knapton's book-

shop at the Crown in St. Paul's Churchyard yet another buccaneer book. It was *A New Voyage and Description of the
Isthmus of America* by Lionel Wafer.

Unlike Thomas Gage, whose bombastic account of the Antilles shared with Wafer's *New Voyage* the distinction of helping
to launch a massive expedition to the Caribbean, Lionel Wafer
intended no propaganda, either about the Golden Antilles or
about himself. Rather, he wrote his book as a hand-maiden to
Dampier's best-selling *Voyage Around the World*. Knapton may
even have intended Wafer's book as nothing more than a pot-
boiler to capitalize on the success of Dampier's publication and
keep the *Voyage Around the World* in the public eye. Wafer's
book went out of its way to praise and recommend Dampier's
already well-known travelogue. Time and again Wafer included
complimentary references to Dampier's writing, and with great
delicacy he took care not to tread on any subjects which the
more famous author had already dealt with. Nevertheless, Wafer's *New Voyage* was an excellent publication in its own right,
and the surgeon's literary efforts stood comparison with those
earlier books about the Antilles written by Sir Walter Ralegh and
Thomas Gage. Wafer shared with Ralegh that vital sense of delight in the aboriginal innocence of the natives and the ability to
explain the thrill of opening the treasure chest of Caribbean
wonders; and, like Gage, the surgeon clearly had an enormous
gusto for those strange lands where the compliant visitor could
be absorbed by the exotic environment.

But the closest parallel with Wafer's *New Voyage* was Esquemeling's *History*, particularly those passages describing the
personal experiences of the earlier buccaneer surgeon. Wafer and
Esquemeling both reacted in the same manner to their adventures
in the Antilles. Their descriptions of the islands struck the same
note; their anecdotes had much the same flavor; and they tackled
their material with the same slightly formal pattern of authorship.
Possibly Wafer's book had been worked over by one of Knapton's editors who deliberately strove for this effect, but the similarities between the two authors ran far deeper than editorial
pruning and gloss. Wafer's comments on the climate, creatures,

plants, and natives of the Caribbean echoed what Esquemeling had said on these subjects, and, like his fellow surgeon, Wafer offered his own version of Esquemeling's strictures on the poisons and medicines of the West Indies. In the *New Voyage*, for example, there were those same warnings which Esquemeling had uttered about the virulence of the machineal tree and the dangers of eating certain, apparently harmless, dishes. Wafer did not plagiarize; it was just that the interests and professional outlook of the two authors overlapped very closely.

But Wafer's medical interests did not prevent him from including homely gobbets of information that would not normally have been found in a plain catalogue of medical advice. For example, in the pages of the *New Voyage* he pronounced that the sacklike membrane of a pelican's bill made a capital tobacco pouch if hung up with a musketball inside it to pull it into shape; that the powdered backbone of a barracuda was antidote against food poisoning; and that dead seagull could be turned into a tasty dish if first buried for eight hours in hot sand in order to lessen its fishy flavor. Similarly, Wafer shared with Esquemeling the ability to pick out those details which would make his scenario come to life. In his description of the tropical rainstorms, for instance, he wrote of the aftermath of the torrential downpours when the thunder and lightning of the storm suddenly pass away, and the ensuing calm is shattered by the sudden chorus of the forest bursting out at full volume. "You shall hear" he wrote, "for a great way together the Croaking of Frogs and Toads, the humming of Moskito's or Gnats, and the hissing or shrieking of Snakes and other Insects, loud and unpleasant." His description of the forest monkeys in Panama was equally memorable: when the buccaneers were laboring across the isthmus, he said, bands of monkeys had kept pace with them, "skipping from Bough to Bough, with the young ones hanging at the old ones Back, making faces at us, chattering, and, if they had the opportunity, pissing purposely on our heads."

But the real value of Wafer's *New Voyage* was his description of the geography of the Panama isthmus. On this topic he was unrivaled, because no other buccaneer author had spent so much time on that part of the mainland, and his observations had all the freshness of an explorer's report. To his fascinated readership Wafer served up a precise, detailed, and orderly synopsis of this strange and immensely strategic neck of land. Topic by topic he discussed the natural vegetation, the drainage, the position and quality of the harbors and their approaches, the fertility of the soil, and the region's economic potential. Indeed, his exposition was so thoroughgoing that in a later edition a "Member of the Royal Society" saw fit to append a botched-up series of portentous footnotes, a typical sample being: "The River Hog: Feeds on grass and divers fruits, can swim and dive well; they make a hideous noise in the Night, braying like an Ass."

Yet for all its orderliness, attention to detail, and good sense, Wafer's account of the isthmus of Panama was marred by one damning flaw—he believed that the area could support a plantation economy of the type established in Jamaica fifty years earlier. According to the *New Voyage*, every condition for such a successful European plantation was there: the area was undeveloped and lay outside the Spaniards' territorial claims; the climate and soil were suitable; there were no noxious diseases; abundant springs of water gushed forth on every hand; bosky countryside beckoned the settler; and the Indians were friendly. Moreover, there were large groves of precious logwood waiting to be felled and carried off at great profit. This last claim, above all, was to attract a good deal of attention, because the dyeing industry of seventeenth-century Europe paid as much as a hundred pounds a ton for logwood, which was one of the most sought-after commodities of the West Indian trade. By contrast, Wafer was singularly cautious about the hoary rumor that there were rich gold mines hidden away in the fastnesses of Panama. He told how Lacenta had taken him one day to spy on a group of Spaniards panning for gold in the streams of the cordillera, but he was not enthusiastic about the result. Apart from paying lip service to the usual vague tales of mineral riches throughout Spanish America, he did not advocate the possibility of making a fortune in gold-mining. Instead, Wafer succumbed to the lesser but equally dangerous temptation of gilding his memories of the isthmus and claiming that he had found a land fit for plantation, trade, and profit. It was this diluted vision that pushed the myth of the Golden Antilles into its next phase.

LIONEL WAFER'S EXAGGERATIONS WOULD PROBABLY NEVER have had any real impact on Caribbean history, but for the fact that before the *New Voyage* was published, Dampier loaned a copy of Wafer's journal to a well-known and highly imaginative company promoter by the name of William Paterson, the man who had helped found the Bank of England. It was Paterson who took up Wafer's recommendations and set in motion the cumbersome machinery that finally deposited wave upon wave of bewildered colonists in Wafer's promised land and cost the lives of some two thousand of them.

William Paterson, promoter of companies, was a colossus of his own day, who somehow left nothing more than a puzzling anonymity behind him. To his contemporaries he was either a financial wizard or an irresponsible parvenu, depending upon the point of view. In London his recommendation of a project was enough to unloose purse strings and attract massive investment, and in the West Indies, it was said, his name commanded such respect that any venture he dreamed up would receive whole-hearted public support. And yet, this renowned pillar of commerce was a frustrating enigma, a font of comment and information with little substance of the real man behind the façade. Any analysis of his career must, from its very beginning, be shrouded in a fog of half-guesses. It was reliably recorded that he was a Scot, that his family lived in Dumfriesshire, and that he was born about 1658. Paterson was therefore much the same age as his acquaintance William Dampier, who was forty-six when the *Voyage Around the World* was first published (Wafer was then about thirty-seven). But just how William Paterson rose to become one of the leading business tycoons of England in the last decade of the seventeenth century is a complete mystery. His family was neither wealthy nor influential enough to engineer his promotion, and there was virtually no information about Paterson's commercial apprenticeship. Later in his life it was said that as a young man he had spent some time in the West Indies, and was thoroughly familiar with conditions there. Very possibly he had founded his fortune in the Caribbean. But nothing is certain, even though this West Indian reputation was to have considerable weight when Paterson became involved with Dampier, and through him with Lionel Wafer. Apart from a smattering of references to the travels he undertook in Europe and a suggestion that he had a hand in the plot that brought William III across the Channel, Paterson's life did not really come into public focus until he abruptly appeared in London in 1691 (the same year as Dampier's return). At that time he was vehemently advocating the establishment of a national bank. Three years later his suggestion was taken up, and William Paterson may thus be credited as one of the founding fathers of the Bank of England.

Paterson was clearly a man of immense energy and wide-ranging enthusiasms. In the next five years his name was to turn up in all manner of unrelated schemes: as a member of the first board of the Bank of England, as a prime mover in a plan to reorganize the London Orphan Fund, and even as a director of the Hampstead Waterworks. In this last capacity Paterson was hoping to persuade the authorities to allow the construction of reservoirs in the north London hills and the laying of pipes so that reliable supplies of water could be brought down to the metropolis. But throughout these hectically busy years, one interest above all others attracted Paterson's ferocious energy—his scheme for foreign trade.

Paterson was one of those merchants who were excluded from the monopoly companies, and this exclusion, together with a genuinely held belief in the merits of free trade, drove the successful young Scottish businessman to advocate a much more competitive mercantile system than existed under the tight grip of the monopoly companies. Again and again during his meteoric business career, Paterson hammered away at this theme of expanding the trade structure. He argued that England's prosperity depended upon the maximum use of foreign markets and foreign materials, and that the latter could easily be processed in her manufactories and handled by her exchanges. He pleaded that it was madness to allow England's foreign trade to rest in the hands of a few privileged companies that were shackled by caution and comparative lack of resources, and he demanded that England's trade should be thrown open to everyone who had the capital and the wit to participate. Even as Lionel Wafer was enjoying the painted life of the Cuna, Paterson was mulling over his grandiose theories. In 1688 he went to Brandenburg to try to persuade the Elector there that a national overseas trading company would guarantee the future prosperity of his state. And when this venture failed, he hawked the same notion to the city fathers of Emden and Bremen. But, again, nothing came of his attempts and he moved back to London to try his luck with the liverymen and boards of directors in the City.

By this time Paterson's scheme had become an obsession with him. He had already made enough money in other lines of business to allow him to live comfortably, but he refused to let the matter drop and was prepared to stake his entire personal fortune on the promotion of his beliefs. In 1689, for instance, he paid over his forfeiture to Company of Merchant Taylors so that he might be admitted directly to the company livery and thus to its inner circle of merchant princes. But, as Paterson well knew, he had to tread daintily. The monopolist trading companies wielded enormous power both in the city and in Parliament, and they were savagely jealous of their privileges. Paterson's theories seemed a direct attack against their position by a greedy outsider, and the great companies, led by the East India merchants, were determined to crush any hint of competition. For a short time they had a breathing space while Paterson's genius was temporarily diverted by the Bank of England affair, but after the new bank had been in existence for scarcely a year, Paterson fell out with his co-directors, sold his qualification of £2,000 stock, and voluntarily resigned from the bank. A few months later he was deep in his scheme for foreign trade, and embroiled in a plot to circumvent the English monopolists by the brilliant maneuver of setting up a rival trade company in Scotland outside English jurisdiction.

The key to Paterson's stratagem lay in the somewhat ambiguous relationship which then existed between the kingdoms of Scotland and England. In theory, at least, the two countries were separate, though they both recognized the same monarch. Scotland had her own, somewhat emasculated Parliament, which met in Edinburgh with the power to raise certain taxes and pass Scots laws. In religious matters, the Scots observed an uneasy truce between the bishops and the synods and presbyteries. Yet the overall result of Scotland's ambivalent position was that she was suffering most of the disadvantages of independence while receiving very few of the benefits. King William took only a passing interest in his northern realm, and left its governance to a clique of royal appointees whose chief interest was in maintaining the status quo through an enervating and elaborate system of patronage. The country's economy was dwarfed by its southern neighbor, and Scots industry was gradually wilting away in the shadow of competition. England's wars disrupted Scotland's traditional foreign trade across the North Sea; yet when England was at peace, the Scots were not granted the same trading privileges as their southern neighbors. To cap it all, Scotland had recently been suffering a series of disastrously bad harvests which had brought misery to thousands of her people. But the Scots, though badly shaken and in decline, had not been entirely crushed. Throughout the land ran a deep sense of pride and identity. And it was this feeling, welling up through a crust of frustration, that was to start the next tragic flow of settlers from the Old World to the glittering mirage of the Golden Antilles. Paterson, Dampier, and Wafer were merely instrumental in breaking open the crust and channeling the direction of the flow; the real enthusiasts were the Scots themselves.

It was a mark of this undertow of Scottish sentiment that the Scots themselves had anticipated Paterson's idea of a trading company sheltering under the protection of Scottish laws. To the Scots the notion of such a company, larger in their imaginations than the great East India Company itself, was the incarnation of hope. The company was to be the symbol of their active and flourishing independence, a chance to display their native talent in commerce, a shop window of Scots manufacturers, and the spearhead of a complete economic resurgence for the country. Of course, the dreams far outstripped reality. There was not enough ready money in all Scotland to float a leviathan of the type they fondly imagined. They needed, and lacked, expert lawyers to defend them against the attacks of the English monopolists who would certainly attempt to strangle a Scots trading company. And before a single share of company stock could be put on the market, they had to have a businessman with special experience in such matters who could organize and plan the unwieldy venture for them. Fortunately, or so it seemed at the time, one man—William Paterson—had a reputation in these affairs. Furthermore, he was himself a Scot by birth. So the cabal of Scots nobles and merchants who wanted the Scots trading company asked Paterson in London for advice and practical assistance.

Paterson was delighted to help. He now had, or so he thought, a heaven-sent opportunity to outflank the London monopolists, to put his scheme for foreign trade into practice, and to show that his economic theories were right. It was this difference of approach—with the Scots intent on national resurgence and with Paterson looking mainly for free trade—that was to blight the venture and have such disastrous consequences. But at the outset the difference was either overlooked or seemed too trivial to be important.

After Paterson had been approached by the Scots faction or, rather, by their agents in London, he wasted no time. First, he warned his new colleagues that their plan would succeed only if they kept their intentions quiet and worked swiftly and secretly to raise the necessary capital and to persuade a favorable lobby in the Scots Parliament. Then he set about the task of drafting the Act, by which the Edinburgh Parliament would bring into existence a trading company of Scotland. This caution and diligence were well advised, for already rumors were circulating in the City of London about the Scots plan, and Paterson feared that King William himself would frown on any venture which angered the London merchants or threatened to disturb his foreign policy. Fortunately for the Scots, however, King William chose to go off campaigning in Europe just when their Act was due to come before the Edinburgh Parliament. Better yet, the King delegated the affairs of his northern kingdom to the Marquis of Tweeddale with instructions that Tweeddale was to comply with Scots aspirations as far as politic. To the delight of the Scots merchants seeking their own trading company, Tweeddale not only took these royal instructions to heart, but allowed himself to become personally associated with the Scots plan. The idea of a national trading company quickly found overwhelming support among the delegates to the new session of the Scots Parliament. So that in the summer of 1695, while England dozed and King William was away on the mainland of Europe, the Scots debated an Act for the establishment of a "Company trading from Scotland to Africa and the Indies." Well greased by its promoters, who lavishly dined and wined key parliamentary committee members, the Act slid through the legislative machinery without a pause. No more than a fortnight after its initial introduction, the bill had been read, discussed, returned to a Committee on Trade for comment, approved, reread, embellished with the names of its Board of Directors (Paterson included) and sent to the Throne for final approval. There it was "touched by the Sceptre" and became law. The Scots had their company (its official name was "The Company of Scotland Trading to Africa and the Indies") and Paterson had the means by which to put his theories into practice.

Then, amazingly, Paterson and his allies threw away the advantage that their lightning campaign had given them. Instead of pressing on as expected, the directors of the new company procrastinated disastrously. The reason for the delay was an unhappy outbreak of bickering among the directors themselves, with Paterson, as deeply involved as anyone, preening himself on his own contribution to the Scots plans and pompously lecturing the northerners on the principles and theories of overseas trade. But the real root of the problem was the atmosphere of rivalry which had sprung up between London and Edinburgh. There was not enough money in Scotland to float the new company, and so the Scots had been forced to borrow money on the London market and they resented the loss of control that this maneuver implied. They did not like to go begging hat in hand to the Londoners. They felt that the Company of Scotland was their creation and should not be meddled with by anyone living in the south. On the other hand, the clique of London directors, a mixture of expatriate Scots, Englishmen, and even one Jew, were risking money in the venture and therefore quite naturally demanded some voice in the councils of the company. The moment the Scots Parliament actually brought the company into existence by the legislative Act, these two factions, Scots and English, split into warring camps. Each accused the other of pettifogging and deliberate lack of cooperation. Very quickly the situation degenerated so badly that each side was ignoring the other's letters, and Paterson was priggishly admonishing the Edinburgh directors that "the life of all Commerce depends upon punctual correspondence."

Paterson and his friends managed to conceal the quarrel long enough to persuade a group of London investors to take up the English share of the capital. But then, when he wrote to Edinburgh requesting that a deputation of Scots directors should come to London to arrange the final details, the Scots turned recalcitrant. Suspicious of the London interests, they saw no reason why they should travel to London when the Londoners could come to them. Several times Paterson wrote north, urging haste. "The people here," he pleaded, "are already as much awaken'd as they are like to be, it become us to strike whilst the Iron is hott, and hasten our pace." But his pleas were ignored and the Scots seemed to take a malicious delight in delaying their final consent for a delegation to attend a board meeting in London. Superficially, the quarrel could not have been more trivial. Yet it was a symptom of a far graver illness. This small-minded bickering was caused not only by the sheer cantankerousness of the Scots directors, but by that same sense of pride and obstinacy which had brought the Company of Scotland into existence. Now that same obstinacy threatened the company's very survival, for even as the niggling quarrel dragged on, Paterson's fragile coalition of London investors weakened and fell apart.

The London investors had every reason for caution. While the Scots were dawdling, the company's enemies had shaken off their torpor and were beginning to mount a formidable counterattack. A pirated copy of the Act establishing the Scots company had been printed and was circulating in the City, and the information it contained jolted the East India Company out of its lethargy. By the terms of the Scots Act it was abundantly clear that the Scots now had a legal right to enter the trade to the

Orient; and the East India merchants, who had recently been suffering a number of bad years owing to shipwreck and enemy action, were determined to stop them. So the monopolists mobilized their forces and turned loose their lawyers on the task of smashing the Company of Scotland. The legal experts quickly pointed out that there was no way of attacking the company's base in the north, for the Act establishing the company was a perfectly legitimate Scots affair. On the other hand, Paterson's position in the south was distinctly vulnerable, and it was against the London investors that the established merchants now struck with extraordinary ferocity.

Shamelessly calling upon its large parliamentary lobby, the East India Company led the chorus of other monopolist organizations in wailing that the Scots were trying to destroy England's entire economy. This upstart northern company, they said, would deprive the English of their rightful markets, dispatch noxious Scotsmen to squirm their carping way into His Majesty's colonies, and even penetrate into England herself to peddle their cheap and shoddy wares in competition with English manufacturers. Overdone though it was, the monopolists' argument was pressed remorselessly, and the House of Lords duly obliged them by summoning Paterson and the other London directors for cross-examination. Paterson managed to evade the worst of the questions, claiming that he was only peripherally engaged with the Scots company and had merely advised the Edinburgh directors on the structure of their new company. But the damage was done. The Lords were in no mood to be satisfied with vague excuses, and their Committee on Trade proceeded to recommend that an Act should be passed forbidding any English subject from investing money in the Scottish venture or even taking part in its management. By the same token any English seaman or shipbuilder (the Lords had a shrewd suspicion that the Scots were planning a merchant fleet of their own) would be liable to prosecution under the law. Meanwhile, in the lower House, there was wild talk of impeaching those Englishmen who had helped bring the Scots company into existence. As a final stroke the board of the East India Company announced that any of its own shareholders who had the temerity to buy stock in the Scots company would "be accounted acting contrary to his oath" and ejected. Thus the doors of the City were firmly slammed shut against Paterson and his colleagues, and his earlier supporters were sent scurrying for cover. All but four of them withdrew their pledges, and Paterson, seeing the hopelessness of the situation, was obliged to pack his bags and move to Scotland. There he hoped to continue the crusade for his great "Scheme for Foreign Trade."

But Paterson's troubles did not come singly. After his trouncing in London the promoter was obliged to leave London so hurriedly that his personal fortune suffered a bad knock, and he arrived in Scotland to find himself at the mercy of a vindictive set of Scots directors, who found their cudgel in an unusual act of greediness by Paterson himself. According to the original resolutions of the company, when a quorum of directors had first met in London, Paterson had been given an extraordinary grant of 2 per cent of the company's original funds and 3 per cent of any profits during the first twenty-one years of the company's operation. This extremely generous gift, it was said, was to reimburse Paterson for his expenses in promoting his Scheme for Foreign Trade in the days before the Company of Scotland was founded. Naturally, when the tightfisted Scots in Edinburgh heard of this arrangement, they raised a mighty outcry and pointed out, with some justification, that Paterson had no right whatever to such preferential treatment. If any early dividend was to be distributed, they demanded that it should be paid to those Scots who had dipped into their own pockets to help the passage of the Act through the Scots Parliament. Paterson, the critics pointed out acidly, had been recruited to the scheme well after the original idea for the company had been launched in Scotland and he should be rewarded only in direct proportion to the benefit he had done the company.

Stunned by this outburst, Paterson backed down and renounced any claim to special treatment, only to have another scandal break over his head at this unhappy moment. He had asked one of his London friends to handle the investment of seventeen thousand pounds of the company's funds, and it was discovered that this friend had embezzled eight thousand pounds of the money entrusted to him. The Edinburgh Scots immediately turned on Paterson and blamed him for the trouble. Smarting from the earlier criticism and with his popularity sinking rapidly, Paterson tried to salvage his position by promising that he would repay the company's loss out of his private funds. But his own fortune would no longer cover the liability, and he was driven to pledge his future salary directly back to the company. Even this offer, which made him little better than an indentured servant to the company, did little good. Henceforth he was pointedly excluded from the company's inner councils; his advice was no longer sought by the men planning the company's overseas program; he was stripped of his company privileges; and there were signs that he himself was on the verge of a nervous breakdown.

WHILE THIS COMMERCIAL DOGFIGHT OVER the Company of Scotland was in progress, Lionel Wafer had been quietly pushing ahead with the preparation of his *New Voyage and Description of the Isthmus of America.* But before the book was ready for press he was approached by agents of the Scots company and asked to attend a meeting of the company's London supporters at Pontack's coffeehouse. There, he was told, the gathering would be glad to receive the benefits of his unique and renowned experiences in Panama.

Actually, the Scots and their allies were hoping to get something for nothing. The story had got around, probably via the better-known Dampier, that Wafer was about to publish a full account of the isthmus of Panama, with his observations on the prospects for trade and plantations there. It was also rumored that the retired buccaneer surgeon had such confidence in the commercial possibilities of the region that he had suggested to a consortium of London shippers that they should send a vessel to the isthmus to harvest certain great stands of logwood which he had observed in the Cuna country. Rumors of this type were of particular interest to the Scots, who were casting about for a likely commercial proposition overseas. Through Paterson's good offices, the Company of Scotland already had on its files a sheaf of reports about the Caribbean, including measurements, maps, and a draft copy of Wafer's journal (probably, once again, obtained through Dampier). The directors felt that if the retired surgeon was on the point of publishing his special knowledge of the area, they wanted to be sure that they knew about any vital intelligence which his book might contain beyond that already found in his journal. Furthermore, they were worried that the publication of the *New Voyage* might attract English rivals to Panama and spoil their own chances for success.

Ironically for Paterson, who was now in disgrace, the Scots enthusiasts for Panama drew their main argument from his Scheme for Foreign Trade. When the East India Company had made it clear that it would brook no interference with its traditional Cape route to the Orient, Paterson had investigated the idea of approaching the riches of the Orient via the New World. Like Columbus and the searchers for the Northwest Passage before him, Paterson had a theory that ships could sail westward from Europe to reach the markets and products of the Indies. But whereas the earlier explorers had hoped to find an all-water route, Paterson envisaged a sea voyage broken into two stages by the land barrier at the isthmus of Panama. European merchants would send their goods to the isthmus to be unloaded and transshipped across to the Pacific shore. There the cargoes would be reloaded onto other vessels and carried to China and the Spice Islands. It was a straightforward plan, and the linchpin of the entire scheme would be the foundation of a great mercantile emporium on the shores of Panama. There the traders would be able to store their inventories, exchange their wares, obtain credit and insurance, set up factors, and make arrangements with the shipmasters. In short, Paterson dreamed of a Baghdad on the isthmus, but wholly underestimated both the difficulties of transporting goods across the land barrier of Panama and the violent opposition of the Spaniards in the area.

For the moment, however, Paterson's arguments had convinced the Scots, who knew nothing of Central America. They were impressed by the promoter's alleged expertise on Caribbean matters and by Paterson's peculiar flair for wrapping his propaganda in an attractive package. According to him, nature had made the Panama isthmus one of the great commercial crossroads

of the world. It was, in his neat phrase, the "door of the seas and
key to the universe," and he argued that if a trade emporium
could be established there, "the time and expense of navigation to
China, Japan, the Spice Islands, and the far greatest part of the
East Indies will be lessened by more than half, the consumption
of European commodities and manufactories will soon be more
than doubled. Trade will increase trade, and money will beget
money, and the trading world shall need no more to want work
for their hands, but will rather want hands for their work." His
grandiloquence dazzled the Scots, worried by the slow death of
their traditional North Sea trade and frustrated and envious of
England's commerce with the fabled Orient. The directors of the
new company made up their minds to reap the benefits of trade
and plantation in this strategic area where the New World would
be a gateway to the East. Among their plans they included a
resolution that Lionel Wafer, living in Wapping, was a valuable
source of information about the region.

But Wafer was not only a prey for the Scots. English
merchants in London had also heard of his adventures in Darien,
and they were equally eager to pick his brains. English mercantile
cartels already controlled the lucrative trade to the West Indies,
and they never turned down a chance to increase their profits,
least of all when there was the nagging thought that Wafer might
perhaps render the new Company of Scotland such valuable
assistance that the Scots would steal a march on the Londoners.
So even as Wafer was being cautiously sounded out by the Scots
faction, he was suddenly important to the English. Again, it was
William Dampier who smoked Wafer out of cover, for Dampier
had been called up before a Committee of Inquiry to comment
on the rumor that the Scots were planning to set up a plantation-
cum-emporium on the isthmus. Dampier told the committee that
in his opinion the only man who really knew anything about the
isthmus was a retired surgeon by the name of Lionel Wafer. A
month later, in July 1696, both Dampier and Wafer were summoned to appear before the committee to answer questions concerning Panama and the Scots plan there. It was a grueling interview conducted by men of caliber, including John Locke, whose
reputation as a philosopher was matched by his experience in

colonial affairs (he had in fact helped to draft the constitution of Carolina), and Wafer was sufficiently impressed to spend some time drawing up a synopsis of his views. This memorandum, entitled "An answer to the Queries proposed by the Honble. Council of Trade," and his replies to their questions helped to convince the English committee that the isthmus of Panama really did have good potential as a future colony and plantation. Soon afterward the Council recommended that an advance party of English settlers should be sent without delay to the isthmus to take possession and, by implication, forestall the Scots.

Meanwhile the Scots company had been closing in on Wafer. At their meeting with the surgeon in Pontack's, the London supporters of the company were so taken with Wafer's evident expertise concerning the isthmus that they immediately raised "a collection of guineas" for him. He received this money on condition that he hold up the publication of his book until such time as the directors in Edinburgh had had a chance to employ him in the capacity of a confidential servant of the company. The ex-buccaneer was not coy about accepting the bribe, and Robert Pennycook, one of the company's leading members, promptly hurried north to inform Edinburgh that Wafer was open to offer. The reply from Edinburgh was typical of that strange mixture of ambition and parsimony which characterized the northern directors. Wafer, they said, was to be taken into the company's employ, but on no account should he be overpaid. Their agent was to approach the surgeon again, make "the easiest bargin he could," and offer him "a modest wage." The ex-buccaneer was hopelessly outclassed during the negotiations which followed. Wafer started by asking for an immediate payment of a lump sum of one thousand pounds to secure his cooperation, but the tight-fisted Scots eventually beat him down to the comparatively paltry amount of 750 pounds, of which only fifty pounds would be paid in advance. The final details of his contract, he was told, rested with the board in Edinburgh. Therefore his first duty was to proceed north as soon as possible and report for interview with the directors in person.

The events surrounding Lionel Wafer's visit to Edinburgh were soon to become a *cause célèbre*, and the popular broad-

sheets, with their accusations and counteraccusations, would effec-
tively cloud the precise nature of that visit. If such charges were
right, the Edinburgh directors had only invited Wafer up to
Scotland in order to treat him as vilely as they had already
treated Paterson. On the other hand, if the company's apologists
were telling the truth, Wafer learned in Scotland that the company was not prepared to pay him as much as he thought he was
worth, and he therefore decided to abandon his contract with
them. Probably there was some truth in each version of the story,
but in the long run it turned out to be singularly fortunate for
Wafer that he, unlike Gage, did not become associated with the
Caribbean expedition which he helped to set in motion.

   According to their English critics, the Scots directors called
Wafer to Edinburgh simply to pump the ex-buccaneer of all
information about Panama. For this reason they made quite sure
that Wafer was kept entirely ignorant of their real plans or his
true value to the company. The Scots agents in London impressed on Wafer that the English authorities might stop the
surgeon from going north to render assistance to the Scots and
that he would therefore have to travel in disguise and stay in
Edinburgh under conditions of the greatest secrecy. Wafer fell in
with the plan and allowed himself to be bundled off to Scotland
incognito as plain "Mr. Brown." Nor was he suspicious when he
was intercepted by Pennycook at Haddington, some twelve miles
outside Edinburgh, and whisked off to a secluded house owned
by one of the company directors. There he was kept a virtual
prisoner for two or three days, while a succession of company
supporters dropped in to cross-examine him about Darien, read
him selections from the manuscript copy of his journal which the
company had obtained earlier, and ask him questions about his
experiences on the isthmus. They even prompted him to tell them
precisely where they would find the vast groves of dyewood he
had reported. Either Wafer was mesmerized by the thought of
his promised company salary or he was uncommonly naïve, for
he answered their questions as fully as possible, and gladly told
them the precise bearings and directions of the dyewood groves.
The Scots, delighted with his helpfulness, then took him under
cover of night to the company's offices in Edinburgh where he

was again kept in confinement while the interrogation continued at the greater convenience of the directors. Eventually, after the Scots felt that they had drained Wafer of every drop of useful information, they brusquely informed him that they were abandoning the idea of a Panama emporium because the English had wind of the venture and were preparing to blockade the Panama coast. Under the circumstances, they craftily pointed out, Wafer's special knowledge was no longer of any great use to them. They regretted that they could not employ him in his original capacity, but perhaps he might consider working for them in South America or the East Indies. As they anticipated, Wafer had no intention of being fobbed off with a minor position in some far-flung company outpost, and he turned down the Scottish offer in a huff. Thereupon the directors promptly dismissed him without any further payment and turned him loose to make his way back to London, even refusing to pay his expenses for the trip.

Two years later, when the failure of the Scots expedition to Panama was the subject of intense debate, Wafer's shabby treatment at the hands of the Edinburgh directors was to be vehemently denied by the company's apologists. Certainly Wafer himself never wrote about the affair. But, of course, he had little reason to advertise his own gullibility and admit that he had been duped. Furthermore, Lionel Wafer was not the sort of person to resurrect a squabble merely to satisfy an old grudge. Yet, in the final analysis, Wafer never received the appointment which the Company of Scotland had hinted at, and the Scots did sail off to plant a colony at precisely the spot that he had recommended in his journal. Fortunately for the ex-buccaneer, however, he was back in London seeing his book through the press when the Scots went ashore in the Golden Antilles, and so he did not share in the next great debacle of the myth.

16.

A Smile on the Face
of the Sun

LAUNCHED IN IGNORANCE AND HANDLED WITH an unhappy blend of incompetence and bad luck, the Scottish attempt to colonize the Golden Antilles was a two-act tragedy, whose prologue began on February 26, 1696. On that day the subscription book of the Company of Scotland was officially placed before the public in Edinburgh; a week later a similar ledger was opened in Glasgow. The enormous sum of four hundred thousand pounds was required to fund the new company, and as all hope of London's financial help had now gone, it was up to the Scots themselves to show their confidence in the project by supplying every penny of the capital fund from their own savings.

But if the Scots company was short on ready cash, it was strong on pomp and circumstance. The trappings and privileges of the embryo company were grand enough to delight the most chauvinistic Scots heart. By the terms of its new charter the company was almost a state within a state. It was empowered to fly its own colors, arm and equip its own ships, declare and wage war against its enemies. It could plant trading stations in any foreign land not yet claimed by a European monarch and where the native population was agreeable to the idea. Once planted, the company could build and defend its own forts, own and operate mines, even take reprisals against interlopers. At home company employees were exempt from military service, and the King's magistrates were obliged to protect the company's interests at all times. Its mercantile privileges were equally sweeping. For thirty-one years all Scotland's trade with Asia, Africa and America was to be a company monopoly, and in its early years most taxes on the company trading would be waived. A single hogshead of tobacco every year would be blench duty for the company's future possessions overseas. All these privileges, prerogatives, and claims to high status were very grand, but of course they were built entirely on air. Nothing symbolized this extraordinary mélange of hope and confidence more succinctly than the company's newly minted coat-of-arms. Supported by a happy-looking blackamoor and an American Indian, each clutching a flowery cornucopia, the company shield was divided into four parts by a large cross of St. Andrew. In the spaces between the arms of the cross were depicted the imagined carriers of the company's future worldwide commerce: a deep-ladened merchant ship wallowing home to port, an elephant complete with howdah, and two Peruvian llamas trotting gaily along beneath their loads of South American wealth. Surmounting the ensemble was the company's crest—a rising sun with smiling image. So, too, it was boasted, would Scotland rise again in just such glory.

If the Court of Directors had planned on using patriotic appeal to unlock the coffers of the Scots, they had calculated shrewdly. The public was swept forward on a wave of national feeling and, as luck would have it, the directors' very failure to raise capital on the London market actually helped them. The withdrawal of the London investors, the Scots felt, had been a deliberate snub; once again the perfidious English had demonstrated their selfishness and their utter lack of interest in the northern kingdom. The Scots would show that they neither wanted nor needed English help.

The creation of their own trading company along the lines of the great trading companies of England, Holland, and France, had touched a nerve of pride and optimism deep within the national character, and the Scottish reaction was not restricted to a handful of rich financiers or a few enthusiastic Scots merchants.

It tinged every layer of Scots society that could scrape together the necessary disposable capital. Apothecaries and wigmakers, as well as landowners and bankers, put their names down in the subscription lists. Forty peers came forward to pledge money to the company; entire city corporations invested municipal funds; guilds, glovemakers, and goldsmiths took up fragments; and at the humblest level small coteries of friends clubbed together to take out the minimum pledge of one hundred pounds allowed under the company's rules. The upper limit permitted to any single individual was three thousand pounds in stock, but there were only eight Scots wealthy or willing enough to invest so heavily, and the vast majority of the 1,400 shareholders who saw the company afloat were financial mice, little men who could not afford the risk they were taking. According to one estimate, they pledged away, in their collective enthusiasm, almost half the floating capital in the country. Certainly, their liberality was the most optimistic investment ever made in the myth of the Golden Antilles. Their ill-conceived involvement made the imminent tragedy all the more poignant.

For, without question, the Scots investors were gambling their money. The directors of the vaunted company, however respectable they might appear on paper, had, in reality, precious little knowledge about either the prospects or the mechanics of trade and plantations, whether in the East or the West Indies. The grand phrases of the company's advertising broadsheets (which conveniently omitted any hint of the anticompany furor building to a head in England) made splendid reading, but they could be interpreted in almost any way the reader might please. When it came to putting theory into practice, the Court of Directors of the company had only the vaguest notion of how to make a profit in foreign trade. It was a mark of their profound and well-concealed ignorance that one of their first resolutions was to send an agent quietly to London with orders to find out exactly what sort of trade goods were popular on the West African coast. At the same time, another correspondent was asked to obtain patterns of the trade items sold in Greenland and Archangel. The Court of the company, it was clear, had not made up its mind whether to risk the public's money in commerce with the Slave Coast or with the Eskimos and Russians.

On the opening day no less than £50,400 worth of support was pledged amid general excitement, and although the final, and vital, total of four hundred thousand pounds was only just reached by dint of urgent last-minute appeals and by allowing the subscription books to stand open for longer hours each day, the initial public reaction to the new company was most encouraging. The directors had reason to feel well pleased with themselves. "They came in shoals from all corners of the kingdom," said one observer, "rich, poor, blind and lame, to lodge their subscriptions in the Company's house. . . ." Her Grace, the Duchess of Hamilton, was the first name on the subscription lists, down for the full three thousand pounds. Behind her came the Countess of Rothes and Lady Hope of Hopetoun, and there followed in descending order of importance rank upon rank of lesser subscribers. Naturally, the shareholders' pledges were not called in at once, for it was obvious that many subscribers were promising away not only their existing capital but their future income as well, and it was understood that the company would only ask its supporters to honor their pledges as necessity demanded. In fact the largest call on the capital subscription was the first, for 25 per cent of the pledge. It raised almost the full one hundred thousand pounds that was theoretically possible. With this cash in hand, the company's directors began to set in motion their rather vague notions on the conduct of trade and plantations.

At first they toyed with their earlier scheme for the African trade, and actually had shipments of bangles, arm rings, brass basins, and the like sent up from England in order to look them over with a view to going into the slaving business. But it was at this crucial time that Paterson was hovering in the background, skillfully prodding the Scots into adopting his cherished scheme for the great emporium at Panama, and seeing to it that the Court of Directors found much to interest them in the maps and charts of the Antilles, the glowing reports of the commercial possibilities in the Caribbean and Central America, and all the usual bric-a-

brac of the myth of the Golden Antilles which the London
company promoter assiduously provided. Some sort of overseas
trade and settlement was implicit in the company's foundation;
and whether it was to East or West Indies, the company needed
first of all a fleet of ships. So the directors, knowing that the
English yards were closed to them by parliamentary hostility and
that Scotland's shipbuilders could not provide the number and
size of vessels they required, turned to the great shipyards of the
Continent. Company agents traveled to Hamburg, Lübeck and
Amsterdam to inspect vessels, negotiate building contracts, and
even hint that the Hansa merchants might like to take stock in
the Company of Scotland, which was so assured of success.

Two full years were spent in this way, constructing the
intricate and enormous mechanism of the company's overseas
endeavor. Item by item, the carefully inscribed ledgers of the
accountants recorded the progress of the enterprise. Four vessels
were ordered at the Lübeck yards and fitted with Swedish
cannon. Special payments were to be made on their launch day
for trumpeters to sound flourishes and for Canary wine to be
distributed among the shipyard workers. In Amsterdam one
vessel was bought at auction and another built new. The latter
was to be the pride of the fleet: thirty-eight guns, oak built, and
aptly named the *Rising Sun*, she would eventually appear in Leith
Roads, gilded and carved with all the lavish ornamentation of her
day, matching sunbursts at stem and poop, and bright yellow
upholstery in the captain's cabin. But naturally the directors
concentrated on placing the bulk of their orders within Scotland
herself, and there the company's substantial purchases created a
small commercial vortex of their own. Paterson's idea of an
overseas emporium had won the day, for the directors began
their preparations on the huge scale that the Panama scheme
implied. Orders went out for medical supplies to be assembled in
sufficient quantity to last 1,500 men for two years, figures which
were to be the common yardstick, from sealing wax to frying
pans. Two hundred cattle were slaughtered and their flesh
pickled in barrels. Coal was purchased for the ships' galley
stoves; various brands of rum bought and stored; and a company

representative went off to London with orders to engage a Spanish-speaking interpreter and buy maps of the Antilles. He found his man, a Jew who claimed to speak six languages, and he also brought back with him a selection of Caribbean sea-charts, books of sailing directions, maps by Mercator, and two azimuth compasses, one of which, it was carefully accounted, was bought new and the other secondhand. The company's warehouses began to fill with consignments of cartridge belts, grenades, nails and anchors, lignum vitae, parchment, sword blades, and company livery. And bearing in mind Lionel Wafer's claim that there was enough logwood in Darien to defray the entire cost of the expedition within six months, the directors ordered a large number of felling axes, saws, and ropes.

The forward movement of Scotland's great overseas adventure was quickening, and as the urgency and bustle increased and minutiae flooded in on the attention of the company's leaders, there was less and less awareness that perhaps something might go wrong with the vast project. Not even Paterson spoke out against the flashes of palpable ignorance and amateurishness which occasionally broke through the sheen of energy and confidence. But he must have known how ill-advised it was when the Scots, in their eagerness to sell only Scots manufactories to the Darien Indians and the other settlers of the Antilles, bought up great boxes of wigs (made, of course, from Scots hair), buckle shoes, mountains of stockings, and rolls of heavy serge, "one fourth part black, one fourth part blue, one fourth part of several sorts of reds, and one fourth part of several sorts of cloth colours." The brightly-colored cloth and the specially ordered hair-combs might perhaps have appealed to the Cuna dandies whom Wafer described in his journal, but the Cuna had little or no money to pay for their purchases—and what would be done with such items as the 380 Bibles, 51 New Testaments, and 2,808 Catechisms which the Scots carefully packed in barrels ready for shipment to the pagan and illiterate heathen?

By March 1698 preparations were far enough advanced for the directors to set about the task of signing on the men who would sail to Darien. It was decided that the company settlement would go in two fleets. The first fleet would make landfall, explore, select a site, negotiate with the Indians, and build houses. Then a second fleet would bring out reinforcements, additional supplies, and consolidate the position. It was all very neat in theory and there was no lack of volunteers to go with the "first equipage," as the directors called it. According to the terms of the recruiting prospectus which was nailed up outside the company offices in Edinburgh, all volunteers with the first fleet would receive fifty acres of plantable land and at least fifty square feet of ground "in the chief City or Town, and an ordinary House built thereupon by the Colony at the end of 3 years." Furthermore, if any colonist should die before he was firmly established in his new home, his family would be shipped out at the company's expense and would inherit his property.

The cream of the expedition was to be three hundred young men of good Scots families, some of whom arrived at the company's offices clutching birth scrolls which testified to their good position in life. Sixty veteran officers also went along to provide a military nucleus (though every colonist was expected to take up arms if necessary to defend the projected colony), and to give the officers something worth commanding, several hundred Highlanders were enrolled. Most of these ex-soldiers were men who had been discharged from the Highland regiments and who spoke only Gaelic, a barrier which immediately set them apart from the rest of the colonists. In addition, there were artisans, craftsmen, and farmers, carefully selected with a view to their skills and future usefulness. The total number of twelve hundred was rounded out with sailors, a number of women, and a few civilian "volunteers." Among the latter was Paterson, now sadly in disgrace, accompanied by his wife and servant. Three pastors also went on the expedition's official strength, and the company gave them a special grant of ten pounds to buy the necessary books and equipment.

Three of the company's newly acquired merchant vessels, the *St. Andrew*, the *Unicorn*, and the *Caledonia* made up the first fleet, together with two much smaller ships, a pink named the *Endeavour* and another vessel of a type known as a snow. The latter was a French prize that the company had been able to buy at Newcastle without arousing the suspicions of the English and had renamed the *Dolphin*. Inevitably a patriotic ballad-monger somehow managed to work the ships' names into his *Caledonia Trimphans*, one verse of which ran:

> *St. Andrew, our first Tutelar was he,*
> *The Unicorn must next supporter be,*
> *The Caledonia doth bring up the rear*
> *Fraught with brave hardy lads devoid of fear;*
> *All splendidly equipt, and to the three,*
> *The Endeavour and the Dolphin handmaids be.*

Commander of the first fleet was James Pennycook, the man who had originally interviewed Wafer in London on the company's behalf and who was now promoted to commodore. But most unwisely he was obliged to share the overall direction of the expedition with a board of ten councillors who were expected to reach joint decisions on the new colony's management. Very soon the quarrels of these councillors were to disrupt the company's plantation in the same way as the split command of the Western Design had set General Venables and Admiral Penn at one another's throats. Yet in their ignorance the Edinburgh directors worried very little about the conditions their Board of Councillors would find in the Golden Antilles. The Scots had read and heard so much of the myth and were so cushioned from the harsh experiences of earlier colonial disasters that they had no perspective on the dangers involved. They accepted Paterson's idea for the emporium at face value, and they sincerely believed that Lionel Wafer's experiences among the Cuna pointed the way to a great commercial coup. The Court of Directors and the company's officers had gone into the matter as thoroughly as they were able. They had exercised all due diligence and care in planning the venture, picked the best men, and provided them with the finest equipment in Scotland. It was difficult to see any reason for failure. As a result, the Company of Scotland was organized as a cumbersome machine, designed to suck men and money through its portals in Scotland and spew them forth into unforeseen catastrophe on the other side of the ocean.

So the curtain rose on the first act of the Scottish Darien

tragedy on July 14, 1698. On that day the first fleet sailed with a tremendous send-off from the populace of Edinburgh. Crowds of well-wishers flocked to the harbor at Leith to wave godspeed, and there was considerable commotion as numbers of stowaways were discovered aboard and had to be put ashore, protesting that they were unjustly robbed of their chance in the Antilles. But the expedition's organizers were firm: the fleet carried only enough supplies to feed the planned number of colonists, and already the colonists had consumed an alarming amount of food as they waited for the fleet to sail. That first day the ships made a short voyage to Kirkaldy on the opposite side of the firth, where a last-minute selection of stores was taken aboard. Then Commodore Pennycook took his command out onto the North Sea and began the long and tedious passage northward around the Orkneys before turning southwest for the inviting Caribbean.

It was a foul trip. A storm scattered the fleet, and the first dews of enthusiasm quickly evaporated under the effects of thick weather and seasickness. Indeed, the only member of the expedition to have any reason for satisfaction was William Paterson himself. Now that he was away from the malign opposition of the Edinburgh directors, his energy bubbled back. Because one of the original councillors had failed to join the fleet at the last minute, Paterson was soon asked to fill the vacancy. Among his first acts was a letter to the directors, in which he wrote: "For God's sake be sure to send the next fleet from the Clyde, for the passage north about is worse than the whole voyage to the Indies."

The Court of Directors received these first dispatches from the fleet when it reached Madeira. There the Scots ships had arranged to rendezvous, and their unexpected arrival off the island caused near-panic among the inhabitants, who did not recognize the strange new company colors at the masthead. Indeed the Madeira garrison mistook the *Caledonia* for an Algerian corsair and the little *Endeavour* as her prize. When this misunderstanding had been straightened out, and the harbor authorities had regained their poise, the Scots could not forbear to rehearse the dignity and privileges of their station. Between Harbor and Fleet there was much dipping of flags, firing of salutes, and the sending of courtesy boats. Commodore Penny-cook, who was solemnly counting the number of guns, proudly noted that the governor of Madeira gave him "as much as he gives to any of the King's Shipps." Rather more sensibly, the cargo of the *Endeavour* was sold for twenty-seven pipes of good Madeira wine, with which to ease the discomforts of the forth-coming Atlantic passage and to enter the Caribbean liquor trade, for the fleet's tropical destination was now common knowledge. In Madeira Roads the councillors had opened the packet of sealed orders that the directors had given them in Edinburgh, and they read that their final destination was to be a point on the American mainland isthmus behind Golden Island in the gulf of Darien. It was exactly the place where the buccaneers had landed on their way to the Pacific and where Lionel Wafer had reported the existence of logwood in abundance.

On September 2, the reunited fleet set sail to follow the same track which Ralegh, Gage, and Penn had taken in their attempts on the legendary Antilles. Deseada Island, near Guadeloupe, was the West Indian landfall, and at Nevis the Scots delighted anew to show off their sovereignty, sailing in close to the island and hoisting their colors to the English fort there. Then they stood away for Crab Island, south of Puerto Rico, and Paterson was detached with the *Union* and *Dolphin* to find a suitable pilot for the Darien Gulf. At the Dutch-held island of St. Thomas he had the good fortune to pick up an old buccaneer, Captain Alliston, who had visited the isthmus with the South Seas expedition, and knew the Darien coast. Under his guidance the first fleet wal-lowed across the Caribbean and 109 days out of Leith dropped anchor off Golden Island (now Isla de Oro). Two days later the *Caledonia*, *Unicorn*, and *St. Andrew*, preceded by leadsmen in the ships's small boats, moved in along the channel behind the island itself. There they discovered an excellent natural harbor where an arm of land curled out into the sea and enclosed a splendid anchorage. The first fleet had reached its destination.

The Scots were delighted with what they found. Conditioned since the start of the great adventure to expect the Golden Antilles in all its wonders, they were disposed to view everything in the best possible light. The harbor was the first gem to draw their praises. "It is large enough," wrote one diarist, "to contain 500 sail of ships. The greatest part of it is landlock'd, so that it is safe, and cannot be touch't by any wind that can blow." He was wrong. A strong northerly wind could raise such seas as to make the entrance impassable. And Mr. Rose, the expedition's official recorder, pronounced with even greater exaggeration that "the harbour is capable of containing 1000 of the best ships in the world, and with no great trouble wharfs may be run out to which ships of the greatest burthen may lay their sides and unload." Clearly, the ardent Scots already saw in their mind's eye the "great emporium" which Paterson had promised them. They congratulated themselves on the vast capacity, splendid aspect, and natural defenses of the place. A single fort on the tip of the peninsula, they calculated, would command both the harbor and the peninsula itself, and another battery on the opposite shore, Mr. Rose belligerently declared, would mean that the place "may be fortify'd against a Navy."

To the same indulgent eyes, the land itself was everything that could be desired. In the first glow of enthusiasm there was wild talk of taking ten thousand hogsheads of sugar every year from the immediate area alone, and the more sanguine colonists spoke as if it were simply a matter of time before they would uncover the fabulous gold mines that the Spaniards were rumored to have kept hidden for so long against all interlopers. "The Soil is rich," wrote one, "the Air good and temperate, the Water is Sweet, and everything contributes to make it healthful and convenient." The same diarist apparently fancied himself as something of a botanist for he added that "this place affords legions of monstrous Plants, enough to confound all the Methods of Botany ever hitherto thought upon" and he boasted that he would need to restrict the number of botanical specimens he collected "because if I should gather all, 'twould be enough to load the *St. Andrew,* for some of their leaves exceed three Ells in length."

But not all the new arrivals were so loftily scientific in their approach to the new settlement. With more mercenary interests at heart, scouting parties went out under Commodore Pennycook and Captain Alliston to search for Wafer's famous logwood groves. It was their first disappointment. The party returned empty-handed, and in his journal the commodore sadly noted: "It was order'd that Captain Pinkerton, and I with Captain Allitson [*sic*] should goe and search the River of Agra for the Nicaragua Wood, being about a micle and a half from Golden Island. On the 27th [of November] Captain Pinkerton and I return'd and told them that we could find none of that wood. And we have reason to believe Captain Allitson does not know it, nor is there any here does." The famous chance of repaying the entire costs of the expedition at one blow had vanished, though the Scots were not yet downcast. Their arrival had been well timed at the end of summer, and the isthmus was looking its best. The intense green of the forest, the succulent leaves of the vegetation, the abundance of wild life and the kaleidoscope of tropical birds enchanted the newcomers from the bleaker surroundings of Scotland. To them Darien was a lotus land where the balmy air and the thick tropical soils promised rich crops and an easy life. They could not know that these luscious tropical soils were in fact easily exhausted by unplanned farming and difficult to maintain in good heart. Nor did the amateur botanist guess that his "monstrous plants" were evidence of a sultry, enervating climate and of an environment that was both hostile to northern agriculture and a breeding ground for fever. Blindly the Scots paid the new settlement the greatest compliment they knew: they named the place "Caledonia" and their embryonic town "New Edinburgh."

On this high note the Scots started to make the wilderness into a fit place to live. To begin with, most of the colonists were ordered to remain on board the ships while gangs of forty men from each vessel went ashore with axes, ropes, and saws to clear away the underbrush and put up temporary shelters for the invalids who had fallen ill on the voyage. Then the sick were landed; tents, furniture, and other tackle were unloaded; and finally the longboats ferried ashore the main body of colonists for their first tasks in their new home. The immediate priority, the council believed, was the construction of a fort at the tip of the peninsula because there were rumors that both the French and the Spanish in the West Indies were considering sending expeditions to dislodge the intruding Scots. Thus the inevitable "Fort St. Andrew" was hastily thrown up, a somewhat amateur effort, as the Edinburgh directors had unaccountably failed to send out a military engineer with the first fleet. Nevertheless, a battery of sixteen 12-pound cannon was borrowed from the fleet, and when these guns had been mounted on a low platform overlooking the approaches to the harbor, the new fort was fully capable of blowing any unwelcome ships out of the water if they tried to force the entrance behind Golden Island. To protect the landward side of the fort, a breastwork and parapet were erected, and a small moat was dug some nine feet deep and twelve feet across. Beyond this perimeter the Scots energetically hacked down any trees and bushes which might give shelter to the enemy. The fort's real weakness, however, was the fact that there was no supply of fresh water within the defenses and the nearest springs were on the far side of the moat. Commodore Pennycook nevertheless felt sufficiently encouraged by these warlike preparations to note in his journal, "we are now in such condition that we wish nothing more than that the Spanish would attack us"; and he ordered the fleet to anchor in line of battle across the mouth of the great harbor.

At least the Caledonians, as they took to calling themselves, did not have to worry about the possibility of an attack from the natives of the region. Lionel Wafer's optimistic predictions about the friendliness of the Darien Indians proved in fact to be embarrassingly correct. The moment the fleet appeared off the coast, the local Cuna chiefs paddled out in their canoes to greet the colonists with a weird garble of Cuna, broken French, bad Spanish, and worse English. From this excited oratory the Scots were able to make out that the Cuna welcomed the colonists as common allies against the Spaniards, who had recently been sending armed posses into Cuna territory. And of course the arrival of the company's fleet was an unparalleled excuse for the parties, feasts, and drinking bouts that the Cuna so dearly loved. So the Scots were treated to the inevitable parade of ceremonial lip plates, adoring concubines, and dazzling body paints, as the Cuna dignitaries began to emerge from the hinterland in order to display themselves and pay their respects to the white men who had come to live in their land. Initially the Scots response was stiffly formal, and they delivered stilted compliments and crisp speeches through their Spanish-speaking interpreter; but then, when the first novelty had worn off, they began to look upon the Cuna as wild, untutored children rather than as serious allies. They gave the aborigines strong drink, saw the effect, and promptly amused themselves by deliberately making the natives drunk in the hopes that they would fall into the water while trying to climb back down from the ships into their canoes. Other colonists took to exchanging manufactured articles and lengths of cloth for curios from the Indians, and started collections of calabashes, necklaces, arrow heads, and the like. One enterprising colonist even managed to obtain a Cuna penis cover, which Pennycook later sent home to a friend, describing it in his accompanying letter as "a little instrument of silver which I beg your Lordship will not expose to the view of the fair sex, for if they measure the country by the magnitude of that instrument I am sure that they'll have no inclination to visit these parts."

But even while the Scots were busily jotting down their admiring references to the nobility, manliness, and good nature of the Cuna, the Council of Caledonia was belatedly realizing that the Cuna had nothing of value to offer in exchange for the company's trade goods. Those parties of hopeful Scots who went out with Cuna guides to look for gold mines returned with blistered feet and crushed hopes, and the other colonists, who visited the Cuna villages hoping to find flourishing fields and crops, came back with gloomy descriptions of simple thatch huts and wretched plantain patches. Then, too, a few of the Scots never quite gave up the notion that the Cuna were a gang of dissembling savages waiting to massacre them in their beds. These Cassandras warned that the Indians were a simple lot who would just as readily give their allegiance to the first Spanish expeditionary force that came to attack Caledonia.

For the moment, however, the councillors felt that it was their duty to fulfill the colony's legal obligations by arranging a treaty with the aborigines, giving the company official permission to possess Caledonia. Accordingly, they persuaded two of the local clan chiefs to put their marks to a paper, by terms of which the Cuna relinquished sovereignty of the immediate area of the colony in return for the company's protection. The Cuna chiefs probably had no real understanding of what they were doing, and actually the treaty was after the fact, since the colonists had already occupied the land and were building permanent structures there. In return for their cooperation, the council gave one of the Cuna signatories a splendid parchment, tied with a magnificent gold-striped ribbon, which stated that he was now an officer of the company's militia. And in keeping with his new post he was presented with a brace of pistols and a fine basket-hilt Scots sword. Soon the lesser folk among the Cuna were flying little Scots flags at the prows of their canoes as they paddled happily around the harbor, gazing up at the European vessels and hopefully trying to wheedle the sailors into offering them another drink.

But the first flaws in "so valuable a Jewel," as Caledonia had been called, were already beginning to cause worry. With each day the colonists were learning that their new home was marred by several fundamental disadvantages. The most depressing discovery was that the weather, which had been wet and stormy since the day of their arrival, showed no sign of improvement. The daily thunderstorms (which Wafer had warned them about) began to sap at the men's patience. The damp was rotting their clothes and molding their provisions; the muggy heat reduced all inclination to work. To dishearten them still more, the field workers saw that their labors against the undergrowth were having little effect, and they began to feel that they would never succeed in clearing land. The construction of Fort St. Andrew had diverted too many men, and the laying out of the fields had been so held up that the council now realized that the colony would have to rely on imported foodstuffs for at least the first season. Then a strange and undiagnosed fever, accompanied by vomiting and an extraordinary lassitude, began to affect many of the working men. There were more and more cases of the bloody flux, from which many victims never recovered. Every week one or two corpses were buried in the cemetery that had been laid out behind the fort, and the constant strain on the colonists became more than some of the Scots could stand. Two of the

workgangs insanely attempted to run away into the forests. They
did not know where they wanted to go, unless it was to live with
the Indians, and so it was not long before they were caught and
brought back to be put in irons. Thefts, drunkenness, and insubordination became daily occurrences, and work on the fields
and storehouses slowed as the Scots lost their enthusiasm for their
new and supposedly happier land.

In fact a good deal of the trouble stemmed from the poor
quality of the colony's leadership. The folly of dissipating the
expedition's command among so many amateurs was now all too
apparent. Several of the councillors had enough common sense
and energy to be able to keep the colony on its feet, but they
were shackled to the deadweight of the indecision of their colleagues. To make matters worse, some councillors had imported
personal squabbles with them, and now these flared into incred-
ible outbursts of bad temper, aggravated by drunkenness. Commodore Pennycook was particularly difficult to deal with, and he
had blazing arguments with both land officers and sea officers.
There were threats of mutiny, and one group of officers began to
talk of seizing command or perhaps stealing some of the ships and
making off for Scotland on their own. Paterson, who might
perhaps have patched up the quarrels in the council, was approaching his second nervous breakdown. His wife had died soon
after the fleet reached Darien; his manservant was also dead; and it
must have been quite obvious to him that his "great emporium"
was a grim specter. Yet, in direct contrast to this deepening
gloom, the council's first formal report to the directors in Edinburgh clung to the myth of the Golden Antilles. Flagrantly con-
tradicting the lengthening death list and the barely scratched
fields around the bay, they bravely reported that "the wealth,
fruitfulness, health, and good situation of the Country proves for
the better, much above our greatest expectation." Caledonia, they
said, was one of the garden spots of the world, where even the
tops of mountains and hills were mantled in three or four feet of
good, rich loam. Fishing, fowling, and hunting were excellent,
and the air was devoid of "those mortal distempers so prevalent
in the English and other American islands." The only hints that
perhaps all might not be going quite so smoothly as the report

made out were requests for two more ministers to be sent out to replace two who had died, and for cargoes of provisions and more suitable trade goods.

To those who had the wit to see it, the Caledonians were caught in a quicksand of impossibilities. According to the directors' original plan, the colony should have begun drawing its subsistence from trade and plantation soon after the initial settlement. Yet it was already clear that agriculture was virtually impossible and that the native population was worthless as a trade partner. Paterson's dream of the trans-isthmian highway to the Pacific was made ridiculous by the looming barrier of the cordillera behind the colony (which Wafer's manuscript had described very accurately, but apparently without effect). Ironically, the only market for Caledonia's manufactures were the other European colonies of the Antilles, places already fettered by trade monopolies with their own mother countries. Smuggling on a massive scale might perhaps have broken through these difficulties, but even so, Caledonia was most inconveniently situated at the extreme western end of the Caribbean. On all sides of the Scots were Spanish colonies whose masters in Madrid were violently opposed to the idea of a foreign power ever setting foot on the mainland of Central America. The Caledonians were isolated and exposed, their ships and storehouses filled with unsuitable and unsaleable trade goods, slowly decomposing in the tropical humidity. Far from being a cornucopia of easy wealth, the Antilles was a place where new European colonies survived only by taming the land itself and by bitter competition with the older European settlements. Now, like lampreys around an enfeebled victim, the better established European colonies moved in to batten on the Scots.

The first large foreign vessel to put in an appearance was the *Rupert Prize,* an English warship operating out of Jamaica. Her captain, Richard Long, was officially surveying the coast for the wrecks of Spanish plate ships which might be worth salvage. But he had been diverted with orders to inspect the Scottish position and report back to the English and Jamaican authorities. The strength of the Scottish defenses impressed him, and he hovered off Golden Island for some time, keeping an eye on the colonists and occasionally sailing up the coast to discover if the Spaniards were mounting a counterforce. Several merchant ships also arrived, sailing into the harbor at Caledonia with cargoes of goods to sell to the colonists. An occasional privateer wandered in by mistake, believing that the traditional buccaneer anchorage was unoccupied, and was welcomed by the council as a potential ally against the Spaniards and as a source of news. These visitors, casual or deliberate, opened a small trade with the Caledonians, selling them beef, flour, and other stores. But it was only a smattering of business because the ship captains wanted payment in cash and would not accept Scottish trade goods that were of little use to them. However, the captain of the *Maurepas*, a French ship reported to have collected much Spanish loot along the coast, did at least agree to carry the colony's dispatches to a place where they could be forwarded to Edinburgh. But the French captain turned out to be a fool, and he insisted on setting out into Caledonia's narrow channel in the teeth of a fresh gale and with his crew half drunk. Pennycook saw the danger and chased after his ship in a cockboat, managing to catch up with him just as the *Maurepas* was being blown broadside onto the rocks. Pennycook got a line aboard the French vessel and towed her into a small bay where she was still exposed to the fury of the gale but could at least put down her anchors. Then Pennycook sent back to fetch more anchors and cables, while he himself went aboard the *Maurepas* to try to persuade her captain to delay. But before the English cockboat could return, the gale freshened, and the Frenchman's anchor cables snapped. The *Maurepas* was driven ashore amid pounding waves and became a total loss. Her captain and chief mate were rescued, but twenty-four of the fifty-four crewmen aboard were drowned. Pennycook survived only by throwing himself into the sea stark-naked and swimming ashore. He was lucky to escape with a slight scratch and some bruises. The loss of the ship was the worst single accident that had befallen the colony; its impact was all the more depressing since it took place on Christmas Eve.

Five days later a substitute vessel, this time a Jamaican sloop, set out with an updated version of the dispatches, a copy of the death list, a duplicate of the expedition's official journal, and one

Alexander Hamilton,* the expedition's accountant-general, who had been selected by the council to see that the dispatches got safely to Scotland. Paterson had voted against Hamilton being sent as the courier, arguing that he was the only man competent to look after the inventories of Caledonia's trade goods—an indication that Paterson was still blindly hoping for the success of his long-awaited emporium. Paterson was overruled, though he had the consolation that a certain Major Cunningham of the council also went off with Hamilton, though in a private capacity. Cunningham had been the most obstreperous member of the council and an outstanding critic of the entire venture. In fact there had been some discussion of arresting him and throwing him into jail, and there was a sense of relief when the prickly major decided to pack up and leave of his own free will.

Hamilton and the dispatches took three months to reach Edinburgh, and during that interval Caledonia's fortunes ebbed even lower. Thus it was all the more tragic that when Hamilton arrived in Edinburgh, he followed his instructions and delivered a sparkling account of life in Caledonia to back up the council's own enthusiastic dispatches. The Court of Directors was so pleased with what it heard that it voted Hamilton a purse of a hundred guineas "as a Compliment for being the first that brought the good news of the Settlement on America," and immediately turned its attention to the matter of equipping the second fleet. This fleet, according to the original plan, was to build on the foundations which the first settlers were reported to have laid so firmly.

If the truth had been known, the situation of the Scots colony had become increasingly desperate with every week since Hamilton's departure. Neither Christmas nor the New Year had brought any excuse for celebration, and the colonists had heard the news that they feared most: the Spaniards had decided to mount a counterattack against them. The first warning came from the English captain, Long, who sent a boat up the coast with information that he had gleaned on his patrols. It was re-

---

* No immediate relative, as far as is known, of Alexander Hamilton, the American statesman, despite the latter's West Indian connection (he was born on Nevis in the British Leeward Islands).

liably reported that the Spanish Windward Fleet was being re-inforced and that an expedition against the Scots was assembling in Cartagena. In January these rumors were confirmed by various scraps of intelligence acquired from the casual stream of mer-chant vessels that continued to drop by the harbor at Caledonia, attempting to hawk their cargoes to the stranded Scots. Then it was learned that the *Dolphin* had struck a rock off Cartagena and had been beached. Her crew had immediately been taken pris-oner by the Spaniards and treated as outright pirates. All these developments spread gloom among the Caledonians, and the colonists braced themselves for a major confrontation with the Spaniards.

These somber rumors filtering into Caledonia were accurate in all but one important respect—they omitted to mention that the Spaniards were pressing forward their preparations with quite extraordinary ineptitude. Indeed, as far as the Caledonians were concerned, the threat was more psychological than real, for despite the apparently massive Spanish maneuvers that were reported throughout the length and breadth of the Caribbean, the Spanish expedition against the Scots was a flabby gesture.

The Spaniards, of course, were not intending anything so feeble. When the government in Madrid had learned that a strong force of Scots was established on the isthmus of Panama, there had been widespread consternation. The English, it was felt, had reneged on their treaties with Spain, and Lord Stanhope, the English ambassador to the court of Madrid, found himself in bad odor. He tried to explain to the Spanish that the Scots had acted without his sovereign's connivance, and that they had set up in Darien as Scots and not as Englishmen. But he made little headway. The Spaniards were not overly impressed with nice distinctions between King William's several realms, and they soon decided that it would be more effective to eject the Scots by force than to argue the matter out with the English ambassador. Accordingly, the Council of the Indies unleashed a swarm of royal instructions, ordering the redeployment and reinforcement of the Windward Fleet, diverting one of their admirals who was on a mission to Pensacola, to go instead to the isthmian coast, and instructing the governors of Spanish colonies in the Antilles to provide all possible assistance in the drive against the Scot "pirates." Even the Church was reported to have agreed to a levy of one million pieces-of-eight to help drive the Protestants into the sea.

But the Spanish colonies around the Caribbean were incapable of mounting an armada at such short notice. The Spanish intelligence officers erroneously estimated that the Scots had landed four thousand well-armed men in Darien, and in consequence the Spanish Americans proceeded with extreme caution. The careful messages between the various Spanish colonies took weeks or even months to circulate, and due to a shortage of transports, the Spanish military authorities had to bide their time while they built their fleet by the simple expedient of commandeering every ship that came into port. Then, too, the Spanish commanders had long since fallen into the habit of expecting their partners to bear the brunt of any costs and fighting. Each colony judged the danger of Caledonia in the light of its own interests. The Scots, as it happened, had settled in an area that was not really a direct threat to any single Spanish settlement; and for the same reason, Caledonia's isolation meant that the Spaniards had no harbor closer than Cartagena where a sizable force might gather and find the necessary supplies. To cap it all, the Spanish commanders were, by and large, a poor lot who were temperamentally inclined to procrastinate. One admiral spent so much of his time asking for clarification of the royal orders that he failed to reach the rendezvous on schedule; the commander of the Windward Fleet was eager enough to attack the Scots, but his fleet had been grossly neglected and was scarcely seaworthy; and the governor of Panama was reluctant to commit his forces against what he considered to be a minor risk while leaving his own city unguarded against an attack from the Pacific.

Thus the Spanish offensive wobbled forward shakily, prodded on by fresh exhortations from the Council of the Indies, which demanded to know why its instructions were not carried out quickly enough. In reply the several overseas commanders sent back so many contradictory excuses and dispatches that it is not easy to untangle the exact course of the campaign that followed. The first move apparently came from the governor of Panama, who reluctantly divested himself of four companies of the city's militia. These troops found their way across the cordillera and an advance party ran into a Scots patrol. A brief skirmish followed, with a handful of losses on each side. The Spanish militia promptly withdrew to the nearest ridge of the cordillera, where they took up their positions to wait for reinforcements and keep an eye on the Scots. But they waited in vain. The Spanish Windward Fleet had arrived at Portobelo in such a sorry condition that two of the leaking ships could not put to sea again until extensive repairs had been made. Since the other Spanish fleet in the Caribbean had failed to show up at the rendezvous, any idea of an amphibious attack against Caledonia was abandoned forthwith.

Instead, the Admiral of the Barlovento Fleet landed five hundred sailors and marched them across to Panama where they joined an additional group of two more companies of militia and a scratch company of gentlemen volunteers. This force then set out to cross the cordillera, which had given Lionel Wafer so much trouble, to reinforce the earlier party of attackers. The Spaniards' trans-isthmian march was a fiasco. Their troops were garrison men, unused to semijungle conditions, and they wore themselves out dragging their equipment over the mountains. They were drenched by the thunderstorms; their food ran low; and finally, when they had at last approached within striking distance of Caledonia and could actually hear the Scots signal guns below them on the coast, they were engulfed by one of those same terrifying floods that had scared Wafer and his friends so badly. To the Spaniards the ordeal was even worse, for they had camped in a narrow gully that was flushed out by the sudden torrent. Swept about like drowning rats, the Spaniards lost their stores, their weapons, and their fighting spirit. A party of Negroes bringing up supplies from the rear had to abandon their equipment and run for their lives. When the flood abated, the Spanish commander held a council of war and decided that it would be hopeless to launch an attack. His expedition turned for home without firing a shot. Its complete failure, however, did not deter him from writing a bombastic report of his campaign. His force, he claimed, had shown extraordinary valor in surmounting the physical difficulties of Darien without losing a man. He even dropped several hints that his own brave conduct and the skillful handling of the entire operation merited some reward.

But the real threat to Caledonia lay much closer to the Scots colony than the pitiful little Spanish force groping its way through the hills. Fever, boredom, and disappointment kept pace with each other and were now joined by famine. As day succeeded day the colonists were realizing that their efforts at agriculture and trade had been futile. Apart from the merchant ships who came to sell and not to buy, Caledonia might as well never have existed for all its success in opening a new trade in the Golden Antilles. There were no crops in the fields and, worst of all, there had been no news from home. The colonists felt neglected and isolated. Caledonia was wrapped in an air of doubt and gloomy speculation. Then, in February, there came a giant thrust of despair when a Jamaican sloop sailed into the harbor with the news that the English government had banned any English colony from rendering assistance to Caledonia. In Jamaica, for example, Governor William Beeston had issued a proclamation forbidding His Majesty's subjects "on any pretence whatsoever, to hold any correspondence with the said Scots, nor to give them any assistance of arms, ammunitions, provisions, or other necessaries whatsoever, either by themselves or any for them, or by any of their vessels, or of the English nation, as they will answer the contempt of His Majesty's command, at their utmost peril."

It was a punishing blow to the occupants of the sad little colony in the far end of the Caribbean. The Scots felt that they had been abandoned, and that every nation's hand was against them. Knowing that the Spaniards would surely attack again, they were convinced that the colony could not possibly survive without massive aid from home. Yet no support squadron had come from over the horizon and, with the colony's storehouses emptied, a third of the colony was dead of disease and malnutrition. To the distraught and beleaguered council the position looked untenable; to the rank and file the increasing difficulties seemed idiotic. The weekly issue of flour was down to two pounds, of which a quarter pound was said to be "moldy maggots, worms, and other such beasts." The beef, pickled in Edinburgh, was black, rotten, and inedible. Only the brandy ration brought temporary relief from hunger and the pain of pustulating boils and rotting teeth.

As backbiting and grumbling gnawed away steadily at the small store of confidence yet remaining between the Caledonians and their leaders, the council began to waver. Paterson, who might have stemmed the collapse, was still ill and was querulous and complaining in his fever. He was blocking out of his mind the failure of his grand design and substituting petty little problems of his own, complaining that some of his belongings were mislaid or stolen. In his clearer moments he opposed the council's wish to evacuate the colony, and was stoutly backed up by Captain Thomas Drummond, a fiery ex-Grenadier who felt that a few men, well led, could hold the position and make a success of the colony. But they were overwhelmed by the solid majority of the council, who voted for evacuation. The first fleet had been sent to establish a beachhead, they said, and it had failed in that purpose. Even if their efforts had been enough, there was no sign that the company was sending out another wave of men to take possession of the land. There seemed no point in holding on while fever decimated the survivors. Caledonia could be settled a second time, and the first fleet should withdraw in the face of Spanish hostility. So in the first week of June the survivors began the re-embarkation in the "great harbor" they had so enthusiastically reached seven months earlier.

But before the tattered remnants of the first fleet could reach home, a second company fleet went out from Scotland for the Antilles. And believing the company's master plan, they sailed forth confident that they would arrive in that happy land which Paterson, Wafer, and Accountant Hamilton had described to the Court of Directors. Thus, even as the survivors of the first failure crept back to Scotland, a fresh sacrifice was delivered to the myth of the Golden Antilles.

17

The Collapse of Darien

E XPECTING TO MEET WITH OUR FRIENDS AND COUNTRYMEN, we found nothing but a vast howling wilderness"—so wrote the Reverend Francis Borland, whose diary was a unique account of the fate of the second Scots expedition to Caledonia. Borland was minister to the company's second fleet, which had arrived off Golden Island on November 30, 1699, and like the fourteen hundred colonists with him, the preacher was utterly dismayed to find the first Caledonians "deserted and gone, their huts all burnt, their fort most part ruined, the ground which they had cleared adjoining the fort all overgrown with weeds." No one with the second fleet had seriously thought that anything could have gone so wrong with proud Caledonia, until they saw with their own eyes the desolation that was Scotland's claim in the Golden Antilles. Yet the second expedition, with its women and children, its fresh stocks of clothes and useless manufactures, was arrived in the New World. The second act of the Darien tragedy was irretrievably on stage.

The colonists of the second fleet did not know half of the full disaster. Only in the company's offices in Milne Square, Edinburgh, was the full horror of the situation becoming apparent as the gloomy dispatches started to come in and the directors began to grasp the magnitude of their blunders.

There was much to regret. Ever since the first euphoric reports of Darien from the colonists of the first fleet, the Scots directors had been priding themselves on the success of the great venture, and in a leisurely fashion they had set about assembling that second "equippage," which was to complete the colonization of Darien. The Caledonians' descriptions of stately parkland, fertile soil, salubrious climate, friendly Indians, and a magnificent natural harbor made excellent reading under the gray skies of Edinburgh, and confirmed the directors' preconceived notions of the Antilles. The letters, it was true, contained disturbing references to feuds among the expedition's councillors, and the death list seemed incomprehensibly long. Yet any needles of doubt which may have pricked the dignitaries of Milne Square had nothing to do with the overall concept of their colonial plan, and there was much praise and little criticism for the actual site of the Scots plantation. So, to meet the Caledonians' immediate requests and gain a little time for themselves, the directors had got together two vessels—the *Olive Branch* and the *Hopeful Binning*—and loaded them with a variety of stores and a further three hundred colonists. These had been sent out to Darien ahead of the second fleet as an interim measure to assist the Caledonians.

It was at this all-important stage—with the *Olive Branch* and the *Hopeful Binning* at sea; the Caledonians actually in the process of evacuating Darien; and the second fleet being made ready on Clydeside (the directors had taken Paterson's advice and moved their depot to the western approaches)—that the problem of inadequate communications began to have very serious consequences. The difficulty was that the several parts of the company's far-flung operations did not really know how any other part was faring. Therefore they could not coordinate their activities. Thus, even as the two relief ships were carrying an extra group of settlers to Central America, the ships of the first fleet were re-embarking the refugee Caledonians because the isthmus was considered to be untenable. And in Edinburgh the directors were looking for artisans, family men, women, and children who would consolidate the position they imagined had been successfully established in the Antilles. The extent of the directors' ignorance can be judged from the fact that they sent with the second fleet such unlikely specialists as an engineer who knew how to make and operate coin-minting machinery, a distiller with his equipment, a group of young scholars from Edinburgh University with their tutor, and a savant with a patent scheme for teaching English to the Darien Indians.

In the great harbor, meanwhile, the re-embarkation of the Caledonians had been a bitter, sad affair. The hopes for Darien had been so high in the beginning that the abandonment now seemed all the more craven. Commodore Pennycook, who supported the idea of evacuation, was scarcely on speaking terms with those councillors who were against abandoning the colony, and in this strained atmosphere it was inevitable that the transfer back to the ships would be scrambled and slipshod. The men squabbled for places in the launches and cockboats; they left most of the equipment to rot where it lay in the huts and half-cleared fields. There was even an argument whether it was worth salvaging the guns of Fort St. Andrew's battery. But to abandon Scots guns to the first Spaniard or privateer who should come into the bay was more than the military veterans could stomach, so they mounted an armed guard while a hole was knocked in the palisades of the fort and the cannon were trundled down to the landing place and ferried out to the ships. Then the four vessels, *St. Andrew*, *Unicorn*, *Caledonia*, and *Endeavour*, weighed anchor and headed for the open sea, intending to sail for New York. There they would take on supplies and medicines, and either cross back to Scotland or await further instructions from the Directors.

The *Endeavour* should never have been allowed to attempt the voyage. She was leaking badly, her mainmast was sprung, and she lurched through the sea like a waterlogged barrel. Yet for twelve days she struggled along behind the *Caledonia*, and when finally her crew could no longer keep pace with the water pouring in through the gaping planks, all her passengers were successfully transferred to the larger ship. But it was only a temporary salvation, for on the already severely overcrowded

Caledonia fever was raging below decks. During the voyage to New York one hundred and sixteen men—just under half her complement—died, and their bodies were casually tossed overboard. A third of the survivors were desperately ill. According to the testimony of some Scots merchants who visited the ship after she arrived in New York, the sufferings of the voyage were due as much to the callousness of the officers as anything else. "Was there any more horrid barbarity," they wrote to the company in Edinburgh, "than in the passage they [the officers] exercised toward their poor men, who no sooner fell sick but were turned out on deck, there exposed to most violent rains; and though most of their provisions consisted in flour, yet they whose distemper was the flux must have nothing but a little sour oatmeal and little water, nor their share of that neither. When they complained, to condole or comfort them . . . [the officers retorted] 'Dogs! It's too good for you.' "

The plight of the *Unicorn*, with a delirious William Paterson on board, was equally pitiable. Short of trained seamen but with 250 refugee colonists crammed into her hold, the *Unicorn* ran into bad weather. A storm ripped away her foremast and mizzen top, and made her a virtual hulk. The crew contrived a jury rig and with every man fit enough to stand on his feet heaving away at the pumps, the *Unicorn* was blown toward Cuba. Arriving off that island's coast, Benjamin Spense, the Jew who claimed to speak six languages, went ashore to treat with the Spaniards, while a watering party looked for fresh water to replace the sour green slime in the *Unicorn*'s water casks. But the Spaniards promptly opened fire on the Scots and they had to beat a hasty retreat, leaving Spense to fall into Spanish hands. Perhaps the Jew was lucky. He was sent to the comparative safety of a Spanish jail, while the wretched passengers of the *Unicorn* were forced to endure a nightmare journey northward. By the time she joined the *Caledonia* in New York, 150 men aboard the *Unicorn* had died of sickness and starvation, "most of them for want of looking after means to recover them." Paterson himself had slipped into such a deep abyss of craziness that the Scots in New York reported to the company that "grief had broke Mr. Paterson heart and brains, and now he is a child."

The third large ship of the first fleet, the *St. Andrew*, never even tried to make New York. Under a feverish Pennycook—he was drinking heavily—she set course for Jamaica, perhaps to seek help, perhaps to refit and turn buccaneer. One hundred and forty of her men, including Pennycook, died during the crossing. By the time she reached the Jamaican coast, the *St. Andrew* was a death ship, carrying mutinous seamen, haggard refugees, and a dazed group of landsmen-officers who had been forced to assume command when the naval officers had died. There, anchored off the Jamaican coast, the *St. Andrew* was left to rot. The English proclamations against the Scots colony in Darien prevented the Jamaicans from helping the refugees. Even the company's official agent in Port Royal refused to go out to visit the ship. Night after night, men from the *St. Andrew* deserted. Slipping over the side, they swam ashore to sell themselves as indentured men to the planters of Jamaica. It was a bitter ending for volunteers who had dreamed of fifty lush acres and a company-built house in Caledonia.

So the empty heart of the Antilles, the deceptively gentle Caribbean, completed the destruction that the green hills and marshes of Caledonia had begun. Of the first fleet only the *Caledonia* and the *Unicorn* escaped the Antilles. For lack of crew, the *Unicorn* was eventually abandoned in New York, and the *Caledonia* was the single ship to reach home, bringing back less than three hundred of the original twelve hundred colonists. The *St. Andrew*, the *Endeavour*, and the *Dolphin* all stayed in the Caribbean. So too did the relief ships, *Olive Branch* and *Hopeful Binning*, for though they reached Caledonia without incident and learned from a gaunt Scots castaway the terrible circumstances of the colony's desertion, they were dogged by bad luck. While still debating whether or not the two ships should stay, the *Olive Branch* caught fire. Her cooper, searching for brandy, had gone below decks with a lighted candle in his hand and set himself and his ship alight. Next day she was nothing but a charred wreck and her cargo of stores was a total loss. The captain of the *Hopeful Binning* had no choice but to withdraw, leaving a tiny party of volunteers to await the arrival of the second fleet. He too sailed for Jamaica, where many of his three hundred colonists were absorbed into the older settlement.

In this apparently endless series of disasters afflicting the Scots, the company's troubles had really all sprung from their first, fundamental misconception of the geography of Central America. Now, however, their continued misfortunes were to be as much the result of sheer bad luck as of any incompetence on their part. By one of the unhappiest coincidences in Scotland's history, the same fortnight which saw the departure of the second fleet for Darien also witnessed the arrival of dispatches in Edinburgh telling the directors of the abandonment of the first colony and the appalling conditions there. It was Scotland's misfortune that the directors only learned the truth after, and not before, their second fleet had sailed.

Paradoxically, the director's chronic inefficiency nearly saved the day. It had been hoped that the second fleet would reinforce Darien in early summer, when the new influx of settlers and equipment would have been of the most use in Caledonia. But the directors' "Committee of Equipping" took so long to outfit the new ships (including the *Rising Sun,* now sent over from Amsterdam where the Czar of Russia had been given a tour of her) that the second fleet was not ready until mid-August. By then, Caledonia had already been abandoned for two months, and the news of the collapse was seeping like a black stain toward the mother country. Indeed, rumors of Caledonia's evacuation had actually reached London via Jamaica before the second fleet sailed. But the reports were vague and unconfirmed as yet, and although the Scots directors were worried by these whispers, they refused to be stampeded. With typical suspicion they sniffed an English plot to discourage the reinforcement of Caledonia, and they continued to make leisurely progress, fortified by much claret at committee meetings, toward the dispatch of four ships and thirteen hundred men to assist the Caledonians.

Once again the company had no difficulty in recruiting colonists. To a nucleus of men who had been denied places with the first fleet was added an assortment of disbanded veterans, gentlemen volunteers, a hundred women (mostly wives of men who, they fondly imagined, were waiting for them in the Antilles), and a nameless horde of what the muster lists described as "Tradesmen, Planters, and Others." Many of these humbler folk were only too glad to be leaving Scotland, where another dismal summer heralded the next in a succession of poor harvests and hungry winters. Several of these hopefuls childishly pinned their faith in a crude little map of Caledonia, which had been printed from a sketch sent back by one of the earlier settlers. In one place some imaginative soul had added the enticing legend: "Place where upon digging for stones to make an oven, a considerable mixture of gold was found in them. . . ." It was a pathetic summary of the enduring Antillean dream.

By mid-August the second expedition was ready, and on the 18th it actually sailed. But then, by a strange twist of fate, the weather turned against them and the ships were forced to take shelter behind the island of Bute, well within range of the directors' message-boats. It was a curious situation, for even as the second fleet lay at anchor awaiting better weather, the news of Darien's disaster was nearing Scotland. On September 22, after a month of waiting, the directors were sufficiently worried by the growing volume of rumors to send a message to the fleet, informing them of the situation. But on the following day, before the messenger could reach the fleet, the weather improved, and the fleet promptly set sail. Only twelve days later the directors heard that Caledonia was definitely abandoned. But it was too late to warn the second fleet that they were sailing toward a deserted plantation.

The raw shock of arriving to find Caledonia derelict and in decay crushed the second expedition from the moment it arrived off Golden Island. If the colonists with the second fleet had been warned, they might possibly have gone ashore determined to succeed where their predecessors had failed so dismally. But as it was, they came prepared to assist, not to pioneer, and the sight of the tumble-down huts and weed-choked fields blighted their enthusiasm immediately. Within hours of their arrival several of the colonists were demanding that the fleet should turn round and head for safety at once, particularly as an inventory of the ships's stores revealed a shortage of food. But the new council, as weak and incompetent as the first, voted that the expedition should stay on, at least until they had taken stock of the situation.

The contrast between the disembarkation of the first and second fleets was remarkable. No one with the second fleet found any occasion to praise the scenery or write glowingly of the great potential of Caledonia. Instead, they landed in a woebegone fashion, gloomily speculating on their own chances of survival. Nor would they, in this frame of mind, apply themselves with any enthusiasm to the hard labor of clearing the fields or mending the lapsed defenses of Fort St. Andrew. They grumbled, drank, and began to pilfer from the colony's stores rather than try to grow food. Within three weeks there was the first desertion—ten planters stole a rowing boat and tried to make for Portobelo—and on December 20, only twenty days after landing in Darien, the council was obliged to hang a carpenter accused (probably falsely) of spreading sedition and mutiny among the colonists. The daily allowance was rationed at a half-pound of meat and a half-pound of bread per man, and it was not surprising that on this diet the demoralized settlers began to succumb to the effects of heat exhaustion and fever. By the New Year their hoes and spades were used as much for digging graves as for tilling the fields. On the anchored ships in the bay the sailors no longer bothered to land the dead for burial, but simply dropped the corpses into the harbor. As usual, the bickering council was impotent. It failed miserably to provide a firm lead. One councillor, who held his position by virtue of the amount of company stock he had bought, somehow arranged a passage back to England aboard a visiting ship. His colleagues could do no better than suggest that all the women and children and half of the men should leave for Jamaica as soon as possible in order to reduce the drain on the food stores and allow the remaining colonists to prepare the position against their return. The chosen evacuees all went back aboard two of the ships, but a north wind, the bane of the "magnificent anchorage," sprang up and raised such seas in the channel behind Golden Island that the ships dared not leave. They were forced to swing idly on their anchors while the evacuees suffered the torments of bad food and overcrowding.

The lethargy of the Scots even infected the Cuna. The Indians had been puzzled and downcast to see their liquor-selling allies of the first fleet abandon the settlement, and not unnaturally the Cuna had lost confidence in the Scottish determination to fight with them against their traditional foes, the Spanish. Now, when an officer from the second fleet went out to visit the Cuna villages, he found the longhouses full of glum reports that the Spaniards were preparing a massive invasion of Caledonia and that the Scots would be expelled once and for all from the mainland of Central America.

In fact the Cuna's intelligence was extremely accurate. The Spanish authorities had been delighted to learn of the abandonment of the first colony from the captain of a wandering Spanish coaster that had visited Darien soon after the Scots withdrawal. Then, just as the Spaniards were beginning to feel that the danger had conveniently eliminated itself, they heard that the interlopers were back, refreshed and in strength. To the Spanish authorities it seemed that only a full-scale punitive expedition would convince the Scots that Spain regarded Darien as her property, and that no alien settlement would be tolerated. Therefore, in the usual cloud of long-winded correspondence, the Spanish authorities dusted off their plans for a military expedition to eject the Scots from Caledonia. This time, however, they had the twin advantages of a military commander who knew his business, and the fund of experience that they had gained from their previous abortive campaign against Caledonia.

The Scots too had at last found themselves a champion, though more by coincidence than deliberate selection. He was Colonel Alexander Campbell of Fonab, a veteran officer who had belatedly gone out to Darien with the directors' frantic dispatches in the wake of the second fleet. Although less than forty years old, Campbell was an experienced and able soldier. He had fought in several of the bloodier battles of the Low Countries, and many of the disbanded soldiers on the second expedition must have known him personally or by reputation. More important, Campbell arrived in Caledonia fully aware that matters had gone badly awry with the first settlement, and he was prepared to put matters right. When, upon reaching Darien, he saw that the same lethargy and general demoralization was already stifling the second settlement, he took immediate action. Acidly pointing out to the dithering council that a Spanish attack could not be far away, he took over command of the colony's military defense. He came just in time; a Spanish cruiser was already hovering off the coast, watching the harbor mouth and spying on the strength of the Scots.

Nevertheless, Campbell had overestimated the Spaniards' ability to launch a swift assault, and when the Spanish campaign finally did get under way, it was not so much a sudden hammer blow as a slow, painful strangulation of Caledonia. Their method was, perhaps, the most effective way to deal with the entrenched Scots, and certainly it cost very few Spanish lives. Yet Don Juan Pimienta, the Spanish commander, probably could not have tackled the Scottish defenses any more briskly had he wanted to, as his troop dispositions were hamstrung by poor coordination. In its essentials, Pimienta's plan was to launch a two-pronged attack. A small diversionary force would cross the cordillera and attack Caledonia from the landward side; and then, while the Scots were drawn off to face that sector, the Spanish fleet would land Pimienta's main force and his heavy guns on the Scots' seaward flank. This main seaborne force was to be protected by the powerful Barlovento fleet, reinforced by royal warships sent out from Spain, and most of its troops were to be drawn from the garrisons of Panama, Cartagena, and Portobelo. The smaller force attacking from the landward side would be led by Don Miguel Cordones, whose post as governor of Darien gave him responsibility for that area. Cordones's rather amateur force of levies and irregulars would be strengthened for the occasion by three companies of militia specially sent up by galley from Panama City. Had Pimienta been a little more daring, or had his knowledge of the Scottish position been a little more exact, he could probably have swept through their meager defenses with a single, bold frontal attack. But the Spanish commander was reluctant to commit his troops so rashly. He had had difficulty in obtaining his garrison drafts and he considered them to be unreliable in a close fight. Moreover, there were rumors that the Scots engineers had contrived an immense mine, which they planned to detonate under the advancing Spaniards to inflict huge casualties.

Of course, the Scots had no such awesome defenses. Indeed, until Alexander Campbell's arrival they had done little to mend the tumble-down defenses they had inherited from the first expedition. They had landed a few guns and placed them in Fort St. Andrew, mounted a handful of cannon to face the landward approaches, and made some desultory repairs to the walls of the fort and its defensive canal. But that was all. No one had thought to organize a reserve of drinking water within the waterless fort, or to prepare a stock of bullets. Campbell's furious energy changed everything. He landed on Sunday, February 11, and within hours he had not only overawed the council into giving him command of the colony's defense but had arranged that all the men waiting to be evacuated to Jamaica should be put ashore again and set to useful work. By Monday evening he was selecting two hundred men to take on a sortie to attack a Spanish column—it was, in fact, Cordones's overland force—which, the Cuna reported, had crossed the cordillera and were now encamped in the hills behind Caledonia. Campbell intended to catch the Spaniards offguard, so next morning, only forty-eight hours after he had first set foot in Caledonia, he was bustling out of the settlement. With him he took two hundred Scots and some thirty Indian irregulars under Lieutenant Turnbull, an enthusiastic officer who had trained the Cuna levies for just such an emergency.

Campbell's miniature campaign was a brief flash of glory in an otherwise ignominious affair, and his boldness and resolution entirely deserved the brief success they brought him. He had never been in the Central American forest before, and he quickly found that it was a grueling experience. His troops were burdened down with cartridge bags, muskets, axes, and swords, and they made slow progress. They sweated in their heavy clothing, and the sheer physical exertion of struggling through the undergrowth, coupled with the debilitating effects of weeks spent cooped up in the colony, made every step difficult. But Campbell and his officers pushed them on mercilessly. By Tuesday night the column had reached a Cuna village, whose chief was one of the Indian dignitaries that the first Scots expedition had enrolled as an officer of militia. This chief—he had been a Spanish slave at one time and the Scots had taken to calling him Pedro—was so impressed with Campbell's belligerence that he put on his war paint, donned the military coat which the company had given him, and grandly promised to add forty of his own warriors to Campbell's command.

The Scots spent that night in the village, and next morning trudged forward into the foothills of the Sierras. Their route took them steadily upward, across occasional streams and over the flanks of the hills. The men were soon exhausted, and by afternoon even the Indians had begun to flag. Pedro, in fact, suggested to Campbell that it would be more sensible to set an ambush and wait for Cordones's men to come to them, rather than go marching over the mountains in the heat. But Campbell was determined to take the enemy by surprise and he insisted that the march continue. Finally, when his men were too tired to go any farther, he allowed them to halt. That second night the Scots slept in the open.

They encountered the enemy the following day when Pedro's scouts located the Spaniards by the sound of Cordones's work parties chopping wood in the forest. Lieutenant Turnbull went forward with his Cuna and twelve gentlemen volunteers to reconnoiter, and discovered that Cordones's force had built themselves a stockade. This stockade made the Scots pause. It was a sturdy affair, placed in a clearing and made of treetrunks embedded upright in the earth with interlacing branches filling the gaps between the uprights. Cordones's only mistake, as far as the scouting party could observe, was that he had built his stockade on the slope of the nearest hill and not on its crest, and so the Scots would not necessarily have to attack uphill. Unfortunately, Turnbull's reconnoitering party had been seen by the Spanish sentries, and Cordones's men had withdrawn into their stockade and were now peering out, waiting for the Scots' next move.

Campbell's attack, or the battle of Touboucanti as it would later be called with considerable exaggeration, was no stroke of inspired generalship. It was, rather, a crude but effective skirmish. Turnbull had begged to be allowed to lead the attack with his Indians, and when Campbell granted him his wish, he charged off with his irregulars and the volunteers. Before the rest of the Scots could catch up with them, this advance party had run out into the clearing, straight into the fire of the Spanish muskets. Turnbull himself received a musketball in the shoulder, and in the mêlée that followed, it looked as if his "forelorn" might be repulsed with heavy loss. But then, in the nick of time, Campbell and his main force came puffing and panting out of the woods, and their impetus carried them to the palisade. There, partially sheltered in the lee of the rampart and with their musketeers giving covering fire, the Scots storming party swung away with their axes until they had hacked a breach, and the attackers could swarm in with lance and bayonet. Cordones's frightened Spanish levies put up only a brief resistance before they broke and ran. Streaming out of the opposite gate of their redoubt, they bolted for the safety of the woods with Pedro's excited Indians yelping at their heels. Behind them they left their cooking pots still bubbling over the campfires, and Cordones's dress uniform, decorated over the left breast with his insignia of the Order of St. James.

The Scots had lost seven dead and fourteen wounded in their headlong charge, and though no one bothered to record how many of their Indian allies had been killed, Pedro himself had been wounded while storming the palisade. In strict military terms the Scots had done well: they had completely routed Cordones's diversionary attack, inflicted heavy casualties, and taken two or three dozen prisoners. Tragically, however, they had paid too dearly for their victory—Alexander Campbell also had been hit in the right shoulder by a musketball as he was leading his troops, and was incapacitated. Henceforth his verve would be curtailed by pain and delirium, and his disablement meant that the only spark of military talent in the colony was perilously dimmed.

The Spaniards took a little more than six weeks to beat the Caledonians to their knees once the Scots had lost Campbell's full talents. In the last days of February, Pimienta and his fleet came lumbering ponderously up the coast of the Golden Island from the south and took up station a few miles offshore. There the great Spanish galleons, their attendant cutters, the troop transports, and the flyboats tacked back and forth, while the Spanish general staff gingerly made arrangements to pluck the thorn of

Caledonia. Oared Spanish launches nosed along the shore and found two small landing beaches that the Scots had overlooked, one to the east and one to the west of the harbor mouth. Here Pimienta landed his troops, boatload after boatload of men in blue-and-yellow uniforms accompanied by their peacock-gaudy officers, cannon, munition, and baggage. Snaking out from the two beachheads, the Spanish columns began to encircle Caledonia, advancing slowly through the dense underbrush and suspecting a Scots ambush in every thicket. But the cornered Scots seemed mesmerized by the danger, and scarcely put up any resistance worthy of the name. An occasional Highlander on forward sentry duty would fire off his musket in alarm before he turned and scrambled for safety, and on one occasion a foolhardy Scots officer attempted a counterattack. It was a costly failure. The Spanish, closing in with textbook thoroughness, had prepared a defensive breastwork against just such a maneuver. Three times the Scots' attacking party threw themselves against the ambuscade and were driven back before they finally had the sense to withdraw, leaving seventeen corpses in the field. Meanwhile, reinforcements of Spanish troops came ashore almost daily, and in Caledonia dysentery and fever took their toll. Campbell, occasionally surfacing through a haze of fever, tried desperately to organize a more intelligent defense. He had the men melt down the pewter tableware to make shot, and he arranged for water barrels to be filled and placed in reserve inside the fort. But his wound was troubling him, and he could not sustain the defense of the colony single-handed.

By the last week of March the Scots were hemmed into a tight perimeter, and in his diary for March 28 and 29, the Reverend Mr. Borland noted: "The Spaniards near us. Some of their musketeers advanced forward near the skirts of the wood contiguous to our Fort, and fired both these days upon our Fort, the bullets flying over our heads. . . . they debarred us from our watering place. . . . so our poor distressed people were necessitate to dig for water within the Fort, which is brackish, puddle-unwholesome water. This was most hurtful and pernicious to our men, especially considering how bad and unwholesome our old, sair, and spoiled provisions now was. And as for other liquors at this time to give to the sick and dying, we had little or none, or any other sustenance that was suitable or comfortable, and moreover our Surgeon's drugs were now almost exhausted, and our Fort indeed like a hospital of sick and dying men."

With illness and despair inside, and Spanish guns outside, Caledonia was doomed. Toward the end of the month, seven weeks after Campbell's arrival had injected a small flare of spirit into the colony, the Caledonians could take the punishment no longer. Rather than wait for Pimienta's militia to rupture the perimeter and sack the settlement, the Scots asked to be allowed to surrender under honorable terms. Pimienta, worried by the impending onset of the rainy season and the gradual deterioration in his own troops' morale in those appalling conditions, agreed gladly. The Articles of Capitulation were drawn up in Latin so that both sides could understand them properly and were signed in a rain-soaked ceremony at noon on March 31, 1700. Pimienta gave the Scots two weeks to return to their ships and prepare for departure. Then, on the next favorable wind, they were to sail away and not return. It was the formal end to their Antillean adventure.

The Caledonians took ten days to get their sick and weary men aboard their fleet, and on April 12, because they were too dispirited to warp themselves out of the great harbor, Spanish rowing boats towed the company's once-proud ships out to sea. The next day an east wind carried the Scots out of sight of Darien.

The fate of the second fleet was even more gruesome than the disasters that had attended the withdrawal of the first expedition. "The poor sick men," wrote Borland, "were sadly crowded together, especially aboard the *Rising Sun*, like so many hogs in a sty or sheep in a fold, so that their breath and noisome smells infected and poisoned one another. Neither was there anything suitable or comfortable to give the sick and dying, the best was a little spoiled oatmeal and water, and poorly were they attended in their sickness." Amid such conditions it was inevitable that the refugees should die like flies. Aboard the *Rising Sun*, it was not uncommon to bury eight men in the sea every morning, to say nothing of the deaths recorded on the other ships. One vessel

leaked so badly that her master refused to attempt the crossing to
Jamaica and ran instead direct to Cartagena where he threw
himself and his crew on the mercy of the Spaniards. Another
vessel was wrecked on the Cuban coast with fearful loss; and
although a couple of the smaller ships managed to limp home to
Scotland, the greatest tragedy struck the *Rising Sun* and her
consort the *Duke of Hamilton*. They were engulfed by a hurricane off the Carolina coast. The *Duke of Hamilton* was already in
imagined safety in Charleston harbor but she went down, while,
out at sea, the *Rising Sun* was lost with all hands.

Only a dribble of the thirteen hundred colonists who had left
Scotland with the second fleet ever returned. Somehow the
injured Alexander Campbell lived through the homeward voyage.
He was lucky enough to have a berth on one of the smaller ships,
which won through, and he came back to a hero's welcome. The
company gave him a medal, one side of which had a fanciful
scene depicting his famous attack on the palisade of Touboucanti.
Minister Borland also escaped the holocaust, for he left the *Rising
Sun* in Jamaica, and went north to Boston aboard a New England
ship, thereby missing the terrible disaster of the hurricane. Other
survivors trickled home months, even years, later. The multi-
lingual Benjamin Spense and his imprisoned colleagues were
eventually set free by the Spaniards, when it was clear that the
Scots would never again try to lay claim to Darien. But these
returnees were no more than the flotsam of the vast catastrophe
which had been Scotland's attempt to graft a colony onto the
isthmus of Central America. In his *New Voyage*, Lionel Wafer
had reported that Darien was a smiling and fruitful land; but
Borland was speaking for all his colleagues when he described the
place as a "wilderness." The critics of the company's failure, he
said, "know little of what it is to be in an American wilderness
under such circumstances, and I would not wish them to be in
sadder circumstances in the world." His words and the deaths of
a thousand Scots pricked the company's bubble of the Golden
Antilles for the last time.

18.

The Turn of the Legend

T HE SCOTS NEVER WENT BACK TO CALEDONIA AGAIN, and neither, for that matter, did the Spaniards. Pimienta, content to have evicted the settlers, sailed away and allowed the huts and fort of New Edinburgh to rot away under sun, wind, and rain. The Cuna, having had their one moment of contact with the outside world, withdrew into their forests and resumed their secretive existence. Everywhere the land of Darien reverted to its primitive state, much as Wafer and his buccaneers had found it. Only the slowly healing scar of Fort St. Andrew's defensive canal remained to show the lives and effort that Scotland had expended in the Antilles.

On the other side of the Atlantic the failure of Darien killed the Company of Scotland, and its death throes were marked by a storm of hate and abuse. Bitter tracts, pamphlets, and circulars spattered the blame for the colonial failure on everyone from the English government to the lackluster council in Caledonia. One Fleet Street hack wrote so scurrilously that his work was burned in Edinburgh by the public hangman. Yet the shareholders, who had so unwisely ventured their money in company stock, suffered in their pride rather than in their purses, for in the Treaty of Union in 1707 England agreed to give Scotland the sum of four hundred thousand pounds, a part of which was to repay the capital stock of the company. Moreover, the money was returned to the shareholders with 5 per cent interest. Unexpectedly, William Paterson's scheme had at last made a profit for its subscribers.

Paterson himself, by some miracle of tenacity and courage, attempted a brief comeback. He returned to Scotland and, regaining his health, stubbornly proposed that instead of winding up the company, the Scots should try to plant another colony, this time with England's collaboration. He even calculated that a capital stock of two million pounds would be enough money for the new scheme. Of course it was a hopeless proposition. The Scots were heartily sick of the whole tragedy, and the company gave Paterson an *ex gratia* payment of one hundred pounds, perhaps to stop his mouth. So the promoter went sadly back to London, where the Crown was decent enough to grant him an annuity of a hundred pounds in recognition for his services to "king and country." But his days as a successful businessman were over, and it was recorded that William Paterson was later driven to eking out his income by taking work as a tutor of mathematics.

Of the original protagonists of the Darien scheme, William Dampier also came back to London. He had never fulfilled his early promise, and his voyage of exploration to the southern continent had turned out to be a scandal. Dampier was, it seems, one of those men who are excellent as lone travelers but totally unsuited to work with a team. To put him in command of a naval expedition was to compound the fault. As a captain he was aloof, overbearing, and suspicious, and his crew hated him. The voyage of exploration degenerated into a farce, and by the time he reached South America on his way to explore Terra Australis and perhaps find new spice islands, his ship was in tumult. He himself had beaten his lieutenant, a regular naval officer, with a cane and, on reaching Bahia, he had thrown the man into the common jail. This officer eventually found his way back to England and, when Dampier returned, promptly laid charges against his former commanding officer. Dampier was court-martialed by the navy, found guilty of "very bad and cruel usage" toward the lieu-

tenant, and ordered to forfeit all his captain's pay. Yet, despite
the disgrace, he was soon given another chance. He was ordered
to take two ships to the South Seas on a voyage that was officially
exploratory but in reality a privateering raid. Once again, Dampier's prickly nature provoked trouble. The voyage was marred
by mutinies, quarrels, and maroonings, including the abandonment of Alexander Selkirk on Juan Fernández Island, an event
which Daniel Defoe was to make famous with his tale of Robin-
son Crusoe. This second failure finished Dampier as a ship's
captain; and his next, and final, voyage was as a pilot aboard the
privateer *Duke* under Woodes Rogers. Ironically, it was Woodes
Rogers's expedition which rescued Selkirk from his solitary imprisonment. Fortunately for Dampier, the *Duke*'s voyage was also
highly profitable, and Dampier's share of the prize money meant
that the traveler, who had by now been several times round the
world, could at last retire. Dampier set up house in London, and
died there at the age of sixty-three. Sir Hans Sloane, that dedicated
collector of Caribbeana, preserved his portrait, which eventually
came to rest in the National Gallery in London.

Lionel Wafer, on the other hand, maintained his cloak of
anonymity. In all probability he continued to live among his
piratical friends in Wapping, though there is no record of his
whereabouts after he had come back from his abortive negotiations in Edinburgh with the directors of the Company of Scotland. Even as the first Scots expedition was discovering the rigors
of life in Darien, Wafer's *New Voyage* was released to the public
in England. The book sold well enough for the publisher to bring
out his revised edition in 1704 with its misleading footnotes from
the "Member of the Royal Society." Interestingly, Wafer's preface in this second edition included a strong appeal to the English
government to plant a colony of their own on the isthmus of
Panama. But the Scots debacle at Caledonia was already infamous,
and it was not surprising that his advice was ignored completely.
The following year, or so it is thought, Lionel Wafer, "Chirurgeon" and friend of the Cuna, died.

In many ways, however, the claims made by Wafer, Paterson,
and Dampier for the economic potential of the Antilles had their
foundations in truth. Certainly their bold campaign for trade and

plantation in the West Indies was far more practical than the earlier schemes put up by Ralegh and Thomas Gage. And the idea of a Panama emporium was not only a considerable refinement of the original legend, but the natural conclusion of the lifecycle of the myth.

In the beginning, the enthusiasts for the Antilles had preached that the Caribbean offered, quite literally, a golden opportunity. Walter Ralegh, whatever his long-term ambitions for English overseas empire, had cleverly distilled this optimism into his projects for gold mines on the Orinoco and the fabled kingdom of El Dorado. Guiana, he said, was the "Magazin of all rich mettells," and his supporters eagerly waited for him to return from that treasure house with shiploads of bullion. A generation later Thomas Gage moved a little closer to reality when he argued that the wealth of the Antilles lay in its agricultural produce, and not in its mineral wealth. Of course Ralegh's theme still lingered, and Gage too spoke of gold mines, just as Wafer later described Spaniards washing gold from the streams of Darien. Yet fifty years after Ralegh, the hope for bullion was no longer the main attraction. In Gage's hands the lure of the Golden Antilles was given a new twist toward the notion of an army of carefree natives who would lovingly present the tribute of a bountiful earth to the English nation. It took the hardships of Cromwell's soldiers, grimly struggling to break open the grudging soil of Jamaica, to show that sweat, toil, and death were the forerunners of the riches of the Caribbean.

Paterson's "emporium"—and the boxes of wigs, shoes, and Bibles—was the third version of the Antillean dream, stressing commercial trade and tropical plantation as the twin pillars of success. The Scots failed because they underestimated the hostility of the Spaniards and planted Caledonia in the wrong place at the wrong time. Yet the next half-century of West Indian history was to show how near they might have come to success. No more than three years after the evacuation of Caledonia, English officers stationed in Jamaica were complaining that the islanders were so wealthy that the cost of living there had reached extraordinary heights. A turkey, they reported, cost ten shillings (this was in 1703); a chicken, three shillings and sixpence; and the smallest coin on the island was worth sevenpence half-penny and would only purchase what one penny would buy in England. Fifteen years later the West Indian trade had exceeded even Paterson's grandest dreams, and the value of Jamaican imports into England was only slightly less than the value of all the imports from all the American mainland colonies added together. It was this burgeoning economic reality which lay behind the English decision at the Treaty of Paris in 1763 to return the island of Martinique to the French, if France would entirely renounce her claim to Canada. Even so, there were violent protests in England, where it was considered in some quarters that the tiny sugar-rich island was a poor exchange for the vast but barren wastelands of Canada.

Nor could Ralegh have guessed the antics of some of the successful colonists who were caught up in this roaring Antillean prosperity. One governor of the Leeward Islands was to insist that all his house servants should daily polish their bare legs with butter so that they shone like jet, and he refused to take any message or object from a servant unless he used a pair of golden tongs especially made for the purpose. By the middle of the eighteenth century, wrote the Jamaican historian Leslie, it was remarkable to see in Spanish Town "the number of coaches and chariots which are perpetually plying, besides those which belong to Private Persons. They have frequent Balls, and lately have got a Playhouse, where they retain a Set of extraordinary good Actors." West Indian society was drunken, ignorant, corrupt, and lusty. Owing to the great heat, the white men seldom wore anything heavier than thread stockings, linen drawers, and a vest, and instead of a wig they tied a handkerchief over their heads. Their wives spent most of the day indoors, languidly draped, said Leslie, "in a loose night-gown, carelessly wrapped about them."

A vast labor force of Negro slaves, rather than the happy Indians whom Gage had suggested, supported this superstructure, together with echelons of indentured men, clerks, and tradespeople. Male slaves, many of them brought straight from the stinking holds of the slave ships, worked stark-naked in the fields and were provided with clothes only if they ventured near the "great houses" or were employed as personal servants. Negro women were given a coarse kind of petticoat, which they usually discarded unless they were obliged to wear it, and "Some of them [the Negro women] there," said Leslie, "go neat enough, but these are the favourites of young 'Squires, who keep them for a certain Use." The penalty for killing a slave out of "Wilfulness, Wantonness, or Bloody-Mindedness" was three months in jail and a fine of fifty pounds paid to the owner.

The dangers and rewards of this pulsating life were equally great. A planter might make a fortune in a few years, or just as quickly be carried away by one of the periodic epidemics that swept the islands. According to the English military authorities, yellow fever made the West India station one of the unhealthiest spots in the world. A regiment sent out from England would have such wastage that within two years every man in that regiment would have to be replaced. Yet the lucky planter fortunate enough to survive the hazards and reap his reward had little reason ever to return to England. Life in the Antilles had indeed become the idyll that the early travelers had described. Vastly wealthy, the successful colonist was lapped about with luxury: Negro mistresses (voluptuousness rather than beauty was prized), superb food, an endless supply of rum, and extraordinary privilege. It is said that one Barbadian planter who was finally threatened with a lawsuit for his misdemeanors neatly solved the problem by arranging his own appointment as judge in the relevant court. Under such circumstances it was inevitable that, when a violent earthquake shook Port Royal so badly that a large part of the town slid off its sandspit and dropped into the bay with enormous loss of life, pious observers compared the event to the fate of Sodom and Gomorrah.

So, in considerable style, the vision of the Golden Antilles had finally come true, and the forecasts of men like Ralegh, Wafer, and Gage were vindicated. Drawing its opulence from rum, sugar, cotton, and molasses, the heyday of the English West Indies was to be a spectacle worthy of the legend. And even when these staples began to lose their value, the glamour remained. The same climate which had decimated Venables's soldiers and the Scots of Caledonia became the subject of local pride. "In Virginia," wrote Leslie, "Mr. Jefferson relates that the mercury in Fahrenheit's thermometer has been known to descend from 92° to 47° in thirteen hours. The West India islands," he pointed out archly, "are happily exempt from those noxious variations." A century and a half later his smugness was to be attested to by the swarms of tourists migrating southward in response to the brochures and travel posters, with which a new generation of promoters was reviving the legend of the Golden Antilles.

Author's
Bibliographical Note

I T WILL BE CLEAR TO THE READER that my starting point for *The Golden Antilles* was to go back to the original narratives of the early travelers to the West Indies. I was delighted to find that Ralegh's *Discoverie* and *Apologie* had been edited very ably by the eminent historian V. T. Harlow. Sumptuously reprinted, these two editions were packed with useful footnotes, bibliographies, and supporting material, which led me effortlessly into the byways of Elizabethan voyages and Spanish-American history of the period.

Departure point for a review of Thomas Gage's escapades in Central America was his own volume of travels, *The English American*. Two excellent editions were my companions—one by A. P. Newton, a very readable historian of colonial expansion, and the other by J. E. S. Thompson, whose more recent work on Thomas Gage has done much to clarify that traveler's adventures and itinerary.

By contrast, the story of Cromwell's Western Design lacks a single contemporary chronicler, and I was therefore obliged to begin by putting together an amalgam of texts, including Sailing Master Whistler's diary, General Venables's *Narrative*, and the Spanish accounts of the invasion of Jamaica.

Of the many books about the Caribbean buccaneers, Esquemeling's *History of the Bucaniers* still stands head and shoulders above its rivals. Lionel Wafer's *New Voyage*, too, has made its mark. Edited by L. E. E. Joyce, who himself spent many years on the isthmus of Panama, Wafer's narrative is to be found on the booklist of the Hakluyt Society, whose careful reprints of early travel narratives are a rich vein of travelogue material.

Understandably, the Scots debacle at Darien has inspired a very long shelf of work, ranging from contemporary ballad sheets to the carefully preserved account books of the Company of Scotland. No better synopsis is to be found than the recent book *The Darien Disaster* by the Scots author John Prebble. Though published after the main draft of *The Golden Antilles* was completed, this book was helpful in drawing together the main threads of the Scots colonial fiasco.

Finally, I should add that throughout my research I was greatly assisted by visits I was able to make to many of the places mentioned in the text. One academic year was spent at the University of the West Indies. There I had access to the collections of Caribbeana at the university library and also at the Jamaican Historical Society in Kingston, as well as being able to visit the scenes of the original British occupation of the island. Earlier I had been to Point Icacos on Trinidad, whence Ralegh made his dash for the Orinoco. Most useful of all was a tour I made with my wife through Central America, paying special attention to the places Thomas Gage had written about. My most vivid memory is of "old" Guatemala City, now sadly reduced by earthquake but still magnificent. The grandeur of the ruins (on one wall a plaque commemorates Thomas Gage, identified as an "Irish" priest) impressed me as much as the place in its heyday had impressed the English American some three hundred years earlier.

INDEX

INDEX

A long-time student of travel and exploration, Timothy Severin has substantiated his research through his own travels. He is an Englishman, born in Assam, India, in 1940. He has lived in the United States and the West Indies, as well as in England, collecting material for his three books: *The Golden Antilles*, about the explorers of the West Indies; *Explorers of the Mississippi*, about pioneers on the Mississippi River; and *Tracking Marco Polo*, the story of his own journey along Marco Polo's trans-Asian route. Mr. Severin, who has a research degree from Oxford University, is now in London, where he is at work on a book on the exploration of Africa.

A NOTE ON THE TYPE

The text of this book was set on the Linotype in Janson, a re-cutting made direct from type cast from matrices long thought to have been made by the Dutchman Anton Janson, who was a practicing type founder in Leipzig during the years 1668–87. However, it has been conclusively demonstrated that these types are actually the work of Nicholas Kis (1650–1702), a Hungarian, who most probably learned his trade from the master Dutch type founder Kirk Voskens. The type is an excellent example of the influential and sturdy Dutch types that prevailed in England up to the time William Caslon developed his own incomparable designs from these Dutch faces.

This book was composed, printed, and bound by
H. Wolff Book Manufacturing Co., Inc., New York, N.Y.